LEARNING POLICY, DOING POLICY

INTERACTIONS BETWEEN PUBLIC POLICY THEORY, PRACTICE AND TEACHING

LEARNING POLICY, DOING POLICY

INTERACTIONS BETWEEN PUBLIC POLICY THEORY, PRACTICE AND TEACHING

EDITED BY TRISH MERCER, RUSSELL AYRES, BRIAN HEAD AND JOHN WANNA

Australian
National
University

PRESS

Published by ANU Press
The Australian National University
Acton ACT 2601, Australia
Email: anupress@anu.edu.au

Available to download for free at press.anu.edu.au

ISBN (print): 9781760464202
ISBN (online): 9781760464219

WorldCat (print): 1241204119
WorldCat (online): 1241204699

DOI: 10.22459/LPDP.2021

Cover design and layout by ANU Press

Contents

Part 2. Putting policymaking theory into practice

Part 3. How can theory better inform practice and vice versa?

Foreword

To govern is to make policy. We can count generations of practical experience of government, but, until recently, little academic study of how and why choices are made.

Indeed, it was not until the 1970s that the first academic research appeared in Australia and New Zealand with a specific focus on policymaking, and a decade later before the first textbooks emerged.

Scholars were keen to demarcate the focus on organisation that characterised the older discipline of public administration, promising instead a new spirit of inquiry about the content of government decisions. Over time this would become a distinction without a real difference, as it became clear that policy is influenced by institutions, and institutions by the purposes they adopt.

Those first textbooks were aimed primarily at undergraduate classes, and were written for students keen to understand the alchemy by which political imperatives translate into programs, and who, perhaps, might one day join the public service.

And then, suddenly, the 1980s saw unprecedented dialogue emerge between academic and practitioner. Public sector reform in a number of state jurisdictions and in Canberra and Wellington sparked sudden debate between senior public servants and academic critics.

Arguments about the nature and merit of 'managerialism' engaged scholars and officials alike, with passionate monographs, numerous conferences and animated controversy the result. National centres to study public management, funded by the Commonwealth, were established at Griffith and Monash universities in Australia, while an influential governance institute developed at Victoria University of Wellington. New Zealand scholars carried news to Australian gatherings of radical change to public sector practices across the Tasman.

This dialogue between practice and theory found practical expression in 2002 with the establishment of the Australia and New Zealand School of Government (ANZSOG), eloquently described by John Wanna in this volume. ANZSOG is significant for the vision it embodies: a desire to educate public officials across state and national jurisdictions, so creating a shared body of knowledge and concepts with deep networks informed by contemporary research.

Nearly 20 years on, ANZSOG graduates occupy agency leadership positions in every jurisdiction served by the school. The ANZSOG governing board continues to attract the most senior officials in both nations, alongside vice-chancellors representing the 15 member universities. The school is an important conduit of ideas and publications.

ANZSOG represents a confluence of academic and practitioner concerns. It must answer the question debated through all those symposia and journal exchanges: how do we understand policymaking, and what skills should be taught to a new generation of public servants? ANZSOG must write and deliver curriculum for its Executive Master of Public Administration and other executive programs; embedded in these courses are hypotheses about the nature of the policy process and the best ways to improve policymaking and administration.

Appropriately, this volume arose from a workshop supported by ANZSOG, and has been edited with skill by a mix of academics and practitioners. Many contributors have worked on both sides of the theory–practice divide during their distinguished careers. They speak to debates about curriculum by exploring the interaction between ideas, case studies and teaching expressed in the classroom.

As the chapters make clear, the debate is not resolved. Arguments continue about how to define policy, explain its variations and educate those entering the field. Here academic criticism meets practitioner need and, in turn, academic models get tested through trial and error in the field. So, even while contributors carefully delineate contending schools of theory, the volume also offers sharp judgements from senior public servants about what works when theory faces ever-shifting political and departmental circumstance. 'No plan survives contact with the enemy' is a well-known military observation, but plan we must, and any plan contains an implicit theory of what will work.

In describing experience in the field, contributors find value beginning with an intellectual framework drawn from the academic literature, even if it must quickly be modified on the run. Policymakers are informed by scholarship, even as they deal with contingency, seeking defensible and robust policy proposals. Decision-making is never perfect but, thanks to theory, it can be better than ad hoc incremental drift.

The dialogue between the academy and public services has enriched both sides, as most contributors to this volume agree. They find plenty to argue about still, in lessons deftly distilled by Allan McConnell in his chapter on synthesising theories and practice. These worlds overlap and yet diverge, sometimes informing each other, other times operating in parallel.

Many students have asked about the value of studying a policy cycle when the circumstances are always different, the steps are often compressed, time is short and politicians are impatient. Yet, if you don't know what 'good' looks like, you have no place to start, no way to proceed and no way to evaluate your recommendations. Certainly, in time, the cycle becomes second nature for those making policy, as they tailor each process to the situation, and learn what can be skipped and what is vital. But policy can be better when informed by theory and the self-awareness about process this provides.

In the meantime, we can learn from movie making and an exasperated Francis Ford Coppola during the filming of *Apocalypse Now*. An actor refused to learn his lines on the grounds that he was better at improvising in the moment than slavishly following the script. Eventually Coppola exploded: 'once you've learned your lines, then you can forget them!'

There is much in this volume to learn, and much that will be absorbed and thereafter forgotten because it is now instinctive. For reminding us of the journey, and providing this rich array of perspectives, academic and practitioner alike—and all who move between these worlds—we are indebted to Trish Mercer, John Wanna, Russell Ayres and Brian Head and the authors they present in this fine volume of reflections.

Glyn Davis
Chair, ANZSOG Research Committee
Distinguished Professor of Political Science,
Crawford School of Public Policy,
The Australian National University

Acknowledgements

The catalyst for this collection came from an Australia and New Zealand School of Government (ANZSOG) workshop held on 9 July 2018 at The Australian National University (ANU). The workshop explored how public servants access and respond to academic research in the form of frameworks and models designed to explain public policy processes. Despite the winter chill, the workshop audience, drawn from Australian and New Zealand academics and current and former public servants, engaged in stimulating and enthusiastic conversations on the day, and our editorial committee was set up as a post-workshop outcome.

The editors would like to acknowledge the encouragement and support provided by Professor John Wanna (former Sir John Bunting Chair of Public Administration at ANU) and the support provided by ANZSOG through the participation of the Deputy Dean (Teaching and Learning), Professor Catherine Althaus. Organisation of the workshop was supported by Jessica Mason (executive assistant to John Wanna) and by Wendy Jarvie, David Threlfall and Isi Unikowski on the day.

The book was informed by conversations both before and during the workshop and subsequently, not only with our contributors but also with a diverse group with interest in this area of public policy. In particular, we thank Michael Di Francesco, Wendy Jarvie, Paul Fawcett, Catherine To, Louise Gilding, Andrew Maurer, Duncan McIntyre, Craig Ritchie, Meredith Edwards, Serena Wilson, Marija Taflaga, Subho Banerjee and Kim Grey. We also thank our reviewers.

Our thanks to Sam Vincent, our ANZSOG editor, for his patient and sage support and advice, to Rani Kerin for her meticulous and judicious copyediting, and the team at ANU Press.

The book benefited from a process of cross-fertilisation, achieved by providing other relevant chapters to individual contributors. We thank our contributors for their sustained commitment to the project and patience with our deadlines and publishing requirements.

List of figures

List of tables

Abbreviations

ACT	Australian Capital Territory
ANZSOG	Australia and New Zealand School of Government
APC	Australian policy cycle
APS	Australian Public Service
APSC	Australian Public Service Commission
BRANZ	Building Research Association New Zealand Ltd
CEO	Chief Executive Officer
DPS	Department of Parliamentary Services
DSS	Department of Social Services
EBPM	evidence-based policymaking
EECA	Energy Efficiency and Conservation Authority
EFP	Executive Fellows Program
EMPA	Executive Masters of Public Administration
EPSDD	Environment, Planning and Sustainable Development Directorate
EQC	Earthquake Commission
HNZ	Housing New Zealand
IPAA	Institute of Public Administration Australia
IPANZ	Institute for Public Administration New Zealand
IPCC	Intergovernmental Panel on Climate Change
IPENZ	Institution of Professional Engineers New Zealand
MHUD	Ministry of Housing and Urban Development
MSA	multiple streams approach
NPM	new public management

NZCIC	New Zealand Construction Industry Council
PC	Productivity Commission
PET	punctuated equilibrium theory
PM&C	Department of the Prime Minister and Cabinet
PMCSA	Prime Minister's Chief Science Advisor
PMO	Prime Minister's Office
PSA	Public Service Association
RCT	randomised control trial
SEMP	Senior Executive Management Program
SES	senior executive services
TSL	Towards Strategic Leadership

Contributors

Catherine Althaus is Australia and New Zealand School of Government (ANZSOG) Chair of Public Service Leadership and Reform, Public Service Research Group, University of New South Wales, Canberra, and ANZSOG Deputy Dean (Teaching and Learning). Catherine held a number of policy posts with the Queensland Treasury and Office of the Cabinet.

Russell Ayres is a policy consultant and Adjunct Associate Professor at the University of Canberra's Institute for Governance and Policy Analysis. His career spanned 30 years in and outside the public sector, including senior policy roles in early childhood education and care, mental health, disability, Indigenous affairs, higher education and research, and research and evaluation.

Val Barrett was recently awarded her doctorate at The Australian National University for her qualitative and interpretive study of the United Kingdom and Australian parliaments from 2015 to 2019. Val held executive and senior management roles in the Parliament of Australia and the Australian Capital Territory (ACT) legislative assembly.

Sarah Hendrica Bickerton was a doctoral candidate with the School of Government, Victoria University of Wellington, her PhD research being political participation construction among Twitter users in New Zealand, which she completed in 2020. She also undertook graduate study in sociology at the University of Illinois, Chicago, and is currently a postdoctoral research fellow at the Public Policy Institute, University of Auckland.

Paul Cairney is Professor of Politics and Public Policy at the University of Stirling, UK. He specialises in British politics and public policy, often focusing on the ways in which policy studies can explain the use of evidence in politics and policy.

Meredith Edwards is Emeritus Professor at the University of Canberra's Institute for Governance and Policy Analysis. From 1983 to 1997, she advised on some major social policy, education and labour market issues in the Australian Public Service (APS), including as deputy secretary in the Department of the Prime Minister and Cabinet.

Louise Gilding is the Chief Executive Officer (CEO) of Housing and Homelessness in the ACT Community Services Directorate, leading the delivery of public housing and homelessness services to 23,000 tenants in 11,700 properties. She has a masters degree in public administration from ANZSOG.

Brian Head is Professor of Public Policy in the School of Political Science, University of Queensland. He previously held senior roles in government, universities and the non-government sector. His major interests are evidence-based policy, complex or 'wicked' problems, program evaluation, early intervention and prevention, collaboration and consultation, public accountability and leadership.

Karl Löfgren is Associate Professor, School of Government, Victoria University of Wellington. His research interests include government and service delivery, democratic auditing of new forms of local democracy, policy implementation, organisational changes and reforms in public sector organisations.

Kathleen Mackie's most recent position was CEO of Karnyininpa Jukurrpa, a non-government organisation working in the Western Desert of Australia with Martu Indigenous people. Kathleen's doctoral study at the University of New South Wales was on environment policy success and failure, drawing on her 25 years experience in environment, energy, employment and Indigenous policy in the APS.

Andrew Maurer had a diverse career in administrative and policy roles in the APS, and led a six-month mission in India for a United Nations agency. He retired in 2017 as a senior executive in the Department of Communications and the Arts, where he worked on policy areas involving the intersection of technology, law and economics.

Allan McConnell is a political scientist at the University of Sydney whose work examines how political factors (large 'P' and small 'p') shape public policy. His research addresses responses to crises and disasters, policy success/failure, policy evaluation, wicked policy problems, placebo policies, hidden policy agendas and the politics of policy inaction.

Trish Mercer is an ANZSOG visiting fellow at The Australian National University. Her 30-year career in the APS encompassed policy, program and service delivery roles in education, employment, social welfare and immigration. Her research interests span early childhood, education and employment, and how to take academic policy theory into practice.

Craig Ritchie, a Dhunghutti man, is the CEO of the Australian Institute of Aboriginal and Torres Strait Islander Studies. He has extensive public sector experience in the APS and the ACT Government, as well as in the community sector as CEO of the National Aboriginal Community Controlled Health Organisation. He is an adjunct professor at the Jumbunna Institute for Indigenous Education and Research, University of Technology Sydney and an ANZSOG Distinguished Fellow. Craig is completing his doctorate on the interaction between Aboriginal culture and policymaking systems.

David Threlfall is completing a PhD on British political rhetoric at the London School of Economics and Political Science. This doctoral project builds on research David commenced as part of an MPhil at the University of Cambridge. Before returning to study, David was chief of staff at ANZSOG, and worked in research and communications in the Vice-Chancellor's Office at the University of Melbourne.

John Wanna is Emeritus Professor in both the School of Politics and International Relations, College of Arts and Social Sciences, The Australian National University, and the School of Politics and International Relations, Griffith University. He was the Sir John Bunting chair in public administration with ANZSOG until 2019.

PART 1

Theorising, teaching and learning about policymaking

1

Public policy theory, practice and teaching: Investigating the interactions

Trish Mercer, Russell Ayres, Brian Head
and John Wanna

In theory, there is no difference between theory and practice. But, in practice, there is. (Eigen quoted in Nature Neuroscience, 2005, p. 1627)

Why investigate these interactions?

This book grew out of a longstanding interest in examining the perceived disconnects between the theory and the practice of policymaking to discover whether insights drawn from theories of the policy process could be—and indeed have been and are being—employed by academics, public servants and practitioner academics. Although real world policymaking is essentially a practical activity, involving government and non-government actors, there have been myriad attempts to construct theory-informed explanations of such practices to better understand their logics. These presumed linkages might arise in many contexts and temporal dimensions, from attempting to analyse past policy episodes through to practical applications in the pressure cooker environment of working within government organisations.

Distilling the myriad issues involved, we see two main problems: practitioners do not see academic insights as directly useful to their policy activities, and theorists tend to write for other scholars and to contribute to existing debates in the literature. While the contrast may be overdrawn, bureaucrats are more interested in solutions while academics are motivated by attempts to define and delineate the problems. The challenge is to see these two perspectives as more synergistic than antagonistic.

The language employed in theories about the making of policy tends to be self-referential, obtuse and dense, studded with conceptual jargon and references to other bodies of theory. From the 1950s and more recently, however, some theories have been developed with a greater focus on practical applications. Some of this theorising is underpinned by normative concepts including rational decision-making, public choice, public value, public integrity and accountability. The development and application of policy theory for practical purposes is indeed a burgeoning field of academic analysis, with policy theorists seeking to translate the insights from complex theoretical constructs to present more immediate value for policymakers and practitioners (Cairney 2015; Cairney & Weible 2017). Some theories are intentionally pitched at a broad or meta level, while others are tackled more narrowly through a case study orientation focused on policy in action.

Yet, the impact of such theories and concepts on the work of practitioners and policymakers has been a largely neglected area of research and analysis. This book seeks to help redress this gap in the literature. To be sure, policy theory has been utilised in particular case studies that can be readily located in the Australian and New Zealand literature; usually the authors are academics and occasionally practitioner academics. There have also been two recent volumes that were deliberately centred upon a particular theoretical approach. The first was a collection edited by Katherine Daniell and Adrian Kay (2017) that examined the concept of multi-level governance and its explanatory power for Australian public policy. This volume included both conceptual chapters (written largely by academics) and case study chapters ranging across social and environmental policy domains (written by practitioner academics).[1] The second was a collection of case studies of successful public policy in Australia and New Zealand, edited by Joannah Luetjens, Michael Mintrom and Paul 't Hart (2019a).

---

1   The theory and practice of multi-level governance has also been extensively developed and researched in the European Union.

This volume outlined a 'policy success assessment map' drawing on academic research into success that the contributing authors used as a template to analyse a diverse and detailed set of policy cases.

This present volume of essays strikes out in a different direction. There is no singular theoretical approach that informs the collection; indeed, we recognise that there are many important policy theories that are not discussed or mentioned only in passing. There are excellent standard texts that outline the wider spectrum of theoretical approaches to policy study, such as Christopher Weible and Paul Sabatier's *Theories of the policy process* (2017 and earlier editions) and Paul Cairney's *Understanding public policy* (2020). Rather, our primary intent is to offer some practical insights from those who research and teach in policy studies, and from those involved in the practices of policy development and implementation, in relation to how public policy theories are presented to individual public servants (practitioners), what we know about how teaching experiences impact on practice, and, conversely, how policy practices influence academic teaching and research.

Policymaking capacity— the interconnections

We see this issue as highly relevant to the issue of policymaking capacity. Since the 1990s, leading politicians, academics and informed commentators have persistently complained about the weak policy capacity of public servants and their departments. This critical judgement about the alleged declining capacity of the public service has also been echoed in international literature across Westminster-style political systems such as the United Kingdom, New Zealand and Canada (Parsons 2004, p. 45; Tiernan 2011, pp. 335, 337). The waves of public sector reforms through the 1980s and 1990s, commonly described as new public management (NPM), resulted not only in the public sector downsizing selected functions and outsourcing its service delivery, but also in the increasing contestability of policy advice to ministers. Governments increasingly obtained policy advice from diverse sources including ministerial advisory staff, consultancy firms and think tanks (Head 2015, p. 54).

Some see claims of declining policy capacity in the Australian Public Service (APS) as lacking an empirical basis or even as the product of 'rumour', as suggested by Janine O'Flynn et al. (2011, p. 310). This 'declinist' discourse concerning public service capability in the contemporary era has also been challenged in recent positive case studies of 'standout public policy accomplishments' in Australia and New Zealand (Luetjens, Mintrom & 't Hart 2019b, p. 3). The truth of the matter is likely to be variable between and within public services, with strong capacity in some departments and agencies and weak capacity in others, as suggested by the Australian Public Service Commission's (APSC) capability reviews (discussed below).

Complaints about policy capacity are particularly associated with the arrival of new governments that have ambitious new policy agendas. In Australia, new ministers in John Howard's Coalition government in 1996 and again in the Rudd Labor government in 2007 were critical of the APS's slow response to their big agendas. Prime Minister Kevin Rudd and the new secretary of his department, Terry Moran, communicated 'a trenchant critique' of the APS, and Moran was tasked with chairing an expert advisory group to develop the blueprint for a world-class public service (Lindquist 2010, pp. 117–18). While our discussion here largely relates to the federal level of government, similar critiques have been made across jurisdictions at the state government level (and in many local government contexts as well).

The report of the Moran advisory group (*Ahead of the game*) identified 'enhancing policy capacity' as a key priority (Advisory Group on Reform of Australian Government Administration 2010, p. ix). The departmental capability reviews recommended in the report, and subsequently coordinated by the APSC in several key departments between 2012 and 2015, also drew attention to weaknesses in strategic policy expertise (e.g. see Australian Government 2013, pp. 209–10). These concerns persist in contemporary debates and discourse: less than a decade after *Ahead of the game*, then Prime Minister Malcolm Turnbull established yet another inquiry—hailed as an independent review of the capability, culture and operating model of the APS, and chaired by David Thodey (CSIRO chair and former CEO of Telstra). Its interim report (*Priorities for change*) highlighted concerns that the APS's underlying policy capacity had been weakened over time (Commonwealth of Australia 2019, p. 15).

Whatever the actual situation, the perception of a decline in policy capacity is frequently raised as a concern, and made a focus for future improvement. Even before the finalisation of Thodey's *Independent review of the APS*, the APS Secretaries Board was galvanised into addressing policy advising weaknesses, with a cross-agency policy capability project producing an insightful *APS policy capability roadmap* in March 2019, built on feedback received across the APS and beyond (Australian Government 2019; Easton 2019a). By November 2019, however, with the Coalition government having recently been returned under Prime Minister Morrison, and with a new secretary for the Department of Prime Minister and Cabinet (PM&C), Philip Gaetjens, the APS's project launch was something of a damp squib: its earlier promise of a 'common policy model' had become a simplified and loose framework consisting of four 'key elements' for delivering great policy, with a policy hub website providing more detail and resources. Further undermining this effort, most of the initiative's secretary-level 'champions' lost their jobs in a major machinery-of-government revamp of the APS.[2]

Under the Morrison government, concern about the policy capacity of its bureaucrats appears to have slipped in priority. The government's underwhelming response to the final report of the *Independent review of the APS* was released in December 2019. The response document, *Delivering for Australians*, reinforced the prime minister's strong view, earlier expressed in his annual address to the APS, that government sets the policy direction and the APS simply delivers (Grattan 2019; Morrison 2019; PM&C 2019a, p. 9).

However, one relevant recommendation in the *Independent review* has been accepted: the establishment of a 'professions' model along the lines of what has been developed in the UK. The APS commissioner, Peter Woolcott, had already signalled that a formal professions model would be established to lift in-house skills and improve capability, looking to models in New Zealand, the UK and Singapore (Jenkins 2019a; PM&C 2019b, p. 20). A professions model for 'policy' might be expected to involve formal policy training with some academic input, whether in the form of accredited tertiary training, such as a masters degree, or short course offerings. Such formal teaching had been recommended both by

---

2   Heather Smith (the principal driver of the project), Mike Mrdak, Renée Leon and Kerri Hartland, who all spoke at the November launch, lost their positions under Morrison's restructure of the APS in December 2019 (Jenkins 2019b; Easton 2019b).

academics and by other experts in the 2012 capability review conducted into the PM&C (Crowley & Head 2015, p. 7; Tiernan 2018). However, the practitioner–academic divide in Australian public policy remains a longstanding challenge, and one that may have been worsening 'to the detriment of both' (Stewart & Buick 2019). The boundaries between what are seen as distinctly separate worlds, while not impermeable, entail different drivers, assumptions and expectations. John Wiseman (who inhabited both spaces at different times) has characterised the challenges to develop effective partnerships between these parallel universes as a case of 'dancing with strangers' (Wiseman 2010).

An essential context for this book is to understand this divide, sometimes referred to as 'two worlds' or 'two separate communities'. This includes understanding how the policy capacity of bureaucratic practitioners in Australia has been built primarily on learning by 'doing' and, correspondingly, how the academic field of policy studies is a relatively recent development in Australia and has been influenced by demands for practical policy analysis instruction for public servants. Our focus is specifically on bureaucratic policy practitioners, even though we recognise that there are many policy advisers outside the APS, both within ministerial offices and in many locations within the business sector, consultancy firms, community bodies and research centres. Broadening the analysis to include other such 'policy workers' may be work for future consideration.

Terminology—different routes to the same destination?

The 'two worlds' of theory and practice can have different terminology and, even more problematically, different meanings for the same terms. Because, as editors, we wanted the authors in this monograph to be able to approach their arguments in their own way, we did not impose a single or uniform nomenclature on contributors. Nonetheless, words matter and it is useful to briefly discuss key terms as they relate to this volume.

As Sabatier (2007, pp. 3–4) suggests, in seeking to understand or improve the practice of public policymaking, we inevitably simplify a highly complex, multifaceted reality. In the following chapters, much epistemological weight is carried by terms such as 'theory', 'model' and 'framework'. In general, a theory is contingent in character, providing a set of propositions that remain open to being disproved through empirical study; a model is more definitive and often aspires to be both empirically sound and normatively useful; while a framework is generally a looser construct of ideas and concepts that seeks to help understanding and guide action, without claiming unerring predictive power or perfect utility in all circumstances. In his text on public policy, Parsons (1995, pp. 57–61) presents a useful typology of policymaking 'frameworks', comprising three non-exclusive categories:

- *explanatory frameworks*, which seek to explain how policymaking happens, with a focus on causation, indicating expected pathways, given specific initial conditions
- *'ideal-type' frameworks*, which classify types or forms of policymaking, using a variety of categorisation methods (e.g. policymaking as an expression of institutional and structural forms and norms)
- *normative frameworks*, which specify how policymaking *ought* to be done, given certain value preferences (e.g. analytical rigour, community engagement and political utility).

The distinctions and interactions between explanatory ('is') and normative ('ought') frames are especially important in this book. Practitioners and academics tend to fall somewhere on the continuum between these two poles; indeed, many are deeply concerned about the gap that can open up between how policymaking should proceed and how it is seen to actually play out in the real world. Perhaps a little paradoxically, many practitioners who venture into the theoretical literature seem to be idealistic or aspirational in their motivations, while many academics are more interested in the empirical evidence. Practitioners are often attracted to frameworks that are normative and ideal in character—for example, the Australian policy cycle or Moore's (1995) public value model—as touchstones for what their deeply pragmatic craft aspires to achieve. Many academics, on the other hand, are uneasy with loose frameworks that seem unreflective of what actually happens in real world policymaking, and they will often prefer more empirical or descriptive models, such as Charles Lindblom's (1959) 'muddling through' or John Kingdon's (2011) multiple streams approach.[3] In this way, practitioners often use 'ought' to improve what 'is', while academics focus on analysing what 'is' to show where it falls short of what it 'ought' to be. Each are, perhaps, on different journeys towards if not the same destination, then to destinations that are closer than either group might imagine.

Learning about policy 'on-the-job'— the infusion approach

Practitioners well versed in policy theory are far from the norm. In the United States, a graduate recruited to undertake policy work for government organisations will, almost certainly, have undertaken accredited courses in public policy and government; however, a graduate recruited to the public sector in Australia is much less likely to have specific training in political science or government. Australian public servants principally learn their policy advising skills 'on-the-job', as do their counterparts in most Westminster countries (Allen & Wanna 2016, pp. 27–8; Head 2015, p. 59). Among our contributors, both Kathleen Mackie and Andrew Maurer reflect on how their policy skills were built and honed through such 'learning by doing'—essentially an infusion approach after being 'thrown in the deep end'. These fundamental 'craft' skills for public servants are gradually acquired through practical learning, through knowledge passed on informally and through direct contact. These processes are also central to how public servants are inducted into the belief structures of their respective organisations, even if the doctrines are not explicitly articulated in detail (Rhodes 2016, p. 643; Rhodes & Wanna 2009, pp. 158–9). While there is general consensus that policy skills are inculcated through this experiential process, there is very limited research into how such learning 'as you go' occurs (Adams, Colebatch & Walker 2015, pp. 102–4).

---

3   Especially insofar as Kingdon builds on the 'garbage can' model outlined by Cohen, March and Olsen (1972).

We do know, however, that academic policy training is subsidiary to this 'in-house' experiential training provided within the APS. This point is aptly illustrated in the recollections of Arthur Sinodinos, who joined the Department of Finance in 1979:[4]

> While I'd had a certain amount of academic training in economics and commerce and all the rest of it, I really started to understand what you need to know when I became a public servant. I had to put that sort of training into operation. (Sinodinos 2017, p. 78)

The 70:20:10 pedagogic model developed by the APSC and adopted within many departments is built around this emphasis on unstructured and practical skills acquisition, with the 70 per cent coming from direct experiential learning, 20 per cent from relationships and networks and 10 per cent from formal education programs (Allen & Wanna 2016, p. 28). Public service training in Australia and also New Zealand has indeed had a piecemeal history: fragmented training and development has been delivered mostly at the individual agency level with some external 'for credit' instruction supported for individual officers.

This emphasis on 'learning as you go' complements what is described as a characteristically Australian administrative trait of pragmatism, arguably linked to the pragmatism observed in the national political style (Edwards this volume, Chapter 7; Hollander & Patapan 2007). Public servants attuned to the importance of practical experience and pragmatic action are therefore likely to be sceptical of theory-based learning and academic analysis. For some, this will be seen as floating in the stratosphere rather than a useful resource to be drawn on. This perception was conveyed by Peter Shergold (former APS 'mandarin' and also an accomplished academic) in his pithy description of public policy skill requirements as 'more in the nature of administrative craft and managerial mystery than political science' (Shergold 2015, p. xx).

In Australia, the various waves of NPM reform in the 1980s and 1990s produced the rise of performance-oriented 'managerialism' and the outsourcing of many traditional public service delivery programs. This was a period in which the public sector at all three levels of government were enjoined to undertake business and management training, with

---

4   Arthur Sinodinos was chief of staff to Prime Minister Howard between 1997 and 2006 and later became a New South Wales senator and government minister under prime ministers Abbott and Turnbull.

accredited masters degrees in business administration becoming popular. The policy orientation of government was also being radically shifted by the rise of 'economic rationalism', with quantitative methods and economics qualifications becoming desirable skills for new graduates (Crowley & Head 2015, p. 5). In Australia, those who acquired public policy training often did so at postgraduate level and not always in accredited training programs; it is not clear whether doing such studies was regarded as career enhancing by their agencies. In their survey of 55 state public servants in three capital cities, David Adams, Hal Colebatch and Christopher Walker (2015, p. 81) found that only half reported any previous formal study of policy, and those who were enrolled in policy-related studies had done so at their own initiative. At the Commonwealth level, the Rudd government's *Ahead of the game* report in 2010 found serious underinvestment by the APS in staff development (Advisory Group on Reform of Australian Government Administration 2010, pp. viii–ix). The *APS policy capability roadmap* released in March 2019 reported that foundational training, while provided by many agencies, was targeted at graduates, and that policy advisory staff generally had to 'go it alone' on professional development (Australian Government 2019, p. 14).

Learning about policy in the 'ivory towers'—academic and applied approaches

The *APS policy capability roadmap* reported that policy advisers were critical of the relevance and 'fit' of training provided by academics and consultants (Australian Government 2019, p. 14). However, Michael Di Francesco (2015, p. 261) has shown that the field of policy analysis instruction in Australia (mainly termed 'public policy') has been 'firmly grounded in an Antipodean proclivity towards pragmatism'. As both an academic and a practitioner field, it encompasses both the academic analysis *of* policy (to explain decisions and their making) and the applied focus of analysis *for* policy (to improve decisions) (Di Francesco 2015, pp. 261–2). This marks a critical point of difference with the United States and Canada, where the nexus between theory and practice is reflected in the professional affiliation of most universities and schools that teach policy with a formal accreditation system incorporating standards for policy programs and a core curriculum for 'professional degrees'.

In Australia, public policy as a university-level field of study within the umbrella of political science is now well established and its growth has seen a corresponding decline in 'public administration' course offerings (Crowley & Head 2015, p. 5). Di Francesco's (2015, p. 270) extensive survey of current structures and programs for public policy in Australia located 18 instances of public policy programs offered in the 41 Australian university-level institutions, including five entities that were classified as standalone 'policy schools'. One of these is the Australia and New Zealand School of Government (ANZSOG), established in 2002 by the Commonwealth and several state governments and New Zealand. It is seen as a dedicated school for building executive capacity—a unique experiment that is the focus of John Wanna's case study in this book.

The growth in policy analysis studies has been linked to the relatively recent expansion in government and individual demand for policy training (Di Francesco 2015, p. 277), of which ANZSOG is the leading organisational example of tailored training. While there is no standard core curriculum in this field across Australian and New Zealand universities, Di Francesco's survey indicated that across both undergraduate and postgraduate levels, some commonalities included standalone subjects on policy theory and public policy, and an emphasis on examining case studies on sectoral policy or public policy process (Di Francesco 2015, pp. 274–5). The use of teaching cases has been taken to a new level within ANZSOG, including the use of case teaching in its two signature programs, the Executive Masters of Public Administration and the condensed Executive Fellows Program.

Policy studies have also morphed into other academic disciplines and fields of inquiry in universities. These tend to be more sectoral in application but still very focused on policy development and implementation. These areas include environmental and climate change policy, water and drought policy, human rights policy, national security policy, demographic and immigration policy, Indigenous policy, health and educational policy, and foreign aid policy etc. Most of these sectoral areas investigate policy options rather than policymaking per se, but may work from disciplinary specific approaches to policymaking.

Exactly what policy theories are offered through the more generic tertiary courses on public policy has not been well documented. However, since the late 1990s, the policy theories offered both through university institutions and also through major textbooks has generated vigorous debate within Australia, especially regarding two particular theories. One is the 'Australian policy cycle'—a modified version of the classic stages or cycle approach originating in North American discussions in the 1960s. It was expounded in a popular textbook, *The Australian policy handbook*, first published in 1998 by Peter Bridgman and Glyn Davis (based on a 1995–96 Griffith University consultancy on policy formulation for the Queensland Government) and now in its sixth edition (Althaus, Bridgman & Davis 2018). This policy cycle model is offered as a 'good process' guide for public servants and the associated handbook is a classic text for both undergraduate policy subjects and graduate courses (Di Francesco 2015, p. 267). Critiqued as an attractive but unrealistic theory of the policy development process (Adams, Colebatch & Walker 2015, p. 108; Gill & Colebatch 2006, pp. 261–2), the Australian policy cycle's perceived strength is its practical approach and comprehensiveness in capturing the entirety of policy development and implementation activities. Its utility is explored extensively in the chapters by Russell Ayres, Meredith Edwards and Trish Mercer in this volume. Institutionally, as Andrew Maurer's contribution demonstrates, such a stages approach continues to hold attraction as a means of underlining the sequence of actions underpinning 'good' policy development. Gary Banks (2018), former head of the Productivity Commission and a supporter of 'an ordered approach' to policymaking, describes the steps in the cycle as differing little from those set out in the regulatory assessment requirements that apply in all Australian jurisdictions. Yet, as the policy theorist Cairney (this volume, Chapter 13) argues, this theory of policy made from the centre via a series of logical stages entails a much too simple understanding of policy processes compared to the far messier realities of a complex system over which policy practitioners have little control.

The second contentious public policy theory is the 'public value' approach for strategic public management associated with Mark Moore from Harvard's Kennedy School of Government. This approach articulates a strategic triangle framework offering three tests of a public policy: whether it is valuable, legitimate and doable (Moore 1995). As a heuristic, the public value approach with these three criteria has been taken up with gusto by public managers, and has achieved wide circulation through being embedded in core elements of ANZSOG's higher level training curriculum (Alford & O'Flynn 2009, pp. 171–2). Whether public value is appropriate within Westminster systems, with their focus on ministerial leadership and public service responsiveness to governmental priorities, has been the subject of robust debate (Alford 2008; Alford & O'Flynn 2009; Bryson, Crosby & Bloomberg 2014; Rhodes & Wanna 2007, 2008, 2009). A recent workshop on understanding public value explored the ambiguities of the concept, noting the wide variety of ideas about where public value is created and by whom. Nevertheless, the concept has resonance for public servants demonstrated through its extensive application:

> Public value … was a term created by academics and then adopted by public managers, a cycle of ideas in which academics try to describe what practitioners do and then practitioners use to describe their work. (Brown et al. 2019, p. 21)

As Di Francesco (2015, p. 268, original emphasis) remarks, these debates are emblematic in drawing attention to the apparent gap between academic and practitioner knowledge about policy: 'the nub of the dispute is that *practitioners* find the concept [of public value] useful'. This is manifested, as Mercer's chapter illustrates, in the willingness of many senior public servants to reference Moore's authorising environment when discussing public policy in external forums. Indeed, in the *APS policy capability roadmap,* a strong authorising environment is posited as a key area of focus to increase the demand for good practice policy development (Australian Government 2019, p. 20; Mercer this volume, Chapter 3). Both of these policy theories, and the debates they have engendered, are explored in several of our chapters, along with another influential policy theory— John Kingdon's (2011) multiple streams approach. This approach, while essentially setting out to explain how the United States Congress makes policy decisions (within a highly entrepreneurial political system and lower party discipline), has been applied in numerous empirical studies (including on parliamentary systems), although sometimes superficially (Cairney & Jones 2016, p. 38).

An associated area of strong academic and practitioner interest in Australasia has been the theoretical exploration of the contested area of policy success and failure. In particular, Allan McConnell (2015, pp. 232–6), also a contributor in this book, has explored methodological difficulties in analysing the maze of what constitutes success or failure, and developed a framework to map the characteristics of different policy outcomes in terms of three analytical categories: process, program, and political success or failure. He underlines the importance of engaging with the real world complexities—the realpolitik—of policy failure:

> We need to accept that failure is bound up with issues of politics
> and power, including contested views about its existence, and the
> power to produce an authoritative and accepted failure narrative.

Mackie, as a practitioner academic, relates in her chapter how she employed McConnell and Marsh's 2010 framework as a useful rubric to analyse 12 policy episodes of environmental policymaking, including the Rudd government's Home Insulation Program, which was the subject of a scathing Royal Commission report commissioned by the succeeding Abbott Coalition government. Mackie's intention was to determine which episodes could be categorised as a policy 'success' or 'failure'. Luetjens, Mintrom and 't Hart's (2019b, pp. 3, 7) study, which aims to reset the agenda for teaching, research and dialogue on public policy performance and success in Australia and New Zealand, adopts McConnell's success framework, with the addition of a fourth, temporal dimension that assesses success over time.

The purpose of this book

Those engaged in policy practice are, then, increasingly being offered policy theory through formal and informal training, and through textbooks and published research. Yet, we have little empirical evidence as to the impact of such policy theory on the individuals or their workplaces. While the Commonwealth's policy capability project has estimated that there are more than 7,000 'policy advisers' in the APS (Australian Government 2019, p. 1), the potential audience for theory-informed practice extends also into public servants involved in service and program delivery, regulation and compliance, given the interconnection between policy design and implementation and monitoring.

This book aims to begin to address this gap in our evidence base by bringing together insights from research, teaching and practice on the relationship between theory and policy practice. Its impetus came from an ANZSOG workshop held in Canberra in July 2018 organised by Trish Mercer and John Wanna with Brian Head's assistance, in order to open the conversation about theory-informed practice.[5] The diverse audience

---

5   The workshop, 'Building communities of practice: exploring how practitioners access and respond to academic policy frameworks', was held at The Australian National University on 9 July 2018. Some of the contributors to this book (Ayres, Althaus, Threlfall, Gilding, Mackie and Mercer) were presenters at the workshop.

of Australian and New Zealand academics, practitioner academics and public servants from the national and capital territory jurisdictions were enthusiastic about the opportunity to hear academic and practitioner presentations on the theory–practice nexus. They were keen to share insights about what we know—and, more often, what we do not know—about 'making theory speak to practice', as David Threlfall and Catherine Althaus subtitled their workshop presentation. A subsequent ANZSOG sponsored visit to Australia and New Zealand in October 2018 by Paul Cairney explored inter alia how we can take lessons from policy theory into practice, including for evidence-based policymaking.

Given the interest expressed at the July 2018 workshop, an editorial committee was formed of Head, Mercer and Wanna, joined by one of the practitioner academic presenters at the October 2018 workshop, Russell Ayres. We have deliberately sought to bring together contributions from the academy with those from former or current public servants to ground this work in the practical experience of real world policy.

To explore how policy theory is transferred and taken into practice, we decided to seek contributions under three broad headings:

1. outlining the landscape for policy training and identifying gaps in our knowledge of how theory and practice have influenced each other in the Australian and also international contexts

2. exploring how current and former practitioners have employed policymaking theory to support their analysis of policy episodes and/or as a sense-making tool for themselves and the people with whom they work

3. tapping into the latest research on how lessons can be taken from policy theory into practice.

These three topics became the basis for the three parts of the volume. The core questions explored by our contributors can be summarised thus:

- How is policy training offered in Australia and what are the challenges?
- What can we uncover about which policy theories have been influential (and why) among practitioners? What is the role of heuristics in reflective policy learning?
- Is the divide between the worlds of academia and policy practice as significant as the literature suggests?

- How have individual practitioners, including practitioner academics, employed—and adapted—policy theory, either for analytical purposes of studying past policy episodes or for their own and their teams' reflective learning?
- How do institutions seek to connect theory and practice implicitly or explicitly?
- How can policy theorists offer insights in a form and through a medium that is relevant and useful for those engaged in policy practice?

Our analytical gaze falls primarily on investigating whether policy theory can speak to practice. However, one of the questions generated through this book, and particularly by Threlfall and Althaus, Mackie and also Cairney, is how we can move towards practice-influenced theory. This is a seminal question for a future research agenda—one that fundamentally addresses the interconnectivity between practice and theory.

This work was completed before the major changes in the operational routines of governments, universities and corporate organisations catalysed by the national and global response to the COVID-19 pandemic. We have not attempted to forecast the possible impacts on working relationships and lessons for dealing with rapidly changing challenges that this crisis has produced. Indeed, the experience of balancing health and economic impacts in a highly uncertain environment and preparing for the aftermath may well change both the practice of policymaking and how it is theorised. However, policy theorists have been quick to offer insights and perspectives for practitioners endeavouring to develop public policy responses to this unprecedented global crisis and to learn from the experience of other governments, including through ANZSOG's 'Leading in a crisis' series of online articles (Macpherson & 't Hart 2020; McConnell, Stern & Boin 2020; Weible et al. 2020).

Overview of the book

This book is addressed to practitioners and academics alike. We see this as an opportunity to open up discussion on this all too hidden area: practitioners rarely volunteer information on how they employ and adapt theory in their policymaking experiences, and academics are more often preoccupied with developing than with offering theory to those involved in policy 'doing'. We seek to investigate this area by structuring our contributions in three parts.

Part 1 examines theorising, teaching and learning about policymaking, drawing on not only academic perspectives but also practitioner academics who bring their knowledge of how theory can translate at the level of policy workers. It explores:

- whether the emphasis on a theory–practice divide obscures the interconnection between these two communities
- what we can discover about how public servants acquire their policy knowledge and skills, and the role played by academic training in building capacity, particularly through the Antipodean experiment of ANZSOG
- what policy theories have been offered, or could be offered, to public servants across all areas of government, including parliament, and what we can discover about the resonance and translation of such theory for policy practitioners.

Part 2 provides access into the insider world of current and former practitioners who bring insights seldom available to academics about their interactions with the processes, documents and relationships that move policy forward. It explores:

- how theory can be applied to offer insights for practical action, and the processes of simplification and distillation that play out in such adaptations
- which theories have been found to offer coherent frameworks (i.e. to strike a chord) and in what circumstances
- whether theories can be adapted by blending or by mixing and matching them to provide greater applicability, and how policymakers might go about this
- whether theory can be employed at an institutional level, and how it is influenced by the culture and environment of a public service agency.

Part 3 examines how theory can better inform practice and vice versa. Two policy theorists offer their perspectives on how policy theory can indeed assist policy practitioners by examining:

- how insights from policy theory can help policy practitioners understand the complex nature of the policy process that they themselves observe and in which they are immersed
- how theories can offer a way of thinking to help set up a new agenda to consider how policy should be made

- the importance of having realistic expectations of what is possible in the worlds of both academic theory and policy practice and avoiding stereotypes of these, and of exploring opportunities for interaction and shared space.

As this structure indicates, our contributors represent the views of a spectrum of writers, from those whose days are spent thinking about policymaking to those who are engaged in the business of fast-paced policy decision-making and implementation to those who inhabit the worlds in-between: policy analysts, public policy researchers and academics, public policy teachers, policy consultants, policy practitioners, and some who juggle more than one of these roles or have worked across the 'two communities'. We see this plurality and diversity as a particular strength of the monograph.

Our chapters and contributors

The rest of Part 1 explores theorising, teaching and learning about policymaking. Chapter 2, by David Threlfall and Catherine Althaus, both of whom have academic and practitioner experience, interrogates the relationship and interconnection between theory and practice and the fundamental role of heuristics in reflective policy learning. In Chapter 3, Trish Mercer, a former APS senior executive and now an ANZSOG visiting fellow, examines the impact of academic theories about policymaking, focusing on four specific theories that traverse the theory spectrum to investigate which have resonated with Australian public servants and why. John Wanna draws on his ANZSOG research and teaching experience in Chapter 4 to explore the issues and challenges (including in offering policy theory concepts) associated with teaching public policy through senior executive education programs and, in particular, through ANZSOG's key programs.

In Chapter 5, New Zealand–based researchers Karl Löfgren and Sarah Hendrica Bickerton consider the concept of two separate communities of theory and practice and, based on their survey into how policy professionals in New Zealand use academic research, conclude that the picture is more complex and dispersed than generally perceived. With the lens of a former parliamentary senior manager, Val Barrett, in Chapter 6, draws on her research into Australia and the UK's national parliaments to argue that the characteristics of public value are as appropriate for parliamentary administration as they are for public administration.

Part 2, as indicated above, delves further into the world of practice seen through a theory lens with contributions by practitioners and practitioner academics. Some have employed policy theory within their workplaces whereas others have employed theory to analyse and reflect on policy episodes or to investigate policymaking as a cross-cultural endeavour. In Chapters 7 and 8, our contributors offer different reflections on their public service careers through the prism of the policy cycle. As one of the 'boundary riders' between the public service and academia, Meredith Edwards puts the policy cycle in a practical context in her reflections on Australia's public policy processes. Russell Ayres describes how his professional practice as a senior APS executive (2004–16) was informed by his academic knowledge of policymaking theory and research, and how he employed his theoretical insights to offer his staff a way of seeing policy through the policy cycle admixed with observed practice.

Assessing success and failure in environment policy through the lens of policy theory was the subject of Kathleen Mackie's doctoral research. Drawing on her interviews with key policy practitioners in the Commonwealth department, assisted by her previous experience as a departmental senior executive, Mackie highlights the significance of the agency exerted by officials as a key to understanding policy success and failure in Chapter 9. In the next chapter, Craig Ritchie, head of a key Aboriginal and Torres Strait Islander cultural and research agency, critiques our reflexively rationalist, Western Enlightenment-inspired approach to policymaking. He argues that this approach leads to mental shortcuts and assumptions that all but guarantee failure when dealing with the deeply different ways of seeing and being manifest among Aboriginal and Torres Strait Islander cultures.

Louise Gilding offers insights into her theory-informed practice as a senior executive in the Australian Capital Territory Government in Chapter 11. Drawing on the public value theory featured in her ANZSOG masters study, she describes the 'blended approach' she employs with her teams and for her own analytical and reflective purposes. In Chapter 12, the final chapter in Part 2, we see how Andrew Maurer employed the rational-comprehensive approach of the policy cycle as an overarching template to develop a policy handbook while working as a senior executive in the then Australian Department of Communications and the Arts. During its development, this 'in-house' guide would come to map the complementary roles of the department's new organisational structure and provide a common language and heuristic guide.

Part 3 presents insights from two leading public policy theorists on the processes underpinning policymaking in the modern state. UK-based theorist Paul Cairney, whose textbooks, blogs and research into policy theory reach an international audience, argues in Chapter 13 that policymakers and practitioners could utilise insights from policy theories if they were communicated more effectively, and that these insights could be used to explore common constraints and ethical dilemmas. In Chapter 14, Allan McConnell, a public policy specialist, synthesises the various authors' contributions, addressing the need for realistic expectations about what academic theory can bring, the dangers of stereotyping the two 'separate' worlds, the potential benefits of sharing the same space and the value of looking beyond the tip of the academic iceberg.

The concluding chapter explores why, and to whom, the debate about policy capacities and skills is important; the contours of the debate; the range of policy skills and practices involved; and future directions for applied research, including how theory can be tested against practice. We end, we hope, by offering something for practitioners looking for ways to improve their craft, academics keen to see future opportunities for applied research, and academic and practitioner partners who want the best of both worlds.

References

Adams, D, Colebatch, HK & Walker, CK 2015, 'Learning about learning: Discovering the work of policy', *Australian Journal of Public Administration*, vol. 74, no. 2, pp. 101–11, doi.org/10.1111/1467-8500.12119.

Advisory Group on Reform of Australian Government Administration 2010, *Ahead of the game: Blueprint for the reform of Australian government administration*, Department of the Prime Minister and Cabinet, Canberra, ACT.

Alford, J 2008, 'The limits to traditional public administration, or rescuing public value from misrepresentation', *Australian Journal of Public Administration*, vol. 67, no. 3, pp. 357–66, doi.org/10.1111/j.1467-8500.2008.00593.x.

Alford, J & O'Flynn, J 2009, 'Making sense of public value: Concepts, critiques and emergent meanings'. *International Journal of Public Administration*, vol. 32, nos. 3–4, pp. 171–91, doi.org/10.1080/01900690902732731.

Allen, P & Wanna, J 2016, 'Developing leadership and building executive capacity in the Australian public services for better governance', in A Podger & J Wanna (eds), *Sharpening the sword of state: Building executive capacities in the public services of the Asia-Pacific*, ANU Press, Canberra, ACT, doi.org/10.22459/SSS.11.2016.02.

Althaus, C, Bridgman, P & Davis, G 2018, *The Australian policy handbook: A practical guide to the policy-making process*, 6th edn, Allen & Unwin, Crows Nest, NSW.

Australian Government 2013, *Australian Public Service Commission state of the service report 2012–13*, Canberra, ACT.

Australian Government 2019, *APS policy capability roadmap: A practical plan to lift policy capability across the APS*, viewed 16 April 2020, www.policyhub.gov.au/sites/default/files/projects/aps-policy-capability-roadmap.pdf.

Banks, G 2018, 'Whatever happened to "evidence based policy making?"', Alf Rattigan Lecture delivered 20 November, Canberra, ACT, viewed 16 April 2020, apo.org.au/node/206646.

Brown, P, Cherney, L, Warner, S with Ugochie CA, Ball, S, Cunningham, LE, Le, LDD, Simpson Reeves, L & Worsoe, H 2019, *Understanding public value workshop: Report on proceedings*, University of Queensland, viewed 16 April 2020, polsis.uq.edu.au/files/22013/understandingpublicvalueworkshopreportcorrected.pdf.pdf.

Bryson, JM, Crosby, BC & Bloomberg, L 2014, 'Public value governance: Moving beyond traditional public administration and the new public management', *Public Administration Review*, vol. 74, no. 4, pp. 445–56, doi.org/10.1111/puar.12238.

Cairney, P 2015, 'How can policy theory have an impact on policymaking? The role of theory-led academic-practitioner discussions', *Teaching Public Administration*, vol. 33, no. 1, pp. 22–39, doi.org/10.1177/0144739414532284.

Cairney, P 2020, *Understanding public policy theories and issues*, 2nd edn, Red Globe Press, London, UK.

Cairney, P & Jones, MD 2016, 'Kingdon's multiple streams approach: What is the empirical impact of this universal theory?', *Policy Studies Journal*, vol. 44, no. 1, pp. 37–58, doi.org/10.1111/psj.12111.

Cairney, P & Weible, C 2017, 'The new policy sciences: Combining the cognitive science of choice, multiple theories of context, and basic and applied analysis', *Policy Sciences,* vol. 50, no. 4, pp. 619–27, doi.org/10.1007/s11077-017-9304-2.

Cohen, M, March, J & Olsen, J 1972, 'A garbage can model of organisational choice', *Administrative Science Quarterly,* vol. 17, no. 1, pp. 1–25, doi.org/10.2307/2392088.

Commonwealth of Australia 2019, *APS Review: Priorities for change,* Department of the Prime Minister and Cabinet, viewed 16 April 2020, www.apsreview.gov.au/resources/priorities-change.

Crowley, K & Head, B 2015, 'Policy analysis in Australia: Context, themes and challenges', in B Head & K Crowley (eds), *Policy analysis in Australia,* Policy Press, Bristol, UK, doi.org/10.1332/policypress/9781447310273.003.0001.

Daniell, K & Kay, A (eds) 2017, *Multi-level governance: Conceptual challenges and case studies from Australia,* ANU Press, Canberra, ACT, doi.org/10.22459/MG.11.2017.

Department of the Prime Minister and Cabinet (PM&C) 2019a, *Delivering for Australians,* viewed 5 February 2020, pmc.gov.au/resource-centre/government/delivering-for-australians.

Department of the Prime Minister and Cabinet (PM&C) 2019b, *Our public service, our future. Independent review of the Australian Public Service,* viewed 5 February 2020, pmc.gov.au/sites/default/files/publications/independent-review-aps.pdf.

Di Francesco, M 2015, 'Policy analysis instruction in Australia', in B Head & K Crowley (eds), *Policy analysis in Australia.* Policy Press, Bristol, UK, doi.org/10.1332/policypress/9781447310273.003.0017.

Easton, S 2019a, 'APS secretaries unveil online collaboration hub in push to improve policy skills', *Mandarin,* 21 June, viewed 16 April 2020, www.themandarin.com.au/110225-aps-secretaries-unveil-new-online-collaboration-hub-in-push-to-improve-policy-skills/.

Easton, S 2019b, 'Four departments and five secretaries cut while one returns, as PM reshapes the public service', *Mandarin,* 5 December, viewed 16 April 2020, www.themandarin.com.au/122170-from-the-desk-of-the-prime-minister-here-is-your-new-public-service/.

Gill, Z & Colebatch, HK 2006, 'Busy little workers': Policy workers' own accounts', in HK Colebatch (ed.), *Beyond the policy cycle: The policy process in Australia,* Allen & Unwin, Crows Nest, NSW.

Grattan, M 2019, 'View from The Hill: Morrison won't have a bar of public service intrusions on government's power', *Conversation,* 13 December, viewed 16 April 2020, theconversation.com/view-from-the-hill-morrison-wont-have-a-bar-of-public-service-intrusions-on-governments-power-128880.

Head, B 2015, 'Policy analysis and public sector capacity', in B Head & K Crowley (eds), *Policy analysis in Australia,* Policy Press, Bristol, UK, doi.org/10.1332/policypress/9781447310273.001.0001.

Hollander, R & Patapan, H 2007, 'Pragmatic federalism: Australian federalism from Hawke to Howard', *Australian Journal of Public Administration*, vol. 66, no. 3, pp. 280–97, doi.org/10.1111/j.1467-8500.2007.00542.x.

Jenkins, S 2019a, 'This APS review will be different, says Commissioner', *Mandarin,* 26 September, viewed 16 April 2020, www.themandarin.com.au/116772-this-aps-review-will-be-different-says-commissioner/.

Jenkins, S 2019b, 'How to deliver great policy advice', *Mandarin,* 5 December, viewed 16 April 2020, www.themandarin.com.au/122114-how-to-deliver-great-policy-advice/.

Kingdon, JW 2011, *Agendas, alternatives, and public policies*, updated 2nd edn, Longman, Crawfordsville, IN.

Lindblom, CE 1959, 'The science of "muddling through"', *Public Administration Review*, vol. 19, no. 2, pp. 79–88, doi.org/10.2307/973677.

Lindquist, E 2010, 'From rhetoric to blueprint: The Moran review as a concerted, comprehensive and emergent strategy for public service reform', *Australian Journal of Public Administration*, vol. 69, no. 2, pp. 115–51, doi.org/10.1111/j.1467-8500.2010.00684.x.

Luetjens, J, Mintrom, M & 't Hart, P 2019a, *Successful public policy: Lessons from Australia and New Zealand.* ANU Press, Canberra, ACT, doi.org/10.22459/SPP.2019.

Luetjens, J, Mintrom, M & 't Hart, P 2019b, 'On studying policy successes in Australia and New Zealand', in J Luetjens, M Mintrom, & P 't Hart (eds), *Successful public policy: Lessons from Australia and New Zealand*, ANU Press, Canberra, ACT, doi.org/10.22459/SPP.2019.01.

Macpherson, R & 't Hart, P 2020, 'Leading in a crisis: Using adaptive leadership to shape the COVID-19 crisis response', ANZSOG, 18 April, viewed 23 April 2020, www.anzsog.edu.au/resource-library/research/using-adaptive-leadership-to-shape-the-covid19-crisis-response.

McConnell, A 2015, 'What is policy failure? A primer to help navigate the maze', *Public Policy and Administration,* vol. 30, nos 3–4, pp. 221–42, doi.org/10.1177/0952076714565416.

McConnell, A, Stern, EK & Boin, A 2020, 'Leading in a crisis: How to learn from others', ANZSOG, 28 April, viewed 3 May 2020, www.anzsog.edu.au/resource-library/research/how-to-learn-from-others.

Moore, MH 1995, *Creating public value: Strategic management in government,* Harvard University Press, Cambridge, MA.

Morrison, S 2019, 'Prime Minister's address to the Australian Public Service', 19 August, Institute of Public Administration Australia ACT Division, viewed 16 April 2020, www.act.ipaa.org.au/2019-pastevent-primeminister.

Nature Neuroscience 2005, '(Editorial) The practice of theoretical neuroscience', Editorial *Nature Neuroscience,* vol. 8, no. 12, p. 1627, doi.org/10.1038/nn1205-1627.

O'Flynn, J, Vardon, S, Yeatman, A & Carson, L 2011, 'Perspectives on the capacity of the Australian Public Service and effective policy development and implementation', *Australian Journal of Public Administration,* vol. 70, no. 3, pp. 309–17, doi.org/10.1111/j.1467-8500.2011.00731.x.

Parsons, W 1995, *Public policy: An introduction to the theory and practice of policy analysis.* Edward Elgar, Cheltenham, UK.

Parsons, W 2004, 'Not just steering but weaving: Relevant knowledge and the craft of building policy capacity and coherence', *Australian Journal of Public Administration,* vol. 63, no. 1, pp. 43–57, doi.org/10.1111/j.1467-8500.2004.00358.x.

Rhodes, RAW 2016, 'Recovering the craft of public administration', *Public Administration Review,* vol. 76, no. 4, 638–47, doi.org/10.1111/puar.12504.

Rhodes, RAW & Wanna, J 2007, 'The limits to public value, or rescuing responsible government from the platonic guardians', *Australian Journal of Public Administration,* vol. 66, no. 4, pp. 406–21, doi.org/10.1111/j.1467-8500.2007.00553.x.

Rhodes, RAW & Wanna, J 2008, 'Stairways to heaven: A reply to Alford', *Australian Journal of Public Administration,* vol. 67, no. 3, pp. 367–70, doi.org/10.1111/j.1467-8500.2008.00594.x.

Rhodes, RAW & Wanna, J 2009, 'Bringing the politics back in: Public value in Westminster parliamentary government', *Public Administration,* vol. 87, no. 2, pp. 161–83, doi.org/10.1111/j.1467-9299.2009.01763.x.

Sabatier, PA 2007, 'The need for better theories', in PA Sabatier (ed.), *Theories of the policy process*, Westview Press, Boulder, CO.

Shergold, P 2015, 'Foreword', in B Head & K Crowley (eds), *Policy analysis in Australia*, Policy Press, Bristol, UK.

Sinodinos, A 2017, 'Innovations awards address', in *IPAA speeches 2017. A year of speeches from public service leaders,* Institute of Public Administration Australia ACT Division, Canberra, ACT.

Stewart, J & Buick, F 2019, 'The academic-practitioner divide in public management: and how to bridge it', *Power to Persuade*, blog 6 June, viewed 16 April 2020, www.powertopersuade.org.au/blog/the-academic-practitioner-divide-in-public-management-and-how-to-bridge-it/6/6/2019.

Tiernan, A 2011, 'Advising Australian federal governments: Assessing the evolving capacity and role of the Australian Public Service', *Australian Journal of Public Administration,* vol. 70, no. 4, pp. 335–46, doi.org/10.1111/j.1467-8500.2011.00742.x.

Tiernan, A 2018, 'Public sector capability. Buy it or build it?', PolicyInnoHub, 20 March, viewed 20 April 2020, medium.com/the-machinery-of-government/public-sector-capability-f4a40fe38739.

Weible, CM, Nohrstedt, D, Cairney, P, Carter, DP, Crow, DA, Durnova, AP, Heikkila, T, Ingold, K, McConnell, A & Stone, D 2020, 'COVID-19 and the policy sciences: Initial reactions and perspectives', *Policy Sciences*, vol. 53, no. 2, pp. 225–41, doi.org/10.1007/s11077-020-09381-4.

Weible, CM & Sabatier, PA 2017, *Theories of the policy process,* 4th edn, Westview Press, Boulder, CO.

Wiseman, J 2010, 'Dancing with strangers: Understanding the parallel universes of academic researchers and public sector policy makers', *ANZSOG Occasional Paper No. 11*, Victorian State Services Authority and ANZSOG.

2

A quixotic quest? Making theory speak to practice

David Threlfall and Catherine Althaus

All models are wrong, but some are useful. (George EP Box, as cited in Box, Hunter & Hunter 2005, p. 440)

This chapter considers the relationship between theory and practice. It seeks to interrogate the historical, professional and ideological underpinnings of theories of the policy process and their utilisation in policy practice. These theories should of course influence practice, but practice should similarly influence theory building. We explore why this connection is commonly seen as unidirectional. To advance both theoretical and practice-based understanding, we argue more attention should be paid to the interconnection of the two. The task of translation from one to the other—in either direction—requires acknowledgement of one's assumptions about knowledge. Knowing *how* (practice, through experience of public problem-solving, or craft) should be recognised as just as valid as knowing *what* (academic or scientific knowledge creation and mastery) (Billett 2009 as cited in Cendon 2016, p. 305; cf. Raadschelders 2004). In public policy and public administration, as in many other fields, this has not always been the case—to the point that apparent divisions have arisen between theoretical questions and their practical application. The professional division of labour between academia and policymaking should not naturally hinder mutually reinforcing knowledge advancement in this way.

Drawing on longstanding debates in educational philosophy about this troubling distinction between theory and practice and applying them to the domain of public policymaking, we urge renewed focus on the interconnection of theory and practice through *critical thinking* and *reflection*. Ideally, there should be a two-way translation effect at play in policy learning. For policy professionals, a theory often becomes valuable knowledge only through the experience—in practice—of how to apply it. Likewise, practice should inform theory development through the insights offered by reflection on the experience of practice. We argue this interconnection between practice and theory is possible through a renewed focus on the educational step required to bridge the space 'in-between' theory and practice: encouragement of critical thinking and reflection as a means to learn from and build on experience of practice, and the use of heuristics in policy learning.

In making our argument, we want to be clear that we employ a broad interpretation of the term 'theory'. At times we are referring specifically to the case of theories of the policy process and their deployment, or otherwise, in relation to practice. For many of our arguments, however, we utilise 'theory' to capture the broader concept of academic scholarship. We recognise that empirical work is not the same as theory building and, in this regard, that 'theory' might be misleading. For the purposes of accessibility, however, we think the term 'theory' resonates with how practitioners often understand the breadth of academic efforts. We prefer to embrace this broad church of academic scholarship and see it as encompassing the endeavours of theory building, rather than split hairs on this occasion and risk losing the thread of our analysis and its key messages.

The chapter proceeds in five parts. First, we explore and argue against any perception of a divide between theory and practice in public administration and public policymaking. Reflective learning on policy experience is explored in the second, drawing on educational philosophy. In the third, we analyse public administration theories and theorists for efforts at theoretical consolidation and connection to practice. The role of heuristics in reflective policy learning is fundamental to our own theoretical approach, explored in the fourth part. Finally, in our conclusion, we call for deeper engagement between theorists and practitioners through mutually reinforcing reflective practice, with a view to improving (together) the policymaking process.

Interrogating the apparent divide between theory and practice

Many commentators argue that the link between theory and practice in public administration has been afflicted by a deep division or has in some way fundamentally broken down. We remain more optimistic. In fact, we go one step further, and reject outright the existence of any such divide. Promotion of this notion will only (continue to) foster potentially antagonistic relationships rather than encourage the important work of translation and mutual understanding that is so necessary to the advancement of the fields of public policy and public administration in a holistic way.

Scholars such as Sandra Nutley (Nutley et al. 2003), Brian Head (2010, 2014), Paul Cairney (2016), Peter Shergold (2013), Meredith Edwards (2010a, 2010b) and Helen Sullivan (2011, 2019) variously propose that more needs to be done to unite scholarship and practice in the name of improving evidence-informed policymaking. The reasons they identify for the disconnect vary: academia is unplugged from the reality of practice, academic incentives do not value practical impact, practitioners do not have time to read or they cannot access academic information due to paywalls, practitioners perhaps do not comprehend theoretical or academic language and doubt its relevance, practitioners do not appreciate the framing of research questions, practitioners are not interested in rigour or simply fail to apply the lessons of academic work (cf. Buick et al. 2016, p. 36; Newman, Cherney & Head 2016). The list goes on (and the topic is explored further in the New Zealand context by Karl Löfgren & Sarah Hendrica Bickerton [this volume, Chapter 5]). While all of these observations contain nuggets of truth, to then interpret their combined pessimistic sentiment into an irreparable gulf, rather than a series of discrete solvable problems, is deeply unhelpful.

In fact, arguments that promote this 'sharp distinction' between theory and practice ensure 'our understanding [of both is] distorted and impaired' (Carr 1986, p. 177). The systematic division of theory and practice artificially separates knowledge from its application and, in doing so, introduces a hierarchy of knowledge based on the division of labour involved in knowledge creation (academia, science) and the application of that knowledge (practice). Writing about this division from the perspective of the higher education profession, Carr (1986, p. 177) argued strongly for a break from this technical rational hierarchy, declaring it a hindrance to the advancement of what should be a shared endeavour:

> Ideas about the nature of educational theory are always ideas about the nature of educational practice and always incorporate a latent conception of how, in practice, theory should be used. Thus the systematic, well-articulated and explicit accounts of educational theory which philosophers are prone to discuss and dissect are, at one and the same time, less systematic, unarticulated and often implicit accounts of educational practice as well. There are not, therefore, theories of theory and theories of practice and yet other theories about the relationship between the two. All education theories are theories of theory and practice.

By separating philosophical questions about theory from pragmatic discussion of the insights drawn from practice, we may advance theory itself but we lose sight of its connection to context: policy practice happens in an environment that is volatile, complex, uncertain and ambiguous (van der Wal 2017, pp. 1–6). Problems in the real world are not ring-fenced and discrete, as theories might have them be. Real-world puzzles are uncertain and changing continuously, and any application of theory requires an understanding of context, which is generally best achieved through lived experience—and thus through practice (Schön 1983; cf. Cendon 2016, pp. 305–7). Doing this well requires reflection on experience fostered by understanding and judgement—hard won expertise of policymaking and the public administration field (Fletcher et al. 2010, p. 490). What this means is that, in the division of theory from practice, we can de-emphasise the practical importance of real-world problem-solving in favour of a strongly normative approach based on generic and concrete theories. Some theories undoubtedly translate to strong application in a policymaking setting, regardless of context, but this is (unsurprisingly) not universally so.

There is a quote often attributed to Kant that reads: 'theory without practice is empty; practice without theory is blind'. Writing more recently, Langeveld (1979, p. 17, as cited in van Manen, 1996, p. 45) took this further and wrote: 'theory without practice is for geniuses; practice without theory is for fools and rogues. But for the majority of educators, the intimate and unbreakable union of both is necessary.' What is really interesting in Langeveld's contribution is the insertion of *educators* into the theory–practice paradigm. We similarly believe there is an essential yet poorly understood educational step—through critical thinking and reflection—in bridging any division between theory and practice today. By taking an education and learning approach to the union of theory and practice, we see much room for hope in minimising practical blindness and avoiding theoretical emptiness.

From theory to practice: Knowledge through reflection on experience

There is, and should be, a fundamental link between knowing and doing, from action to reflection and back again, a point made by Russell Ayres in this volume (Chapter 8). To argue practice is free from theory is either to divorce critical thinking from action, or to overlook the ideological sleight of hand in laying claim to theory-free practice. When put to the test—as Carr (1986) does in his analysis of theories of theory and practice—it becomes clear it is nonsensical to believe that any set of human practices, like any set of human observations, would be free from theoretical preconceptions. In other words, we can all be seen to hold some theory or assumptions about the relationship between theory and practice, whether implicit or explicit. The assumptions themselves are not missing, but rather their conscious or unequivocal recognition. Understood in this light, rival views of policymaking or public administration embed opposing views of how theory relates to practice. Perhaps what critics are bemoaning, then, is the loss of *their* worldview and its articulation of how theory ought to relate to practice.

While acknowledging that vested interests underlie debates about theory and practice is an important step, the challenge of theoretical and practical advancement remains. Carr (1986, pp. 180–3) sought to solve this problem by categorising four major competing approaches in educational theory and their differing views of practice. He argued through this categorisation that all theory contains an account of practice and all practice embeds theory.

These approaches are:

Common sense: generalisations are acquired through 'observation and analysis of practice and tested pragmatically in practical situations'. Any notion that theory could be developed independently or objectively is rejected; practice establishes the accuracy of theory rather than theory establishing soundness of practice. The role of theory is to uncover or recover concepts, principles and skills implicit in 'good' or 'successful' practice, with the arbiter of such practice being the tradition embodied in, and by, revered practitioners in the field in question (in our case, public administration and policymaking).

Applied science: with its focus on behaviourism and scientific standards, this approach sees practice as essentially a technical endeavour designed to bring about particular, specifiable ends. Good practice is determined not by practitioners through some sort of common sense or tradition but by their measurable adherence to higher order scientific principles.

Practical: Practice does not serve fixed ends but is a fluid activity in which choice of both means and ends is guided by values and criteria immanent in the process itself. Theory and good practice, in this approach, neither encourage conformity to a given practice tradition nor scientific prescription. Instead, they encourage attention to the disposition and character of the practitioner as engaged in moral acts. Thus, in our case, public administration and policy practice relies on 'practical wisdom' (Kane & Patapan 2006) and the informed, committed action and moral judgement of practitioners.

Critical: Theory is meant to help practitioners become self-conscious about the causal determinants of their beliefs and practices, often expressed as ideology, in order to increase their rational autonomy within a social endeavour. This is achieved through 'critical self-*reflection*' (Carr 1986, p. 183, emphasis added). The stress is on moving not between theory and practice but between irrationality and rationality, and from ignorance and habit to knowledge and reflection.

The common sense and practical approaches articulate a familiar model of public policy learning—on-the-job, through experience of the policymaking process, guided by traditional (common sense) or moral (practical) principles. The technical rational model in the applied science approach sits at the other end of the spectrum, where practice has little to offer. We find the fourth, critical approach promising in assisting the transition from knowing what (theory) to knowing how (practice) and back again. Carr's argument here links directly to the concept of critical thinking and reflective learning in educational philosophy. To expand on this concept and define terms, reflection in this usage follows Cendon (2016, p. 309): 'a critical stance towards [one's] own learning, actual situation, and influencing circumstances'. It is 'an evidence-based examination of the sources of and gaps in knowledge and practice, with the intent to improve both' (Ash & Clayton 2009, pp. 27–8). A shared language with the policy profession is evident in this second quotation, and yet the interlinkage between policy practice and theory on these terms is not. 'We may [then] use existing theories to *make further sense of*' our policy experiences (van Manen 1991, p. 100, emphasis added). The order that van Manen articulates for the learning process is central to our argument: existing theory supplements experience of practice and reflection on practice. By placing greater weight on this reflective task in policy learning, we should be able to make progress towards a clearer interconnection of theory and practice.

While this may sound like a time-consuming or complex ask, both Carr and van Manen are simply asking for a more conscious approach to learning that values reflection in both theory and practice. Whereas Carr's categorisation identifies the prior assumptions we bring to our thinking about practice, van Manen's (1991, p. 100) model of reflective learning asks practitioners to be critical as they act in the present. For van Manen, insight can be drawn from four levels of reflection: 1) common sense thinking, or intuition and routines; 2) reflection on day-to-day incidents; 3) reflection on one's own experience and the experience of others, or conscious thought to create insights (theories) about action and interaction with others; and 4) reflection on the nature of knowledge, or 'meta-reflection', interrogating the way we think and the way we learn (cf. Cendon 2016, pp. 311–12, 315).

The translation of Carr's and van Manen's work is that policymakers are more influenced by theory than they might believe, and simultaneously more capable of creating sound theory than theorists might expect. While the fast pace or the daily grind of the policy arena may render this task challenging, if we are to advance both theory and practice in a holistic way, practitioners and theorists should be similarly self-critical and reflective, and pursue engagement with one another to exchange these insights. In this way we can develop the most effective theory-informed practice, and successfully tackle the significant translation exercise and effort required to develop practice-informed theory.

There is one further element to add to this discussion of knowledge creation about practice: the concept of *emergence*, or what we might term the 'Harry Potter maze effect'. In the fourth instalment of this now famous book and movie series, *Harry Potter and the goblet of fire* (Rowling 2000), the by-now teenage wizard, Harry, is selected to compete in the Triwizard Tournament. This is a competition that sets a number of young wizards on a dangerous quest of self-discovery to complete a range of tasks and secure points for their respective wizard schools. The final challenge is to enter a magical maze on the Hogwarts grounds to secure the goal of the Triwizard cup at the centre of the maze. What happens to the wizards after they enter the maze is that it actually shifts around them as they move through it, simultaneously challenging them by revealing their fears and drawing out their courage to confront negative aspects of themselves. As they wade into the maze, not only does the maze change, but also the wizards. They become affected in different ways by the impact of the maze—and their fears and own selves. Thus the wizards become enmeshed in a very dramatic moral dilemma, as they physically move through the maze and simultaneously engage with decisions as to how to respond to their shifting feelings and decisions.

Lessons from the world of practice tell us that, in a similar vein, it is oftentimes very bewildering navigating the maze of policymaking life. There are two basic responses when we find ourselves affected by this kind of complexity: one is to be bewildered and seek out sense-making tools to bring order to the analytical task and to the gathering of evidence and potential solutions. We might call this the *closed mode* of rational evidence gathering and analysis. The other route is to be more creative and secure mechanisms that foster innovation and help develop new ways to frame policy challenges, including new narratives or meta-values that might encourage diverse communities to break through impasses (such as how to define problems and reimagine what solutions might be possible for them). We might call this the *open mode* of craft and creativity. Both closed and open modes are important and of value to the policymaking endeavour, but they involve dissimilar processes and embed different philosophies and goals. They speak to a variety of ways that the literature, too, explains how to do public administration and policymaking (the art, craft or science debate explored by Raadschelders (2004) provides a good introduction).

The maze metaphor captures an important point about theory and practice—as you are engaging in different ways of looking at policymaking and public administration, you are simultaneously changing yourself and policymaking as you perform this policy work. The processes of thinking and doing policy are unavoidably intertwined and reflexive.

Theory and practice in public policy and public administration

We have argued that policy learners must be reflective and critical practitioners if they are to succeed. As such, the wide array of policy models, frameworks and theories that exist in academic literature should be a boon for practitioners (a brief study of recent additions includes Althaus, Bridgman & Davis 2018; Birkland 2016; Colebatch 2009; Dye 2007; Gerston 2010; Haigh 2012; Head & Crowley 2015; John 2012; Knill & Tosun 2012; Kraft & Furlong 2013; Pal 2014; Sabatier & Weible 2014; Scott & Baehler 2010; Wilson 2016). While at times underutilised or misunderstood, these resources are at practitioners' disposal—and it should not require magic to turn their insights into practical benefit. Similarly, practitioner insights and experiences offer tremendous encouragement towards improvements in policymaking processes and outcomes, feeding the development and testing of new ideas by theorists and prompting policymakers to deliberate reflectively on assumptions, values and priorities.

Elinor Ostrom (1999, pp. 39–41) provides a valuable contribution by distinguishing between frameworks, theories and models (cf. Schlager 1999). These conceptual terms operate on three descending and increasingly detailed levels of abstraction. At the most general level, *frameworks* set the architecture for analysis and comparison of identified concepts. *Theories* set out propositions about the relationships between those concepts. *Models* then make specific assumptions about the operation of elements, structures or outcomes within the broader explanatory framework. 'Several theories are usually compatible with any framework … [and multiple] models are compatible with most theories' (Ostrom 1999, p. 40). Many theories in particular attempt to establish causality, explanation or prediction. That these are measures of theoretical strength favoured by many *academics* underlines that most theories emphasise an academic perspective, highlighting in particular the complexity of policymaking. For practitioners, the risk is that, in highlighting complexity, we forget the connection to the object of study, that is, policy practice, not just understanding of it. Practice demands action, even in the face of complexity.

For example, Paul Cairney and Paul Sabatier both focus on the comparison and advancement of theories (Cairney & Heikkila 2014; Sabatier 1999b). In Sabatier's writing, in particular, scholars are the sole audience; there is little emphasis on practitioners. Instead, we read of the 'analyst' or the 'observer' (Sabatier 1999a, p. 4). Cairney (2015; Cairney & Oliver 2018) is more aware of the domain of practice, but the direction of knowledge creation in his writing is from academic insight to practical application. If we were to map this academic inclination to Carr's categorisation described earlier, we might say that the implicit assumption about practice in such writing aligns best with the applied science approach: a hierarchy whereby scientific knowledge is valued above practical experience and problem-solving. With knowledge use and application so divided, the task of thinking through and advancing connection to practice remains incomplete. The reflection encouraged by van Manen is not yet leveraged let alone optimised.

There is nevertheless a strong vein of public policy and public administration literature devoted to holistic theoretical consolidation and advancement. Authors such as Cairney (2013) and Graham Allison (1971) speak of the value brought by applying different lenses to the scholarship of public administration and policymaking. Cairney (2013) suggests three possible approaches for combining theories (or aspects thereof): synthesis, contradiction and complementarity. Members of the complementary camp support the use of different theories to gain breadth of insight, seeing multiplicity of views as both helpful and desirable. Synthesisers, meanwhile, believe that a grand theory is both desirable and attainable through a combination of the array of models, frameworks and theories on offer. The contradictory approach is perhaps better termed comparison—the contribution of each theory and its assumptions are compared, and the most useful theory selected over others, in a 'policy shootout' (Cairney 2015, p. 10).

To us, it seems pointless and self-defeating to pit different theories against each other in this way. We sit squarely in Cairney's complementary camp. Putting our practitioner hats on, and acknowledging the myriad structural, resource and political challenges of the policy world, we see similarities between, and diverse application possibilities for, the widest range of theories, models and frameworks. We believe practitioners are comfortable with complexity and that they can apply whatever model helps them to understand their task more clearly in order to leverage processes and institutions for a better policy outcome. As theorists, this means understanding the underlying assumptions of our own standpoint and interrogating how we can contribute to practical knowledge as well. Thus, as theorists, we believe that we should not discard theoretical advancement as an act in itself, given it offers a means to inspire potential innovation or improved practice.

This position promotes a more conscious view of where we sit in relation to Carr's categorisation of approaches to the intertwining of theory and practice. Complementarity advocates would support a diversity of approaches whereas synthesisers and those in favour of contradiction are more likely to sit within the applied science or common sense approach. In his conclusion, Cairney (2013, pp. 14–15) argues that we generally share a desire to advance theories of policymaking, but disagree as to the methodology that will allow us to do so. From the standpoint of building *academic* knowledge of policymaking, it is hard to argue against his first recommendation (pp. 15–16) for acceptance of 'methodological pluralism' and 'sophistication', supported by 'interdisciplinary collaboration'. However, from the standpoint of impact on *practice*, there is a translation effort lacking even in this liberal approach. How do we make the jump to practical application?

From knowing what to knowing how: The policy cycle and the role of heuristics

The policy cycle has been much maligned in public policy and public administration theory. Yet, Lasswell's (1956) core idea—a staged process through which policy issues progress, and a means to analyse each stage—remains an important contribution. It 'offer[s] a way to think about public policy in concept and, just as important, in operation' (deLeon 1999, p. 20). It sharpens focus on policy problems and the way they work through policy systems, and promotes a multidisciplinary approach to policy problem-solving (Althaus, Bridgman & Davis 2018).

The key point made by critiques of the cycle is that it is an oversimplification—that policymaking is always more complex and does not work in a linear fashion (deLeon 1999; cf. Jenkins-Smith & Sabatier 1993, pp. 3–4; Colebatch 2006). We argue that this criticism misses the point. Neither theorists nor practitioners are looking for an elegant solution with something like the policy cycle. In fact, we believe the very reason practitioners find value in the policy cycle, and the core reason for its longevity, lies in the simplicity of its message and the ease with which it is taught. The policy cycle is a learning aid, or *heuristic*, a 'process or method' by which someone can 'discover or learn something for themselves' (Oxford Dictionaries 2019). As a heuristic, the policy cycle serves to prompt reflection on prior experience of practice and offers a framework for learning about future experience (see e.g. the arguments and application of Meredith Edwards and Russell Ayres in Chapters 7 and 8, respectively). It allows practitioners to step back from the complicated work of the day-to-day policy world with the aid of a framework that they can internalise, learn from and then work with (often unconsciously) in the future.

This is particularly what motivated the development of the Australian policy cycle as a specific interpretation of Lasswell's staged policy process. Figure 2.1 provides a visual of the Australian policy cycle conveying the cyclical and interconnected nature of the various steps. The text associated with the Australian model deliberately conveys its heuristic nature and the proactive and reflective contributions needed from practitioners to bring its application alive and fruitful for policymaking outcomes.

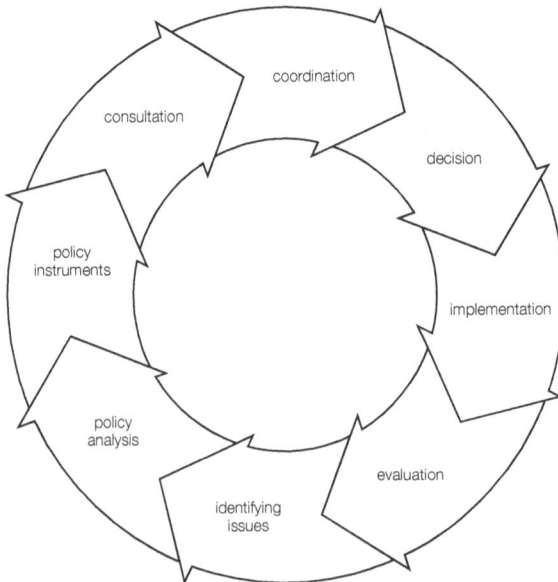

Figure 2.1. The Australian policy cycle.
Source: Althaus, Bridgman and Davis (2018).

Essentially, we are following the Harry Potter maze metaphor—theory and practice are emergent, and policy and public administration protagonists are pivotal as active agents of change. Both policymakers and theorists, as well as policy itself, shift and change as we engage in thinking about policy and making policy. In this fluid environment, a heuristic serves as a guide for those who need to learn about the challenges of their roles. Seen in this light, then, the policy cycle is focused on the teaching, learning and reflection process. It provides a means to make sense of experience, as well as a tool to inspire creativity as policymakers navigate the policy maze they inevitably confront.

A useful analogy here is the London underground (the 'tube'). London in real-life or on a map does not look like the tube map does. Instead, the tube map is a heuristic to help us navigate from one place to another. It is deeply practical; it gets you from A to B. It is not to scale, nor is it physically or geographically accurate, but it can be helpful to travellers. The policy cycle and other heuristics serve the same purpose. Heuristics work because they focus on putting theory and practice at the service of one another, rather than in opposition. They focus on reflective and reflexive learning, and turning knowledge into application in practice. We might argue that a heuristic like the policy cycle is the step from pedagogy (the method and practice of teaching) to andragogy (the method and practice of teaching *adult learners*) (Knowles 1984). Thinking through this interconnection between the theory of practice and the teaching of practice is vitally important in ensuring policy learning continues to improve in future.

As a learning tool, the policy cycle articulates an approach to solving public policy 'puzzles' on both systemic and process levels. It also sets the *routines* of policy work for practitioners, a critical element of the governance process (Davis 1995). Cendon (2016, p. 318) writes that a 'central contribution of teachers is supporting the handling of routines, patterns, or assumptions students have developed as "inner and outer framework conditions"'. Inner framework conditions should be understood as personal biases that may hinder learning or action in new environments, while outer framework conditions are the elements of the public sector that may or may not be susceptible to change. The task of the teacher (or the policy cycle) is to help practitioners learning their craft to understand what they must change in themselves, what can change around them and what cannot. In understanding these routines and the reality of the confines of their environment, they understand how to direct their efforts for maximum impact. The combination of a heuristic like the policy cycle (a tool for at first conscious but increasingly implicit action) and the idea of reflective learning (a very conscious act) leads to a continuum of thought-informed practice that both incorporates theory and is cognisant of the realities of practice. We can map this onto Donald Schön's (1983) distinction between *knowing in action* (at times unconscious yet clearly thought-informed action, like intuition and implicit knowledge—the 'main characteristics [of which] are routines'); *reflection in action*, more conscious yet immediate thought during practice; and *reflection on action*, or 'systematic and critical review and continuous development of one's practice' after the fact (Cendon 2016, p. 307).

Perhaps, then, the best approach to the use of the policy cycle is to acknowledge its strength in assisting practical learning, and to build on its theoretical weaknesses with a view to consolidation rather than competition. Howlett, McConnell and Perl (2017) make just such a contribution to 'moving policy theory forward' in their synthesis of the policy cycle with the multiple streams and advocacy coalition frameworks of Kingdon (1984) and Sabatier and Jenkins-Smith (1993), respectively. By bringing together the insights of three parallel approaches, we derive a richer analysis within the stages of the cycle, with a clearer view of the actors and forces at play in the policy process.

The task of connecting theory to practice is clearly complicated. However, through its careful application as a heuristic, the policy cycle is able to tap both the technocratic closed mode of analysis and evidence gathering, underpinned by the rational-comprehensive approach to policymaking, and also the open mode recourse to practitioner application and judgement. The heuristic embedded in the policy cycle embraces and deploys many of the adult learning principles outlined above. It encourages practitioners and theorists to be pluralistic, active, intrinsically motivated, goal oriented and somewhat pragmatic in how they apply judgement to particular circumstances as well as develop more generalist principles drawn from experience. A key point in our discussion of the cycle is that practitioners and theorists have freedom and should be supported to exercise their own initiative and creativity to progress the discipline as well as societal outcomes. For us, the point of the policy cycle is to spur improvement of practice, a goal far removed from militant argument on the relative merits of different research paradigms.

Conclusion

This chapter has explored and argued against the existence of a theory–practice divide in public administration and public policymaking. There is no value in perpetuating belief in, or perceptions of, a divide. Rather, we should pursue the interconnection of theory and practice in order to advance knowledge and improve practice for those working in either domain. We draw on education philosophy and reflective learning on policy experience to make this case. A brief overview and analysis of public administration theories and theorists indicates various attempts at theoretical consolidation and connection to practice; however, these attempts often perpetuate a hierarchy of knowledge generation from academia into practice. If we are to move to a position whereby both fields are self-reinforcing, this implicit hierarchy would no longer exist or assumptions about the relationship/s between theory and practice would be made transparent.

While it is natural that there may be a certain division of labour and specialisation for academics and policy professionals, those working in both fields must possess a shared language and desire to critique, learn and reflect together with a view to improving the policymaking process and outcomes. This two-way task of translation and knowledge creation is vital. Theory building and practice improvement are a *shared enterprise*. The more we can promote this joint enterprise, and the more we encourage both parties to exercise their agency, the better for policy processes and outcomes.

One way of stimulating this interconnection and reflective practice is through heuristics. We argue that a turn to education and its tools (such as heuristics) is beneficial for both policy practitioners and scholars committed to the improvement of practice. As Box (Box, Hunter & Hunter 2005, p. 440) argues in our epigraph, no single heuristic captures the true operation of policy processes or political systems. Nor should it. Rather, the intent and benefit is to cut through a perfect description or an accurate prediction in order to assist in the task of learning and doing that policy practitioners face on a daily basis. This makes for truly reflective practice for scholars and practitioners. We hope this assessment of the field might inspire others equally to join this endeavour.

References

Allison, G 1971, *Essence of decision: Explaining the Cuban missile crisis*, Little Brown, Boston, MA.

Althaus, C, Bridgman, P & Davis, G 2018, *The Australian policy handbook: A practical guide to the policy-making process*, 6th edn, Allen & Unwin, Crows Nest, NSW.

Ash, SL & Clayton, PH 2009, 'Generating, deepening, and documenting learning: The power of critical reflection in applied learning', *Journal of Applied Learning in Higher Education*, vol. 1, pp. 25–48.

Billett, S 2009, 'Realising the educational worth of integrating work experiences in higher education', *Studies in Higher Education*, vol. 34, no. 7, pp. 827–43, doi.org/10.1080/03075070802706561.

Birkland, TA 2016, *An introduction to the policy process: Theories, concepts and models of public policy making*, 4th edn, Routledge, New York, NY, doi.org/10.4324/9781315717371.

Box, GEP, Hunter, W & Hunter, S 2005, *Statistics for experimenters: Design, innovation, and discovery*, 2nd edn, Wiley, New York, NY.

Buick, F, Blackman, D, O'Flynn, J, O'Donnell, M & West, D 2016, 'Effective practitioner-scholar relationships: Lessons from a coproduction partnership', *Public Administration Review*, vol. 76, no. 1, pp. 35–47, doi.org/10.1111/puar.12481.

Cairney, P 2013, 'Standing on the shoulders of giants: How do we combine the insights of multiple theories in public policy studies?', *Policy Studies Journal*, vol. 41, no. 1, p. 21, doi.org/10.1111/psj.12000.

Cairney, P 2015, 'How can policy theory have an impact on policymaking? The role of theory-led academic-practitioner discussions', *Teaching Public Administration*, vol. 33, no. 1, pp. 22–39, doi.org/10.1177/0144739414532284.

Cairney, P 2016, *The politics of evidence-based policy making*, Palgrave Macmillan, London, UK.

Cairney, P & Heikkila, T 2014, 'A comparison of theories of the policy process', in PA Sabatier & CM Weible (eds), *Theories of the policy process*, Westview Press, Boulder, CO.

Cairney, P & Oliver, K 2018, 'How should academics engage in policymaking to achieve impact?', *Political Studies Review*, vol. [Special Is.], pp. 1–17, doi.org/10.1177/1478929918807714.

Carr, W 1986, 'Theories of theory and practice', *Journal of Philosophy of Education*, vol. 20, no. 2, pp. 177–86, doi.org/10.1111/j.1467-9752.1986.tb00125.x.

Cendon, E 2016, 'Bridging theory and practice: Reflective learning in higher education', in W Nuninger & J-M Châtelet (eds), *Handbook of research on quality assurance and value management in higher education*, IGI Global, Pennsylvania, pp. 304–24, doi.org/10.4018/978-1-5225-0024-7.ch012.

Colebatch, HK (ed.) 2006, *Beyond the policy cycle: The policy process in Australia*, Allen & Unwin, Sydney, NSW.

Colebatch, HK 2009, *Policy*, 3rd edn, Open University Press, Maidenhead, UK.

Davis, G 1995, *A government of routines: Executive coordination in an Australian state*, Macmillan Education Australia, South Melbourne, Vic.

DeLeon, P 1999, 'The stages approach to the policy process: What has it done? Where is it going?', in PA Sabatier (ed.), *Theories of the policy process*, Westview Press, Boulder CO.

Dye, T 2007, *Understanding public policy*, 12th edn, Prentice-Hall, Upper Saddle River, NJ.

Edwards, M 2010a, 'In search of useful research: Demand and supply challenges for policy makers', *Public Administration Today*, no. 24, pp. 56–64.

Edwards, M 2010b, 'Making research more relevant to policy: Evidence and suggestions', in G Bammer, A Michaux & A Sanson (eds), *Bridging the 'know–do' gap: Knowledge brokering to improve child wellbeing*, ANU E Press, Canberra, ACT. doi.org/10.22459/BKDG.08.2010.04.

Fletcher, M, Zuber-Skerritt, O, Bartlett, B, Albertyn, R & Kearney, J 2010, 'Meta-action research on a leadership development program: A process model for life-long learning', *Systemic Practice & Action Research*, vol. 23, no. 6, pp. 487–507, doi.org/10.1007/s11213-010-9173-5.

Gerston, L 2010, *Public policy making: Process and principles*, 3rd edn, ME Sharpe, Armonk, NY.

Haigh, Y 2012, *Public policy in Australia: Theory and practice*, Oxford University Press, Melbourne, Vic.

Head, BW 2010, 'From knowledge transfer to knowledge sharing? Towards better links between research, policy and practice', in G Bammer, A Michaux & A Sanson (eds), *Bridging the 'know–do' gap: Knowledge brokering to improve child wellbeing*, ANU E Press, Canberra, ACT, doi.org/10.22459/BKDG.08.2010.08.

Head, BW 2014, 'The collaboration solution? Factors for collaborative success', in J O'Flynn, D Blackman & J Halligan (eds), *Crossing boundaries in public management and policy: The international experience*, Routledge, Abingdon, UK.

Head, B and Crowley, K (eds) 2015, *Policy analysis in Australia*, Policy Press, Bristol, UK, doi.org/10.1332/policypress/9781447310273.001.0001.

Howlett, M, McConnell, A & Perl, A 2017, 'Moving policy theory forward: Connecting multiple stream and advocacy coalition frameworks to policy cycle models of analysis', *Australian Journal of Public Administration*, vol. 76, no. 1, pp. 65–79, doi.org/10.1111/1467-8500.12191.

Jenkins-Smith, HC & Sabatier, PA 1993, 'The study of the public policy process', in PA Sabatier & HC Jenkins-Smith (eds), *Policy change and learning: An advocacy coalition approach*, Westview Press, Boulder, CO.

John, P 2012, *Analyzing public policy*, 2nd edn, Routledge, Abingdon, UK, doi.org/10.4324/9780203136218.

Kane, J & Patapan, H 2006, 'In search of prudence: The hidden problem of managerial reform', *Public Administration Review*, vol. 66, no. 5, pp. 711–24, doi.org/10.1111/j.1540-6210.2006.00636.x.

Kingdon, JW 1984, *Agendas, alternatives and public policies*, Little, Brown and Company, Boston, MA.

Knill, C & Tosun, J 2012, *Public policy: A new introduction*, Palgrave Macmillan, Basingstoke, UK.

Knowles, MS 1984, *Andragogy in action: Applying modern principles of adult learning*, Jossey-Bass, San Francisco, CA.

Kraft, ME & Furlong, SR 2013, *Public policy: Politics, analysis and alternatives*, 4th edn, Sage, Thousand Oaks, CA.

Lasswell, HD 1956, *The decision process: Seven categories of functional analysis*, University of Maryland Press, College Park, MD.

Newman, J, Cherney, A & Head, BW 2016, 'Do policy makers use academic research? Reexamining the "two communities" theory of research utilization', *Public Administration Review*, vol. 76, no. 1, pp. 24–32, doi.org/10.1111/puar.12464.

Nutley, S, Walter, I & Davies, HTO 2003, 'From knowing to doing: A framework for understanding the evidence-into-practice agenda', *Evaluation*, vol. 9, no. 2, pp. 125–48, doi.org/10.1177/1356389003009002002.

Ostrom, E 1999, 'Institutional rational choice: An assessment of the institutional analysis and development framework', in PA Sabatier (ed.), *Theories of the policy process*, Westview Press, Boulder, CO.

Oxford Dictionaries 2019, 'Heuristic', British & World English online, viewed 18 March 2019, en.oxforddictionaries.com/definition/heuristic.

Pal, L 2014, *Beyond policy analysis: Public issue management in turbulent times*, 5th edn, Nelson Education, Toronto, Canada.

Raadschelders, JCN 2004, 'A model of the arena of PA-theory: Bogey man, doctor's bag and/or artist's medium', *Administrative Theory & Praxis*, vol. 26, no. 1, pp. 46–78, doi.org/10.1080/10841806.2004.11029430.

Rowling, JK 2000, *Harry Potter and the goblet of fire*, Bloomsbury, London, UK.

Sabatier, PA 1999a, 'The need for better theories', in PA Sabatier (ed.), *Theories of the policy process*, Westview Press, Boulder, CO.

Sabatier, PA (ed.) 1999b, *Theories of the policy process*, Westview Press, Boulder, CO.

Sabatier, PA & Jenkins-Smith, HC (eds) 1993, *Policy change and learning: An advocacy coalition approach*, Westview Press, Boulder, CO.

Sabatier, PA & Weible, C (eds) 2014, *Theories of the policy process: Theoretical lenses on public policy*, 3rd edn, Westview Press, Boulder, CO.

Schlager, E 1999, 'A comparison of frameworks, theories, and models of policy processes', in PA Sabatier (ed.), *Theories of the policy process*, Westview Press, Boulder, CO.

Schön, DA 1983, *The reflective practitioner: How professionals think in action*, Basic Books, New York, NY.

Scott, S & Baehler, K 2010, *Adding value to policy analysis and advice*, UNSW Press, Sydney, NSW.

Shergold, P 2013, 'Why economists succeed (or fail) to influence policy', *Policy: A Journal of Public Policy and Ideas*, vol. 29, no. 1, pp. 16–20.

Sullivan, H 2011, '"Truth" junkies: Using evaluation in UK public policy', *Policy and Politics*, vol. 39, no. 4, pp. 499–512, doi.org/10.1332/030557311X574216.

Sullivan, H 2019, 'Building a knowledge-sharing system: Innovation, replication, co-production and trust—a response', *Australian Journal of Public Administration*, vol. 78, no. 2. pp. 319–21, doi.org/10.1111/1467-8500.12370.

van der Wal, Z 2017, *The 21st century public manager: Challenges, people and strategies*, Palgrave Macmillan, London, UK.

van Manen, M 1991, *The tact of teaching: The meaning of pedagogical thoughtfulness*, Althouse Press, London, UK.

van Manen, M 1996, 'Phenomenological pedagogy and the question of meaning', in D Vandenberg (ed), *Phenomenology and educational discourse*, Heinemann Higher and Further Education, Durban, South Africa.

Wilson, RC Jr 2016, *Rethinking public administration: The case for management*, 2nd edn, Melvin & Leigh, Irvine, CA.

3

What can policy theory offer busy practitioners? Investigating the Australian experience

Trish Mercer[1]

Introduction

> When you come into a policy area and don't have the content knowledge, a model can help when you're digesting and making sense of a new area. Compared to an economic framework, it's much more accessible … Our brains need this type of framework to navigate policy. (Catherine To, interview, 12 February 2019)[2]

Since leaving the Australian Public Service (APS), and subsequently offering policy training for public servants, I have become curious to explore what insights academic theory could offer on the often confusing, ambiguous and turbulent policy world that I experienced from 1980 to 2010—having progressed from graduate entry to senior levels without the benefit of any formal training about the policy process! Public servants in Australia tend to learn the craft of policymaking as I did, through immersion in the workplace rather than building on an underpinning

1   Acknowledgements: Adjunct Professor Russell Ayres, Professor Brian Head, Adjunct Professor Wendy Jarvie and Professor John Wanna are thanked for their very helpful comments on earlier drafts.
2   Catherine To was a policy officer in the then Commonwealth Department of Communications and the Arts at the time of her interview. All interviews were conducted by the author.

academic training. In recent years, more public servants have undertaken formal study (usually at the postgraduate level) or short course training that has introduced them to academic theories of the policy process. Yet, the effect of such exposure to policy theory is an understudied area. This chapter seeks to explore how public servants—practitioners—learn about, and apply, different theoretical models or frameworks in their workplaces.

There are four parts to the chapter. First, I explore how public servants principally learn their jobs 'on-the-job', and how this has begun to change in recent decades. Second, I investigate the world of policy theory and frameworks, concentrating on the different approaches presented in four well-known policy theories and academic debate regarding their merits and limitations. Third, I examine what we know about how practitioners have responded to such frameworks, and what sources of evidence we have as to how they employ these theoretical constructs. The concluding section considers what we have learnt about how policy theory has been put to work to enhance practice and what future appetite there may be to strengthen this theory–practice nexus. My gaze is primarily on public servants at the national level in Australia, but I draw on state and territory examples, and the New Zealand public service where available.

'Policy' is a concept that can evade easy definition. As Wanna, Butcher and Freyens (2010, p. 6) remind us, it is 'a live, unfinished endeavour' during both its development and implementation. There is also no agreed term to describe what policy workers do. I concentrate on the bureaucratic skill of being a 'policy adviser', a broad term that goes beyond the sometimes fashionable 'policy analyst' to encompass the policy work involved from policy analysis and advice through to delivery and implementation of adopted policies.[3]

Learning to do policy

Academics and practitioners concur on how public servants in Australia learn their policy advising skills. In line with the Westminster tradition, these skills (and institutional culture) are acquired primarily through 'craft knowledge' (Rhodes 2016, p. 638). Such craft knowledge is 'something that you learn as you go' (Adams, Colebatch & Walker 2015, p. 104). In this semi-apprenticeship form of training, seizing practical, experiential

---

3   This definition is informed by that employed by Lindquist and Tiernan (2011, p. 444) in their investigation of the APS and policy advising.

opportunities is critical—a chord that resonates in the valedictories and other speeches by current or retiring public service secretaries published by the Institute of Public Administration Australia (IPAA). To cite two recent examples: Andrew Podger (2012, p. 7), a former secretary, had 'serendipitously worked in a series of remarkable teams' in different agencies, while another former secretary, Jane Halton (2016, p. 61), evocatively described how she acquired her policy skills:

> I was well-schooled in the craft of the public sector. There was time for this to happen. I was given increasing responsibility, sent to explain very difficult policy to very angry stakeholders on more than one occasion, spent a lot of time working with state governments developing and then implementing new policy. None of this I learnt at university … People coached me and I was able to make mistakes.

Specific training in policy and the administrative vocation is predominantly learnt once you arrive in the public service, not from what you bring with you, and there is little acknowledgement of underlying value sets and theoretical preconceptions that individuals inevitably hold. At both the national and state levels, the focus has been firmly on 'training for purpose', usually devolved to the individual agency, expressed at the national level through the Australian Public Service Commission's 70:20:10 pedagogic model: 70 per cent from work-based learning, 20 from relationship-based learning and the remaining 10 from formal education programs (Allen & Wanna 2016, pp. 23, 28). This has endured at the policy level, as shown by the recent *Social policy capability plan* developed by the Commonwealth Department of Social Services (DSS) that employed the 70:20:10 standard and described 'experiential learning' (the 70 per cent) as 'the core way' in which policy capacity is developed (DSS 2015, p. 16).

A former senior bureaucrat captured this sense of learning policy as an 'insider':

> My observation was, when I was working in the service, [that] there is almost a wish to keep the policy process secret, the notion that it cannot be taught. This is something that you have to be anointed into; it is a different kind of knowledge. (Comment made at an ANZSOG workshop, 9 July 2018)

Indeed, it is still unusual for Australian public servants, unlike their North American or European counterparts, to enter the public service with any formal training in public administration, public policy or political science

(Di Francesco 2015, pp. 262, 277). Peter Shergold, former secretary of the Department of the Prime Minister and Cabinet (PM&C), may well have reflected the view of many of his senior colleagues when he described the skill requirements for public policy as 'more in the nature of administrative craft and managerial mystery than political science' (Shergold 2015a, p. xx). Following successive waves of public sector reform from the late 1970s, collectively labelled 'new public management' (NPM), economic qualifications together with law and business management have been a high priority in APS recruitments (Crowley & Head 2015, p. 5). In 2017, for example, economics qualifications were 'by far the dominant pedigree' for APS secretaries, followed by law; only the finance secretary held a degree in political science.[4] A consequence of this experiential focus, as Kate Crowley and Brian Head (2015, p. 15) have observed, is that there is no readily accepted concept of a policy analysis profession in Australia.

This readiness to learn on-the-job and to seize opportunities is congruent with another trait that is seen as characteristically Australian: a well-honed pragmatism (Edwards this volume, Chapter 7). The policy workers David Adams, Hal Colebatch and Christopher Walker interviewed for their study of state public servants described policy in terms of constructing programs of action and consequent negotiation. In one interviewee's words: 'Policy is people trying to work out what they should *do* about a problem' (Adams, Colebatch & Walker 2015, p. 103, emphasis added). Pragmatism is also seen as a characteristic of the Australian approach to the public sector reforms that were carried out in the 1980s and 1990s as part of NPM, in contrast to the more sharply theoretical frame initially adopted in New Zealand, for example (Christensen & Lægreid 2001, pp. 21–2).

Teaching and learning about theory

Teaching policy skills

The effects of NPM reforms—such as rapid turnover of staff, emphasis on contract management skills and diversified sources of policy advice—are seen to have created a 'hollow crown' within Westminster public

---

4   This was the conclusion of Tom Burton (publisher of the *Mandarin*) in his analysis of a major reshuffle of the 18 portfolio secretaries announced in September 2017 (Burton 2017). My own check of the secretaries' biographies confirms this assessment.

administrations (Weller, Bakvis & Rhodes 1997), or at least what Tiernan and Wanna described as a 'discourse of declining policy capacity' (as cited in Tiernan 2011, p. 336). This has created a strong interest in actively rebuilding policy capacity in the APS, and a recognition that, in today's time-pressured and adversarial political environment, an ad hoc apprenticeship model is insufficient to accelerate policy skills development: instead, 'we need to school our people more formally and ensure their ongoing professional development' (Halton 2016, p. 61).

Economic approaches and quantitative skills remain highly valued: an economic perspective is the starting point to much policy development rather than a more broadly based analytical framework. However, in the post-NPM world, there is more recognition of the broader skills that are also required 'to develop and manage policy within increasingly distributed service delivery networks' (Di Francesco 2015, p. 265). With a record of significant underinvestment in staff development (Advisory Group on Reform of Australian Government Administration 2010, pp. viii–ix), the APS has belatedly begun encouraging and supporting staff to undertake postgraduate policy instruction.

Public policy training through postgraduate qualifications such as masters degrees and/or more informal policy training is now widely available, particularly at tertiary level through standalone public policy schools such as the Sir Walter Murdoch School of Public Policy and International Affairs, the University of Melbourne's School of Government, The Australian National University's Crawford School of Public Policy, and, since 2002, the Australia and New Zealand School of Government (ANZSOG). As a bi-national and multi-jurisdictional school dedicated to building executive capacity, ANZSOG offers signature programs such as its Executive Master of Public Administration (EMPA) and the shorter Executive Fellows Program (EFP). Yet, there remains a deep scepticism among Australian public servants about the value of academic learning (and, accordingly, policy theory), reflecting what Hal Colebatch has acknowledged as a 'long-running disconnect between the theory and practice of policy-making' (Adams, Colebatch & Walker 2015, p. 106; Colebatch, as cited in Mackie 2016, p. 291). This, presumably, at least partly explains what Di Francesco (2015, p. 261) has termed the 'distinctively pragmatic' Australian approach to teaching policy analysis.

Learning about policy theory

Broadly speaking, we know that more middle- and senior-level public servants have been exposed in the last two decades to policy concepts and tools (although we have neither quantitative data nor qualitative evidence as to the comparative numbers or impact on practice). Within such policy training and through current public policy texts, practitioners who seek to learn about the policy process discover an extensive theoretical literature, aimed primarily at academics, often requiring deep training to be fully understood, and conveyed in a jargon that is not easily translatable (Cairney 2015, p. 23; Maddison & Denniss 2009, p. 82).

This literature is also characterised by vigorous, indeed often acrimonious, debate over the limitations of certain theories or models, frequently driven by philosophical differences among academics. These 'duelling analytical frameworks' (Howlett, McConnell & Perl 2017, p. 65) tend to be seen as contrasting:

- a 'rational-comprehensive' and structured view of the policy world and centralised decision-making (such as a cycle approach), with
- a focus on the myriad of policy actors in a complex policy environment.

Paul Cairney (2015, pp. 26–7) has encapsulated the shift in modern policy theory as the move from an emphasis on top down decision-making pursued by a sole central actor to action by many actors (people and organisations) within a complex policy process. While recognising the many hybrid theories, this spectrum is well represented in the four policy theories discussed below. All are North American in origin: in Australasia, we tend to adapt rather than create our own theories. Unfortunately, and perhaps significantly, none address directly the underlying cultural nature of the policy enterprise examined in Chapter 10 by Craig Ritchie. From the plethora of available theories, these four have been selected because they:

- are accessible for practitioners in terms of language employed, explanation of concepts and focus on practical application
- range from *normative* (i.e. deriving from a standard or norm, especially of behaviour) to *empirical*, and in emphasis from *process-directed* to *relational* (i.e. focusing on multiple actors and organisations)
- have traction in Australia (either with practitioners, academics or both).

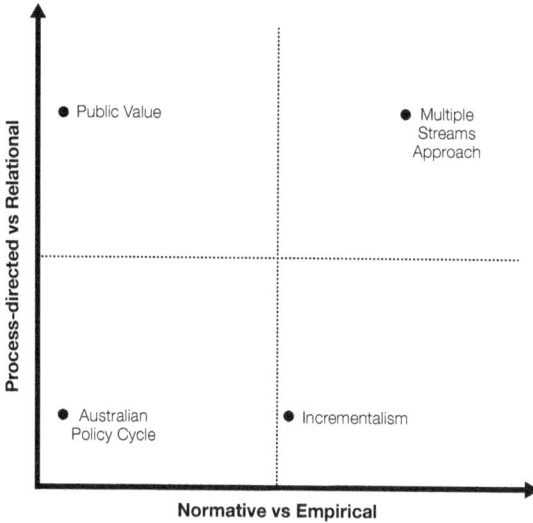

Figure 3.1. Typology of theories investigated.

Figure 3.1 illustrates where these different theories are situated in terms of the range described above, and Table 3.1 summarises each theory and its intended benefit for practitioners.

Table 3.1. Investigating four major policy theories taught in Australia.

Theory and brief description	Intended benefit for practitioners
Australian policy cycle: Policy as a sequence of stages, some of which may be skipped or repeated; a logical approach.	**Normative:** To offer a practical and comprehensive understanding of the policy process and a 'good process' to serve as 'a foundation for good policy'.
Incrementalism: 'Muddling through'; policymakers tend to work through consensus and trial and error rather than through radical change.	**Empirical and normative aspects:** To understand that, in reality, most policy development involves small-scale, gradual modification of existing programs.
Multiple streams approach: Three separate 'streams' (problem, policy solution and politics) must come together during a brief 'policy window' for significant policy change to occur.	**Empirical:** To explain how government agendas are set enabling radical policy change, and how 'policy entrepreneurs' can influence this by having policy solutions ready even before problems emerge.
Public value – strategic triangle: Managers should aim to deliver 'public value' by managing up and out ('authorising environment') and down (operational).	**Normative:** To detail what managers 'should think and do', employing a 'strategic triangle' concept as a tool for strategy development and emphasising stakeholder engagement.

Each of these theories are considered to have strengths and weaknesses. Some of the academic debates swirling around them are discussed in more detail in the chapters by Cairney (Chapter 13) and McConnell (Chapter 14) in this volume. The discussion below seeks to distil the approach and key academic critiques of each theory.

Australian policy cycle: A normative heuristic[5] to offer a 'good process' guide

The first is the classic policy cycle, seen as the epitome of the 'rational-comprehensive' approach and a highly enduring conceptual construct (Howlett, McConnell & Perl 2017, p. 65). In the 1990s it was adapted for an Australian audience and then published by Peter Bridgman, Glyn Davis and later Catherine Althaus (all with practitioner experience) as the core framework in their textbook, the *Australian policy handbook* (now in its sixth edition).[6] Shown in Figure 3.2 below, the Australian policy cycle (APC) is regarded as the cycle's most prominent modern example. The APC follows policy development through eight stages and the authors are quite explicit that 'good policy should include the basic elements of the cycle' (Althaus, Bridgman & Davis 2018, pp. 2, 45, 49).

The APC has many supporters, especially among practitioners, but has drawn strong academic criticism on the grounds that it is:

- a 'revival of rationalism', idealistic and highly normative (Di Francesco 2015, p. 267; Wanna, Butcher & Freyens 2010, p. 194)
- lacks agency and is misleading by 'suggesting a more linear and logical progression of policy activities than could be observed in practice' (Paul Sabatier, as cited in Howlett, McConnell & Perl 2017, p. 69; Maddison & Denniss 2009, pp. 87–9; Scott & Baehler 2010, p. 29)
- is not a guide to practice given the complexity of policy and policy actors (Adams, Colebatch & Walker 2015, p. 108; Colebatch 2006, pp. 1, 26; Gill & Colebatch 2006, pp. 261–2).

---

5   Heuristic is a term frequently employed in academic theory as both a noun and an adjective; it means to enable a person to discover or learn something for themselves (a 'hands-on' or 'rule of thumb' approach to learning).

6   Originally developed by Bridgman and Davis as a handbook for Queensland public servants, this became a national text in 1998, and Althaus became involved as the third author from the fourth edition. Another well-known example is Eugene Bardach's *Eightfold path of policy analysis*, based on his Berkeley teaching experience of over 30 years (Althaus, Bridgman & Davis 2018, pp. 3–4; Bardach 2009).

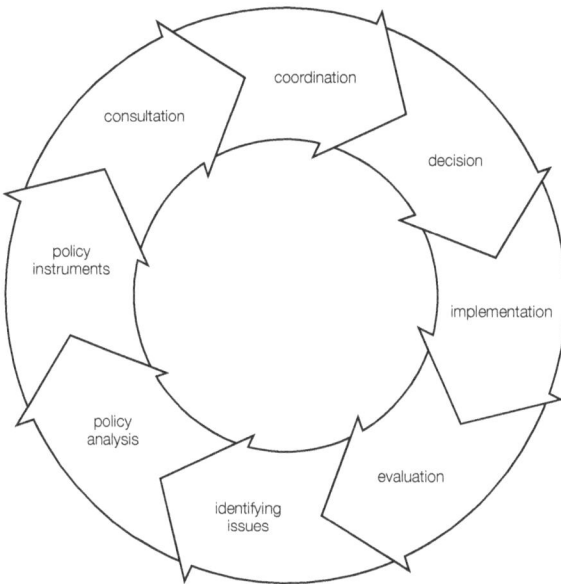

Figure 3.2. The Australian policy cycle.
Source: Althaus, Bridgman and Davis (2018).

Althaus, Bridgman and Davis (2015, p. 112) dispute these criticisms: 'The policy cycle does not assert that policy making is rational, occurs outside politics, or proceeds as a logical sequence rather than as a contest of ideas and interests.' They argue that the critics misinterpret the purpose of the cycle, which is a heuristic that 'can help public servants to develop a policy and guide it through the institutions of government' (Althaus, Bridgman & Davis 2003, p. 102).

Incrementalism: A realistic but limited behavioural approach

Incrementalism, or the art of 'muddling through', is the second theory—a behavioural and pragmatic approach developed by the American political scientist Charles Lindblom in the late 1950s and refined over the next two decades as 'disjointed incrementalism'. It was a critique of the rational-comprehensive approach, drawing on Herbert Simon's concept of 'bounded rationality' that recognised the cognitive limitations in information processing and use (Cairney 2015, pp. 27–8). Lindblom argued that complex problems can never be fully analysed; therefore, policymakers require incremental analytical strategies 'to make the most of our limited abilities to understand', employing such strategies as:

- a sequence of trials, errors and revised trials
- limiting analysis to only a few policy alternatives
- a greater focus on ills to be remedied than positive goals to be sought (Lindblom 1979, pp. 517, 519).

From an incrementalist perspective, policymakers rarely attempt radical policy change as they choose instead to build on past policies that have been developed through a painstaking process of building consensus among diverse interests. It does not appear to be employed frequently in Australian case studies, although Cockfield and Botterill (2013, pp. 138–9), in their study of rural and regional policy, concluded that such policy over the last 50 years was a story of 'punctuated incrementalism'.

Incrementalism, as the *Australian policy handbook* recognises, 'probably most accurately describes how policy making proceeds', given that it builds on bureaucratic expertise and familiarity with programs (Althaus, Bridgman & Davis 2018, p. 95). Among the criticisms levelled at such a 'small steps' incremental approach are that it encourages conservatism, inertia and the adoption of risk-averse approaches (Althaus, Bridgman & Davis 2018, p. 95; Wanna, Butcher & Freyens 2010, pp. 195–6). John Kingdon (2011, p. 80) has argued that such an approach does not account for how agendas can change suddenly and that significant problems facing governments may require more radical interventions. Incrementalism lost support (as a normative prescription, if not as an empirical description) during the NPM reforms and in the turbulent economic and political environment of recent years (Wanna, Butcher & Freyens 2010, p. 196).

Multiple streams approach: An explanation for agenda-setting

One of the acknowledged limitations of the policy cycle is that it does not seek to generate causal explanations for how policy develops (Althaus, Bridgman & Davis 2018, p. 47). Explaining the puzzle of how and why 'an idea's time has come' was taken up by Kingdon in 1984 through his multiple streams approach (MSA), which focuses specifically on how agendas are set, using the metaphor of three independent streams:

- problem—attention lurches to a policy problem
- policy—a solution to the problem is available
- politics—policymakers have the motive and opportunity to turn a solution into policy (Cairney & Jones 2016, p. 40).

These streams come (flow) together and become coupled at critical junctures, which Kingdon (2011, pp. 78, 165) depicted as a 'policy window' opening in the political system, enabling a marked, even radical change in policy.[7] MSA thus offers a counterintuitive strategy for policy advisers—for example, by producing solutions before chasing problems, because there will be no time to produce a solution when a policy window (briefly) opens. 'Policy entrepreneurs' who display qualities such as persistence can employ a policy window to secure government attention, but are dependent on the environment being right, like 'surfers waiting for the big wave':

> Advocates lie in wait within and around government with their solutions at hand, waiting for problems to float by to which they can attach their solutions, waiting for a development in the political stream they can use to their advantage … Sometimes, the window opens quite predictably … At other times, it happens quite unpredictably. (Kingdon 2011, p. 165)

MSA draws on Cohen, March and Olsen's (1972) 'garbage can' model of policymaking and seeks to capture the complexity, ambiguity and occasional chaos in policy episodes (as cited in Colebatch 2006, p. 14; Kingdon 2011, p. 78). As a flexible approach, it has a big fan club within academia globally, and has influenced policy theory and been employed in numerous case studies (Cairney & Jones 2016, pp. 43, 45, 49). Howlett, for example, in employing MSA in a Canadian context, found that routine policy windows, such as elections, arose more frequently than other more random opportunities (as cited in Cairney & Jones 2016, p. 48).

However, MSA has also been criticised on a number of fronts, including:

- it was distilled by Kingdon from observing deliberations of the United States Congress; therefore, its applicability for Westminster systems is questionable (although it is also argued that, by being built on the highly abstract 'garbage can model', its insights extend beyond the original focus of study) (Cairney & Jones 2016, p. 38)

---

7   Kingdon (2011, p. 3) defines the 'agenda' as 'the list of subjects or problems to which governmental officials, and people outside of government closely associated with those officials, are paying some serious attention at any given time'.

- it offers the flexibility and ability to inspire empirical studies; however, the number of studies in which Kingdon is cited superficially is 'more than troubling' (Cairney & Jones 2016, pp. 38, 51–2)
- it may be tautological when used to provide post-hoc explanations
- it would require substantive stretching 'to move from agenda-setting activity to encompass the entire policy process' (Howlett, McConnell & Perl 2017, p. 71).

Public value: Aspirational and normative heuristic aimed at individual managers

The fourth policy theory was created by Mark Moore, a Harvard Kennedy School of Government professor (*Creating public value: Strategic management in government* 1995; *Recognizing public value* 2013). Public value is seen as a post-NPM paradigm, offering a model of management in an era of 'networked governance' (Stoker, as cited in Alford & O'Flynn 2009, p. 179). Rhodes and Wanna (2009, p. 180)—strong critics of public value—see its attraction as due to the 'high esteem' attributed to the public sector, with middle to senior public servants responding to this acknowledgement of their contribution following years of top down NPM reforms. The following example gives a sense of this value-oriented perspective, and of how public value has entered into the language of practitioners. Andrew Nicholls, a New South Wales public servant and EMPA graduate who received a Public Service Medal in the 2018 Australia Day honours list, described what motivated him: 'I have a strong commitment to the ethic of public service and I've always been attracted to the roles which focus on generating *public value* not private value' (ANZSOG 2018, emphasis added). Moore's approach, created specifically for public sector managers, was developed as a normative theory of managerial (rather than organisational) behaviour: 'it details what managers *should* think and do' (Moore 1995, p. 2, original emphasis). The core idea in public value theory is the 'strategic triangle', represented in Figure 3.3.

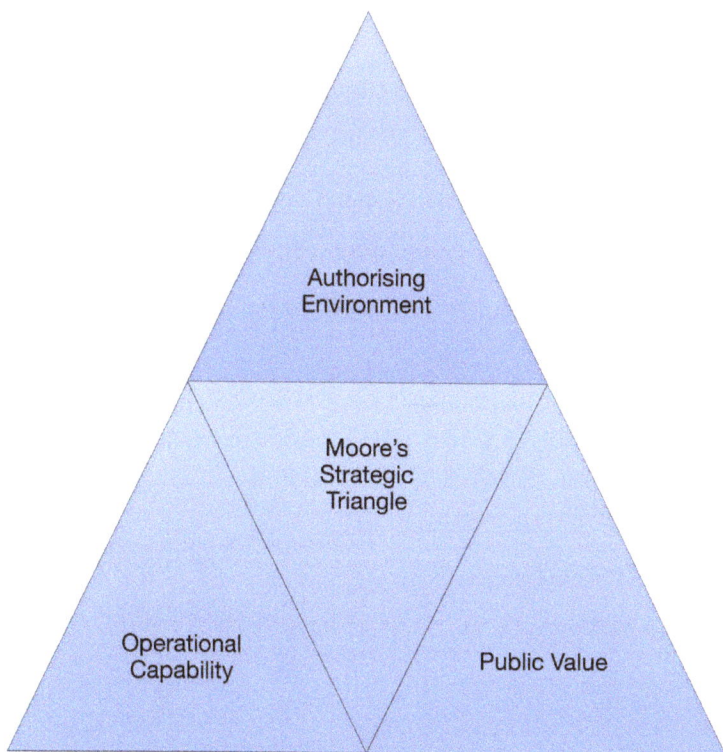

Figure 3.3. Moore's strategic triangle.

Source: Louise Gilding (Chapter 11, this volume), based on Moore (1995).

Public value: managers need to develop 'public value propositions' for their agencies/areas/programs, akin to a 'business case', but also drawing in the public's aspirations and concerns.

Authorising environment (legitimacy and support): managers need to 'manage up' and 'manage out' by actively gathering legitimacy and support for their value propositions from their political leaders and also many other actors (such as parliament, interest groups, media, clients).

Operational capabilities: managers need also to 'manage down' to ensure that there would be the requisite resources, people and processes for the task.

(Alford et al. 2017, pp. 590–1)

Public value has been influential among senior public servants in Australia and New Zealand and, to a lesser extent, in the UK (Di Francesco 2015, p. 267; Rhodes & Wanna 2009, p. 161). A major contributing factor has been its centrality in public management courses in Australasia, particularly in ANZSOG's EMPA and EFP in the last 15 years, which included personal presentations by Moore until recent years (Alford et al. 2017, p. 592; Scott & Baehler 2010, p. 15). Moore has also presented in ANZSOG chief executive officer forums.

In Australia and New Zealand, public value has drawn much greater interest from public management academics and business schools than from those in public policy (Alford et al. 2017, p. 592; Bryson, Crosby & Bloomberg 2014, p. 452). Public policy texts in Australia tend to ignore public value (Colebatch 2006; Maddison & Denniss 2009) or criticise it (Wanna, Butcher & Freyens 2010, pp. 41–4). Two exceptions are short discussions in the *Australian policy handbook* (Althaus, Bridgman & Davis 2013, p. 34, 2018, p. 13) and longer coverage in a textbook written by Scott and Baehler (2010, pp. 15–17), two New Zealand academics who taught in the early ANZSOG programs.

As with the policy cycle, public value has prompted robust academic debate—in particular, between two public policy academics, Rod Rhodes and John Wanna, who argued that it is not appropriate for Westminster systems of government, and public value supporters (and ANZSOG teachers) such as John Alford and Janine O'Flynn, who came to Moore's defence (Alford 2008; Alford & O'Flynn 2009; Rhodes & Wanna 2007, 2008, 2009). One consequence has been more theoretical work by Moore, Benington and others to clarify definitions and terms: for example, 'public value' is characterised as 'a broad portmanteau phrase expressing ideals and aspirations about public service, but capable of meaning many different things to different people' (Benington 2009, p. 233; Bryson, Crosby & Bloomberg 2014, pp. 453–4). In July 2019, a number of public policy academics came together at the University of Queensland, Brisbane, to workshop the concept of public value and its theoretical and practical application: participants were generally agreed 'that public value has wide application, but as a concept it is messy' (Brown et al. 2019, p. 22).

While these four theories are all intended for practical application, their views on policy are quite sharply differentiated. The APC seeks to guide public servants—particularly the inexperienced—through policy development processes within a centralised Westminster system of government. By contrast, incrementalism presents policy development as one of gradual evolution whereby public servants seek to achieve change through small steps; the emphasis is on incremental analytical strategies to progress policy action. The other two theories place greater emphasis on complexity and multiple actors. Under MSA, the intersection of three independent streams (problem, policy and politics) can explain how a policy window opens to enable a significant policy change. The public value approach, with its key concept of a strategic triangle, was constructed by Moore as a tool to guide managers in determining what they should think and do within their own policy environments.

Applying theory to practice

Given the dominant vein of pragmatism among public servants, and the equally strong vein of scepticism of academic discourse, it could be expected that academic theories of the policy process would not meet with a receptive audience. Yet, in their admittedly small survey of how state public servants learnt about policy work, Adams, Colebatch and Walker (2015, p. 105) found that those who had taken up study after several years on-the-job found a significant benefit, as articulated by one of their respondents:

> What interested me … I was trying to get a better understanding
> of what the heck I'd been doing for the last 20 years because
> I didn't have a vocabulary or a framework to explain it.

As we have also seen with public value, practitioners can display enthusiasm and interest, at least when such theory is offered in an interactive setting such as ANZSOG's EMPA and EFP.

In terms of policy process theory, the four approaches examined here were all intended to 'speak' to policy advisers, with language and imagery that could be understood relatively easily—and readily recalled. Based on the literature and practitioner feedback, the following section explores what we know about how public servants have accessed and responded to such policy theory.

Australian policy cycle: Impact

With cumulative sales of over 30,000 and now in its sixth edition, the *Australian policy handbook* has become a 'staple' for undergraduate policy subjects and required reading for graduate courses (Althaus, Bridgman & Davis 2018, p. 4; Di Francesco 2015, p. 267). One of its authors (Bridgman) has, for many years, delivered two-day policy workshops in capital cities (Brisbane, Canberra and Sydney), with participants receiving a copy of the handbook.[8] The APC's success has been attributed to its practical approach, simplicity, comprehensiveness and 'analytical scope and range' (Howlett, McConnell & Perl 2017, p. 66; Scott & Baehler 2010, p. 34).

Using the cycle as a guide for policy action

The APC's value as a practical guide is explored by two pracademics[9] in this monograph:

- Meredith Edwards (2001, p. 4), who employed the APC in her case study of major social policy reforms, reflects in Chapter 7 (this volume) on its use as a heuristic for practice—'a valuable, if rough guide to action in pursuing success for a policy position'
- Russell Ayres in Chapter 8 (this volume) relates how he adapted the APC, with tweaks for complexity, in 'under the radar' information sessions with his own staff on the theory of policymaking.

The cycle approach has many supporters. Gary Banks, former dean of ANZSOG and former head of the Commonwealth's Productivity Commission, has recently stated that the policy cycle, notwithstanding critiques of its sequential aspects and rationalist conception of policymaking, remains a useful 'good process' test in the way its components match up with standard requirements in the policy process. He employed a small number of 'good process' indicators to assess (not favourably!) recent government policy initiatives such as the National Broadband Network and emissions trading scheme (Banks 2018).

Given that the policy cycle sits naturally with an emphasis on centralised decision-making, it is not surprising that examples located within institutional frameworks of policy processes tend to draw on the cycle as their organising construct:

- Andrew Maurer in Chapter 12 (this volume) demonstrates this affinity in his exploration of how he developed a policy handbook for his department (Communication and the Arts).

---

8   Bridgman is a former practitioner in the Queensland public service and delivers these workshops with another ex-practitioner. Their website provides course details and feedback from participants (see policyskills.com.au).

9   A pracademic (or practitioner academic), while not appearing in dictionaries, is a term that has been in use for some 30 years and is defined as someone who is both an academic and a practitioner in their subject area.

- Another example can be taken from the DSS's *Social policy capability plan,* which described understanding the policy cycle as a characteristic of capable social policy officers (DSS 2015, p. 3).

An exception to this use of the cycle in institutional frameworks is a policy development toolkit developed for staff in the then Commonwealth Department of Industry, Innovation and Science in 2014, and placed on their intranet site. The toolkit provides an introduction to the fundamentals of policymaking and pointedly offers a 'realistic policy model' that presents policy as an iterative and adaptive process rather than a logical progression of separate and distinct steps (Department of Industry, Innovation and Science 2014, pp. 3, 13).

Beyond Australasia, Cairney (2015, p. 26) notes that UK departments, such as the Cabinet Office, have maintained versions of the policy cycle model of policymaking. The World Bank (2019) also employs a project cycle approach that has similar stages to the policy cycle, although this may involve multiple overlapping cycles that emphasise the complexity of their processes.

As a normative model, the policy cycle implies a prescription for a rational-comprehensive plan of action that aligns with the centralised decision-making seen as integral to Westminster systems and democratic politics. A staged approach to policymaking is deeply embedded in public service practice. A policy proposal being put forward to Cabinet, for instance, needs to be able to be presented, discussed and recorded as having undergone careful consideration of the issue or problem, the options available to government, the views of key stakeholders and the likely consequences of any decision taken; that is, a proposal that has encompassed all the dimensions of policy development envisaged in the cycle, even where the actual process in all likelihood will not have followed such a 'rational' path! In Chapter 13 (this volume), Cairney discusses the 'far messier reality' of policymaking compared to this projection of centralised policy made through orderly stages. He argues that perhaps the most we can expect of the policy cycle's stages is 'to treat them as a *checklist* of functions to carry out at some point'; in other words, not applying them rigidly or in order, and with an appreciation of the bigger picture.

Incrementalism: Impact

The incrementalist explanation of policy development emphasises that we can only ever have imperfect knowledge; therefore, we need strategies for 'skillful incompleteness' (Lindblom 1979, p. 524). Lindblom's emphasis on building from existing policy understandings and arrangements is likely to feel intuitively familiar for public servants, especially those involved in implementation. Moreover, the APC's authors have noted that, when exercising judgement about how much time and thought to devote to a problem, agreement based on the 'quick and rough calculations of incrementalism' may be 'the most effective way to proceed' (Althaus, Bridgman & Davis 2018, p. 95). Lindblom (1979, p. 520) argues that it is also possible to achieve rapid and significant change under incrementalism, precisely because, by their very nature, such changes 'do not rock the boat, do not stir up the great antagonisms and paralyzing schisms as do proposals for more drastic change'.

An element of Lindblom's work that continues to resonate is his emphasis on a 'trial and error' strategy. Shergold's (2015b, pp. 6–7) report for the Abbott Coalition government in 2015 on *Learning from failure* recommended such a 'learning by doing' strategy for Commonwealth public servants, involving testing out ideas on a small-scale, trialling different delivery options and making rapid adjustments as necessary.

Cairney (2015, p. 31), drawing on his conversations with UK civil servants in policy training seminars, suggested that incrementalism, with its familiar, practical qualities, 'translates well' from theory to practice. There is no direct Australian evidence, but the story here may be similar. Certainly the feedback from public servants in policy workshops that I have conducted has been that incrementalism is immediately familiar to them, and many have indicated that this best describes their current work environment.[10] Indeed, the former secretary of the Department of Foreign Affairs and Trade, Peter Varghese (2016, p. 35), made a personal plea for what he termed 'radical incrementalism':

> If I were to give one piece of advice to the next generation of public service leaders it would be to advocate the virtues of radical incrementalism … The only sustainable change is change that is

---

10   With Adjunct Professor Wendy Jarvie, I have jointly offered workshops on 'policy essentials' through the ANU Crawford School of Public Policy Executive Education program, which includes a session exploring the insights from key policy process theories such as incrementalism.

understood and then accepted ... And that takes persuasion and vision and the hard yards of incremental improvements in pursuit of a bigger agenda.

However, one of the newer secretaries, Heather Smith[11] (2018, p. 40), then head of the Department of Industry, Innovation and Science, questioned whether, because these are 'not ordinary times', such radical incrementalism 'will now get us to where we need to be'.

In making these claims, it is unlikely that these senior bureaucrats were systematically drawing on academic theory. Nevertheless, for many public servants who have studied policy theory, incrementalism may appear as a status quo option—too passive in a policy world beset by 'wicked' problems requiring multidimensional responses[12]—even while it may continue to be an accurate description of how a significant body of policy work is quietly achieved, particularly in Commonwealth–state contexts.

Multiple streams approach: Impact

While many public servants may not recognise that they are drawing on Kingdon's work, his evocative descriptions of the policy process have been taken into the policy vocabulary: notably, 'policy window' and 'policy entrepreneurs'. MSA's coverage in major textbooks and the number of Australian case studies employing the approach indicate its influence among academics (Althaus, Bridgman & Davis 2018, p. 47; Colebatch 2006, p. 14; Fawcett et al. 2018; Lancaster et al. 2017: Rodwell 2016). Two examples from individuals who have bridged the academic and policy worlds are illustrative. First, the doctoral study by Kathleen Mackie (which she draws on in Chapter 9, this volume) examined 30 years of environmental policy development by bureaucrats in the Commonwealth department (in which she had been a senior executive). An unexpected finding from her extensive interviews with policy officers was the, at times, covert role adopted to pursue success and avoid failure, which she found:

---

11 Heather Smith lost her position under Prime Minister Morrison's restructure of the APS in December 2019.
12 Alford and Head (2017) have investigated how 'wicked' has become an inflated and overused term that obscures distinctions between different forms of problems.

> More akin to the kind of agency found in Kingdon's (1984) exploration of the role of policy entrepreneurs to determine why issues did or did not get on to the US government's policy agenda. (Mackie 2016, p. 300)

Second, Edwards, who adopted a modified policy cycle in her study of major social policy, also dipped briefly into MSA when she compared the behaviour of a group of DSS officials during the internal development of the Keating government's Working Nation initiative to Kingdon's 'entrepreneurs':

> The group of DSS officials who had been working on a particular set of policies for some years found the right angle and right timing to have a significant influence on the income support policies contained in Working Nation. (Edwards 2001, p. 188)

Intriguingly, no specific examples of MSA being employed by current practitioners have yet come to light. While its concepts are vivid and readily explained, it may not be frequently taught in formal or informal public policy training.[13] Moreover, MSA does not offer a clear template for practical application and there is a risk that it could be backwards fitted by practitioners wishing to make a messy process of policy development seem more coherent. Yet, Kingdon's concept of being ready for a policy window to open is a strategy that policymakers may understand instinctively; consequently, they may be drawn to his counterintuitive strategy of developing solutions in advance of problems emerging.

Public value: Impact

Notwithstanding academic critiques, senior public servants in Australia and New Zealand have responded with interest and enthusiasm to public value and, specifically, to the heuristic tool of the strategic triangle (Alford et al. 2017, p. 592; Alford & O'Flynn 2009, pp. 171–2; Prebble 2012, p. 392). The 2018 edition of the *Australian policy handbook* somewhat diplomatically noted that 'traction between public value ideas, theorists

---

13 Discovering this would require a survey of the various institutions offering public policy courses. I am aware of two examples: 1) Brian Head (University of Queensland) has drawn on MSA for a masters course on policy analysis; 2) Paul Fawcett (now at the University of Melbourne) has employed this framework in policy training, including with policy officers from the then Commonwealth Department of Communications and the Arts, and he believes that public servants can get a handle on this theory relatively quickly and intuitively (Brian Head, personal communication, 23 June 2019; Paul Fawcett, personal communication, 5 July 2018).

and practitioners is strong' (Althaus, Bridgman & Davis 2018, p. 13). More directly, Di Francesco (2015, p. 268, original emphasis) commented that 'the nub of the dispute [about public value] is that *practitioners* find the concept useful'. A recent academic workshop on public value agreed that this was 'a term created by academics and then adopted by public managers' to describe their work (Brown et al. 2019, p. 21). The term 'public value' is frequently employed in public policy discussions, not only at bureaucratic and academic levels, but also, occasionally, at political levels (Alpers & Ghazman 2019, p. 211; Australian Government 2019, p. 1; Gallop 2018; Tiernan 2011, p. 343). For public managers, the public value approach offers recognition of their ability to influence policy and decisions and encompasses earlier respected concepts such as the public interest and the common good (Bryson, Crosby & Bloomberg 2014, pp. 449–51).

In academic circles, the current status of public value management has been described as 'mainly heuristic' (Althaus, Bridgman & Davis 2018, p. 13; Brown et al. 2019, p. 9; Hartley et al. 2017, pp. 670–1)[14] given the lack of empirical studies of this approach in action. Therefore, there is no strong body of evidence to demonstrate its strengths and weaknesses, including whether public managers are being careful to balance discretion and responsiveness in any coalition-building, as Rhodes and Wanna (2008, p. 368) urged.

Nevertheless, examples have not been difficult to find as to how practitioners have adapted the public value framework of the strategic triangle to their particular environment and circumstances. In IPAA and ANZSOG forums, and in presentations at public policy conferences and workshops, senior bureaucrats have publicly referenced the strategic triangle and its 'authorising environment' concept, presumably expecting that at least some of their audience will make a connection.[15] Senior public servants have also shared how they have adapted Moore's framework. Duncan McIntyre, a division head in the then Commonwealth Department of Industry, Innovation and Science who was in the first EMPA cohort,

---

14   To my knowledge, the only Australian study of implementing public value management is by Edwards, Soo and Greckhamer (2016, p. 188). Their case study of disability sector reform in Western Australia concluded that public value approaches had enabled the development of community networks and the trialling of co-created innovations.

15   Two examples of events in Canberra at which current or past senior executives employed Moore's concepts were hosted by the IPAA: 'Future leaders', 22 November 2018, and 'Prioritising reform', 18 September 2019.

amended the strategic triangle's descriptors as the language failed to resonate with his staff. He used the following questions to talk his people through the concept of public value and strategy development:

- What *should* we do (to achieve public value)?
- What *can* we do (the organisation's capacity)?
- What are we *allowed* to do (by the political layer)?

In McIntyre's (personal communication, 22 March 2018) experience, most people know more about the first question, which means that more attention needs to be focused on the last two.

Louise Gilding, an EMPA graduate and senior executive in the ACT Government, explains in Chapter 11 (this volume) how she developed a 'blended approach' to employ with her team, involving the use of four questions and the strategic triangle. Her framework is a kind of hybrid, in that it begins with the early stages of the policy cycle (such as identifying and analysing the problem) before incorporating a public value approach by asking if it will 'make a difference', achieve support and be implementable. Moreover, as Gilding notes, her framework is flexible: 'scalable across problems, timeframes and resources'.

Employment of the public value approach is not restricted to ANZSOG graduates. Catherine To, the policy officer quoted at the start of this chapter, considered that the unit on public value in her masters degree in communications from Griffith University provided her with a reflective tool: 'I use Mark Moore's strategic triangle as a means of stepping back— as a kind of template, how should I address this issue' (Catherine To, interview, 12 February 2019).

What can we learn about taking policy theory into practice?

This exploration of the response to four well-known policy theories has indicated that, in these early decades of the new century, public servants, albeit at an individual level, are receptive towards policy theory offerings. Their knowledge appears to have been principally acquired through short or longer-term policy training offered by universities or other training institutions specialising in executive education, and probably reinforced at times by short pieces in grey literature now available in online public policy sites such as the *Mandarin, Per Capita,* the *Conversation,* and *Analysis and Policy Observatory.*[16]

The policy vocabulary employed by many practitioners now contains some of these academic concepts, which are sometimes jarring in an Australian context—for example, muddling through, policy window, policy entrepreneur and, above all, authorising environment. At a recent IPAA event in Canberra, the keynote speaker (head of a prominent think tank), a panel member (former head of department in both Commonwealth and state arenas) and audience member (head of a statutory agency) engaged in an animated conversation drawing on Moore's framework and authorising environment concept to discuss the contemporary difficulties of prosecuting policy reform (IPAA 2019). At an institutional level, however, there appears to be an implicit and longstanding bias towards a cycle or stages approach for depicting policy development, not only for its coverage of policy from start to finish, but also, perhaps, for its utility 'to help ministers project a sense of central control' (Cairney this volume, Chapter 13).

Among ANZSOG graduates, the public value theory has caught the imagination of senior public servants at both Commonwealth and state levels and in policy and delivery roles. This underlines the medium of interactive discussions as a conduit for offering policy theory in an accessible way, as Cairney (2015, p. 33) also emphasises, based on his experience of offering policy training to UK civil servants: 'It is the discussions, beginning with limitations of cycles and exploring policy theory alternatives, that make the difference, not the reading materials.'

Possibly the strong focus on public value offered in ANZSOG's EMPA and EFP has avoided the risk of participants drowning in a sea of academic theory and debates. Direct academic (or pracademic) engagement can certainly help with the translation of theory, as reflected in a participant's feedback in 2018 on an Australian policy training course employing the policy cycle: the course offered 'anecdotes that connected theories to real life experiences' (Bridgman & Malone 2019).

---

16   For examples of such grey literature see Katsonis (2019), Mainwaring (2019) and Threlfall (2018).

A common feature of the four theories explored here is that they tend to eschew jargon and complicated presentations of the theory, and to offer evocative images and/or language that provides memorable hooks to cut through and speak to the direct experiences of public servants, as Gilding (this volume, Chapter 11) captures: 'reflecting on my policy successes and failures, there is a correlation with whether the [strategic] triangle is aligned or misaligned'.

For practitioners looking to take theory into the workplace, the approach needs to be readily communicated to other public servants who, in most cases, will not be familiar with the language or underpinning concepts, and who are working in high-stress, rapidly changing circumstances.

From an academic perspective, Howlett, McConnell and Perl (2017, p. 65) describe the value of policy frameworks in terms of their ability to help 'both students and practitioners make sense of the complex set of socio-political activities that constitute policy-making'. Weible and Cairney (2018, p. 186) similarly recognise that, while the complexity of policy processes prevents scholars offering 'precise predictions' for policy actors, scholars nevertheless can:

> Help them to make sense of policy theories so that they can think more critically about how they make their choices [in specific instances of policymaking] and how they make sense of their complex context.

Congruent with developing a greater appreciation of complexity, Cairney has also drawn attention to how practitioner–academic discussions can encourage the type of 'intelligent policymaking' promoted by Ian Sanderson, which, at its heart, involves a commitment to experimentation and policy learning (Cairney 2015, p. 33; Sanderson 2009, p. 713).

Employing a lens of 'intelligent policymaking' provides new perspectives into how practitioners apply theory. While there is no simple metric, what we might expect is that a deeper understanding of policy theory could lead to new ways of thinking and/or be employed in critical reflection back in the workplace. From the examples discussed in the previous section, and other chapters in this monograph, we gain some insight into how policy theory has indeed been put to work to enhance practice, including its use as:

- a *'sense-making tool'* when immersed in a policy agenda that can appear chaotic or indeed shambolic
- a *policy review framework* to reflect on past or current policy episodes, individually or with others, and garner policy learnings
- a means of facilitating conversations through a *shared policy vocabulary*, even if this may only connect with certain colleagues
- a *heuristic or broad guide* for leaders to employ individually or with their teams for more strategic policy development processes.

These can occur not only at an individual level, but also at the institutional level, as Maurer (this volume, Chapter 12) demonstrates with the policy handbook that he developed for his department.

We also gain a sense of how policy theory is modified in light of the particular circumstances and institutional culture in which public servants operate. A common thread among the cited examples of practitioners (current and former) is their readiness to adapt theory to their particular environments. Indeed, Ayres in Chapter 8 (this volume) (and it would seem Gilding in Chapter 11), have grafted complexity onto a cycle model in order to create the 'sense-making tool' that policy theorists describe. Presumably, this is the type of professional growth that the authors of the *Australian policy handbook* suggest is likely to occur with experience and confidence (Althaus, Bridgman & Davis 2018, p. 5).

While we have Australian examples of theory tested empirically, such as case studies drawing on the MSA, we have no examples of practice directly informing theory, notwithstanding that academics acknowledge that practice can be 'a great stimulant of good theory' (Hartley et al. 2017, p. 671). Improving knowledge exchange between the policy and academic worlds exercises those on both sides (Sullivan 2019, p. 319). Yet, being frank in an academic environment as to how they apply theory in practice may be daunting for practitioners, even for pracademics. The former practitioners who constructed the APC have needed 'broad shoulders' given ongoing academic disparagement. It was also perhaps inevitable that Edwards's employment of a modified policy cycle in her book on social policy case studies would be critiqued by academics (e.g. Gill & Colebatch 2006, pp. 243–4) for what they saw as tensions between the theory and Edwards's account of her own experience, demonstrating 'the limitations of the model'. Reflecting the trenchant debate over public value, Gilding (Chapter 11), in her contribution to this volume, is careful to note that the strategic triangle 'has caused disagreement between public managers and academics'.

From the perspective of practitioners, insights can be gleaned from multiple theories notwithstanding what may appear to be arcane academic disputes. Indeed, in an initiative to move beyond these longstanding debates, Howlett, McConnell and Perl (2017, pp. 67–9) have proposed a new 'five streams framework of the policy process', which would synthesise the strengths in three of the key meta-frameworks: the policy cycle and MSA discussed in this chapter, and also the advocacy coalition framework proposed by Sabatier.

At present, we only have tantalising glimpses into how existing policy theory has been put to work and tested for its relevance and utility in practice. While government support for ANZSOG has helped to expose considerable numbers of Commonwealth, state and New Zealand senior executives to policy theory such as public value, largely it has been left to individuals to bring their learnings back to their workplaces. A practitioner–academic partnership could further our understanding of how this occurs, including any cultural dissonance, through a well-designed research project or projects to extend our understanding of theory-influenced practice (and vice versa):

• by tapping into public servants' knowledge and application of policy theory, including inchoate understandings of 'policy'

• by investigating what policy theory is offered, particularly in postgraduate public policy offerings, and what resonates with practitioners.

However, this begs the question of the APS's appetite, particularly at senior levels, to recognise that training in policy theory, delivered in an interactive environment, can support the skills development of policy advisers. Apart from the initiative of individuals, we have only uncovered the occasional adoption at particular times by particular institutions of a policy theory or framework. Yet, as highlighted in this book's first chapter, the policy capacity of federal public servants has been in the spotlight again with the independent review of the APS (PM&C 2019b). In the Coalition government's response to the independent review's final report, the strong message conveyed by Prime Minister Morrison was that government 'sets the policy direction' for the nation and the APS delivers through implementation (PM&C 2019a, p. 9). Only 15 of the 40 recommendations were accepted in full.

Notwithstanding this lukewarm response, the review's recommendation for a new 'professions model' aimed at deepening capacity and expertise has been accepted and APS Commissioner Peter Woolcott has already begun work on this, focusing on human resources, data, digital and procurement areas (PM&C 2019b, p. 20; Jenkins 2019). In the UK, 28 professions have been established in the Civil Service, and the 'policy profession' has its own professional standards and learning curriculum, with externally accredited courses including masters in public policy (PM&C 2019b, p. 194; Policy Profession Board 2019). We wait to see whether this international model and others, such as New Zealand's public service 'policy profession', will influence the development of a policy 'standard' for the APS that recognises the value of practitioner–academic interaction.

References

Adams, D, Colebatch, HK & Walker, CK 2015, 'Learning about learning: Discovering the work of policy', *Australian Journal of Public Administration*, vol. 74, no. 2, pp. 101–11, doi.org/10.1111/1467-8500.12119.

Advisory Group on Reform of Australian Government Administration 2010, *Ahead of the game: Blueprint for the reform of Australian government administration*, Department of the Prime Minister and Cabinet, Canberra, ACT.

Alford, J 2008, 'The limits to traditional public administration, or rescuing public value from misrepresentation', *Australian Journal of Public Administration*, vol. 67, no. 3, pp. 357–66, doi.org/10.1111/j.1467-8500.2008.00593.x.

Alford, J, Douglas, S, Geuijen, K & 't Hart, P 2017, 'Ventures in public value management: Introduction to the symposium', *Public Management Review*, vol. 19, no. 5, pp. 589–604, doi.org/10.1080/14719037.2016.1192160.

Alford, J & Head, BW 2017, 'Wicked and less wicked problems: A typology and a contingency framework', *Policy and Society*, vol. 36, no. 3, pp. 397–413, doi.org/10.1080/14494035.2017.1361634.

Alford, J & O'Flynn, J 2009, 'Making sense of public value: Concepts, critiques and emergent meanings'. *International Journal of Public Administration*, vol. 32, nos 3–4, pp. 171–91, doi.org/10.1080/01900690902732731.

Allen, P & Wanna, J 2016, 'Developing leadership and building executive capacity in the Australian public services for better governance', in A Podger & J Wanna (eds), *Sharpening the sword of state: Building executive capacities in the public services of the Asia-Pacific*, ANU Press, Canberra, ACT, doi.org/10.22459/SSS.11.2016.02.

Alpers, P & Ghazman, Z 2019, 'The "perfect storm" of gun control: From policy inertia to world leader', in J Luetjens, M Mintrom & P 't Hart (eds), *Successful public policy: Lessons from Australia and New Zealand*, ANU Press, Canberra, ACT, doi.org/10.22459/SPP.2019.09.

Althaus, C, Bridgman, P & Davis, G 2004, *The Australian policy handbook: A practical guide to the policy-making process*, 3rd edn, Allen & Unwin, Crows Nest, NSW.

Althaus, C, Bridgman, P & Davis, G 2013, *The Australian policy handbook: A practical guide to the policy-making process*, 5th edn, Allen & Unwin, Crows Nest, NSW.

Althaus, C, Bridgman, P & Davis, G 2015, 'Learning about learning: Discovering the work of policy', *Australian Journal of Public Administration*, vol. 74, no. 2, pp. 112–13, doi.org/10.1111/1467-8500.12145.

Althaus, C, Bridgman, P & Davis, G 2018, *The Australian policy handbook: A practical guide to the policy-making process*, 6th edn, Allen & Unwin, Crows Nest, NSW.

Australia and New Zealand School of Government (ANZSOG) 2018, 'Public value or profits? Why I chose a career in the public sector', *ANZSOG News*, 12 February, www.anzsog.edu.au/resource-library/news-media/andrew-nicholls.

Australian Government 2019, *APS policy capability roadmap: A practical plan to lift policy capability across the APS*, viewed 5 February 2020, www.policyhub. gov.au/sites/default/files/projects/aps-policy-capability-roadmap.pdf.

Banks, G 2018, 'Whatever happened to "evidence based policy making?"', presentation delivered at Alf Rattigan Lecture, Canberra, ACT.

Bardach, E 2009, *A practical guide for policy analysis*, CQ Press, Washington, DC.

Benington, J 2009, 'Creating the public in order to create public value?', *International Journal of Public Administration*, vol. 32, nos 3–4, pp. 232–49, doi.org/10.1080/01900690902749578.

Bridgman, P & Malone, N 2019, *Policy skills,* viewed 5 February 2020, www.policy skills.com.au.

Brown, P, Cherney, L, Warner, S, Abazie, UC, Ball, S, Cunningham, LE, Le, LLD, Simpson Reeves, L & Worsoe, H 2019, *Understanding public value workshop: Report on proceedings,* University of Queensland, viewed 5 February 2020, apo.org.au/node/252741.

Bryson, JM, Crosby, BC & Bloomberg, L 2014, 'Public value governance: Moving beyond traditional public administration and the new public management', *Public Administration Review,* vol. 74, no. 4, pp. 445–56, doi.org/10.1111/puar.12238.

Burton, T 2017, 'Canberra clones itself', *Mandarin,* 8 September, viewed 5 February 2020, webarchive.nla.gov.au/awa/20180313181456/https://www.themandarin.com.au/83422-tom-burton-canberra-clones/.

Cairney, P 2015, 'How can policy theory have an impact on policymaking? The role of theory-led academic-practitioner discussions', *Teaching Public Administration,* vol. 33, no. 1, pp. 22–39, doi.org/10.1177/0144739414532284.

Cairney, P & Jones, MD 2016, 'Kingdon's multiple streams approach: What is the empirical impact of this universal theory?', *Policy Studies Journal,* vol. 44, no. 1, pp. 37–58, doi.org/10.1111/psj.12111.

Christensen, T & Lægreid, P 2001, 'A transformative perspective on administrative reforms', in T Christensen & P Lægreid (eds), *New public management: The transformation of ideas and practices,* Ashgate, Aldershot, UK.

Cockfield, G & Botterill, LC 2013, 'Rural and regional policy: A case of punctuated incrementalism?', *Australian Journal of Public Administration,* vol. 72, no. 2, pp. 129–42, doi.org/10.1111/1467-8500.12016.

Cohen, M, March, J & Olsen, J 1972, 'A garbage can model of organisational choice', *Administrative Science Quarterly*, vol. 17, no. 1, pp. 1–25, doi.org/10.2307/2392088.

Colebatch, HK 2006, *Beyond the policy cycle: The policy process in Australia*, Allen & Unwin, Sydney, NSW.

Crowley, K & Head, B 2015, 'Policy analysis in Australia: Context, themes and challenges', in B Head & K Crowley (eds), *Policy analysis in Australia,* Policy Press, Bristol, UK, doi.org/10.1332/policypress/9781447310273.003.0001.

Department of Industry, Innovation and Science 2014, *Policy development toolkit*, internal document, Canberra, ACT.

Department of the Prime Minister and Cabinet (PM&C) 2019a, *Delivering for Australians*, viewed 5 February 2020, pmc.gov.au/resource-centre/government/delivering-for-australians.

Department of the Prime Minister and Cabinet (PM&C) 2019b, *Our public service, our future. Independent review of the Australian Public Service*, viewed 5 February 2020, pmc.gov.au/sites/default/files/publications/independent-review-aps.pdf.

Department of Social Services (DSS) 2015, *Social policy capability plan*, internal document, Canberra, ACT.

Di Francesco, M 2015, 'Policy analysis instruction in Australia', in B Head & K Crowley (eds), *Policy analysis in Australia*, Policy Press, Bristol, UK, doi.org/10.1332/policypress/9781447310273.003.0017.

Edwards, M 2001, *Social policy, public policy: From problem to practice*, Allen & Unwin, Crows Nest, NSW.

Edwards, MG, Soo, C & Greckhamer, T 2016, 'Public value management: A case study of transitional change in disability sector reform in Western Australia', *Australian Journal of Public Administration*, vol. 75, no. 2, pp. 176–90, doi.org/10.1111/1467-8500.12193.

Fawcett, P, Jensen, M, Ransan-Cooper, H & Duus, S 2018, 'Explaining the "ebb and flow" of the problem stream: Frame conflicts over the future of coal seam gas ("fracking") in Australia', *Journal of Public Policy*, vol. 39, no. 3, pp. 521–41, doi.org/10.1017/S0143814X18000132.

Gallop, G 2018, 'Empowering our senior public servants with political skills', *Mandarin*, 14 December, viewed 5 February 2020, www.themandarin.com.au/102310-empowering-our-senior-public-servants-with-political-skills/.

Gill, Z & Colebatch, HK 2006, '"Busy little workers": Policy workers' own accounts', in HK Colebatch (ed.), *Beyond the policy cycle: The policy process in Australia*, Allen & Unwin, Crows Nest, NSW.

Halton, J 2016, 'Secretary valedictory', in IPAA, *Twelve speeches 2016: A year of speeches from public service leaders*, IPAA, Canberra, ACT.

Hartley, J, Alford, J, Knies, E & Douglas, S 2017, 'Towards an empirical research agenda for public value theory', *Public Management Review*, vol. 19, no. 5, pp. 670–85, doi.org/10.1080/14719037.2016.1192166.

Howlett, M, McConnell, A & Perl, A 2017, 'Moving policy theory forward: Connecting multiple stream and advocacy coalition frameworks to policy cycle models of analysis', *Australian Journal of Public Administration,* vol. 76, no. 1, pp. 65–79, doi.org/10.1111/1467-8500.12191.

IPAA 2018, *Future leaders series*, ACT Division, 22 November, viewed 5 February 2020, www.act.ipaa.org.au/futureleaders-1.

IPAA 2019, *Prioritising reform*, ACT Division, 18 September, viewed 5 February 2020, www.act.ipaa.org.au/2019-pastevent-prioritisingreform.

Jenkins, S 2019, 'This APS review will be different, says Commissioner Peter Woolcott', *Mandarin,* 26 September, viewed 5 February 2020, www.themandarin.com.au/116772-this-aps-review-will-be-different-says-commissioner/.

Katsonis, M 2019, 'Putting value creation back into public value', *Mandarin,* 8 July, viewed 5 February 2020, www.themandarin.com.au/111206-value-creation/.

Kingdon, JW 2011, *Agendas, alternatives, and public policies*, 2nd edn, Longman, Crawfordsville, IN.

Lancaster, K, Ritter, A, Hughes, C & Hoppe, R 2017, 'A critical examination of the introduction of drug detection dogs for policing of illicit drugs in New South Wales, Australia using Kingdon's "multiple streams' heuristic"', *Evidence and Policy,* vol. 13, no. 4, pp. 583–603, doi.org/10.1332/1744264 16X14683497019265.

Lindblom, CE 1979, 'Still muddling, not yet through', *Public Administration Review*, vol. 39, no. 6, pp. 517–26, doi.org/10.2307/976178.

Lindquist, E & Tiernan, A 2011, 'The Australian Public Service and policy advising: Meeting the challenges of 21st century governance', *Australian Journal of Public Administration,* vol. 70, no. 4, pp. 437–50, doi.org/10.1111/ j.1467-8500.2011.00743.x.

Mackie, K 2016, 'Success and failure in environment policy: The role of policy officials', *Australian Journal of Public Administration,* vol. 75, no. 3, pp. 291–304, doi.org/10.1111/1467-8500.12170.

Maddison, S & Denniss, R 2009, *An introduction to Australian public policy: Theory and practice,* Cambridge University Press, Cambridge, UK, doi. org/10.1017/CBO9781139168656.

Mainwaring, R 2019, 'What will the Turnbull-Morrison government be remembered for?' *Conversation,* 8 April, viewed 5 February 2020, theconversation.com/what-will-the-turnbull-morrison-government-be-remembered-for-114618.

Moore, MH 1995, *Creating public value: Strategic management in government,* Harvard University Press, Cambridge, MA.

Moore, MH 2013, *Recognizing public value,* Harvard University Press, Cambridge, MA, doi.org/10.4159/harvard.9780674067820.

Podger, A 2012, 'My fortunate career and some parting remarks', in J Wanna, S Vincent & A Podger (eds), *With the benefit of hindsight: Valedictory reflections from departmental secretaries, 2004–11,* ANU Press, Canberra, doi.org/10.22459/WBH.04.2012.02.

Policy Profession Board 2019, 'Looking back to look forward: From "twelve actions" to "policy profession 2025"', *Mandarin,* 2 June, viewed 5 February 2020, www.themandarin.com.au/people/sir-chris-wormald/.

Prebble, M 2012, 'Public value and the ideal state: Rescuing public value from ambiguity', *Australian Journal of Public Administration,* vol. 71, no. 4, pp. 392–402, doi.org/10.1111/j.1467-8500.2012.00787.x.

Rhodes, RAW 2016, 'Recovering the craft of public administration', *Public Administration Review,* vol. 76, no. 4, pp. 638–47, doi.org/10.1111/puar.12504.

Rhodes, RA & Wanna, J 2007, 'The limits to public value, or rescuing responsible government from the platonic guardians', *Australian Journal of Public Administration,* vol. 66, no. 4, pp. 406–21, doi.org/10.1111/j.1467-8500.2007.00553.x.

Rhodes, RA & Wanna, J 2008, 'Stairways to heaven: A reply to Alford', *Australian Journal of Public Administration,* vol. 67, no. 3, pp. 367–70, doi.org/10.1111/j.1467-8500.2008.00594.x.

Rhodes, RA & Wanna, J 2009, 'Bringing the politics back in: Public value in Westminster parliamentary government', *Public Administration,* vol. 87, no. 2, pp. 161–83, doi.org/10.1111/j.1467-9299.2009.01763.x.

Rodwell, G 2016 'Re-examining the curriculum development centre: Coordinative federalism and Kingdon's agenda-setting (1975–87)', *Education Research and Perspectives,* vol. 43, pp. 1–35.

Sanderson, I 2009, 'Intelligent policy making for a complex world: Pragmatism, evidence and learning', *Political Studies,* vol. 57, no. 4, pp. 699–719, doi.org/10.1111/j.1467-9248.2009.00791.x.

Scott, C & Baehler, K 2010, *Adding value to policy analysis and advice,* UNSW Press, Sydney, NSW.

Shergold, P 2015a, 'Foreword', in B Head & K Crowley (eds), *Policy analysis in Australia,* Policy Press, Bristol, UK.

Shergold, P 2015b, *Learning from failure: Why large government policy initiatives have gone so badly wrong in the past and how the chances of success in the future can be improved,* Australian Public Service Commission, Canberra, ACT.

Smith, H 2018, 'Doing policy differently: Challenges and insights', in IPAA, *IPAA Speeches 2018: a year of public sector speeches,* IPAA, Barton, ACT.

Sullivan, H 2019, 'Building a knowledge-sharing system: Innovation, replication, co-production and trust—a response', *Australian Journal of Public Administration,* vol. 78, no. 2, pp. 319–21, doi.org/10.1111/1467-8500. 12370.

Threlfall, D 2018, 'From walk to talk: Academics and practitioners join forces for public policy learning', *Mandarin,* 10 September, viewed 5 February 2020, www.themandarin.com.au/98387-from-walk-to-talk-academics-and-practitioners-join-forces-for-public-policy-learning/.

Tiernan, A 2011, 'Advising Australian federal governments: Assessing the evolving capacity and role of the Australian Public Service', *Australian Journal of Public Administration,* vol. 70, no. 4, pp. 335–46, doi.org/10.1111/j.1467-8500.2011.00742.x.

Varghese, P 2016, 'Parting reflections', in IPAA, *Twelve speeches 2016: A year of speeches from public service leaders,* IPAA, Canberra, ACT.

Wanna, J, Butcher, J & Freyens, J 2010, *Policy in action: The challenge of service delivery,* UNSW Press, Sydney, NSW.

Weible, CM & Cairney, P 2018, 'Practical lessons from policy theories', *Policy and Politics,* vol. 46, no. 2, pp. 183–97, doi.org/10.1332/03055731 8X15230059147191.

Weller, PM, Bakvis, H & Rhodes, RAW (eds) 1997, *The hollow crown: Countervailing trends in core executives,* Macmillan Press, New York, NY, doi.org/10.1007/978-1-349-25870-3.

World Bank 2019, *World Bank project cycle,* viewed 16 August 2019, projects.world bank.org/en/projects-operations/products-and-services/brief/projectcycle.

4

Delivering public policy programs to senior executives in government—the Australia and New Zealand School of Government 2002–18

John Wanna[1]

Leadership and executive development programs have a long trajectory in the Australian and New Zealand public sectors, but there is currently a growing concern that many of the skills and capacities of leadership and policy advice have been eroded and/or neglected (Tiernan 2011, 2015). In recent times, dedicated leadership development programs have become intrinsically important in enhancing individual and collective organisational capacities, often integrated within formal staff appraisal processes and performance review systems. The prevailing pedagogical philosophies behind such programs have centred on developing organisational human resource capabilities and encouraging leadership potentialities in a team-based context aimed at problem-solving and performance results. This chapter examines the origin and development of the Australia and New Zealand School of Government (ANZSOG), which, for almost 20 years, has delivered executive developmental

1   The author wishes to thank Catherine Althaus, Trish Mercer, Val Barrett, Isi Unikowski and Robert McMahon for comments and suggestions on an earlier draft, and Peter Allen for his contribution to an earlier version of this chapter.

programs to middle and senior executive public policy practitioners across both countries and to the wider geographic region. It also discusses many of the persistent dilemmas and challenges faced by those engaged in executive training more generally.

The evolution of specialised executive education

Australia and New Zealand have both established permanent-based civil services that enjoy formal statutory status while preserving their separation (and protection) from politics and minimising ministerial involvement in senior appointments. Public service organisations (departments and statutory authorities) are administratively interdependent with government, working professionally with Cabinet and its ministers, requiring staff to become politically savvy without being politically active. Over time and through experience, senior public servants have developed considerable administrative expertise (the 'craft'), advisory skills ('mastery') and effective relations with elected (and frequently changing) ministries. Even from colonial times, these public services have become career services, generally unified as a jurisdictional workforce, enshrining the principles of continuity, neutrality, anonymity and relying on largely internal notions of merit. The entrenchment of tenure for officials has largely established the current structure and cultures of public service. Typically, public servants learnt their vocation and were trained in the art of administration through constant on-the-job experiences, acquired competencies and some occasional training ('training for purpose').

Throughout most of the twentieth century, public services across Australasia were staffed by a combination of predominantly generalist administrators with some specialist professions or scientific grades. They were highly insular and not open to 'strangers' (with very little lateral recruitment or 'lateral entry' from outside), becoming increasingly bureaucratically industrial in their employment orientations (with strong public sector unions organised by administrative categories). For decades, governments and their central personnel management agencies (the public service boards in Australia or state services commissions in New Zealand) were preoccupied with improving the quality and reliability of administration, including economy and efficiency, routinisation and consistency of administrative practice, due diligence, compliance accountability and ethics (Public Service & Merit Protection Commission [PSMPC] 2001). More recently, these perennial bureaucratic issues have tended to be overshadowed (but not totally displaced) by the imperatives of improved management, greater reliance on business techniques, performance and program effectiveness over results and outcomes, capacity-building, developing outward-oriented cultures of responsiveness and client-focused forms of service delivery, and consultative practices and public engagement. However, the turn towards new public management (NPM) from the 1980s onwards led to accusations that managerial imperatives had severely impacted on policy capabilities and 'hollowed out' state capacities.

Training and development for public servants was not a statutory requirement (and is not mentioned in the Australian *Public Service Act 1999* and no longer in the New Zealand *State Services Act 1988*) but service-wide bodies and individual agencies maintained an enduring interest in 'training for purpose'. Most of the larger agencies tended to operate their own training activities (often contracting external providers for specific programs or workshops), while central agencies (public service boards or commissions) retained some overall service-wide responsibilities, including coordination, and ensuring agencies fulfil their training and executive development obligations. Accordingly, most training and development was fragmented and conducted at the individual agency level, with considerable 'in-service' delivery and customised on-the-job training. Taken together, these training regimes formed a matrix of self-administered, 'job-focused' training, generally characterised by piecemeal internal provision, short-term foci, stop-start delivery and lack of credit (i.e. 'not-for-credit', meaning that the training did not count as an upper-secondary or tertiary qualification). These 'in-service' offerings, resourced primarily at the individual agency level, could be supplemented at the individual officer level by formal 'out-service' instruction 'for credit' (qualification-based programs delivered by business and secretarial colleges, night schools and further education colleges, dedicated training institutes and universities).

Historically, no Australian or New Zealand jurisdiction chose to invest in a single, monopoly provider to deliver training services across the entire public sector (although both armed forces did so with specialist training institutes). One of the main considerations may have been the recurrent direct costs likely to be involved, with agencies preferring to allocate smaller amounts from general staff budgets year by year. There has never been an equivalent in Australia or New Zealand to the central civil service colleges, such as the centrally funded Singapore Civil Service College or Taiwanese National Academy of the Civil Service with service-wide responsibilities for training and development. This is not to say that there have not been constant tensions between and debates over the merits of agency-specific 'competency training' and the 'holy grail' of devising centrally coordinated generic training regimes.

As the number of graduates entering the various services increased, demands for more externally provided training and education grew. Once graduates rose through the ranks, these more educated public servants stressed the importance of knowledge and intellectual and analytic abilities. By the 1980s, attention turned to middle management training and business and management training, often with graduates undertaking subsequent graduate diplomas and masters courses in professional areas, including business administration, law and accounting. Internal training tended then to focus on competency-based training, gap analysis for required skills and selective recruitment. A frequent structure for courses was based on three themes: technical skills, interpersonal skills and self-management skills (Public Service Commission [PSC] 1992, pp. 37–8). A government mandated training guarantee program in the early 1990s requiring agencies to spend 2 per cent of their budgets on training saw the proliferation of many private sector training organisations and providers of organised conferences on work-related topics under the banner of training. In addition, a number of 'senior executive services' (SES) had been created by the early 1990s across Australian jurisdictions, and specialist development programs were devised for this cohort, including a dedicated induction program called SEMP (Senior Executive Management Program). Executive development relied on a formal leadership capability framework to broaden capabilities and develop high performance leadership (by encouraging participants to develop executive capabilities to shape strategic thinking, cultivate productive working relations, communicate with influence, exemplify personal drive and integrity, and achieve results) (see Australian Public Service Commission [APSC] 2004). At the same time, a 'cooperative venture' between all the Australian jurisdictions and a consortia of universities provided middle management development instruction with formal university qualifications (graduate certificate) in the public sector management course (PSMPC 2001, p. 191). As the

2000s progressed, many jurisdictions adopted forms of an 'integrated leadership framework' applying to their SES and other executive levels (see APSC 2004; APSC 2014).

Government departments and individual public servants energised the demand for formal qualifications (e.g. tertiary degrees, advanced diplomas, graduate diplomas or masters by coursework) as endemic 'credentialism' manifested itself in the public service. By the 1990s, almost all new recruits now possessed graduate qualifications (or were close to graduating), and many were sponsored to undertake (relevant) higher level studies, especially vocationally oriented masters courses (e.g. public policy, policy studies, public management, administrative law, accounting or generic business studies). Universities and further education colleges expanded their vocational offerings and began to tap the part-time student and distance education markets. However, at the same time, traditional courses in the building blocks of public administration tended to decline as academic specialisations, replaced by more generic courses in business techniques, organisational design, human resource management, computing studies and information technology (Davis & Wanna 1997). The number of Australian institutions offering master of business administration (MBA) courses increased from two in the 1970s to over 30 by the late 2000s, and in New Zealand from one in the 1970s to eight in 2019, and, for a while, these business-oriented higher degrees were remarkably popular with public servants and their departmental supervisors (despite their frequent lack of fit). Eventually, rivalling this development of generic business credentialism was the establishment of a number of dedicated public policy tertiary courses; some were offered at the undergraduate level but most were provided at the masters level to graduates (see Di Francesco 2015). Enrolments across tertiary institutions in Australia increased from 200,000 in 1985 to 600,000 by 2014, forming a huge pool of educated jobseekers from which to recruit staff.

New Zealand tended to concentrate public management training at Victoria University of Wellington in the postgraduate public management courses in the School of Government, and through the policy-applied Institute for Policy Studies. The University of Auckland also developed a popular masters in public policy. Australia saw the growth of specialist professional institutions delivering executive education to public servants. Most noticeably, there arose dedicated training centres such as the Australian Administrative Staff College, a residential executive college established in 1954 that later became the Mount Eliza Business School (and then merged in 2004 with the Melbourne Business School of the University of Melbourne). There was also increased provision from leadership academies and from various professional bodies, such as the various public service commissions, the Australian Institute of Management, the Institute of Public Administration of Australia and New Zealand's Institute of Public Administration. These professional bodies tended to provide professionally oriented and vocational training, and also concentrated on some generic capabilities (e.g. public policy skills, business and management techniques, accounting and specialist law programs, and health and safety training). A host of private sector training and executive development providers also sprang up from the 1980s, often headed by former top executives from the public and private sectors.

A unique Trans-Tasman experiment in developing senior executive capabilities

In the early 2000s, a significant innovation occurred in the Australian and New Zealand context in the formation of a dedicated executive development institution jointly owned by government jurisdictions with member universities—the Australia and New Zealand School of Government (see Allen & Wanna 2016). ANZSOG's stated purpose was to become:

> A world-class centre providing cutting-edge research and tailored learning opportunities for future leaders of the public sector. ANZSOG's purpose is to encourage improved public sector leadership, decision-making, policy outcomes and performance for the benefit of the community. ANZSOG plays a crucial role in promoting public service as a vocational profession of great social value to the public interest. (ANZSOG n.d.)

To achieve these ambitious objectives ANZSOG concentrated on three core functions:

1. to provide executive education development including the Executive Fellows Program (EFP) for senior executives and the Executive Master of Public Administration (EMPA) degree for mid-career government officials

2. to produce a high-quality inductive 'teaching case' collection available for training and executive development (currently around 200 cases are available for use)

3. to undertake an active research program investigating topics of immediate relevance to public sector managers in order 'to deepen knowledge and understanding of government and to disseminate that understanding throughout the community'.[2]

The creation of ANZSOG was actually brought about because other specialist or tertiary institutions were not providing these functions, or not providing them to the satisfaction of key public sector leaders. There was an ambition in both countries to improve public sector capabilities and performance in delivery (Fels 2003). There was also a sense of a perceived policy capability gap afflicting both countries as a direct result of nearly 20 years of NPM (Boston & Eichbaum 2014; Podger 2003; Tiernan 2015). With regard to the existing university programs, ANZSOG was the response to the perception of various Australian governments that there was a 'market failure' in the provision and quality of training and development programs available for public sector executives, especially focused on public leadership and management. Governments, therefore, took the initiative (and made the necessary investments) to create, with the collaboration and support of leading Australian and New Zealand universities, their own multi-jurisdictional school of government to which they could send their mid-senior executives identified as likely future leaders.

The establishment of the school in 2002

The establishment of ANZSOG in 2002 reflected a proactive recognition that the task of designing, delivering and maintaining the quality of professional development for future public sector leaders was challenging governments and specialist educational providers across the world. Existing approaches ranged from reliance on dedicated government-owned institutions (such as the Singapore Civil Service College and the French Ecole Nationale d'Administration) to specialist institutes attached to leading universities. In this latter category the United States, for example, had a number of world-class providers such as Harvard's John F Kennedy School of Government, the Brookings Institute, the

---

2   These objectives have changed only slightly since 2002–03. The most recent statement of the school's objectives state that its purpose is 'dedicated to creating value for citizens by providing world-class education for public sector leaders, conducting research and facilitating informed discussion on issues that matter for public sector performance, and promoting and supporting innovation in the public sector' (ANZSOG 2013). Only the last phrase is an augmentation on earlier statements.

Woodrow Wilson School of Public and International Affairs (Princeton) and the Goldman School of Public Policy at California's Berkeley University. Recent United Kingdom experience has witnessed the demise of the government-owned National School of Government in 2012 (Civil Service College and Cabinet Office), although new initiatives have emerged as replacements, such as the Oxford University Blavatnik School of Government as well as continuing roles for established providers such as the London School of Economics and Warwick University. Against this background, public sector leaders in Australia and New Zealand determined to pursue a distinctively different approach to executive development, one that attempted to harmonise and build on the respective capacities of governments and universities across the two nations.

While many universities had graduate programs aimed at public officials, they were all constrained by limited demand; comparatively small, regionally focused academies; and limited, highly conditional, support from public service leaders. There was also a growing concern that the executive development of public executives was becoming a case of 'market failure': a dissipated and fragmented pattern of tertiary education institutions not investing in the required intellectual perspectives and teaching expertise to produce the required specialist courses and training opportunities that governments needed and requested. Accordingly, a new consolidated model was needed to provide customised high-quality public sector executive education to meet the governments' specific needs.

The decision to establish a bi-national school of government occurred almost by accident. A small group of senior officials led by the head of the Victorian Premier's Department, Terry Moran (also former CEO of the Australian National Training Authority), began discussing the possibility of a dedicated teaching institution across several Australian states. New Zealand officials heard of this development and expressed a keen interest to join. In many ways, this unplanned enhancement crystallised the opportunity and pedagogic benefits of collaborative action across government and universities. However, this necessitated the Commonwealth coming in, which, under the Howard government, it was at first disinclined to do, but later it agreed to join and augment the funding.[3]

---

3   In fact, the final agreement to form ANZSOG was reached at a Council of Australian Governments dinner in 2002 when a group of heads of first ministers' departments convinced the Commonwealth to join and send officers to the programs. John Howard's head of the Department of Prime Minister and Cabinet, Max Moore-Wilton, gave an undertaking to join, provided the state heads stopped badgering him about it.

By mid-2002, five 'foundation members' had been identified with commitments for three years to fund the agreed intake for two initial ANZSOG executive development programs. One was the EMPA aimed at executive level officers with between five and 10 years public sector experience, and largely taught in block intensive mode. The second was a three-week intensive EFP targeted at SES officers. In November 2002, an agreement was signed by the founding governments and with the associated university partners.[4] The member governments were themselves responsible for nominating participants for ANZSOG programs in addition to fully paying for them, ideally selecting those they believed to have considerable potential and leadership capabilities. Significantly, all participants to the main educational programs were government sponsored, meaning individual public servants could not voluntarily enrol in ANZSOG or personally pay tuition fees, nor could private sector managers elect to enrol.

Enrolment of the initial 130 public sector managers in the inaugural EMPA was completed and the first week-long course ('Delivering public value') was presented in May 2003, with the balance of the 10-course masters program delivered through 2003 and 2004. The inaugural delivery of the more senior EFP occurred across October and November 2003, with an enrolment of 80 senior public officials from across Australia and New Zealand, and a faculty drawn from Australian, New Zealand, United States and United Kingdom universities, and Australian and New Zealand public sector leaders. Gradually, the other jurisdictions (South Australia, Tasmania, Western Australia, the Northern Territory and the Australian Capital Territory) joined, bringing with them additional university partners. ANZSOG programs have expanded to include a program for public sector managers making the transition from operational to strategic leadership roles ('Towards Strategic Leadership' [TSL]), an extensive range of executive education short courses, programs aimed at building public sector capability in the Asia-Pacific region, a leadership development program for local government and an increasingly active

---

4   The five original jurisdictional members comprised the governments of the Commonwealth of Australia, New Zealand, Victoria, Queensland and New South Wales. The nine founding university members were The Australian National University, the University of Canberra, the University of Victoria, Monash University, the Melbourne Business School, Griffith University, the University of Queensland, the University of Sydney and the University of New South Wales. Subsequently, all other Australian governments (South Australia, Western Australia, Tasmania, the Northern Territory and the Australian Capital Territory, and seven additional universities agreed to join ANZSOG).

research program (see ANZSOG 2013, 2016). By 2019, the total number of alumni across the school's three main programs (EMPA, EFP and TSL, but not including executive education short courses) was over 4,000.

An important feature distinguishing ANZSOG from other international public service training institutes, such as the former UK National School of Government, has been the role of, and investment in, research, which both underpinned the core curriculum and informed teaching. This has generated an extensive research and publications program, including supervision of doctoral students, some of whom may develop as future teachers of ANZSOG programs. This was followed by a series of other government-sponsored senior academic research posts in other member jurisdictions, as well as joint teaching–research appointments. ANZSOG has also invested heavily in the development of 'teaching cases' aimed at executive education, with an available library now of more than 200 written case studies; these are all available to member governments and university partners at no cost.

While ANZSOG naturally shares many characteristics with other 'schools of government', it also has several distinctive features. These can be summarised as follows:

- ANZSOG is a not-for-profit consortium of stakeholder governments and universities designed to achieve economies of scale and scope in addressing the needs of government.
- It is a collaborative partnership between two nations (Australia and New Zealand).
- Governments identify and nominate emerging leaders from around Australia and New Zealand, and support them financially during their engagement with ANZSOG.
- The school has the capacity to attract first class teachers from Australia, New Zealand and overseas.
- Its rigorous EMPA is accredited by Australian and New Zealand universities.
- The school offers a research-driven, practitioner-oriented curriculum.
- Its pedagogic philosophy stresses innovative and engaging program delivery.
- It has managed around 20 major international conferences on topics of direct interest to practitioners and many workshops and seminars.
- It has strategic linkages with other prestigious international schools of government in Europe, America and Asia.

Six significant factors have contributed to ANZSOG's institutional progress and the continuing high level of support it enjoys from both its government members and university partners. First, the school has prioritised a continuing focus on meeting governments' needs in senior executive development, with the corollary that continuing support from government stakeholders has required maintaining relevance and high levels of customer satisfaction. Second, it has invested in, and provided dedicated educational programs to, its stakeholder governments. Third, it has demonstrated a commitment to teacher development focused on effective postgraduate/mid-career teaching and learning. Fourth, it has actively utilised an extensive network of scholars and practitioners, across Australia and New Zealand and internationally, to provide input into programs and courses. Fifth, the school has maintained an active engagement with, and support from, alumni, including providing ongoing educational refreshers and network opportunities. Finally, the school has operated within a robust business model designed to maximise its effectiveness and influence, while providing value for money for governments and participants.

ANZSOG's distinctive participant population and teaching innovations

Participants in ANZSOG's executive development programs were generally middle to senior officials with significant experience and embedded practice backgrounds. They were highly engaged, motivated and possessed a high performance culture in the commitment they put into the learning environment. They were energised through reflecting on a range of theoretical insights and explanations of best practice presented to ensure they were serving the demands of government and the needs of the community. These features placed unique demands on the teaching and learning process. Teaching was not simply a matter of delivering content in traditional lecturing modes. Learning had to take place in a realistic and dynamic environment, pitched at the right level to connect with participant experiences and capabilities, and developed with tangible takeaway messages that deliver benefit to the participants in their practice environment.

ANZSOG has developed over time its distinctive learning-centred pedagogical approach to respond to the opportunities presented by this challenging cohort and the important roles they already play in promoting good public policy outcomes and good public management practices. ANZSOG has worked collaboratively with the Kennedy School of Government at Harvard University to develop a practically oriented structure of developmental learning that builds on a core set of foundations, namely delivering public value, managing organisations, governing in a market economy, designing programs, decision-making under uncertainty, governing by well-designed rules and regulations and leading public sector change. Initially, in the masters program, the school promoted the interactive 'teaching case' pedagogical approach, but over time it developed in tandem with innovations in pedagogy drawing on interactive learning. The aim of interactive education was to broaden and diversify the learning experience through deploying a range of 'teaching methods' or sources of information. 'Teaching cases' became complementary to a range of other available teaching approaches including guest expert presenters and greater use of digital-based learning to promote active applied learning by all participants in the learning environment (see Alford & Brock 2014).

Another innovation ANZSOG has developed has been the 'immersive case' as a pedagogic experience to stretch participant learnings. Immersive cases are 'live issues' that demand policy attention and involve participants (instructors and learners) performing site visits and working 'in the field' with policy or management issues in a real world context, especially nominated by owner governments of ANZSOG who might be grappling with a particular matter at a point in time, and are seeking the 'wisdom of the crowd' from participants in how to address intractable challenges or 'wicked' issues. For example, the TSL program divided participants into groups to address the particular challenges of dealing with homelessness in Victoria. This pedagogy was also employed on an inter-jurisdictional level to expand comparative learnings across Australia and New Zealand. It is now a crucial component of ANZSOG's international collaboration, with program participants in the EMPA and EFP travelling to Singapore and investigating 'live thematic issues' pertinent to Singaporean society, and working on presentations to project sponsors attached to the 'live policy challenges'. EFP participants have also been engaged in immersive case experiences in New Zealand concerning the film industry, with students matched with project sponsors, subject matter experts, instructional coaches and live site visits. A variety of practical proposals were generated that were communicated back to industry and government sponsors.

ANZSOG's work-based project in the EMPA serves as the capstone collaborative project with research topics nominated by agencies within member governments. Groups of five to six participants investigate policy problems or topics, frame their analysis and methodologies, and report their findings in oral presentations and written reports, often in seminars back to the nominating agency. While research-based projects have been employed in courses in other universities, ANZSOG began systematically to mine the topics and information gathered to inform the school about the main issues of concern to governments and extract policy learnings across time and across the federation and Trans-Tasman setting.

Under a new dean, ANZSOG refreshed its teaching and learning strategy in 2018–19 as part of its new *ANZSOG 2025 strategy review,* which was initially approved by the board in late 2018 with the implementation plan approved in May 2019. An additional investment of resources up to $9 million was committed to the strategy over three years. The strategy called for greater stakeholder engagement, new marketing channels, revised curriculum and course offerings, more immersive experiences and 'adaptive offerings', greater use of innovative digital and online platforms in 'blended delivery' modes, customised support for instructors and institutional accreditation for tertiary-level courses. A key aim was to make learning increasingly active, curated and personalised. It also prioritised a greater focus on inclusion and diversity, including developing Indigenous peoples in the school's programs and incorporating Indigenous perspectives and cultures across the education programs.

Together, the distinctive participant populations and the pedagogic initiatives undertaken by ANZSOG were aimed at injecting direct value to actual public policymaking as well as better public management practices across the region. Internal ANZSOG research on the school's alumni suggested that participants found great value in the school's programs, and regularly rated their educational experience highly, averaging 4.2 out of 5 between 2012 and 2016 cohorts (ANZSOG 2019). Many frequently cited important aspects of learning that they operationalised at their places of work (such as the strategic triangle concept, adaptive leadership, the authorising environment, responsive regulation and collaborative leadership). Participants also greatly appreciated a number of by-product benefits associated with ANZSOG's cross-jurisdictional educational structure, including building networks and developing expert communities of practice. Alumni reported that they were better able to work within complex organisations, frame and interrogate problems, converse with colleagues, demonstrate self-awareness, use contacts and inter-jurisdictional networks, and promote collegiality and public sector camaraderie. In short, respondents have deepened their expertise and knowledge as well as enhanced their inspirational commitment to what the present board chair has called the 'spirit of service' (Hughes 2018).

Dilemmas and challenges in delivering high-quality executive development programs

The discussion that follows draws on extensive experience from academics working closely with senior public servants and government employees in educational environments. It is evident that, for many public sector executives, executive education opens new horizons, provides new knowledges and understandings, provides windows into alternative ways of thinking, and challenges them to translate theories and models into applicable learnings. It is often the case that inspirational presenters can transform the learning environment in class and leave lasting impressions on participants. Applied adult education can unleash the potentiality of higher learning in those with ample experience of work and professional development. In particular, schools like ANZSOG help program participants to transition from backgrounds in technical knowledge into public policy and policymaking, and provide an awareness of the imperatives of political governance, including developing a stronger sense of professional coherence. However, there are some very real challenges in directing education to these senior career public officials, not all of which are unique to the ANZSOG participants. First, government executives, especially those with more seniority and responsibilities, are a very particular type of course participant. Many undertaking executive development opportunities think they 'know it already'; they believe they cannot be taught much from formal programs and/or that academics cannot 'teach' them anything of importance. Many are not as curiosity-driven as they could be but instead view executive education as a way of gaining formal competencies, accumulating frameworks to deploy as modus operandi and investing in networking. Recipients as well as presenters often prefer the intensive or concentrated mode of learning, where they are corralled into training courses for about a week (three to six days) often with a residential component, or for repeated intensive days some weeks apart. Intensive modes can assist new learnings to resonate and readily be built upon in subsequent classes; however, they also allow relatively little time for wider contemplation, genuine reflection, wider reading, written assignments or demonstrated comprehension. Class-based delivery in teaching venues (even when interactive participation is encouraged) is typically an unreal environment in which busy executives have taken time out to contemplate and reflect on the curricula. Many participants are time-poor, and already have intensive work-life balance challenges in their lives. Reading time is often restricted, leading to cramming and skimming, and almost always limited to the readings provided by the course presenters. Most of all, many executives are not allowed to (or cannot) 'leave work' behind and are constantly focused on problems or crises at work, on their mobile phones or heading back to the office, all of which reduces their concentration levels and attention spans. Too many participants in executive programs have a 'completion' mentality and requirement for credentialism, gaining higher degree credits or maintaining attendance to gain proof of completion and perhaps certification.

Second, there is the issue of what course participants themselves bring to the educational programs. Many executives bring considerable practical experience to the classes, gained from years of professional engagement within the sector. Indeed, this factor may be precisely why they have been nominated by their agencies for further executive development. The experience, however, may be in relatively circumscribed niches, leaving them with relatively little broader policy or managerial expertise or abilities. Hence, there may be some caution warranted when considering someone's experience in senior management of say 15 years: it may span 15 complex years in many challenging environments or consist of one year 15 times over. Class participants tend to attract both sorts of experiences, which serves to complicate the learning environment.

There is also the issue within agencies of which age cohorts should be trained for maximum benefit. Twenty to 30 year olds generally do not have the required experience and are not usually in substantive positions to be able to use the imparted knowledge. Those in their late 30s and 40s are the primary target group for executive development, but may not be intending to remain in the public sector in five or 10 years. Those over 50 or approaching 60 may need and appreciate executive training but there is a declining marginal utility in the investment. So, how to identify the next generation of future leaders remains a major problem for elite executive schools of government, as it is for public service departments and agencies. Historically, many 'fast-tracking' or 'hot-housing' schemes have reported limited success, with those officials eventually reaching senior posts often not having been selected into the hot-housing programs.[5] Occasionally, executive training may be regarded by agencies as a reward for past service, going to those who have 'earned' kudos or met targets, and not necessarily those most likely to succeed, innovate or lead the agency in the future. Having said that, it should be recognised that ANZSOG is perceived as a prized program and competition in jurisdictions for places is often intense.

Third, on the supply-side, instructors, many of whom are academic class teachers and guest presenters, may be less familiar with the world of the practitioner and not comprehend the pressures they may be under. Often academics have never worked in the administrative public sector or performed routine bureaucratic jobs. Many of the executives these instructors hope to motivate are ingrained with agency cultures and bureaucratic norms, accustomed to hierarchical decision-making practices, too harried to be reflective or to undertake the necessary research, working with difficult bosses, and often filling in for others who may be away from the job. Academics tend to draw from what they know best: bodies of literature, critiques and key debates, explanatory concepts or precepts, simplified modelling, familiar articles or current academic preoccupations. These are real bodies of knowledge to them and frame the way they see the world. Academics may be able to teach for the allotted time in class sessions, but not necessarily translate or tailor their material to highlight the applicability to practical situations. For instance, many representations of classical incrementalism present the main aspects of the theory, limitations of knowledge, limited sequential comparisons of action, 'muddling through' and trial and error tactics, and root and branch adaptations, but fail to concretise the heuristic modelling for

---

5   The classic example in Australia was the deputy secretary scheme (intended to develop promising deputies into the next generation of secretaries, then called permanent heads), which ran throughout the 1960–70s. However, when the succession planning scheme was reviewed, very few of the deputies had made it to the top, and those that had had typically not done the fast-tracking scheme. Interestingly, ANZSOG has established its own deputy leaders program in 2018 available to member governments.

audiences. Practitioners often recognise the model, not as normative 'best practice' or an ideal way of doing policy, but as an academic descriptive version of what they often see at work: the messiness of decision-making, people making it up as they go along and reactions to expedient stimuli. Too often, the applicability of abstracted models often has to take place in the minds of the recipients. Guest presenters with practical experience can 'ground' the learning opportunities, but they are often restricted to their own personal experiences, which are typically anecdotal; consequently, they struggle to translate their observations to broader contexts.

Fourth, in pedagogic terms, instructors and participants can resemble strangers dancing with strangers or ships passing in the night that are unlikely to bump into one another, with academics more interested in theoretical debates (assumptions, approaches, worldviews or *weltanschauung*) and practitioners interested in how to get their jobs done. Academics tend to be focused on problems and critiques of performance, while practitioners tend to be interested in proposing solutions in relation to salient issues on the agenda. In formal programs, the expectations of teachers is that participants will absorb learnings, be able to apply models and theories and contextualise learnings, and respect the expertise of those with knowledge. The expectations of the learners are to be challenged, reassured and entertained; they expect to enjoy some 'time out' from work and clear their head space and, above all, that their instructors will respect practical experience. Participants often have difficulty, not with following a given presentation, but with relating what has been presented with other approaches or interpretations, or into other contexts. At worst, presentations from practitioners can descend into a series of 'war stories' related from the distant past, with no help provided to ground the learnings, put them into context or help participants apply the learning (where, when and how). Required course readings authored by academics can be less 'mind opening' and may soon become a chore for participants who may not know what 'learnings' to draw from them. The use of simplified theories, models or key concepts is often presented in the abstract, devoid of real context, meaning that these heuristic devices typically airbrush out the messiness and complexities of real-life engagement with public policy (e.g. 'bounded rationality', 'market failure', the 'authorising environment', the 'strategic triangle', 'policy stages' or 'policy cycles', 'punctuated incrementalism', 'multi-streams analysis' and 'program logics'). Simplified models become stylised heuristics, arguably misleading as much as they inform (e.g. the debate over the 'policy cycle' heuristic is far removed from the real world of practitioners [see Cairney 2015]).

Fifth, 'teaching cases' are specially designed as problem-oriented learning exchanges, using background readings that condense aspects of a particular incident, issue, scenario or controversy. They can be excellent forms of pedagogy and are a renowned format of applied learning (although they can be a 'high wire act' for presenters unsure of where they may go). The pedagogic philosophy behind 'teaching cases' is that the smartest person in the room is the room itself (i.e. liberating the collective knowledge and experiences of capable participants). Most 'teaching cases' are written in parts to narrate a particular problem though various stages (pretending it is a live scenario) to allow for compartmentalised class discussion of alternative ways of proceeding or explaining proposed actions. However, there can be problems associated with the over-reliance on 'teaching cases'. Cases typically date quickly, become mainly of historical interest and are highly contextual. Participants need certain bodies of content knowledge and context before they can analyse a given case appropriately. Often classes divide between those that are very familiar with the case information, and participants for whom it is a bewildering puzzle with incomprehensible aspects, a phenomena that policy expert Professor Patrick Weller once called 'pooled ignorance'. If an experienced instructor discovered a class full of participants who knew little about the topic, how could they expect them to make sense of the case? Many participants will typically make naive or simplistic suggestions, politically unfeasible options or venture implausible proposals that would not gain realistic support. To illustrate this point, a few years ago, a group of transport executives exploring a case about traffic congestion in metropolitan cities discussed options and reported that the best way forward was to introduce road pricing for entry into the CBD; when a media leak occurred, the then premier stated that it was the most preposterous proposal he had ever heard and that it would not be happening under his watch.

It takes great skill from presenters to bring out the complexity and ambiguity of teaching cases and allow participants to reflect on the learnings. 'Teaching cases', while drawn from real world experiences, are somewhat artificial in classroom contexts. They are predictably post-hoc rationalisations, with the authors having the luxury of being wise after the event. Many signpost dilemmas and pitfalls, highlight misjudgements or shortcomings, and include some form of 'narrative closure' making endings predictable and the pitfalls readily avoidable by class participants. Many cases present clear examples of policy failure or poor judgement and no one in a course discussion will admit that they would repeat the decisions to allow that unfortunate scenario to eventuate. With the benefit of hindsight, class participants, when asked to make comments or assessments of case scenarios, often say that 'they wouldn't have done that', which makes them more circumspect and erodes the learning experience. Indeed, the 'wisdom of hindsight syndrome' is a really difficult quality to dislodge. In addition, with 'teaching cases', there is rarely any truly right or wrong answers; any nominated course of action or suggested solutions could be right or wrong, better or worse, depending on the context, prevailing imperatives and implications. Negotiating how to proceed in teaching cases is usually more a question of appropriateness and prudence. Post course follow-ups and alumni master classes can be part of the learning journey, as offered regularly by ANZSOG, and these can provide valuable updates and refreshers to former participants who may have attempted to apply executive learnings in their places of work.

Sixth, role-playing scenarios provide a sense of drama and entertaining interludes; they are good ways to get participants talking and engaged. However, even when 'real-life' scenarios are re-created, they do not replicate a real world situation when reprised in the class context. Such role-playing exercises are one-off exercises in which no one is really responsible for what they say or do, there is no real hierarchy or power disparity, and no repeated occurrences as would occur in ministers' offices or bureaucracies. Many role-playing exercises see participants merely wanting to seal the case, complete the exercise or find narrative closure, and, in learning terms, there is often a danger that participants will interpret this to mean that one comment is as good as another. Other gaming exercises, such as brainstorming and thinking outside the box scenarios, may also not be realistic representations, as they tend to find participants who 'know the patter' but do not consider the risks or alternative perspectives. It is hard to game a scenario when no one has skin in the game and no responsibility for any conclusion or consequence. ANZSOG's adoption of 'immersive cases' in real-life contexts (which are similar to UK executive development experiences) aims to make case work far more realistic and powerful in terms of learning.

Seventh, there is a broader problem of whether the content of programs is 'fit for purpose' and germane. How do we know if the focus on leadership, for instance, is a priority for agencies or the profession of public administration and whether it will enhance the capabilities of officials? Are notions of 'market failure', 'competitive advantage' or 'rent-seeking behaviour' useful concepts for non-economist public servants doing graduate courses? Training programs designed for senior executives (both in the public and private sectors) can become fixated on particular conceptions (such as strategic leadership, corporate planning, change management or an emphasis on 'public value'). Many public policy schools have now endorsed a normative 'public value' approach to public management, advocating a malleable concept encouraging various experiments in bureaucratic interventionism often more suited to US-style policy entrepreneurialism. The danger here is that the endorsement of a particular normative concept risks creating disciples rather than critical thinkers or sceptics. Critics may argue that the adoption of a pedagogy about administrative experimentation and the advocacy of a licence to go 'value-adding' by policy entrepreneurs can take precedence over more 'hard-edged' managerial education, stakeholder management, quantitative skills, data analytics and interpretations, implementation and project management capabilities. Often, too much emphasis on policymaking can neglect an exploration of the art and craft of public administration.

Finally, in the wider domain of executive education, there is frequently an overuse of PowerPoint presentations, with information-laden slides listing notable points and providing visual hooks. PowerPoint is generally a passive form of pedagogic learning, with presentations delivered as authorial scripts, often with little time to digest or discuss the contentious points. It is a convenient but unsatisfactory way of delivering complex information, usually with no explanation as to why a presenter has chosen to select certain information and exclude other information or rival approaches. Often many of the crucial explanatory variables are hidden in the white spaces between the bullet points or linked (somewhat mystically) between slides in the presentation. Unless the presenter is very skilled at narrative and explanation, PowerPoint slides tend to recite canon not analysis.

Conclusions

Delivering high-quality training and development to senior executives across the public sector from different jurisdictions, different agencies and at different stages of career progression has its challenges and rewards. The intensive mode of teaching, which is typically associated with senior practitioner executive development, suits their work-life balance and busy work schedules. Classes become 'semi-retreats' away from the workplace, providing relatively 'safe spaces' where executives can share experiences, learnings and indiscretions, and speak honestly while benefiting from the interactive exchanges of a cohort of relatively similar level executives. However, there are distinct challenges in taking the learnings and insights gained through such classes and translating them into real practice.

Forty years ago very little of this intensive block executive education was delivered in Australian tertiary institutions, with the exception of a handful of graduate schools and institutes of management experimenting with intensive MBA programs. Now it has become the norm. So, where to from here? We might wonder whether such forms of intensive executive training and development will still be around in the next 20 or 30 years? Will they have been displaced by other more customised, self-paced forms of interactive learning, perhaps delivered closer to the real work environment? Or will there be a much-welcomed metamorphosis in which greater immersive experiences are widely adopted, with greater buy-in from agencies and supervisors, greater evaluation of the impact of executive development, and revised and improved pedagogical approaches?

Executive development programs have to find better ways of blending traditional 'hard' managerial skills with 'soft' relational skills. Specialist providers such as ANZSOG have to constantly recalibrate their course content, preferred curricula and chosen pedagogies. They need to explicitly clarify and justify the intended impacts of their delivery modes and monitor the out-year effectiveness of whatever developmental programs are undertaken. They need to reframe their offerings regularly to maximise impact and value for money, especially for the sponsoring agencies and participants. There is a clear imperative to engage more fully with public executives about how best to extend their individual and collective capabilities. Above all, as 'suppliers', specialist providers must ensure that they satisfy demand and continue to meet or exceed member government expectations.

References

Alford, J & Brock, J 2014, 'Interactive education in public administration', *Teaching Public Administration*, vol. 32, no. 2, pp. 144–57, doi.org/10.1177/0144739413515491.

Allen, P & Wanna, J 2016, 'Developing leadership and building capacity in the Australian public services for better governance', in A Podger & J Wanna (eds), *Sharpening the sword of state: Building executive capacities in the public service of the Asia-Pacific*, ANU Press, Canberra, ACT, doi.org/10.22459/SSS.11.2016.02.

Australia and New Zealand School of Government (ANZSOG) n.d. [c. 2003], *The establishment of the school*, ANZSOG, Melbourne, Vic.

Australia and New Zealand School of Government (ANZSOG) 2013, *Annual report 2012*, ANZSOG, Melbourne, Vic.

Australia and New Zealand School of Government (ANZSOG) 2016, *Annual report 2015*, ANZSOG, Melbourne, Vic.

Australia and New Zealand School of Government (ANZSOG) 2019, *ANZSOG 2025 strategy review*, ANZSOG, Melbourne, Vic.

Australian Public Service Commission (APSC) 2004, *Integrated leadership capability framework*, APSC, Canberra, ACT.

Australian Public Service Commission (APSC) 2014, *The integrated leadership system*, APSC, Canberra, ACT.

Boston, J & Eichbaum, C 2014, 'New Zealand's neo-liberal reforms', *Governance*, vol. 27, no. 3, pp. 373–6, doi.org/10.1111/gove.12092.

Cairney, P 2015, 'How can policy theory have an impact on policymaking', *Teaching Public Administration*, vol. 33, no. 1, pp. 22–39, doi.org/10.1177/0144739414532284.

Davis, G & Wanna, J 1997, 'Does the teaching of public administration have a future?', *Australian Journal of Public Administration*, vol. 65, no. 4, pp. 1–5, doi.org/10.1111/j.1467-8500.1997.tb02482.x.

Di Francesco, M 2015, 'Policy analysis instruction in Australia', in B Head & K Crowley (eds), *Policy analysis in Australia*, Policy Press, Bristol, UK, doi.org/10.1332/policypress/9781447310273.003.0017.

Fels, A 2003, 'The Australian and New Zealand School of Government', *Canberra Journal of Public Administration*, no. 108, June, pp. 75–6.

Hughes, P 2018, 'The spirit of service', ANZSOG Patterson Lecture, Melbourne, Vic.

Podger, A 2003, 'Trends in the Australian Public Service, 1953–2003', *Canberra Bulletin of Public Administration*, no. 109, September, pp. 14–18.

Public Service Commission (PSC) 1992, *Accounting for your training dollar*, PSC, Canberra, ACT.

Public Service & Merit Protection Commission (PSMPC) 2001, *Serving the nation: 100 years of public service*, PSMPC, Canberra, ACT.

Tiernan, A 2011, 'Advising Australian federal governments: Assessing the capacity and role of the Public Service', *Australian Journal of Public Administration*, vol. 70, no. 4, pp. 335–46, doi.org/10.1111/j.1467-8500.2011.00742.x.

Tiernan, A 2015, 'Craft and capacity in the public service', *Australian Journal of Public Administration*, vol. 74, no. 1, pp. 53–62, doi.org/10.1111/1467-8500.12134.

5

How do policy professionals in New Zealand use academic research in their work?

Karl Löfgren and Sarah Hendrica Bickerton[1]

Introduction

How do policy professionals in New Zealand use academic sources and find good evidence for their policy analysis and advice to governments and other stakeholders? A few years ago, one of the authors was delivering a methods course for post-experience masters students in public policy at Victoria University of Wellington. The methods presented in the course included classics, such as systematic reviews, cost–benefit analysis and basic statistics, as well as prescriptive ideas around the importance of utilising academic outputs to enhance the quality of policy solutions. While the students valued and appreciated this evidence-based approach to policy using academic research, it seemed like their work practice was not embodied by any systematic and rigorous pursuit of academic evidence. During a discussion session, participants were asked how they normally responded to a call for evidence in practical policymaking situations. The typical response was to 'see what they know, and do, in overseas jurisdictions' (especially in Victoria, New South Wales, the UK and Canada) and 'ascertain if we can copy that'. Although this is just

1   The authors wish to thank Building Research Association New Zealand Ltd (BRANZ) for the financial support, and all the respondents that volunteered to be part of the study.

anecdotal evidence, and probably should not be overstated, it nevertheless tells us something about the use of social science research among policy professionals in New Zealand (and probably elsewhere).

In this chapter, we analyse how different policy workers inside and outside government perceive and use different forms of research-based sources. The overarching research question is: how do policy professionals in New Zealand utilise academic outputs? We examine constraining and enabling factors for using research outputs, the accessibility and usefulness of different forms of research sources, and the demand, need and relevance of different forms of research outputs. The results are based on two empirical studies: 1) a survey of New Zealand policy analysts/ advisers working for government conducted in 2015 with 220 valid responses; 2) 15 focus groups held in 2018 with different stakeholders in the housing policy field in New Zealand. These studies show that the ideal of evidence-based policymaking (EBPM) is far from prevalent in day-to-day policy work; instead, political considerations, crises and 'narratives' guide the operations.

In the next section, we briefly review some of the academic discussion on 'two communities' and the existing body of knowledge relating to practitioner–academic interaction. In Section 3, we present the data and the methods employed for the two empirical studies. Section 4 examines themes identified from the studies. In the final section, we consider what can be achieved to enhance the utilisation of academic outputs in the policy professional communities.

'Two communities'

The global EBPM movement, with its rational promise of policy decisions based on the best available evidence, has been around since the 1990s and still attracts a large number of proponents (and governments) despite its critics (Kay 2011; see also Cairney 2016; Cairney, Oliver & Wellstead 2016; Head 2008). In New Zealand, this movement has been institutionalised through the establishment of the Office of the Prime Minister's Chief Science Advisor (PMCSA), which seeks to improve 'the government's ministries and agencies use of evidence in both the formation and evaluation of policy' (PMCSA 2013, p. 3; see also PMCSA 2011). However, despite numerous attempts to achieve a higher degree of evidence-based policy, once we leave the symbolic level and reach the 'beltway' of policy professionals actually doing policy work, this has proven to be more challenging than anticipated (Colebatch 2006). There appear to be numerous barriers between academics and policy professionals in terms of utility, time horizons, language, communication etc., such that they have been described as belonging to 'two separate communities' (Caplan 1979; Amara, Ouimet & Landry 2004). According to this representation, academics in their 'ivory towers' can afford to probe into esoteric matters divorced from real world problems (because they enjoy the time and resources), while 'beltway' policy workers are subjected to executive decisions, tight time constraints and electoral cycles (Caplan 1979; see Mercer this volume, Chapter 3).

The 'two communities' metaphor seems to have gained currency among both academics and policy workers over the years; however, its applicability has been questioned on several grounds (Newman 2014; Newman & Head 2015; Newman, Cherney & Head 2016). First, technological and digital developments have advanced policy workers' access to academic research findings. In particular, the evolution of information and communication technologies has made it easier and less expensive for policy workers in government to access vast reservoirs of academic knowledge, to identify and make direct contacts with academics, and to review the existing body of academic knowledge, all from their office desks. Although university libraries and academic publishers still do not offer full and free access to all academic publishing, much research of relevance to policy advice is often only a Google search away.

Second, even though several studies empirically confirm the gloomy narrative of 'two communities' (with policy workers not utilising academic research), there are notable individual exceptions. Policy workers do not constitute a homogenous group; they comprise diverse communities (Colebatch 2006). One major distinction that some of the earlier literature on the 'two communities' missed was the difference between those in the policy community acting as 'politicians' (i.e. ultimate 'decision-makers') and those acting as 'bureaucrats' (Newman, Cherney & Head 2016). Moreover, and to make matters even more complicated, while it is easy to discern these two roles in a theoretical and/or official sense, in practice, they are usually conflated.

Third, some policy domains are, by tradition (or perhaps necessity), more connected to the academic world and disciplinary reasoning than others, and have built both infrastructure and capabilities to tap into the abundance of existing knowledge and evidence (e.g. health, economics, the environment and education). Meanwhile, other domains, such as land use, regulatory functions, incarceration or local government, lack this capability for a number of reasons, and remain isolated from academic research. In a similar vein, it should be emphasised that both the original 'two communities' literature, and the more recent debates, have usually focused on social science knowledge rather than a broader understanding of evidential science (Caplan, Morrison & Stambaugh 1975; Cherney et al. 2013). As pointed out by Wehrens (2014, p. 548), 'the two communities approach overemphasizes both the heterogeneity between domains and the homogeneity within the domains of research and policy'.

Fourth, policy rests on several different components of which evidence or 'knowledge' in the classical analytical sense is just one (Majone 1989). Following Flyvbjerg's (2001) Aristotelian categories of knowledge, Tenbensel (2006) distinguishes between three type of knowledge: 1) *episteme*—the analytical rational type of knowledge, 2) *techne*—the practical-technical or 'applied' type of knowledge and 3) *phronesis*—the value/normative type of knowledge (see also Head 2010; Cairney this volume, Chapter 13). These can be seen both as sources of knowledge production and different forms of demand for types of knowledge. While combinations of all these types of knowledge are essential for producing strong policies, the scientific community is predominantly producing epistemic knowledge, as that is the convention. Consequently, policy workers' demand for knowledge (in the sense of practical skills, experience and normative guidance) also needs to be met from sources other than purely academic ones.

Finally, and as pointed out by some of the critics of the 'two communities' model, while the idea resonates well with the experiences of academics and policy professionals, it fails to adequately explain *why* problems exist in the relationship (Lin & Gibson 2003). The premise of 'two communities' is borne by an *a priori* proposition that it is possible to clearly distinguish policy from academic activities, that power is located in the policy world (with the academic world detached from politics), and that the interface between value laden policy and an 'objective' academic world operates through translation and persuasion (Lin & Gibson 2003). By contrast, science, technology and society researchers (e.g. Bijker, Bal & Hendriks 2009; Jasanoff 2013) point to how academic research and policy are co-produced. While evidence-based or scientific knowledge is embedded in all societal institutions, politics and policy equally affect such notions of evidence or knowledge.

Methodology

This chapter draws from two empirical studies: the first is based on a quantitative survey and the second on qualitative focus groups. The two studies also differ in terms of scope, with the first seeking to capture the broad community of policy analysts and advisers mainly working inside different government agencies, and the second focusing on the broader community of policy workers both inside and outside government within a specific policy sector (housing).

The survey

The survey was undertaken online in March and April 2015 using Qualtrics software. The sampling frame was identified with the active support of the Institute for Public Administration New Zealand (IPANZ) and the Public Service Association (PSA) using their membership database to identify relevant respondents. Based on the notion of 'policy workers' (Colebatch 2006) rather than the narrow concept of 'policy analysts', the study sampled members of the two associations with job titles including 'policy' and/or 'researcher' (however, the related title 'business analyst' was excluded). Among those invited to participate, the most frequent job titles were (senior) policy advisers/analysts. In terms of organisations, the study included all New Zealand ministries, statutory Crown entities (excluding secondary schools), Crown research institutions, state-owned enterprises, district health boards and local governments (the two last categories comprised small groups, and the local government memberships almost exclusively included members working for the major local councils). In total, 49 per cent of respondents worked for government departments or Crown entities, with smaller groups working for local and regional governments and others.

The questions asked in the survey replicated an earlier UK study (Talbott & Talbott 2014) that sought to identify enablers and barriers for utilising academic outputs, useful disciplines and methods, the relevance and usefulness of different academic sources, and the role of academics in policymaking. A total of 383 invitations to participate were sent to members of IPANZ (14 failed recipients) and 998 invitations were sent to PSA members (four failed recipients). In total, 220 valid responses were obtained during the four weeks the survey was up and running, generating a response rate of 16.6 per cent. Although this was a low response, one should bear in mind that our total sampling frame captures the views of a large proportion of the total number of policy professionals in New Zealand. This study was originally published in Löfgren and Cavagnoli (2015).

The focus groups

The views of a small group of organisational representatives in the housing policy sector were surveyed in May–September 2018. The study design was based on a research project commissioned by Building Research Association New Zealand (BRANZ). Based on previous knowledge and external advice from professionals engaged in housing policy (not all of whom were in government), a number of relevant organisations, including local governments, professional and trade associations, and government agencies, were identified. Through personal approaches to individuals with leading roles within the organisations, small groups were set up within the organisations. These became our focus groups. Following initial contacts via email and phone, the team ended up conducting 14 focus groups and a single one-on-one interview. There were between two and seven participants in each focus group (45 participants overall) and the conversations normally lasted 45–60 minutes. In most cases, the focus groups were conducted on the premises of the organisations. Despite working for the same organisations, most participants had different educational and professional backgrounds and performed different functions, including policy advice/analysis, engineering, architecture, urban planning and economics. NVivio software was used for the coding phase. Prior to the study, the research team received human ethics approval from their university.

The participants worked for the following organisations:

- Auckland City Council
- Building & Construction Industry Training Organisation
- Christchurch City Council
- Dunedin City Council
- Earthquake Commission (EQC)
- Energy Efficiency and Conservation Authority (EECA)
- Hamilton City Council
- Housing New Zealand (HNZ)

- Institute of Architects (IA)
- Institute of Landscape Architects
- Institution of Professional Engineers New Zealand (IPENZ)
- Lower Hutt City Council
- Ministry of Finance
- Ministry of Housing and Urban Development (MHUD)
- New Zealand Construction Industry Council (NZCIC)
- Wellington City Council.

Two factors out of the control of the research team and related to timing affected the results. First, when we conducted our field studies, the government decided to reorganise the housing policy area by removing housing from the Ministry of Business, Innovation and Employment and relocating the policy sector to a new ministry, MHUD. We managed to get an interview with representatives from MHUD much later, but not in time to include their views in this chapter. Second, our study coincided with the government science advisor's report in June 2018 that found there was no health danger to humans residing in houses in which the narcotic substance methamphetamine had been consumed, but not manufactured—the so-called 'meth myth' report (PMCSA 2018). The previous health recommendation had prescribed that any indoor consumption of methamphetamine would render the dwelling uninhabitable; this had resulted in forced evictions from a number of HNZ properties. Consequently, questions around the utilisation of academic research by people working with housing policy was slightly sensitive. The original qualitative study was published in an internal report (Löfgren & Bickerton 2019).

Themes

Three themes from the 2015 survey and 2018 qualitative focus group study provide insight into how policy professionals in New Zealand utilise academic outputs:

- use and usefulness of academic outputs
- enabling and constraining factors
- the role of academic outputs in policy.

Whereas the survey and the focus groups were similar with respect to the overall objectives and (subsequently) themes, the actual design differed between the two studies. The survey operated with predefined options for answers; although there were open-ended alternatives, the questions were funnelled down to specific responses. Conversely, the qualitative focus groups/interviews allowed the respondents to make sense of the themes in their own way and converse around concepts (such as policy work, knowledge, usefulness etc.) based on their own experiences and practice. This is in contrast to predefined alternatives based on an academic approach to both the research–policy relationship and the linear and stagist policy models.

Understanding the practitioner perspective

Use and usefulness

One of the first questions in our 2015 survey sought to determine the extent to which respondents felt that academic outputs were important sources of evidence in their policy work. Perhaps unsurprisingly, the vast majority felt that academic outputs were an important source (41 per cent to a large extent and 57 per cent to some extent). We asked about the sources of academic outputs (Figure 5.1) and, not surprisingly, articles, books, lectures and personal contacts scored highest. That articles in peer-reviewed journals ranked the highest is interesting given that we had anecdotal evidence suggesting that there were obstacles to accessing these. We also asked respondents what kind of disciplinary academic outputs they made use of (see Figure 5.2).

One response in Figure 5.1 that is worth further exploration is 'other websites' and 'other forms of social media'. This category includes co-produced sources such as Wikipedia. Several of the respondents indicated other sources. However, the vast majority of these sources are clearly not academic, but 'grey literature' from governments, think tanks and internal library collections.

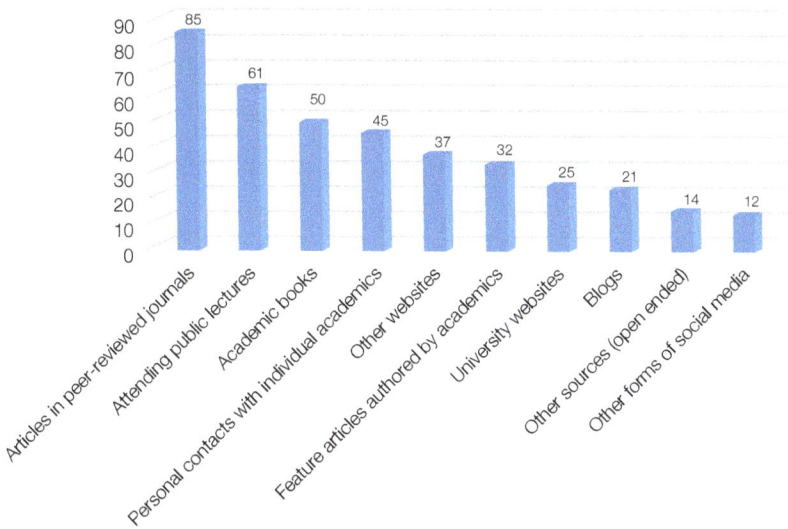

Figure 5.1. Sources of academic outputs (%).

There were several options available for some of the survey questions, including several possible options for Figure 5.1.

A second set of questions sought to establish which disciplines and methods were considered to be useful in respondents' daily policy work (see Figure 5.2). That the output of traditional social science disciplines (e.g. economics, political science/public policy, statistics and demography) should be at the top, followed by sector specific disciplines (e.g. education and health) was something we anticipated. It should also be mentioned that among 'others' we found several open-ended responses listing disciplines such as 'law', 'history' and 'environmental sciences'. We were not completely sure whether those who registered 'law' as an open-ended answer were referring to actual academic legal research, or whether they just listed law as a prerequisite for policymaking.

Our survey respondents, when prompted to discuss qualitatively what sources they used for gathering research and evidence around their policy work, almost universally described academic research (or that which was perceived as academic) as research that was 'separate' from their policy work. While there were exceptions to this (notably those who worked in areas of regulatory assessment or the more technical foci), academic (or, rather, 'university') research was deemed less useful to respondents, for a variety of reasons.

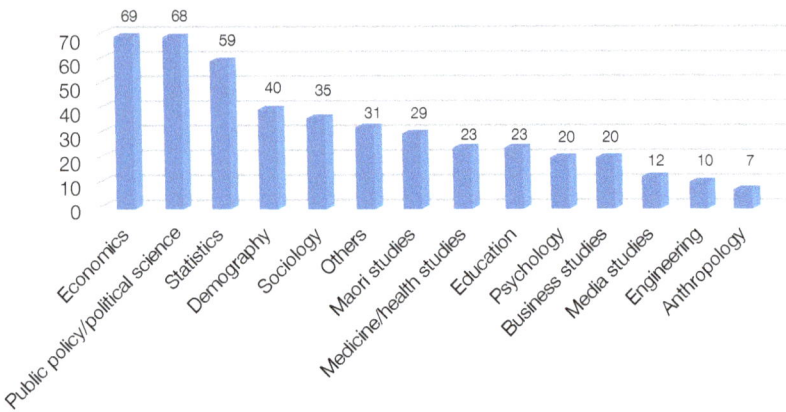

Figure 5.2. Useful academic disciplines in daily work (%).
More than one answer possible.

We asked the same question of our focus groups and, while there were some areas of overlap, their voices nuanced the overall picture slightly. In terms of useful sources of knowledge, the overwhelming leader was Google Scholar. It was considered a key go-to simply because of its lack of a paywall. While some of the articles Google Scholar highlighted were behind paywalls, the benefit of being able to search and read abstracts gave respondents access to a far wider pool of research than normal.

Another preference among focus group respondents was attendance at conferences and public lectures. Their reasoning was that research presentations were often short, digestible and engaging, while discussions with presenters could increase relevancy and connect to wider policy issues. Further, conferences allowed networking and personal connections to be formed, in addition to research being discussed, which respondents found to be particularly useful.

Respondents also valued peer-to-peer networks. These networks could involve members within similar organisations (such as city councils) or external organisations. Another possibility for these informal networks involved contacting academics directly for copies of their research. If an article or articles were identified behind paywalls as being relevant, respondents would contact that academic directly to see if they could get a copy of the article:

> If there's someone's research that I've read who's overseas, I will just email them, say this was really good, can you tell me a bit more about it, is there anything more along these lines you know. (Auckland City Council)

Other sources included clearing houses that provided annotated bibliographies of recent research, as this fitted with respondents' lack of time for research. Respondents also listed organisations such as BRANZ, the New Zealand Green Building Council, EECA and other professional organisations as sources of both research and information on research done elsewhere. A few of respondents had access to their own libraries and/or research staff/librarians, and some commissioned their own research. Generally, the larger the organisation (e.g. Auckland City Council and Treasury), the more likely it was to have its own library and/ or commission research.

In terms of sources not found to be particularly useful by respondents, the generic category 'universities' was identified. This does not include individual academics (who were seen as quite responsive), but rather academic institutions and their communication channels such as websites or social media platforms. Universities were perceived as mainly pursuing their own goals—goals that did not fit well with what was needed by policymakers.

Enabling and constraining factors

The enabling and constraining factor of utilising academic outputs mirrored the results in the quantitative survey results. While policy workers made use of academic outputs, many did so infrequently. Questions regarding the enabling and constraining factors for using arguments from academic publications were also asked (Figure 5.3).

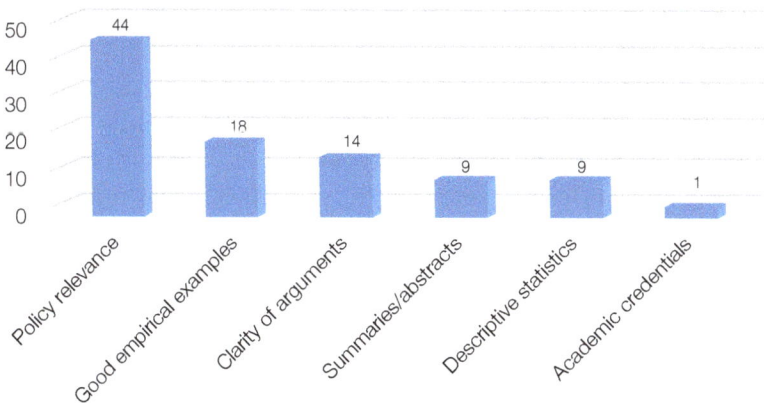

Figure 5.3. Enabling factors (%).
One alternative.

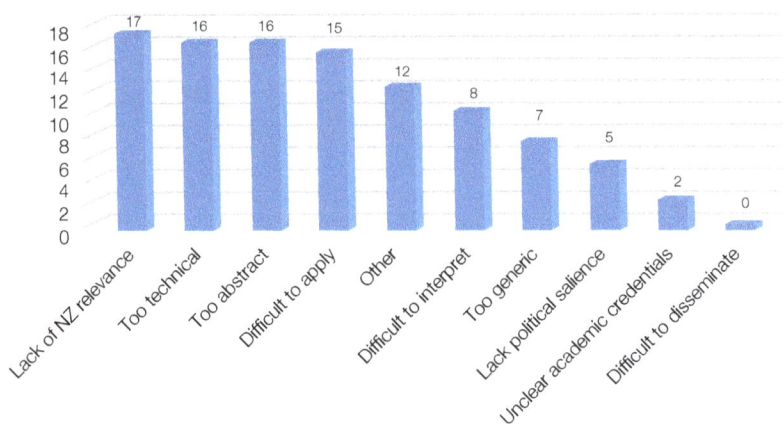

Figure 5.4. Constraining factors for using academic arguments (%).

It is perhaps not surprising that 'policy relevance', 'good empirical examples' and 'clarity of arguments' represent the answers with the highest number of respondents. However, that 'academic credentials' plays almost no role is perhaps something worth further investigation. The question regarding constraining factors for using academic arguments shows a less clear-cut result (Figure 5.4).

While 'lack of relevance' seems to represent the largest proportion of survey answers, arguments based on the 'two community' metaphor (i.e. too abstract, technical and difficult to apply) seem to be an important theme.

The voices from the qualitative focus groups provided similar responses. Much of the conversations revolved around access in various forms. The format and language of academic outputs was something that all the groups mentioned. Concise summaries and abstracts were highly appreciated for professionals not having the time to read lengthy research studies. Equally, the language used in academic journals was often seen as inaccessible and lacking in applicability to the policymaking process:

> I have never read anything like this in my life; it was so weird. Thankfully our academic partners could translate it to us, because we were going—'what is this?' (IA)

However, access was also considered a barrier in a more traditional sense. Academic journals behind paywalls were considered a severe impediment to accessing research, with many respondents just giving up on accessing journals as their organisation could not afford to pay for journal database use:

> I think there is an inherent contradiction at the heart of academia, whereas you want to publish in a journal, but then people are not allowed to read them unless they purchase at a relatively high cost. (IPENZ)

One group of respondents who found journals useful were policymakers interested in highly technical details; they tended to skim read articles, determining the rigour of the research based on the methodology and references.

A different, broader, theme is the importance of contextual relevance and compatibility. The issue of relevance can become a barrier for using research in many different forms. The first, and perhaps most understandable, issue is whether the research output is relevant for 'my organisation' (i.e. the individual stakeholder). The challenges that different respondents faced are localised specificities that differ in character. For example:

> I guess the advantage of something like that [research] is that we have a particular issue and it is in Wellington and it is now, whereas the research that might have gone on might be in Edinburgh in 2013. (Housing policy team in Wellington City Council)

> You really need to live in New Zealand to understand the intricacies. (EECA)

Academics and policy workers in the housing policy community are typically working within separate time frames. Whereas the practitioners are seeking solutions to their imminent problems and have to comply with budget and electoral cycles, academics are following their separate systems of funding and reporting mechanisms. As one respondent described it, academic outputs often reflect a single observational point in time, mainly because of funding opportunities and academic fashion:

> I find the academic stuff tends to, you know it just has a longer time frame, and tends not to touch on the issues that directly affect our businesses. (NZCIC)

However, it is worth mentioning that a few of the respondents stated that the academic world should not be blamed for the incompatible time periods. They felt that such challenges were also and equally caused by policy cycles. Moreover, good research is time-consuming:

> So, the policy framework is far too short term and reactive and so I wouldn't even say it is the research time frame that needs to shift, it is actually the policy time frame that needs to get real. (IPENZ)

The role of academic outputs in policy

One of the chief themes in the quantitative survey concerned the views of policy workers regarding the underlying conditions of using academic outputs, and whether academics should be more active. We asked respondents to rate the importance of academic outputs and general academic expertise to their work on a five-graded Likert scale. The mean value for contribution through outputs was 2.73 and for contribution through general academic expertise was 2.90. Yet, we may conclude that the role of the academic as an (available) expert is perceived as more important than their publications. Questions about the work environment's attitude to using academic outputs produced less encouraging results. Asked about whether public sector managers were encouraging the use of academic support on a five-graded Likert scale, the mean was 2.75 (n = 161). Although the evidence is not especially compelling, it nevertheless provides an indication that 'management' is not overwhelmingly supportive of using academic outputs and may in fact be directly negative. When asked whether there were other requirements (legal, terms of references instructions etc.), the support for using academic outputs was even less. The mean value on a five-graded Likert scale was 2.15 (n = 161). This suggests that institutional support for using academic outputs among policy workers is not prodigious.

Other questions dealt with the involvement of academics in policy work. An overwhelming majority of respondents (80 per cent) responded positively to academics being active in policymaking. However, when asked at what stage academics should be involved, the answers were more varied (see Figure 5.5).

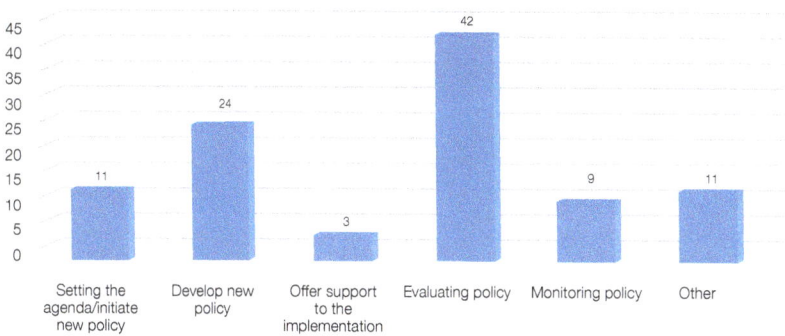

Figure 5.5. 'At what stage in the policy process should academics get involved?' (%).

The assigned role of 'evaluator' is an interesting finding. One possible interpretation is that academics are conceived as neutral and non-biased in the political game, and therefore represent an obvious choice for appraising outputs and outcomes of policy. Equally, the low indication for academics taking part in the implementation process could probably be an indication of distrust in the managerial skills of academics. The category 'other' was full of qualitative responses that not only criticised the underlying premise of the question (i.e. that the policy process could be divided into discrete stages), but also addressed the need for impartial advice. In addition to asking respondents about the role of academics, we also asked them about their general appreciation of the most important 'informers of policy expertise' (Figure 5.6).

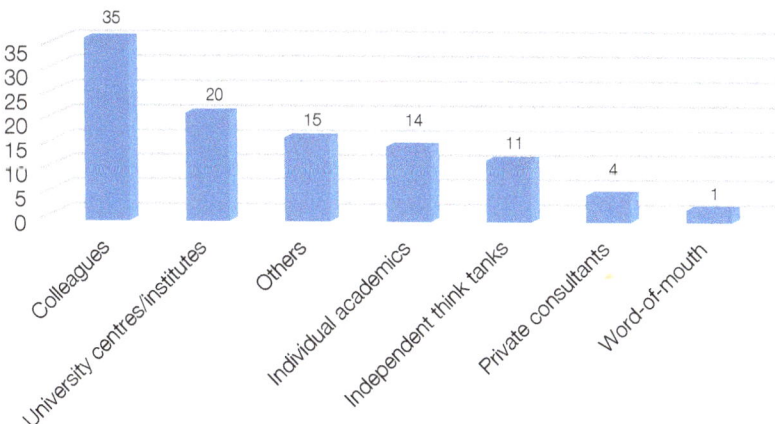

Figure 5.6. Perceptions on the most important informers of policy expertise (%).

Unsurprisingly, most respondents turned to their colleagues when they needed policy advice. University centres or specific university institutes were second best on the list of 'good informers'. Less preferred were private consultants who were not considered to be good informers. The broad category 'others' comprised an interesting mix of informers including 'sector', 'stakeholders', 'ministers' and 'departmental experts'. Some respondents stressed that sources of 'policy expertise' needed to understand the policy process (in which their colleagues were usually most important) and policy content (in which academics were seen as the most important informers).

In conjunction with this question, we also asked respondents about what prevented them from using academic outputs.

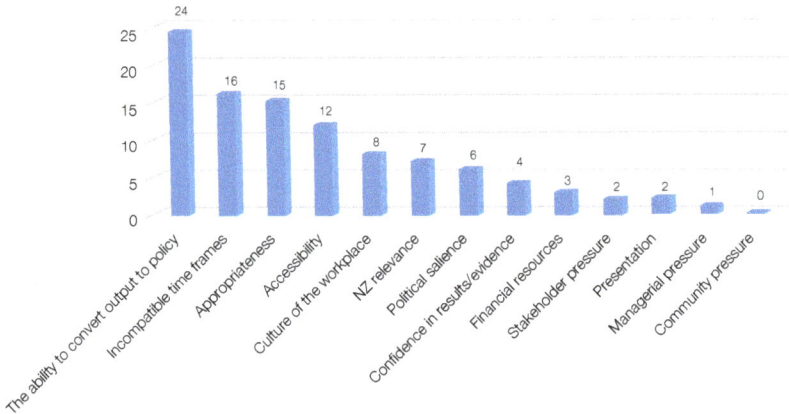

Figure 5.7. 'What prevents you from using academic outputs?'(%).

Our survey data showed that the main problem appeared to be the two different communities of academia and policy workers. Still, it is somewhat disconcerting that 8 per cent of respondents mentioned the culture of their workplace as a reason not to use academic outputs.

Turning to the qualitative study, we asked the focus groups to discuss their specific needs and demands. The biggest driver of demand was research that was holistic. By this, respondents meant research that was interdisciplinary: 'Yeah, housing is just so multidisciplinary' (Ministry of Finance). This involved such things as intersections of the social aspects of housing, such as affordability, or the mixed nature of communities, or how transport intersects with housing:

> So there's a whole lot of literature on the way in which gentrification actually impacts, not in a positive way in particular existing communities, and there's a whole body of literature internationally on that, but then there's all this other literature on why you want to do economic development, or development in a particular way. But the more you need to ensure that there's quality intensification, you need to ensure the normal standards, and you want to think about affordable housing, and you know we provide advice on a whole range of things and so, if it's so isolated that it's very theoretical, then you know sometimes it doesn't then translate into, so yeah I guess the answer would be yes, that around a range of housing topics, or areas if you can't really apply it, or if it's not the reality. (Auckland City Council)

Some found housing research isolated from this context to be less than desirable:

> They're going to give me the sort of the heart and the head. Not just the facts, but also the emotion and the impact, the 'so what?' factor, you know, and … look at the number of people that are being injured or hurt or the disadvantaged or, equally, in the personal stories through the way our urban form influences people. (Christchurch City Council)

A related response was that policymakers want research that tells a policy 'story' or, as one respondent explained, can 'take the public with you'. This means not merely reporting the facts, but also explaining why the research and results are relevant, how they fit with other pieces of research, how they fit with wider policy narratives and why they might be important to the public:

> I think another big thing is also storytelling. Everyone is doing it; I know it is a bit yawny. But you know, it's translating the complex into a story. (EQC)

The policymaker's work is not just the crafting and implementation of policy, but also presenting the policy to the public—justifying or making a case for it. Having researchers that understand that drive and know the import of their research to the wider policy/political world is important and, ultimately, very helpful to policymakers. Conversely, being unaware of the impact of one's research—not knowing or anticipating the problems that releasing it might cause, or leaving it up to others to craft the narrative around such problems—was seen as damaging to the work of policymakers.

Our respondents felt that more research was needed on monitoring and evaluating policy initiatives. Once a piece of housing policy was implemented, there was often insufficient monitoring to ensure it achieved its intended goals. Nor was research usually undertaken to evaluate the application of research to assess if it was correctly applied over the long-term:

> And we have really very little way of actually monitoring how effective we are in doing that, apart from, you know, the usual statistics, which don't actually give us the detailed level that we need to understand what we're actually doing it. (Christchurch City Council)

In fact, long-term longitudinal research was also found to be lacking in the New Zealand context. Understanding housing and communities over longer periods and over multiple indices was seen as crucial for good housing policy planning, not least because housing planning could be better informed with such research:

> Then also the consistency in that sort of longitudinal study that we really had very little of ... which was the point I said to [name] before, that often the academic outputs are a point in time. Yeah. When the research project has funding. It is really important that we have those longitudinal trend data supporting policy decision-making as well. And so how we balance point in time with trend-type academia. (Christchurch City Council)

Given that the consistent refrain from all our respondents was that attempting to find time to access and review research in their fields was important but difficult, it is not surprising that one of the major desires from respondents was some form of annotated research digest:

> The fact that the construction industry is so busy, they haven't got time to understand what the latest research is and can't incorporate it into their practice because, and this is where it's almost like the clearing house, it needs somebody to be working full time to say 'well that's a bit academic, but that's actually really useful, and that could really help your business'. (EQC)

Effectively, research digests would serve as replacements for the research units that used to be part of many organisations, while also freeing up policy practitioners' time. Research digests would allow policy practitioners to spend time reading appropriate texts, rather than trying to find them. Being responsive, with quick turnarounds, to literature requests would continue this knowledge-broker function.

Concluding remarks

With the necessary caveats about generalising from two smallish samples across the public sector, we think it is safe to suggest a few propositions regarding New Zealand policy workers' utilisation of academic outputs.

First, while it is difficult to avoid the metaphor of 'two communities', there is good reason not to exaggerate the gaps between academia and the policy world. Despite some of the strong voices expressed here, academic outputs were being utilised by policy professionals and there were institutionalised channels for communication. Moreover, if one takes a wider look, these findings resonate well with the findings of similar international studies of the policy sector in terms of culture, 'language', time frames, rigour and incentives (Talbot & Talbot 2014; Oliver et al. 2014; Cairney 2016; see also Cairney this volume, Chapter 13). Having said that, the two New Zealand studies presented here, and the differences between the findings, also reflect research from Australia where organisational factors do play an important role (Head et al. 2014). While the survey respondents mainly had specialised and professional policy analyst/advisory functions in government organisations, and thus were more inclined to use academic outputs, the 'jack-of-all-trades' professionals within housing policy approached academic research differently.

Second, access to peer-reviewed material in the form of academic journal articles appeared to be unevenly distributed. While most of the survey respondents had access to digital databases of academic journals, those working for professional associations, local governments and others were generally locked out from this type of material. Several respondents mentioned problems of timeliness, policy relevance and reader accessibility as constraining factors for using academic outputs.

Third, in terms of usefulness, we may construe that, in addition to identifying relevant disciplines and methods based in the individual policy sector, there are concerns around the applicability of international research findings in a New Zealand and/or local context. It is also noteworthy that one of the more appreciated methods for identifying relevant academic outputs was to use digital search engines such as Google, whereas universities' specially designated external engagement and research entry points were not considered especially useful.

Finally, we must conclude that, although there were signs of an active use of academic outputs within the community of policy workers, there were equally signs endorsing the metaphor of 'two distinct communities'. Yet, we must conclude that the vast majority of respondents did make some use of academic outputs and most appreciated peer-reviewed academic sources. This demonstrates that the connection between the professor and the policy worker is probably more complex than we assume, thereby highlighting the need for further research.

References

Amara, N, Ouimet, M & Landry, R 2004, 'New evidence on instrumental, conceptual and symbolic utilisation of university research in government agencies', *Science Communication*, vol. 26, no. 1, pp. 75–106, doi.org/10.1177/1075547004267491.

Bijker WE, Bal, R & Hendriks, R 2009, *The paradox of scientific authority: The role of scientific advice in democracies*, MIT Press, Cambridge, MA.

Cairney, P 2016, *The politics of evidence-based policy-making*. Palgrave Pivot, London, UK, doi.org/10.1057/978-1-137-51781-4.

Cairney, P, Oliver, K & Wellstead, A 2016, 'To bridge the divide between evidence and policy: Reduce ambiguity as much as uncertainty', *Public Administration Review*, vol. 76, no. 3, pp. 399–402, doi.org/10.1111/puar.12555.

Caplan, N 1979, 'The two-communities theory and knowledge utilization', *American Behavioral Scientist*, vol. 22, no. 3, pp. 459–70.

Caplan, N, Morrison, A & Stambaugh, R 1975, *The use of social science knowledge in policy decisions at the national level*, Institute for Social Research, Ann Arbor, MI, doi.org/10.1177/000276427902200308.

Cherney, A, Head, B, Boreham, P, Povey, J & Ferguson, M 2013, 'Research utilization in the social sciences: A comparison of five academic disciplines in Australia', *Science Communication*, vol. 35, no. 6, pp. 780–809, doi.org/10.1177/1075547013491398.

Colebatch, HK 2006, 'What work makes policy?', *Policy Sciences*, vol. 39, no. 4, pp. 309–21, doi.org/10.1007/s11077-006-9025-4.

Flyvbjerg, B 2001, *Making social science matter: Why social inquiry fails and how it can succeed again*, Cambridge University Press, Cambridge, UK, doi.org/10.1017/CBO9780511810503.

Head, B 2008, 'Three lenses of evidence-based policy', *Australian Journal of Public Administration*, vol. 67, no. 1, pp. 1–11, doi.org/10.1111/j.1467-8500.2007. 00564.x.

Head, B 2010, 'Reconsidering evidence-based policy: Key issues and challenges', *Policy and Society*, vol. 29, no. 2, pp. 77–94, doi.org/10.1016/j.polsoc. 2010.03.001.

Head, B, Ferguson, M, Cherney, A & Boreham, P 2014, 'Are policy-makers interested in social research? Exploring the sources and uses of valued information among public servants in Australia', *Policy and Society*, vol. 33, pp. 89–101, doi.org/10.1016/j.polsoc.2014.04.004.

Jasanoff, S 2013, *States of knowledge: The co-production of science and the social order*, Routledge, London, UK.

Kay, A 2011, 'Evidence-based policy-making: The elusive search for rational public administration', *Australian Journal of Public Administration*, vol. 70, no. 3, pp. 236–45, doi.org/10.1111/j.1467-8500.2011.00728.x.

Lin, V & Gibson, B (eds) (2003), *Evidence-based health policy: Problems and possibilities*, Oxford University Press, Melbourne, Vic.

Löfgren, K & Bickerton, S 2019, *Use of academic research and other sources of knowledge in New Zealand housing policy*, BRANZ Study Report SR416, Judgeford, NZ.

Löfgren, K & Cavagnoli, D 2015, 'The policy worker and the professor— understanding how New Zealand policy workers utilise academic research', *Policy Quarterly*, vol. 11, no. 3, pp. 64–72. (Subsequently reprinted in *New Zealand Science Review*, vol. 72, no. 3, pp. 67–74, doi.org/10.26686/ pq.v11i3.4546.)

Majone, G 1989, *Evidence, argument and persuasion in the policy process*, Oxford University Press, Oxford, UK.

Newman, J 2014, 'Revisiting the "two communities" metaphor of research utilisation', *International Journal of Public Sector Management*, vol. 27, no. 7, pp. 614–27, doi.org/10.1108/IJPSM-04-2014-0056.

Newman, J, Cherney, A & Head, BW 2016, 'Do policymakers use academic research? Reexamining the "two communities" theory of research utilization', *Public Administration Review*, vol. 76, no. 1, 24–32, doi.org/10.1111/ puar.12464.

Newman, J & Head, BW 2015, 'Beyond the two communities: A reply to Mead's "why governments often ignores research"', *Policy Sciences*, vol. 48, no. 3, pp. 383–93, doi.org/10.1007/s11077-015-9226-9.

Office of the Prime Minister's Chief Science Advisor (PMCSA) 2011, 'Towards better use of evidence in policy formation', Discussion paper, PMSA, Wellington, NZ.

Office of the Prime Minister's Chief Science Advisor (PMCSA) 2013, *The role of evidence in policy formation and implementation*, PMSA, Wellington, NZ.

Office of the Prime Minister's Chief Science Advisor (PMCSA) 2018, *Methamphetamine contamination in residential properties: Exposures, risk levels, and interpretation of standards*, PMSA, Wellington, NZ.

Oliver, K, Innvaer, S, Lorenc, T, Woodman, J & Thomas, J 2014, 'A systematic review of barriers to and facilitators of the use of evidence by policymakers', *BMC Health Service Research*, vol. 14, p. 2, doi.org/10.1186/1472-6963-14-2.

Talbot, C & Talbot, C 2014, 'Sir Humphrey and the professors: What does Whitehall want from academics? A survey of senior civil servants' views on the accessibility and utility of academic research and expertise', Working paper, Policy@Manchester, Manchester University.

Tenbensel, T 2006, 'Policy knowledge for policy work', in HK Colebatch (ed.), *The work of policy: An international survey*, Lexington Books, Latham, MD.

Wehrens, R 2014, 'Beyond two communities—from research utilization and knowledge translation to co-production?', *Public Health*, vol. 128, no. 6, pp. 545–51, doi.org/10.1016/j.puhe.2014.02.004.

6

The dilemmas of managing parliament: Promoting awareness of public management theories to parliamentary administrators

Val Barrett

Introduction

This book focuses on the apparent disconnect between practice and theory in the development of public policy. One might ask why it would include a chapter on managing parliament: the role of parliament and its internal administration might be considered irrelevant to public policymaking.[1] Indeed, the parliamentary departments in Australia's national parliament were specifically excluded from the recently concluded Thodey review of the Australian Public Service, and an opportunity for an independent review of parliament's capability, culture and operating model was thereby missed (PM&C 2019). But, the effectiveness of parliament's multifaceted role in our Westminster system, the way in which it is managed and its capacity to influence public policy, is important to all public administration scholars, not just those who are attracted to parliament's

---

1   But see Russell and Cowley (2016) who present empirical evidence of the UK parliament's significant policy influence at successive stages of the policy process.

political dimensions. In the context of this book, then, parliament can be seen as a special case in the practice of policymaking, and understanding how it relates to the theory of policymaking is important not only in its own right but also for the light it throws on the broader project of policymaking in Westminster systems.

There has been longstanding debate about an identity crisis within the study of public administration and particularly between academics and practitioners (Peters & Pierre 2017; Raadschelders 1999; Sowa & Lu 2017). Prominent UK parliamentary scholar Bernard Crick (1968) suggested that theory and practice should be one field. Raadschelders's (1999, p. 289) critical point was that, despite differing opinions about what government should do, its legitimacy 'rests with the swiftness and adequacy of its response to changing environmental conditions'—a reasoning that would also apply to parliament.

Drawing on my own research, this chapter discusses parliamentary administration in the UK and Australia's national parliaments.[2] It does so in the context of parliament's key roles: to form government and pass legislation; to scrutinise government; and, in particular, to deliberate on and influence public policy in response to rapidly changing environmental conditions—in Crick's view, the most important role of all. First, it describes an insular and agonistic parliamentary culture that has resisted management reforms; second, it provides an overview of governance in the UK and Australian parliaments before presenting dilemmas relating to their governance, management and procedural and cultural reform. Finally, it considers the relevance and potential of public management practice and theory to improve parliament's capacity to influence public policy and meet public expectations. In this respect, it looks beyond traditional and bureaucratic 'old' public administration featuring hierarchy, specialised knowledge or craft, beyond 'new' public management and a narrow focus on efficiency, and towards newer concepts of public value, collaboration and co-production with a concomitant focus on motivation, agency and relationships.

---

2   The chapter is derived from a qualitative and interpretive doctoral study of the two parliaments from 2015–19. The thesis title is 'Parliamentary administration: what does it mean to manage a parliament effectively?'. The award was approved on 27 March 2020. The study included interviews with more than 90 parliamentary actors—members of parliament, officials, academics and others—analysis of historical and contemporary parliamentary material, and public administration and management literature.

Why do parliaments resist management reform?

Contemporary concerns about the management and governance of the UK and Australian national parliaments have been widely documented (Australian National Audit Office [ANAO] 2015; Hansard Society 2015; House of Commons Governance Committee [HOCGC] 2014; Senate Committee of Privileges 2014; Senate Finance and Public Administration Legislation Committee [SFPALC] 2012a, 2012b, 2015). Reviews and commentaries have pointed to a lack of managerial expertise and/or competence, inadequate and/or complex governance arrangements, inherent conflict between specialist procedural and management roles, resistance to change, an absence of strategic thinking and a limited appreciation of parliamentary norms from would-be reformers. There is also a continuing decline in public trust in parliamentary effectiveness (Hansard Society 2019; Stoker, Evans & Halupka 2018) and a lack of public understanding about how parliament works (Leston-Bandeira & Thompson 2018). Public perceptions suggest that politicians are consumed by adversarial politics and personal advancement and that parliament is a members' club that operates in the interests of its 'elite' insiders (Fox 2009; Snow & Robertson 2015).

Parliamentary administration is complex—a constitutional terra incognita. Parliaments are collective institutional bodies with different and opposing agendas and strong public accountability. Those who can legitimately exercise a powerful administrative role on behalf of their parliaments—elected members—are ultimately accountable to the people who elect them. These characteristics help to explain why decision-making in parliaments in relation to their management and structure is slow and risk-averse. Understandably, Westminster parliaments see themselves as unique political institutions. They are bent on retaining their sovereignty and independence from executive government, even though in reality their powers are closely intertwined (Benwell & Gay 2011). Parliaments are also perceived as agonistic institutions, defined by contest between two of their principal purposes—on the one hand, securing a government's legislative program, on the other, facilitating effective scrutiny and calling the government to account. Inevitably, competition—for status, resources, influence and control—has, over time, pervaded the practice of parliamentary administration and impeded reform

(Geddes & Mulley 2018; Reid & Forrest 1989). Despite intermittent crises followed by reviews and some rhetorical commitment to reform, the 'exceptionalism' of parliament as a political institution continues to diminish its role in policymaking and administrative oversight.

While acknowledging the singular dimensions of parliamentary administration, I argue that a greater appreciation and application of public management theory *and* practice could help parliaments to strengthen their internal and external relationships, restore their reputation and enhance their capacity to facilitate public debate and contribute to policy deliberation. This requires challenging the notion that parliamentary administration is 'unique'—that is, that it is inherently 'parliamentary' and only coincidentally 'public'. The dilemmas and challenges explored in the following sections provide the foundation for a subsequent discussion of practice and theory in parliamentary administration.

Governance dilemmas

Parliaments lack the singular leadership of most public sector organisations; no one is officially in charge (HOCGC 2014). As Speaker Lenthall famously opined in 1642 when Charles I entered the House of Commons chamber to arrest five members of parliament for high treason:

> May it please your majesty; I have neither eyes to see nor tongue to speak in this place, but as the house is pleased to direct me, whose servant I am here. (UK Parliament 2019a)

Presiding officers are appointed to chair parliamentary sessions and manage politics but they also inherit administrative responsibilities without a clear mandate or interest in such matters. They do not have the formal authority of a minister of state in administering their own Houses. Their principal roles are to interpret the rules and practice of their Houses and to maintain order in debate.[3] Presiding officers must retain the confidence of the House, even if they have renounced their party affiliations (as occurs in the UK but not in Australia) and their impartiality can be called into question if their actions are not supported

---

3   As the House of Lords is self-regulating, the Lord Speaker does not control or manage the House during debate. He/she has no power to call members to order, to decide who speaks next or to select amendments (UK Parliament 2019b).

by members, which can limit their inclination to propose reforms.[4] In the UK, both the House of Lords and House of Commons have established commissions to oversee their administration, chaired by their respective Speakers and supported by advisory committees. In practice, however, even when Speakers are independent from their party and the executive, they are limited by the interests of other members in what they can achieve. Day-to-day responsibility is delegated to line officials.

The Parliament of Australia does not have equivalent formal governance structures, although each House has an administrative advisory committee that is chaired by the president of the Senate and the Speaker of the House of Representatives, respectively.[5] These committees can meet jointly, as can the two House committees set up to consider issues related to their facilities, which are also chaired by their respective presiding officers, but such joint meetings appear to be non-existent. A key structural difference between the two parliaments is the existence in the Australian parliament of a separate services department, the Department of Parliamentary Services (DPS), supporting both Houses, which has tended to further distance the administration role from the procedural and political functions. Historic rivalries between the Houses and between departments have also reflected the influence of a powerful Australian Senate (Reid & Forrest 1989).

Notwithstanding the Parliament of the United Kingdom's more formalised governance arrangements, serial reviews of the House of Commons administration have demonstrated a lack of management capacity. The House of Lords administration has also been slow to change. Scholars have suggested that until the Blair government reforms, the non-elected and subordinate nature of the Lords provided little pressure for change (Petit & Yong 2018). A string of reviews aimed at streamlining the Lords governance and administration culminated in the establishment in 2016 of the House of Lords Commission—a 'small cadre of Members with the time, interest and expertise' to engage strategically with administrative matters on behalf of the House, in partnership with the staff, and with two external members (Torrance 2017, p. 19).

---

4   In the UK parliament, former Speaker Bercow was an exception but he has attracted regular criticism from conservative members of the House of Commons and media commentators (see e.g. BBC News 2019; Swinford 2017; Wintour 2014).

5   These are the Senate Standing Committee on Appropriations, Staffing and Security and House of Representatives Committee on Appropriations and Administration.

While the history of the governance and administration of the Australian parliament is less well documented, there are similarities in terms of the slow pace of change and the institution's insularity. Historically, members and senators have been indifferent to staffing and administrative arrangements for the two Houses and have shown fragmented loyalties towards individual departments rather than to the parliament as a whole. As well, jealousies, suspicion and politicking between departments have, historically, stymied attempts at reform (Reid & Forrest 1989, pp. 416–17). The Australian parliament was subjected to numerous reform attempts between 1901 and 2004 (Adams 2002),[6] largely directed at structural changes. Parliamentary departments eventually achieved legislative separation from the Australian Public Service in 1999 with the passage of the *Parliamentary Service Act* and DPS, the combined services department, was created in 2004. Tensions among departmental heads and some well-publicised management failures led to extensive criticism from senators, two performance inquiries by the Senate Standing Committee on Finance and Public Administration, and an investigation into a breach of privilege (Senate Committee of Privileges 2014; SFPALC 2012a, 2012b, 2015). Despite these apparent 'crises', no substantive reform ensued.

In the UK parliament, the clerks of the two Houses are still the official authorities and accounting officers. However, since 2015 many of the responsibilities of the House of Commons clerk have been delegated to a director-general. The clerks tend to have little formal management training or experience; their management functions relate largely to supervision of staff and financial accountability, assisted by professionally qualified managers with financial and other management skills. The House of Commons director-general is the most senior management position in the House. He is a member of the commission and chairs its executive committee, which is responsible for delivery of the strategy. The position holds considerable autonomy and is supported by a number of teams delivering communications, governance, research and information, participation, in-house services, building services, digital and security services (House of Commons 2018).

In Australia, the two House departments have been 'hollowed out' in terms of management responsibilities and are now seen by their clerks as providing a 'secretariat' to the two Houses, specialist procedural advice and some administrative support to members. Nonetheless, they are

---

6   Adams cited at least 20.

'accountable authorities' under the *Public Governance, Performance and Accountability Act 2013*, responsible for the proper use and management of the public resources of their departments. The DPS secretary shares the same accountabilities as the clerks, with responsibility for shared services, such as the parliamentary library, information services, building facilities and security, and internal finance and governance (DPS 2018). There is no overarching coordinating structure that brings the presiding officers, members and officials together with joint responsibility for determining and implementing a collective strategic direction.[7]

The structural differences between the two parliaments make comparison of their relative effectiveness problematic. In any case, the prospects for international adaptation may be limited: what works for one parliament may not be politically acceptable for the other. There may not be 'one best way' of organising a parliament to achieve its conflicting purposes of both enabling and scrutinising parliamentary government while facilitating public debate and contributing to policy deliberation. Effectiveness may depend on the extent to which the parliaments can resolve the dilemmas of authority and collective responsibility, related below.

Who speaks for parliament? The impact of collective responsibility

As has been noted, in parliament the 'authorising environment' (Moore 1995) is problematic. Establishing a commission comprising the presiding officers, members and senior officials will not, of itself, offset the diffuse nature of authority in a representative political body. Many factors would influence its effectiveness, in particular the willingness of all members to engage with administrative issues and to 'convey a sense of public service' (Norton 2016, p. 203). Neither will it ensure a consistent whole-of-parliament approach from two constitutionally separate Houses. However, in the UK the two Houses' overarching commissions appear to encourage a greater appreciation of the increasing need for integration between the political, procedural, cultural and managerial requirements of an effective parliamentary administration. Administrative leadership and advocacy is less apparent in the Australian parliament.

---

7   The Parliamentary Budget Office, established in 2012, is an independent office of experts providing specific economic and policy costing advice primarily to members and senators. Its work falls outside of this study; however, it is a good example of parliamentary reform, reflecting political motivation and agency, achieved by collaboration between crossbench members and the 2010–13 minority government.

The UK House of Commons generally displays a greater potential for collective decision-making balanced with strategic focus. There is legislative recognition of the strategic function in the *House of Commons Administration Act 1978*.[8] The House of Lords Commission provides high-level strategic and political direction for its administration on behalf of the House. In contrast, under the Australian *Parliamentary Service Act 1999* responsibility for leadership, 'stewardship'[9] and strategic direction falls to departmental secretaries and the clerks. The parliamentary service commissioner also gives advice to the presiding officers on the management policies and practices of Parliamentary Services. The less formalised structures in the Australian parliament do not reflect the diversity and complexity of the management services provided by DPS, particularly in its public facing role, nor do they specify a strategic role for members. Recommendations following Senate committee inquiries for a more collaborative, whole-of parliament and strategic focus, which may have engaged members more fully, have not been taken up (Baxter 2015; SFPALC 2017).

In my research, I did not detect in either parliament a high level of enthusiasm for public management theory in general or, specifically, public value. However, in the UK, recent scholarly attention to the problems of legitimacy and authorisation and the need for collective action appears to be gaining traction (Leston-Bandeira & Thompson 2018; Norton 2016).

Management dilemmas

It would not be fair to say that the two parliaments have avoided management reforms entirely. Reform *has* occurred in both over several decades, albeit incrementally and principally in response to exogenous calls for greater efficiency, transparency, accountability and responsiveness. These 'new public management' reforms relate principally to more routine aspects of operational management, including procurement, financial and human resource management and structural changes. More elusive, however, have been strategic cultural and behavioural reforms to reduce public perceptions of incompetence, self-interest, insularity, inertia or unrepresentativeness (Petit & Yong 2018).

---

8   Section 1 of the *House of Commons Administration Act 1978* sets out the membership and functions of the House of Commons Commission; Section 2 provides that the commission must set strategic priorities and objectives in connection with services provided by the House departments.
9   The term is undefined in the legislation.

In both parliaments, regardless of organisational structure, a hierarchy between 'procedural' and 'management' functions has existed, limiting the potential for a collective parliamentary identity and increasing the likelihood of a silo mentality. Three related management dilemmas are discussed below.

Who are the customers? Multiple roles, multiple stakeholders

The achievement of shared goals is complicated by the multiplicity of stakeholders and whether the focus of parliamentary actors is internal or external. Members of parliament are both the overseers and the recipients of services. Parliamentary officials in the UK revealed that the line of sight is not always clear: members expect officials to do what members want but it is not always easy to discern what members want and members complain when they think the officials are 'running the show' (House of Lords clerk, personal communication, 24 May 2016). Some officials think they should not 'just lie down and do what the members want' (House of Commons manager, personal communication, 9 June 2016). Some actors also expressed concern about 'new' parliamentary officials who felt that they owed responsibility more to the public than to members and who might 'dismiss members as being part of the equation'.[10]

In the Australian parliament, the challenge of responding to multiple stakeholders, often at the expense of others, was also prominent. While officials appreciated the central purpose of a parliament was to enable democracy to work, some believed they had been engaged to help the community and the parliament to get closer together; others were wholly committed to the physical building housing parliament, its preservation and its maintenance. But, in both parliaments, management and its associated tasks tended to be viewed in some quarters with disdain, reducing the potential for greater collaboration.

Business as usual or strategically securing the future?

Operational management requirements are common to both parliaments and require oversight of a large span of activities, such as information technology and communications advice, support and security; public

---

10   These views were expressed by various interviewees.

access to the work of the parliaments; sustaining a working parliamentary building; human resources and financial services; and providing accommodation and facilities for members and staff. It is not difficult to understand why daily pressures can overwhelm longer-term strategy.

Notwithstanding the UK parliament's delineation of a strategic management role for members, there was a strong sense among officials that members were reluctant to set a strategic direction and accept ownership, but neither were they content to leave this to officials. The long-delayed restoration and renewal of the Palace of Westminster provides many examples of a lack of political agency and coordination (House of Commons Commission 2016; House of Lords 2016; Meakin 2017). On the 10-year anniversary of the UK parliamentary expenses scandal, scholars drew parallels between the decrepit state of the building and the decline in British democracy, with the chance of a catastrophic failure in both growing by the day (Flinders 2019; Hansard Society 2019).

In both parliaments there is an (often unacknowledged) interrelationship between management and procedural issues, and the public is unlikely to distinguish between them when scandals arise. There are also many missed opportunities to open a debate on how a parliamentary building and associated management issues can change the institutional culture.

Australia's 'new and permanent' Parliament House was conceived, designed and constructed in perhaps a more benign political period and was officially opened in 1988. Managing a new, iconic building carries its own challenges and controversies. An attempt in 1989 by the then government to establish a Parliament House Advisory Panel was resisted by the Senate, and subsequent attempts by interested external parties to place the building on the national and Commonwealth heritage lists have been unsuccessful (SFPALC 2012a).[11] There are continuing conflicts around the procedural, symbolic or public representation of parliament and continuing criticisms, at Senate estimates committees and in the media, of the department charged with its ongoing care.

---

11   The Walter Burley Griffin Society voiced concern about the use of the 'separation of powers' argument, noting that the same argument had not affected the heritage listing of the Houses of Parliament in the UK.

An abundance of scrutiny or excess of criticism?

The apparent subordination of the importance of management skills in favour of procedural knowledge and processes does not suggest that the procedural departments in each parliament are not in themselves well managed, particularly from a routine perspective. Clerks are well regarded by members of parliament and academics for their professional expertise, discretion and integrity. As 'accountable authorities' under their respective legislation and as procedural experts they are not usually found wanting. Conversely, officials in both parliaments are under intense scrutiny. Parliamentary administration in the Australian parliament has been subjected to a number of severely critical audit reports over decades (Auditor-General 1990a, 1990b; ANAO 2015). Members appear to distance themselves from their responsibilities to oversee an effectively run parliament, often seizing opportunities to criticise its management rather than contribute to improved practices.

The media revels in bringing the public's attention to almost every management problem, no matter how trivial (Kenny 2013; Walker 2019). Every expenditure on the parliamentary building or on the services it provides for members and staff is closely scrutinised; taxpayers resent politicians 'feathering their nests'. In the UK, freedom of information laws have helped promote a higher level of transparency and openness; however, they have also increased public distrust of parliamentarians, most notably in the wake of the 2009 expenses scandal (Winnett & Rayner 2009). The Australian parliament is not covered by Australia's *Freedom of Information Act 1982*, but the requirement to disclose the use of parliamentary entitlements is cause for much malign publicity. A lack of awareness, poor administration or hubris on the part of some politicians has led to public outrage, increased external oversight and, arguably, more complexity and inefficiency in the systems that support all politicians in their representational roles.

The absence of a cohesive parliamentary identity, conflicting demands on officials, and a lack of constructive engagement by members and public perceptions of their behaviour, are key contributors to the dilemmas of parliamentary management. Tensions arise from different beliefs about the primary duties and accountabilities of parliamentary actors. For members of parliament (especially in the lower Houses), whose main focus is on serving their constituents and their party, it is perhaps understandable that their interest in management relates narrowly to their own partisan interests in obtaining advice and resources that will help them to achieve these objectives. But, a disregard for the wider institution in an era of increasingly cynical media and public scrutiny and perceived shortcomings in parliamentary self-regulation has had negative repercussions.

The dilemmas of procedural and cultural reform

If the primary purpose of parliament is to enable democracy to work, in the public's view it does not appear to be working well. According to a global survey conducted by the Pew Research Centre (Wike et al. 2017), only 52 per cent of people in the UK were satisfied with the way democracy is working; for Australia, the figure was slightly higher at 58 per cent. The *Trust and democracy in Australia* report (Stoker, Evans & Halupka 2018) found that satisfaction with how democracy works in Australia had fallen from 71 per cent in 2013 to 41 per cent in 2018, suggesting an even starker picture. In this section I address three factors that appear to contribute to the poor public standing of both parliaments and their capacity to play an influential role in deliberation and policymaking: the extent and pace of procedural reform to meet public expectations, members' behaviour and workplace culture, and limited public engagement.

Procedural reform and public expectations

Without established precedent and formalised procedures to provide 'order, decency and regularity' when parliaments are sitting, chaos would ensue (Hatsell as cited in Evans 2014). However, as well as interpreting procedures based on centuries of precedent, there needs to be a capacity to anticipate change and to identify and adopt parliament-wide cultural and behavioural reforms that cross internal boundaries. According to Norton (2000), three conditions must be present for procedural reforms to succeed: a window of opportunity, political will and a coherent reform agenda. A window of opportunity often follows a crisis; the last two conditions are more relevant to planned strategic change.

Both parliaments have a long history of attempts at procedural reform; some succeed, others do not. Some are described as efficiency reforms (Kelso 2009), while others focus on improving effectiveness or scrutiny. Of particular interest are reforms aimed at the public interface with parliament, such as e-petitioning and greater opportunities for public participation. A recent example is the House of Representatives Procedure Committee's call for public comments on how question time could be improved (House of Representatives Standing Committee on Procedure 2019).[12]

Key messages from the public to the Speaker's Commission on Digital Democracy in the UK parliament (Digital Democracy Commission 2015) included: 'we care about issues, not politics', 'speak in plain English', 'stop broadcasting at us', 'to take part in parliament you need to understand it', 'we don't have time to read everything' and 'we want genuine dialogue'. Emerging technologies, including social media, also pose a threat to parliament's ability to articulate and determine collective ideas of public interest (Judge, Leston-Bandeira & Thompson 2018). Initiatives designed to enhance parliamentary control and public involvement have been only partially successful (Goodwin & Atkins 2018). In Australia, parliamentary clerks have lamented members' diminishing enthusiasm for procedural reform, and have claimed that their own authority or ability to contribute is limited.

Members behaviour and workplace culture

Scholars in the UK have suggested that processes of parliamentary modernisation have generally been internally directed much more at the relationship between parliament and government than towards the external environment, in terms of adapting to societal change or sharing power more widely among citizens (Goodwin & Atkins 2018). Longstanding rituals and norms have helped to secure the prevailing dominant social relations (Rai 2010), leading to calls for more effective representation of women and minorities, behavioural and cultural reform, and cross-party support for a concord regarding 'unacceptable and unprofessional behaviour in the chamber and more widely in the House' (Childs 2016, p. 11). Undoubtedly, the public's perceptions are also influenced by the behaviour of politicians, such as the misuse of parliamentary entitlements (Fels 2015; Winnett & Rayner 2009) and reports of bullying and harassment in both parliaments (Cox 2018; Ellenbogen 2019; Murphy 2018a). The Australian Parliament House has been described as a 'prison', characterised by high stress, intense competition and long hours, where the parties are determined to hide

---

12 Forty-one submissions were received, many reinforcing the perception that current practices have a negative influence on public engagement and limit accountability.

any hint of scandal (O'Malley 2018). Parliament is isolated from voters and its occupants are disconnected from each other, compounded by the parliamentary building itself (Murphy 2018b).

The dilemmas of procedural and cultural reform might be seen as challenges to be overcome by political will and a coherent reform agenda. Members of parliament, however, face difficult choices in addressing competing allegiances to their parties, constituents and the parliamentary institution. The dilemma lies in how to achieve a more participatory approach in an environment of public distrust and disengagement, especially when it is not clear whether parliament actually wants to foster greater participation (Hansard Society 2019; Kelso 2007; Uberoi 2017). The role of parliamentary committees in providing opportunities for broader participation in policy development, democratic renewal and citizen engagement is widely acknowledged (Gaines et al. 2019; Halligan, Miller & Power 2007; Hendriks & Kay 2019; Marsh 2016; Russell & Cowley 2016), but more radical measures involving institutional design and processes are increasingly being called for (Ercan, Hendriks & Dryzek 2019; Leston-Bandeira & Walker 2018). Parliament needs to do more than continue with one way communication of its work or rely on the usual contributors to committee inquiries. To achieve greater public involvement and participation, gain greater influence over the public narrative on parliament and manage public expectations of what parliament can and should deliver, may well require ceding some control. A public management approach may help in this process.

Towards a public management approach to parliamentary administration

Attention to the practice as well as the theory of contemporary public management has been limited in the two parliaments I studied, with implications for both institutions' actual and perceived success in influencing public policy and deliberation. Most of the management reform discussion has been concerned with the retention of traditional professional skills, structural efficiency and operational performance. We can recognise here elements of the tension between 'traditional' public administration with its emphasis on specialised knowledge, hierarchy and preservation of the status quo (Albrow 1970; Lindquist & Wanna 2011; Osborne et al. 2015) and new public management (NPM), which saw a shift in values towards efficiency and professional public sector management (Hood 1991; Pollitt 2003). The principles of NPM have undoubtedly influenced parliamentary administration through numerous reviews (in the UK) and legislative requirements (in Australia), and incremental progress has been achieved. Some practitioners have described this as 'muddling through', with one recalling the days when 'administration was something to be done on a Friday afternoon' (House of Representatives clerk, personal communication, 7 April 2017).

Less attention has been devoted to strategic management in the two parliaments, including in the context of procedural and cultural reforms that could be expected to enhance parliament's public standing, relevance and effectiveness. There is clearly a need to rethink the roles of parliamentary actors and parliament's internal and external relationships to achieve an effective balance between enabling and scrutinising a government's legislative program and enhancing public confidence and participation. The discussion below draws particularly on the literature relating to public value, collaboration and co-production.

The relevance of 'public value' to parliamentary administration

Broadly applied, the public value concept aims at administration that creates substantive value, is legitimate and politically sustainable, and is operationally and administratively sustainable (Alford & O'Flynn 2009; Moore 1995). These tests equate with Lynn's (2005) dimensions of responsible public management, which must be constitutionally authorised, performed skilfully and efficiently, and reflect the values of a wider society. Bryson, Crosby, and Bloomberg (2015, p. 239) advocated public value management as a way of moving philosophically, theoretically and practically beyond older public interest debates towards public value governance across multiple sectors and stakeholders and involving multiple conflicting and contentious value judgements (see also Bevir & Rhodes 2006; Stoker 2006; Bryson, Crosby & Bloomberg 2014). In applying this broad approach to parliamentary administration, I make four observations.

- First, the 'substantive public value' of the parliament is difficult to identify and promote in an environment of public disaffection, where public engagement efforts are not always effective. If parliament is to compete with and engage with many emerging players, then new forms of democracy and of public engagement and participation will be required. Importantly, Fukumoto and Bozeman (2019) distinguish between public *value*, whereby public managers determine what is substantively valuable, as envisaged by Moore (1995), and public *values*, which are determined more democratically by improving parliament's representativeness and encouraging public participation.

- Second, strategic parliamentary administration that is 'legitimate and politically sustainable' requires an effective 'authorising environment'. While this exists in practice in the UK parliament, it has not always been considered effective (House of Commons Public Administration and Constitutional Affairs Committee 2019). UK scholars are, however, devoting more attention to administrative effectiveness. Attempts to establish overarching formalised internal governance arrangements in Australia have so far been resisted (Baxter 2015; Senate Select Committee on Parliament's Appropriations and Staffing 1981; SFPALC 2017). Interviewees have confirmed continuing resistance.

- Third, notwithstanding that a 'managerialist' focus on achievement and performance has taken hold in the two parliaments, and certainly within operational or 'management' functions, efforts to ensure whole-of-parliament organisational strategies have been hampered by competition for status and resources (Department of the Senate 2004; HOCGC 2014; Reid & Forrest 1989). In such cases, power and politics are inevitably involved (Geddes 2019). That the Australian parliament does not set its own budget independently of the executive has further influenced competition for resources, impeding the potential to align resources and goals to achieve greater public value.

- Fourth, measuring the value of parliamentary administration (particularly public engagement and outreach) has always been difficult (Weerasinghe & Ramshaw 2018). Measuring parliament's broader impact and effectiveness is also problematic (Russell & Cowley 2016; Leston-Bandeira & Thompson 2017). Moore (1995, 2013, 2016), however, provides valuable insights into how public managers, including officials and elected representatives, can recognise and account for valuable collective social outcomes in a dynamic external environment.[13] This would entail a focus not just on outputs, efficiency and cost reduction, but also on social values such as democratic representation and effective deliberation on important social issues.[14]

---

13   In contrast, see Horner and Hutton (2011), who argue that 'public value is defined … through political and social interaction' and that 'any search for an absolute measure' should be avoided.

14   Evidence presented to the House of Commons Liaison Committee inquiry into the influence and effectiveness of the select committee system emphasised the need to recognise the 'public value dynamic' of the work of select committees (House of Commons Liaison Committee 2019).

Antipathy towards the public value concept has often stemmed from a concern that unelected public officials would overstep the political-administrative divide (Rhodes & Wanna 2007, 2009; Shergold 1997). Yet, as has been recognised in the UK, in the parliamentary environment this may be more likely to occur *in the absence of* well constituted governance arrangements (Judge & Leston-Bandeira 2018; Norton 2016). Stoker (2006) also recognises the pitfalls of public value, such as limits to the extent to which politics can be 'managed' and remain legitimate. He believes, however, that its strength lies in providing a motivational force for reform that does not rely on rules or incentives but on interpersonal relationships within networks and partnerships.

Those who remain sceptical about the potential commitment of politicians to an administrative or management role can also point to a lack of enthusiasm by many presiding officers and members for their administrative roles. There is, however, a constructive role for parliament's officials in managing upwards and outwards to gain political support for proposed reforms within a legitimate authorising environment. The public value approach has advantages for parliamentary actors, principally by engaging both officials and members to think of themselves as public managers as well as parliamentary custodians, exercising agency in focusing on strategic as well as operational tasks, identifying and responding to diminishing public regard for parliament, and responding constructively to external challenges to parliamentary sovereignty rather than using parliament's 'uniqueness' as a defensive shield or barrier to reform. This would require changing internal governance arrangements to mobilise authorised and legitimate decision-making.

If it is possible to relate the broad characteristics of public value to parliamentary administration, what else might be needed for it to become a 'motivational force' designed to overcome resistance to change and encourage mutual respect and shared learning (Petit & Yong 2018; Stoker 2006)? The benefits from a public value approach might become more achievable if pursued in the context of, or in concert with, approaches based on collaboration and co-production.

The potential for engagement, collaboration and co-production

In the two parliaments, internal resistance to change has in the past stymied collaboration among parliamentary actors. For example, in the UK a joint working program set up to achieve further efficiencies between the two Houses has fallen off the political radar (Petit & Yong 2018). Among interviewees there was a strong sense of the need for efficiency and reduced wastage, but this was accompanied by scepticism about the extent of efficiencies that could be harvested from joint initiatives. In Australia, parliamentary departments have traditionally competed to displace the effect of budget cuts or to acquire additional resources (Department of the Senate 2004). Public engagement functions do not appear to be as well funded or prioritised as they are in the UK.

There is room for more concerted cross-parliament deliberations in both parliaments. Arguably, this could be achieved without introducing superfluous management layers. Existing governance bodies could move towards a new norm of meeting collaboratively to discuss matters of mutual and public interest as to how the parliament might operate. The Australian parliament could formalise a collaborative governance structure across the parliament, while the UK parliament could strengthen its collaborative governance across both Houses—the mechanisms are already in place. To be effective they need the continued involvement of parliament's elected representatives.

The skills required for effective collaboration within parliaments would not be vastly different than those expected from senior managers working within their own functional areas; any deficit in collaborative skills would probably indicate shortfalls in management skills per se. Indeed, Bartelings et al. (2017) found that, in large part, the activities of managers still fall within the 10 traditional managerial roles identified by Mintzberg (1973) in his seminal study on managerial work: figurehead, liaison, leader, monitor, disseminator, spokesperson, entrepreneur, disturbance handler, resource allocator, negotiator. They added a new role—orchestration— which emphasises the inter-organisational aspects of management. Whereas Mintzberg describes the manager above all as a leader, Bartelings et al. (2017) define the role as a spokesperson—an observation that resonates with the parliamentary governance dilemmas considered above. Also relevant is the work of Sullivan, Williams and Jeffares (2012) on the need to bring subgroups together to maintain internal cohesion without dissolving diverse identities. Parliamentary actors would collaborate as 'situated agents', each capable of independent action using their existing skills, experience and expertise, but their actions would be mediated by wider influences rather than limited by a narrow span of attention (Bevir & Rhodes 2006; Simon 1977). Finally, the pursuit of greater engagement with external actors and the wider community would call on tangible skills and factors, such as integration, central coordination and information sharing to achieve substantive outcomes, and on 'soft', or less tangible, skills and factors, including personal relationships, trust and a shared collaborative language (Page et al. 2015; Cristofoli, Meneguzzo & Riccucci 2017).

What would be the main pitfalls of such an approach in the parliamentary context and how could these be overcome? Concerns include the differences in motivation, or the influences of politics and public administration, on the effectiveness of partnerships and networks (Prebble 2015); that collaboration is a fad 'that everyone believes but few practise' (O'Flynn 2009); that collaboration is 'highly resource consuming and often painful' (Huxham 2003); and that collaboration needs to overcome blind spots (Wegrich 2019). Barriers to fostering the deep engagement required for collaboration include a reluctance to redistribute power from managers to citizens, lack of trust, uncertainty over political support, diffused accountability and raised expectations (Holmes 2011). Few authors, however, dismiss the benefits of collaboration altogether; many offer strategies to address these and other challenges, and there are examples of attempts to move in this direction. These include the UK parliament's collaboration with external organisations in its public engagement activities, including with the Hansard Society, Institute for Government and universities. Some evidence has also emerged within the Australian parliament of recently forged internal collaboration, but there has been little sign of an 'authorised' and supportive collaborative space or the type of collaborative governance that could provide oversight and assurances. There has also been little evidence to date of parliament collaborating with external pro-democracy organisations.[15]

Co-production is another public management approach that may be useful, in practice as well as reflexively, in parliamentary administration. This is true, despite criticisms that the concept is 'woolly' or 'muddled' and some confusion among academics and practitioners as to what co-production actually means and where it could be usefully applied (Dewey, Blackman & Dickinson 2018; Nabatchi, Sancino & Sicilia 2017). Setting these concerns to one side, co-production would require public engagement at the highest level, including interactions, dialogue

---

15   Although there seems to be a willingness to move in this direction. Democracy 2025 reports on a survey of Australian federal politicians on how they would like to reform democracy (Evans, Stoker & Halupka 2019). The survey was sponsored by the Joint Standing Committee on Electoral Matters.

and deliberation, allowing for the possibility of opinions being changed, rather than a simple exchange of information (Holmes 2011). Bryson et al. (2017) also highlight the role that politicians, political leadership and politics can play in public value production in a democratic society. Co-production can offer advantages in the face of challenges from the media and 'gotcha' journalism.

Scholarly discussion on whether co-production is unavoidable in public service provision (Alford 2016) suggests that citizens derive value from the opportunity to participate in deliberative processes and share in shaping society, and that the greater the skills and knowledge they possess the more likely the extent and quality of their co-production. Trust based on identification can also be restored through co-production provided self-efficacy is increased (Fledderus, Brandsen & Honingh 2014; Thomsen 2017). Citizens would need to identify more closely with parliament and feel that they are influential. Greater efforts at making parliament more representative of society as well as involving citizens in policy deliberation would also appear to be crucial.

To take the collaborative and co-production approaches beyond a focus on how parliament works, particularly in representing its citizens, greater public involvement in actual policymaking could be garnered through citizens' assemblies or similar arrangements. A basis for collaboration has already been established in the UK parliament in the form of the citizens' assembly on adult social care (Allen & McKee 2019), and has continued in the context of the recent citizens' assembly on climate change commissioned by six parliamentary committees and funded jointly through the committees' research budget and philanthropic donations (Webster 2020). Parliaments could thus move closer to Crick's ideal role as a 'broker of ideas' experimenting in public discussion with citizens, ideally in averting rather than responding to crises.

It is important to be aware of the pitfalls of co-production, particularly in light of confusion over its definition. These include difficulty identifying the benefits, particularly when distinguishing self-interest from common interests (Bryson et al. 2017; Dewey, Blackman & Dickinson 2018); and the need to establish and maintain citizens' interaction (Thomsen & Jakobsen 2015).

There is no guarantee that co-production automatically leads to greater trust, particularly when those with low levels of political efficacy, who are more likely to gain from a greater sense of control, are harder to reach, having perhaps already disengaged from politics (Fledderus, Brandsen & Honingh 2014). The challenges of co-production include conflicting values, institutional rigidity, risk aversion, lack of accountability and the conflicts inherent in all group processes. Yet, there is hope for success if managers can review their professional norms, institutional processes and past practices, appreciate the environmental interactions that impact their daily operations and avoid resentment towards the new co-producers (Williams, Kang & Johnson 2016). From a practical perspective, this would suggest a need for sustained internal reform, innovative approaches to public engagement, and greater collaboration with external organisations and citizens.

Conclusion

The theory and practice of public and parliamentary administration offers a rich field for parliamentary scholars in Australia. This is in part because the differences between parliaments and other public institutions are not as great as might be supposed. Contemporary public management theories can, therefore, offer benefits to parliamentary managers beyond the important but narrow requirements of management competence and efficiency. A key factor is parliament's role as a deliberative forum for discussing and achieving some consensus on key policy issues (as opposed to its highly politicised legislative and scrutiny roles).

Parliamentary practitioners can appear dismissive of public management theory (as can other public managers), influenced by a sense of separation from mainstream public service and policymaking and parliament's 'unique' role in the Westminster system. This separation has also been exacerbated by a lack of public or academic attention to parliamentary administration and a tendency among many parliamentary administrators to see their roles through lenses of 'administrative craft and managerial mystery' (Shergold 2015). However, for both governments and parliaments, engendering public confidence and trust in their institutions, and realising the potential to harness the collective capacity of citizens to support and/or accept policy reform necessitated by changing environmental conditions, would seem to be key factors in sustaining their legitimacy (Raadschelders 1999).

Parliament's greatest challenge is to win ongoing public support and approval while fulfilling its roles of enabling and scrutinising policy and legislation and also providing a deliberative forum for policy responses. The problem is not new. The question of parliament's public standing has been raised again and again over decades. While most members of parliament have not been actively engaged in advocating for institutional reform, either administrative or procedural, and traditional parliamentary administrators are reluctant to cross the political-administrative line (at least publicly), external actors are increasingly assuming advocacy roles.

Although incremental management reforms have been achieved in both parliaments, there has been resistance towards internal and external collaboration and a continuing focus on preservation and stewardship rather than strategic reform. External organisations are assuming a greater role in engaging with the public to restore confidence in our democratic system, including through increasing participation, and parliaments are in danger of losing their relevance in this respect. The characteristics of public value and its associated paradigms—building legitimacy, addressing public concerns and ensuring operational capacity and resources— lend themselves as well to parliamentary administration as to public administration.

The skills required for effective collaboration are not dissimilar to readily understood leadership and management skills but place an added focus on internal cohesion taking account of wider influences. Collaboration also requires greater partnership with external organisations with similar aspirations. Perhaps the greatest conceptual challenge is to think of parliamentary deliberation as a form of co-production with citizens, with parliamentary actors providing a legitimately authorised service to a collective citizenry.

Inevitably, there are barriers to the acceptance and take up of policy or management reforms. In parliament these include governance arrangements, diffused authority, the lack of an overall parliamentary identity and political conflict as well as scepticism by practitioners and a preference for learning on-the-job. There are encouraging signs, however, at least in the UK parliament, where the characteristics, practices and skills inherent in the approaches I have outlined are now being applied, albeit often as a result of external pressures.

References

Adams, J 2002, *Parliament: Master of its own household?* Australian Public Service Commission, Barton, ACT.

Albrow, M 1970, *Bureaucracy*, Pall Mall Press, London, UK, doi.org/10.1007/978-1-349-00916-9.

Alford, J 2016, 'Co-production, interdependence and publicness: Extending public service-dominant logic', *Public Management Review*, vol. 18, no. 5, pp. 673–91, doi.org/10.1080/14719037.2015.1111659.

Alford, J & O'Flynn, J 2009, 'Making sense of public value: Concepts, critiques and emergent meanings', *International Journal of Public Administration*, vol. 32, no. 3–4, pp. 171–91, doi.org/10.1080/01900690902732731.

Allen, S & McKee, R 2019, 'Why do citizens' assemblies work? Evidence from the citizens' assemblies on Brexit and Social Care', *Constitution Unit*, blog, 28 February, viewed 3 March 2019, constitution-unit.com/2019/02/28/why-do-citizens-assemblies-work-evidence-from-the-citizens-assemblies-on-brexit-and-social-care/.

Auditor-General 1990a, *The Department of the Parliamentary Reporting Staff*, report no. 21 1989–90, AGPS, Canberra, ACT.

Auditor-General 1990b, *An investigation of an unofficial account operated by Parliamentary Information Systems Office*, report no. 25 1989–90, AGPS, Canberra, ACT.

Australian National Audit Office (ANAO) 2015, *Managing assets and contracts at Parliament House: Department of Parliamentary Services*, ANAO report no. 24 2014–15: Performance audit, Commonwealth of Australia, Canberra, ACT.

Bartelings, JA, Goedee, J, Raab, J & Bijl, R 2017, 'The nature of orchestrational work', *Public Management Review*, vol. 19, no. 3, pp. 342–60, doi.org/10.1080/14719037.2016.1209233.

Baxter, K 2015, *Review of the Department of Parliamentary Services*, in Parliament of Australia, 'Answers to questions on notice', no. 111, 13 April 2017, viewed 25 May 2017, www.aph.gov.au/Parliamentary_Business/Senate_Estimates/fapactte/estimates/add1617/parliamentary/index.

BBC News 2019, 'Newspaper headlines: Bercow 'out of order' over Brexit?', viewed 21 January, 2019, www.bbc.com/news/blogs-the-papers-46818717.

Benwell, R & Gay, O 2011, *The separation of powers*, House of Commons Library Standard Note, SN/PC/06053, 15 August.

Bevir, M & Rhodes, RAW 2006, *Governance stories*, Routledge, London, UK, doi.org/10.4324/9780203969090.

Bryson, JM, Crosby, BC & Bloomberg, L 2014, 'Public value governance: Moving beyond traditional public administration and the new public management', *Public Administration Review*, vol. 74, no. 4, pp. 445–56.

Bryson, JM, Crosby, BC & Bloomberg, L (eds) 2015, *Public value and public administration*, Georgetown University Press, Washington, DC.

Bryson, J, Sancino, A, Benington, J & Sørensen, E 2017, 'Towards a multi-actor theory of public value co-creation', *Public Management Review*, vol. 19, no. 5, pp. 640–54, doi.org/10.1080/14719037.2016.1192164.

Childs, S 2016, *The good parliament*, University of Bristol, Bristol, UK.

Cox, L 2018, 'The bullying and harassment of House of Commons staff', Independent inquiry report, 28 October, viewed 28 November 2018, www.cpahq.org/cpahq/cpadocs/CWP%20Workshop%204%20The%20Bullying%20and%20Harassment%20of%20Parliamentary%20staff.pdf.

Crick, BR 1968, *The reform of parliament*, 2nd edn, Weidenfeld & Nicolson, London, UK.

Cristofoli, D, Meneguzzo, M & Riccucci, N 2017, 'Collaborative administration: The management of successful networks', *Public Management Review*, vol. 19, no. 3, pp. 275–83, doi.org/10.1080/14719037.2016.1209236.

Department of Parliamentary Services (DPS) 2018, *Annual report 2017–18*, viewed 11 May 2019, www.aph.gov.au/About_Parliament/Parliamentary_Departments/Department_of_Parliamentary_Services/Publications/Annual_Reports/Annual_Report_2017-18.

Department of the Prime Minister and Cabinet (PM&C) 2019, *Our public service, our future. Independent review of the Australian Public Service*, viewed 4 June 2018, www.apsreview.gov.au/about.

Department of the Senate 2004, *Annual report 2003–04*, Clerk's review, Canberra, ACT.

Dewey, L, Blackman, D & Dickinson, H 2018, 'Co-production and innovation: Creating better solutions for future public service implementation', UNSW and Public Service Research Group, issues paper no. 3, viewed 6 February 2019, www.unsw.adfa.edu.au/public-service-research-group/sites/cpsr/files/uploads/288554001%20-%20PSRG%20paper%20series%20no.%203_FA%2020200317.pdf.

Digital Democracy Commission 2015, 'Open up!', report of the Speaker's Commission on Digital Democracy, 26 January, viewed 12 April 2015, www.digitaldemocracy.parliament.uk/.

Ellenbogen, N 2019, *An independent inquiry into bullying and harassment in the House of Lords*, report, 10 July, viewed 19 July 2019, www.parliament.uk/documents/lords-committees/house-of-lords-commission/2017-19/ellenbogen-report.pdf.

Ercan, SA, Hendriks, CM & Dryzek, JS 2019, 'Public deliberation in an era of communicative plenty', *Policy & Politics*, vol. 47, no. 1, pp. 19–36, doi.org/10.1332/030557318X15200933925405.

Evans, M, Stoker, G & Halupka, M 2019, 'Democracy 2025: How Australian federal politicians would like to reform their democracy', report no. 5, viewed 16 October 2019, www.democracy2025.gov.au/documents/Democracy2025-report5.pdf.

Evans, P 2014, 'A rule to go by: What is the point of parliamentary procedure', UK parliament open lecture, Aberystwyth University, 7 February.

Fels, A 2015, 'Wanted: An independent umpire to set and enforce clear parliamentary entitlement rules', *Conversation*, 3 August, viewed 16 August 2015, theconversation.com/wanted-an-independent-umpire-to-set-and-enforce-clear-parliamentary-entitlement-rules-45571.

Fledderus, J, Brandsen, T & Honingh, M 2014, 'Restoring trust through the co-production of public services: A theoretical elaboration', *Public Management Review*, vol. 16, no. 3, pp. 424–43, doi.org/10.1080/14719037.2013.848920.

Flinders, M 2019, 'Palace of Westminster is falling down—but government's renewal plans are just as decrepit', *Conversation*, 8 May, viewed 9 May 2019, theconversation.com/palace-of-westminster-is-falling-down-but-governments-renewal-plans-are-just-as-decrepit-116766.

Fox, R 2009, 'Engagement and participation: What the public want and how our politicians need to respond', *Parliamentary Affairs*, vol. 62, no. 4, pp. 673–85, doi.org/10.1093/pa/gsp027.

Fukumoto, E & Bozeman, B 2019, 'Public values theory: What is missing?', *The American Review of Public Administration*, vol. 49, no. 6, pp. 635–48, doi.org/10.1177/0275074018814244.

Gaines, BJ, Goodwin, M, Bates, SH & Sin, G 2019, 'The study of legislative committees', *The Journal of Legislative Studies*, vol. 25, no. 3, pp. 331–9, doi.org/10.1080/13572334.2019.1662614.

Geddes, M 2019, 'The explanatory potential of "dilemmas": Bridging practices and power to understand political change in interpretive political science', *Political Studies Review*, vol. 17, no. 3, pp. 239–54, doi.org/10.1177/147 8929918795342.

Geddes, M & Mulley, J 2018, 'Supporting members and peers', in C Leston-Bandeira & L Thompson (eds), *Exploring parliament*, Oxford University Press, Oxford, UK, doi.org/10.1093/hepl/9780198788430.003.0004.

Goodwin, M & Atkins, M 2018, 'Parliament and modernization', in C Leston-Bandeira & L Thompson (eds), *Exploring parliament*, Oxford University Press, Oxford, UK, doi.org/10.1093/hepl/9780198788430.003.0028.

Halligan, J, Miller, R & Power, J 2007, *Parliament in the twenty-first century: Institutional reform and emerging roles*, Melbourne University Press, Melbourne, Vic.

Hansard Society 2015, *Audit of political engagement 12: The 2015 report*, Hansard Society, London, UK.

Hansard Society 2019, *Audit of political engagement 16: The 2019 report*, Hansard Society, London, UK.

Hendriks, CM & Kay, A 2019, 'From "opening up" to democratic renewal: Deepening public engagement in legislative committees', *Government and Opposition*, vol. 54, no. 1, pp. 25–51, doi.org/10.1017/gov.2017.20.

Holmes, B 2011, 'Citizens' engagement in policymaking and the design of public services', research paper no. 1 2011–12, Parliamentary Library, Canberra, ACT, viewed 23 February 2020, www.aph.gov.au/about_parliament/parliamentary_ departments/parliamentary_library/pubs/rp/rp1112/12rp01#_Toc299 099873.

Hood, C 1991, 'A public management for all seasons?', *Public Administration*, vol. 69, no. 1, pp. 3–19, doi.org/10.1111/j.1467-9299.1991.tb00779.x.

Horner, L & Hutton, W 2011, 'Public value, deliberative democracy and the role of public managers', in J Benington & M Moore (eds), *Public value: Theory and practice*, Palgrave Macmillan, New York, NY, doi.org/10.1007/978-0-230-36431-8_6.

House of Commons 2018, *Annual report and accounts 2017–18*, viewed 11 May 2019, www.parliament.uk/documents/commons-expenditure/Admin%20 Annual%20Accounts/Administration_Annual_Report_and_Accounts_ 2017-18.pdf.

House of Commons Commission 2016, *Strategy for the House of Commons Service 2016–2021*, viewed 25 April 2018, www.parliament.uk/documents/Strategy-for-the-House-of-Commons-Service-2016-2021-long-version.pdf (site discontinued). (For updated strategy see www.parliament.uk/documents/commons/CEB/House-of-Commons-Service-strategy-2019-25.pdf, viewed 17 April 2020.)

House of Commons Governance Committee (HOCGC) 2014, *House of Commons Governance*, 17 December, HC 692, 2014–15.

House of Commons Liaison Committee 2019, 'The effectiveness and influence of the select committee system', 9 September, HC 1860, 2017–19, SCA0053.

House of Commons Public Administration and Constitutional Affairs Committee 2019, *Oral evidence: The role of parliament in the UK constitution: Role of the Speaker*, October 2019, HC 32, 2017–19, data.parliament.uk/writtenevidence/committeeevidence.svc/evidencedocument/public-administration-and-constitutional-affairs-committee/the-role-of-parliament-in-the-uk-constitution-role-of-the-speaker/oral/106560.html#Panel3.

House of Lords 2016, *Strategy for the House of Lords Administration 2016–2021*, viewed 11 March 2019, www.parliament.uk/globalassets/documents/lords-information-office/2017/Strategy-Implementation-plan-2016---2021.pdf.

House of Representatives Standing Committee on Procedure 2019, *Committee questions question time*, media release 1 August, viewed 12 August 2019, www.aph.gov.au/About_Parliament/House_of_Representatives/About_the_House_News/Media_Releases/Committee_questions_Question_Time.

Huxham, C 2003, 'Theorizing collaboration practice', *Public Management Review*, vol. 5, no. 3, pp. 401–23, doi.org/10.1080/1471903032000146964.

Judge, D & Leston-Bandeira, C 2018, 'The institutional representation of parliament', *Political Studies*, vol. 66, no. 1, pp. 154–72, doi.org/10.1177/0032321717706901.

Judge, D, Leston-Bandeira, C & Thompson, L 2018, 'Conclusion: The future of parliamentary politics', in C Leston-Bandeira & L Thompson (eds), *Exploring parliament*, Oxford University Press, Oxford, UK, doi.org/10.1093/hepl/9780198788430.001.0001.

Kelso, A 2007, 'Parliament and political disengagement: Neither waving nor drowning', *The Political Quarterly*, vol. 78, no. 3, pp. 364–73, doi.org/10.1111/j.1467-923X.2007.00865.x.

Kelso, A 2009, *Parliamentary reform at Westminster*, Manchester University Press, Manchester, UK, doi.org/10.7228/manchester/9780719076756.001.0001.

Kenny, M 2013, 'Terracotta pots go missing from Parliament', *Sydney Morning Herald*, 18 November, viewed 13 May 2015, www.smh.com.au/politics/federal/terracotta-pots-go-missing-from-parliament-20131118-2xq72.html.

Leston-Bandeira, C & Thompson, L 2017, 'Integrating the view of the public into the formal legislative process: Public reading stage in the UK House of Commons', *The Journal of Legislative Studies*, vol. 23, no. 4, pp. 508–28, doi.org/10.1080/13572334.2017.1394736.

Leston-Bandeira, C & Thompson, L (eds) 2018, *Exploring parliament*, Oxford University Press, Oxford, UK, doi.org/10.1093/hepl/9780198788430.001.0001.

Leston-Bandeira, C & Walker, A 2018, 'Parliament and public engagement', in C Leston-Bandeira & L Thompson (eds), *Exploring parliament*, Oxford University Press, Oxford, UK, doi.org/10.1093/hepl/9780198788430.001.0001.

Lindquist, E & Wanna, J 2011, 'Co-production in perspective: Parallel traditions and implications for public management and governance', paper presented to ANZSOG, Canberra, 1 March.

Lynn, L 2005, *Public management: Old and new*, Routledge, New York, NY.

Marsh, I 2016, 'The Commons Select Committee system in the 2015–20 parliament', *The Political Quarterly*, vol. 87, no. 1, pp. 96–103, doi.org/10.1111/1467-923X.12223.

Meakin, A 2017, 'Who is in charge of the Palace of Westminster? Big Ben and parliamentary governance', Hansard Society blog, 8 September, viewed 6 October 2017, www.hansardsociety.org.uk/blog/who-is-in-charge-of-the-palace-of-westminster-big-ben-and-parliamentary.

Mintzberg, H 1973, *The nature of managerial work*, Harper Collins Publishers, New York, NY.

Moore, M 1995, *Creating public value: Strategic management in government*, Harvard University Press, Cambridge, MA.

Moore, M 2013, *Recognising public value*, Harvard University Press, Cambridge, MA.

Moore, M 2016, 'Recognising public value: Strategic uses of performance measurement in government', presentation to Australia and New Zealand School of Government workshop, Melbourne, 25 February.

Murphy, K 2018a, 'Why parliament still tolerates thuggery not acceptable in broader society', *Guardian,* 28 November, viewed 29 November 2018, www.theguardian.com/australia-news/2018/nov/28/why-parliament-still-tolerates-thuggery-not-acceptable-in-broader-society.

Murphy, K 2018b, 'Anthony Albanese on how MPs' loneliness feeds parliament's coup culture', *Guardian*, 5 December, viewed 5 December 2018, www.theguardian.com/australia-news/2018/dec/05/anthony-albanese-on-how-mps-loneliness-feeds-parliaments-coup-culture.

Nabatchi, T, Sancino, A & Sicilia, M 2017, 'Varieties of participation in public services: The who, when, and what of coproduction', *Public Administration Review*, vol. 77, no. 5, pp. 766–76, doi.org/10.1111/puar.12765.

Norton, P 2000, 'Reforming parliament in the United Kingdom: The report of the Commission to Strengthen Parliament', *The Journal of Legislative Studies*, vol. 6, no. 3, pp. 1–14, doi.org/10.1080/13572330008420628.

Norton, P 2016, 'Speaking for parliament', *Parliamentary Affairs*, vol. 70, no. 2, pp. 191–206, doi.org/10.1093/pa/gsw031.

O'Flynn, J 2009, 'The cult of collaboration in public policy', *Australian Journal of Public Administration*, vol. 68, no. 1, pp. 112–16, doi.org/10.1111/j.1467-8500.2009.00616.x.

O'Malley, N 2018, 'Total systems failure', *Canberra Times*, 11 August, p. 6.

Osborne, SP, Radnor, Z, Kinder, T & Vidal, I 2015, 'The SERVICE framework: A public-service-dominant approach to sustainable public services', *British Journal of Management*, vol. 26, no. 3, pp. 424–38, doi.org/10.1111/1467-8551.12094.

Page, SB, Stone, MM, Bryson, JM & Crosby, BC 2015, 'Public value creation by cross-sector collaborations: A framework and challenges of assessment', *Public Administration*, vol. 93, no. 3, pp. 715–32, doi.org/10.1111/padm.12161.

Peters, BG & Pierre, J 2017, 'Two roads to nowhere: Appraising 30 years of public administration research', *Governance*, vol. 30, no. 1, pp. 11–16, doi.org/10.1111/gove.12229.

Petit, S & Yong, B 2018, 'The administrative organization and governance of parliament', in C Leston-Bandeira & L Thompson (eds), *Exploring parliament*, Oxford University Press, Oxford, UK, doi.org/10.1093/hepl/9780198788430.003.0003.

Pollitt, C 2003, *The essential public manager*, Open University Press, Maidenhead, UK.

Prebble, M 2015, 'Public value and limits to collaboration', *International Journal of Public Administration*, vol. 38, no. 7, pp. 473–85, doi.org/10.1080/01900 692.2014.949742.

Raadschelders, J 1999, 'A coherent framework for the study of public administration', *Journal of Public Administration Research and Theory*, vol. 9, no. 2, pp. 281–304, doi.org/10.1093/oxfordjournals.jpart.a024411.

Rai, SM 2010, 'Analysing ceremony and ritual in parliament', *The Journal of Legislative Studies*, vol. 16, pp. 284–97, doi.org/10.1080/13572334.2010.4 98098.

Reid, GS & Forrest, M 1989, *Australia's Commonwealth parliament: 1901–1988: Ten perspectives*, Melbourne University, Melbourne, Vic.

Rhodes, R & Wanna, J 2007, 'The limits to public value, or rescuing responsible government from the platonic guardians', *Australian Journal of Public Administration*, vol. 66, no. 4, pp. 406–21, doi.org/10.1111/j.1467-8500. 2007.00553.x.

Rhodes, R & Wanna, J 2009, 'Bringing the politics back in: Public value in Westminster parliamentary government', *Public Administration*, vol. 87, no. 2 pp. 161–83, doi.org/10.1111/j.1467-9299.2009.01763.x.

Russell, M & Cowley, P 2016, 'The policy power of the Westminster parliament: The "parliamentary state" and the empirical evidence', *Governance*, vol. 29, no. 1, pp. 121–37, doi.org/10.1111/gove.12149.

Senate Committee of Privileges 2014, *160th report: The use of CCTV material in Parliament House*, 5 December, Parliament of the Commonwealth of Australia, Canberra, ACT.

Senate Finance and Public Administration Legislation Committee (SFPALC) 2012a, *The performance of the Department of Parliamentary Services: Interim report*, June 2012, Commonwealth of Australia, Canberra, ACT.

Senate Finance and Public Administration Legislation Committee (SFPALC) 2012b, *The performance of the Department of Parliamentary Services: Final report*, 28 November, Commonwealth of Australia, Canberra, ACT.

Senate Finance and Public Administration Legislation Committee (SFPALC) 2015, *Department of Parliamentary Services: Final report*, 17 September, Commonwealth of Australia, Canberra, ACT.

Senate Finance and Public Administration Legislation Committee (SFPALC) 2017, *Additional Estimates 2016–17 (February and March 2017)*, viewed 17 April 2020, www.aph.gov.au/Parliamentary_Business/Senate_estimates/ eetctte/estimates/add1617/index.

Senate Select Committee on Parliament's Appropriations and Staffing 1981, 'Parliament's appropriations and staffing', report of the Senate Select Committee, Canberra, ACT.

Shergold, P 1997, 'The colour purple: Perceptions of accountability across the Tasman', *Public Administration & Development (1986–1998)*, vol. 17, no. 3, p. 293, doi.org/10.1002/(SICI)1099-162X(199708)17:3<293::AID-PAD950 >3.0.CO;2-R.

Shergold, P 2015, 'Foreword', in B Head and K Crowley (eds), *Policy analysis in Australia,* Policy Press, Bristol, UK.

Simon, HA 1977, *Administrative behaviour: A study of decision-making processes in administrative organizations*, 4th edn, The Free Press, New York, NY.

Snow, D & Robertson, J 2015, 'Choppergate puts politicians' perks under scrutiny', *Sydney Morning Herald*, 24 July, viewed 25 July 2015, www.smh.com. au/politics/federal/choppergate-puts-politicians-perks-under-scrutiny-2015 0724-gijj5o.html.

Sowa, J & Lu, J 2017, 'Policy and management: Considering public management and its relationship to policy studies', *Policy Studies Journal*, vol. 45, no.1, pp. 74–100, doi.org/10.1111/psj.12193.

Stoker, G 2006, 'Public value management: A new narrative for networked governance?', *The American Review of Public Administration*, vol. 36, no. 1, pp. 41–57, doi.org/10.1177/0275074005282583.

Stoker, G, Evans, M & Halupka, M 2018, 'Trust and democracy in Australia: Democratic decline and renewal', report no. 1, Museum of Australian Democracy, Institute of Governance & Policy Analysis, University of Canberra, December, viewed 20 December 2018, apo.org.au/node/208536.

Sullivan, H, Williams, P & Jeffares, S 2012, 'Leadership for collaboration: Situated agency in practice', *Public Management Review*, vol. 14, no. 1, pp. 41–66, doi.org/10.1080/14719037.2011.589617.

Swinford, S 2017, 'Up to 150 Conservative MPs will support motion to oust John Bercow as Speaker after his comments about Donald Trump', *Telegraph*, 9 February, viewed on 13 February 2017, www.telegraph.co.uk/news/2017/ 02/09/conservative-mps-begin-bid-oust-john-bercow-speaker-criticism/.

Thomsen, MK 2017, 'Citizen coproduction: The influence of self-efficacy perception and knowledge of how to coproduce', *The American Review of Public Administration*, vol. 47, no. 3, pp. 340–53, doi.org/10.1177/027507 4015611744.

Thomsen, MK & Jakobsen, M 2015, 'Influencing citizen coproduction by sending encouragement and advice: A field experiment', *International Public Management Journal*, vol. 18, no. 2, pp. 286–303, doi.org/10.1080/109674 94.2014.996628.

Torrance, M 2017, *Governance and administration of the House of Lords*, House of Lords Library Note, 2017/0078, 6 November.

Uberoi, E 2017, *Public engagement in the UK parliament: Overview and statistics*, House of Commons Library briefing paper no. CBP 8158, 24 November, viewed 20 December 2018, researchbriefings.files.parliament.uk/documents/CBP-8158/CBP-8158.pdf.

UK Parliament 2019a, *Speaker Lenthall defends Parliament against the King*, viewed 22 April 2019, www.parliament.uk/about/living-heritage/evolution ofparliament/parliamentaryauthority/civilwar/collections/speakerlenthall/.

UK Parliament 2019b, The Lord Speaker's role, viewed 9 May 2019, www. parliament.uk/business/lords/lord-speaker/the-role-of-lord-speaker/.

Walker, P 2019, 'House of Commons suspended after water pours through ceiling', *Guardian*, 5 April, viewed 23 April 2019, www.theguardian.com/politics/2019/apr/04/house-of-commons-suspended-water-pours-through-ceiling.

Webster, B 2020, 'Citizens' assembly set to devise climate action plan', *Times*, 22 January, viewed 23 January 2020, www.thetimes.co.uk/article/citizens-assembly-set-to-devise-climate-action-plan-lnv7qr7t5.

Weerasinghe, A & Ramshaw, G 2018, 'Fighting democratic decline through parliamentary communications: The case study of the UK parliament', Political Studies Association Specialist Group on Parliaments blog, 31 January, viewed 20 March 2018, psaparliaments.org/2018/01/31/communications-uk-parliament/.

Wegrich, K 2019, 'The blind spots of collaborative innovation', *Public Management Review*, vol. 21, no. 1, pp. 12–20, doi.org/10.1080/14719037.2018.1433311.

Wike, R, Simmons K, Stokes, B & Fetterolf, J 2017, 'Globally, broad support for representative and direct democracy: But many also endorse nondemocratic alternatives', Pew Research Centre, October, viewed 20 December 2018, assets.pewresearch.org/wp-content/uploads/sites/2/2017/10/17102729/Pew-Research-Center_Democracy-Report_2017.10.16.pdf.

Williams, BN, Kang, SC & Johnson, J 2016, '(Co)-contamination as the dark side of co-production: Public value failures in co-production processes', *Public Management Review*, vol. 18, no. 5, pp. 692–717, doi.org/10.1080/14719037. 2015.1111660.

Winnett, R & Rayner, G 2009, *No expenses spared: The inside of the scoop which changed the face of British politics—by the team that broke it*, Bantam, London, UK.

Wintour, P 2014, 'Retiring clerk of Commons makes plea for Speaker to remain neutral', *Guardian*, 25 July, viewed 27 March 2017, www.theguardian.com/politics/2014/jul/24/retiring-clerk-commons-speaker-sir-robert-rogers-john-bercow.

PART 2

Putting policymaking theory into practice

7

Public policy processes in Australia: Reflections from experience[1]

Meredith Edwards[2]

Introduction

I spent 14 years (1983–97) as a senior Commonwealth public servant, mostly as a policy adviser. This was a relatively narrow public service perspective, in that it did not include implementation or corporate roles, yet my experience was broad in other ways. As a public servant, I was twice employed as a ministerial consultant. I was responsible to the secretary of the department while also working to a minister and, unusually, worked from within the bureaucracy rather than on the minister's personal staff.[3] Contributing to a broader view, I came to the public service from academia as a researcher with radical policy ideas, having also built up strong links with non-government organisations. I was therefore more comfortable as a 'boundary player' and being a catalyst for change than were many of my public service colleagues.

---

1   This chapter is a revised and extended version of a contribution commissioned for *Power, parliament and politics: Essays in honour of JR Nethercote*, edited by Henry Ergas and JJ Pincus (forthcoming).
2   I am grateful for insightful comments I received on an earlier draft of this paper from Russell Ayres, Alison Smith, Trish Mercer, Jonathan Pincus and Pamela Burton. I remain responsible for any errors and all views expressed.
3   From 1984, ministers were able to appoint consultants who were not under the Public Service Board. In addition, 'consultants can, with the agreement of the department head, work within the department itself as additions to the public service staff numbers' (Wilenski 1986, p. 194).

I was most fortunate to work in the Hawke–Keating era of activist reform and, in that context, I was able to provide policy advice on a number of major (mainly social) policy changes—which I would call reforms in the true sense of the word[4]—notably:

- simplifying youth allowances
- developing a child support scheme
- introducing the Higher Education Contribution Scheme
- developing a national housing strategy
- assisting long-term unemployed people back into work.

Following the period in which I was most active as a policy adviser, there have been many significant changes in the policy environment that tend to render policy outcomes more uncertain, such as:

- global forces are more influential on domestic issues
- technology is advancing in unanticipated directions
- a 24/7 media cycle has become entrenched and magnified or distorted by social media
- tight budgets, not helped by an ageing population
- society is more networked
- power is more dispersed (including to ministerial advisers and non-government players)
- a blurring of boundaries across sectors
- growing citizen distrust in governments
- increasingly rapid and unpredictable changes in party political leaderships
- parliaments are less stable and minority governments are more common.

In addition, within public services it is now commonly argued that the capability to develop policy and to coordinate responses across government(s) has declined alongside a loss of institutional memory (see e.g. Banks 2014a, p. 14; Donaldson 2018). Not unrelated is an apparent lack of courageous political leadership (Edwards et al. 2017). Despite rhetoric to the contrary, there is much evidence of a risk-averse

---

4   I use reform in the way that Gary Banks (2010, pp. 4–5) does: he suggests 'reform' be used only to refer to policies that lead to change that is likely to lead to a net benefit to the community over time.

public service environment with middle management becoming less, and not more empowered, holding back innovative policy initiatives (Behm 2015, pp. 198–200; Productivity Commission 2017). The then head of the Department of the Prime Minister and Cabinet, Martin Parkinson, called on public servants to: 'Think big. Aim high. Experiment. Be ruthless. Ask the simple questions if something is not working' (as cited in Dennett 2017). But there remains a big gap between the talk and the action.

These factors indicate a very different and more challenging policymaking environment from the 1980s and 1990s. However, most of the fundamentals of good policy process remain, and it is still true that 'good process makes not only for good policy, but ultimately for good politics too' (Banks 2013, p. 2). As such, the 'fundamental principles of good policy processes should be timeless, even if the manner of their execution must adapt to the times' (Banks 2014b, p. 43). Effective policy development still requires good analysis combined with an artful mix of process, people and politics.

The fundamentals remain constant for the three main but related roles of a policy adviser: analytical, administrative and relational. Head (2015, p. 53) describes these roles well:

- The analytical role includes examining and comparing policy options, as well as evaluating current policies and programs.
- The administrative role is about how to proceed with developing policy including coordinating across relevant agencies and paying attention to organisational processes and structures.
- The relational role involves testing how acceptable might be policy choices, consulting, negotiating and ultimately taking into account political and financial constraints.

What follows are my reflections as a policy adviser who played these roles in developing policy in the 1980s and 1990s—reflections that should resonate with policy advisers of today. They may also help inform researchers interested in the practicalities of the policy process.

Seven reflections

Any good policy development process will follow some form of organising framework. Many have appeared in the relevant literature over the past 50 years or so.[5] Despite the complexities of the real world, an attempt at a systematic approach to policy development can deliver significant benefits in addressing policy problems.

In my practice, I used a policy cycle framework that is a variant of Bridgman and Davis's so-called 'policy cycle model' (Althaus, Bridgman & Davis 2018). This framework is reflected in my book on the policy process (Edwards 2001) and is outlined below. But there are several possible levels and modes of analysis of the policy process. What follows, therefore, goes beyond the policy cycle approach to encompass other factors important in achieving successful policy outcomes:

- placing the problem in a broader economic, social and political context
- choosing carefully appropriate organisational processes and structures
- the role of players and the value of their networks
- the role of values and, of course, politics as paramount in achieving policy outcomes.

Considering the context

A policy proposal that is tied to the government's current priorities is likely to get a better hearing than if it is not. A good starting point is the party policy platform and party ideologies, which set the boundaries as to what may and may not be possible in both the short- and longer-term. As a former federal Labor minister, Nicola Roxon, remarked: 'Neglecting to provide advice that reflects the government's platform is one of the biggest ministerial pet peeves' (as cited in Donaldson 2018). This does not require public servants to compromise on providing impartial advice, but they do need to be attuned to the government's agenda.

The economic, social and political context was highly relevant in the policy development processes around the introduction of Australia's Child Support Scheme in the 1980s. This scheme was introduced at a time

---

5   See, for example, Chapter 11 by Louise Gilding in this volume on the use of a blended framework with a strategic triangle as its centrepiece.

of a large budget deficit and government was searching for new revenue sources. But it was also a time of concern about poverty among those on low incomes, particularly sole parent families. Therefore, the ministers for Social Security and Finance at the time both had a stake in a scheme that would reduce pressure on the budget as well as assist in alleviating child poverty. It was the right policy at the right time. Contrast this with the environment that faced the development of a national housing strategy in the late 1980s and early 1990s, when policies put forward to assist low income households in housing stress into rental accommodation failed, despite a comprehensive research process, because the focus of government and the public at that time was on high interest rates that inhibited people from gaining a foothold into home ownership.

Other factors may be relevant in a policy context, such as:

- timing (e.g. when an election is likely to occur)
- institutional arrangements (e.g. 'how' different agencies or levels of government relate to each other)
- the key actors to influence within relevant organisations.

And, of course, political leadership is crucial: Hawke and Keating were leaders who demonstrated political courage by making tough decisions alongside being good communicators and, above all, great persuaders. (How different the scene has been over the last decade!)

Covering all policy stages

The policy environment can be likened to a stormy sea, with the policy adviser trying to take a small boat across choppy waters (Edwards 2010a, p. 425). The effort required is great, and there can be considerable risk, but there can be successful ways to navigate a course.

In the 1980s and 1990s, complex policy issues required involvement of a diverse range of players across sectors. It was a messy policy environment and, at times, politically chaotic. In spite of this, my experience was that identifying stages in policy development as a guiding framework, if used flexibly, can assist considerably in policy advising. In other words, a systematic approach to policy development, such as the policy cycle approach, can deliver significant benefits of order and process in addressing policy problems (see e.g. Althaus, Bridgman & Davis 2018; Banks 2010; Edwards 2004).

Using a policy cycle framework, my book on policy development (Edwards 2001) explained how four major policies developed through each policy stage:

a. clarifying the problem (defining and articulating the issues)
b. understanding key values and other questions
c. policy analysis (collecting relevant data and information and clarifying objectives)
d. undertaking consultation
e. moving towards decisions
f. implementation
g. evaluation.

Because these policy initiatives were significant, complex, cross-departmental and involved politically sensitive issues, it was important to cover each of the policy stages. However, far from being a linear process, it was more like an improvised dance (Althaus, Bridgman & Davis 2018, p. 31). Stages were often visited in a different order, or revisited, and there were backward as well as forward movements across stages, or even overlapping stages. The process can be iterative and adapted to circumstances. In some cases, it would have been inefficient to backtrack; in other cases, backtracking seemed to be the only way through to a solution.

Backtracking on original intent occurred when, for political reasons, the child support proposal needed to be introduced in two phases rather than all in one go. Problem identification can overlap with a policy idea when the policy idea gives momentum to the reform agenda. Similarly, overlaps can occur between policy analysis and consultation, or policy analysis and clarifying the problem. It was clear to me, however, that unless each stage is covered, major policy proposals would have less chance of emerging into reality. A good policy process is necessary, though not sufficient, in most instances, to ensure policy objectives are achieved (Althaus, Bridgman & Davis 2018, p. 52; Banks 2010, p. 63; Keating 1996, p. 63).

Some political scientists have been sceptical of the policy cycle approach. Hal Colebatch, for example, has suggested that it fails to consider the full range of policy actors involved and their relative importance in policymaking (Colebatch 2006). But consultation—tailored to the sensitivity of the issue and who is to be consulted as well as when—is, in fact, taken into account in both the Bridgman and Davis version as well as my own (see below).

It has also been argued, for example by Everett (2003), that the policy cycle is a form of 'rationalism'. Given that policy environments are full of complexities, it is not likely that anything approaching classical rationality in the decision-making process will be observed. As Bridgman and Davis (2003, p. 100), both with public service policy experience, have remarked: 'The policy cycle is logical—each step leads to the next—but does not embody formal rationality'. They would also agree with Banks (2018) that, far from a rigid sequential approach, there will be loops and iterations and that models of 'good process' are about 'what should be rather than what is'.

Despite being controversial among political scientists, in my experience the policy cycle framework can serve as a bridge between the ideal of the process and the practice: as a valuable, if rough, guide to action in pursuing success for a policy position. It certainly was a concept familiar to fellow public servants, and sharing the same language helped us work out together where we were at and what might be the next steps (see Ayres this volume, Chapter 8).

Clarifying the problem: the policy problem needs to be identified and well-articulated for it to be owned by the public. Only once the problem is clarified do people tend to ask: 'what can we do about it?'

In the radical child support reforms of the 1980s, it was relatively easy to articulate the problem: why should kids suffer and taxpayers foot the bill just because parents decide not to live together? By way of contrast, as mentioned above, while there was general agreement that housing affordability was an important issue, there was no agreement on which aspect needed to be addressed.

Sometimes the power of a simple idea assists the articulation of the problem and gets it on the policy agenda. For example, in developing policies to assist the long-term unemployed in the first half of the 1990s, the idea of a 'job compact' provided the necessary underpinnings for policy, and imposing some obligation on the part of the long-term unemployed helped make the policy acceptable to the public (Edwards 2001, p. 178).

The notion of a 'policy window' is relevant here: that window occurs when the acknowledgement of the problem is combined with ideas on a solution that responds to political interest (Kingdon 1995). In this way, the problem, policy proposal and politics all came together. Of course, the language used to communicate to and influence a broad audience about these issues also mattered.

Agenda-setting matters here too. Policy issues can emerge from within as well as outside of government. Ministers are generally better able to place policy problems on a crowded agenda. This might be at their own initiative, although often they react to external pressures.

Understanding values before putting options: too often policy development stalls because policy advisers put policy options to ministers without taking account of the values that will govern their decisions.[6] This is particularly the case when the problem is complex and where there is electoral sensitivity. The trade-off between efficiency in spending and more equity in outcomes is often framed by values (Edwards 2001, p. 181). In cases where decision-makers have deeply held beliefs (e.g. on euthanasia or same sex marriage), then no number of policy options or amount of evidence to support them is likely to make a difference.

Politics ultimately determines whether a policy progresses from stage to stage and at what pace, and values link policy and politics (see e.g. Behm 2015, p. 202; Botterill & Fenna 2019). It may be a frustrating realisation that politicians might be driven more by values and emotion than 'rational' analysis of the evidence before them (Cairney & Kwiatkowski 2017; French 2012). However, as Bromwell (2017, pp. 95–6) has remarked:

> Relying on evidence and empirical analysis alone is like trying to sit on a one-legged stool—it is neither stable nor comfortable for any length of time. Effective policy advisors therefore have to engage not only with relevant data and empirical analysis, but also with emotions and social psychology, and with values and moral argument.

Public servants, therefore, are not in a good position to weigh value-based criteria. This means the policy process can be assisted by ministers giving some direction on values, such as through a set of guiding principles. A statement of principles from ministers can inform the criteria by which options are assessed.

---

6   For example, in the case of the reform of youth allowances in the 1980s, in the absence of such ministerial guidance, at one stage, the relevant interdepartmental committee put before ministers 16 options also referring to numerous other options that could be considered (see Edwards 2001, p. 29).

My experience was that, where it was possible, confronting ministers early with key issues before presenting them with policy options helped them to clarify their objectives and speeded up the policy process. The issues stage could be made easier if the process started with possible areas on which ministers could agree and then moved onto harder decisions from which principles were derived, and that took into account political values. This is often a point in the process that is missed in traditional textbooks on the policy process. In the case of child support, whether to use an administrative or a court-based system needed to be argued and decided before dealing with the issue of whether to use a formula and, in turn, that issue was to be decided before the critical issue of what government agency should assess, collect and enforce payments (Edwards 2001, p. 72).

The *policy analysis* phase is where policy advisers can really show their expertise. Relevant data and research are analysed and options are assessed for likely consequences, based on an understanding of the decision-maker's value framework and on key criteria, such as efficiency, equity and administrative feasibility.[7] This is also the stage at which key players—internal to government as well as external stakeholders—can be expected to participate closely, and where their differences are likely to emerge.

It is unrealistic to expect pure 'evidence-based policy' when policy and politics mix. A purist approach is flawed if it does not take into account people and their values or beliefs, or the politics, including where power lies. However, evidence-*influenced* policy can lead to both good policy and good politics (Head 2015). When the environment is receptive, evidence can be powerful both in clarifying a problem and in moving towards a solution.

Once ministers have decided what they want to do—as a consequence of their political values and/or pressure from their electors or party supporters—they will seek evidence to support their decision so that they can justify the policy in public (see e.g. Strangio, 't Hart & Walter 2017, pp. 227–8). Often what is sought, therefore, is more 'policy-influenced evidence' or 'values-influenced evidence' rather than evidence-influenced policy. This challenges public servants who want to stay clear of values and politics in selecting evidence.

---

7   For example, see criteria used for Child Support and HECS in Edwards (2001, pp. 75–6, 115–16, 118).

Apart from the need to tailor evidence to the nature of the policy issue, I found different forms of evidence were needed at different stages of the policy cycle.[8] Evidence about better practice, especially overseas comparisons, I found to be of great benefit in developing policies. There is substantial value in policy transfer from other countries, if ideas are adapted appropriately to local circumstances.

It is also important to 'curate' the evidence: to decide who should get the evidence and why, from whom it should come and why, as well as deciding what the decision-makers need and when, and the best ways to communicate it. This is particularly challenging today as the public appears more selective about what evidence to trust in a 'post-truth' world.

In the *consultation* phase, participation by stakeholders and, more broadly, citizens who are potentially affected by a possible decision, will vary depending on the nature of the issue, its complexity and sensitivity. Processes could be formal or informal, continuous or episodic. Who to consult, why, when in the policy process and how, are critical process issues (see Edwards et al. 2012, pp. 53–172). Good judgement is needed. Today, engaging stakeholders, if not co-designing with them, is recognised as more important; yet, at the same time, there appears to be a disjuncture between that recognition and reality (see e.g. Beauchamp 2016, p. 90; Burgess 2017).

Moving to policy decisions: ultimately, following refinement of original proposals, the pivotal stage occurs and policy decisions emerge in what can be a highly political context. This is where the political, policy and administrative impacts of a proposal are weighed and Cabinet consideration brings all perspectives together and 'arguments translate to a decision' (see Althaus, Bridgman & Davis 2018, p. 169; Shergold 2015, pp. 26–30).

In all my major policy experience, *implementation* of Cabinet decisions was the most neglected and poorly performed policy stage. Too often, ministers announced their decisions but then lost interest as they refocused on new issues on the agenda. There are many factors that can derail policy intent, including lack of clarity around interpretation of the decision as well as respective responsibilities in the implementation process, insufficient resources allocated, insufficient attention to coordination and

---

8   See *Working Nation* example in Edwards (2010b, p. 59).

collaboration across agencies, or a shortage of time (Edwards et al. 2012, pp. 223, 230). Despite recent focus on policy implementation, there often still appears to be a disconnect between policy aims and delivery reality.

Evaluation is the final stage in policy development in which questions of effectiveness, efficiency and continued appropriateness of objectives are assessed. Ideally it is also a stage of policy learning. A good evaluation process, as occurred in the early 1990s on long-term unemployment issues, is incorporated into the policy process before the decision stage. Evaluation needs to be timely, involve a range of people who hold a stake in the policy or program, and ensure a wide dissemination of results (Edwards 2010a, p. 421; Keating 2017, p. 2).

Evaluation can be highly political. For example, evaluation documents can be changed as they proceed from technical experts and ultimately on to the minister. In addition, those best able to assess the impact of a change, such as frontline workers, are not necessarily involved.

A welcome recent sign is the greater acknowledgement of the need to experiment with new approaches and 'learning from failure' alongside the monitoring of outcomes (Althaus, Bridgman & Davis 2018, p. 14; Shergold 2015, pp. 63–82; Productivity Commission 2017, p. 203).

Attending to organisational structures and processes

A framework of stages in developing policy is only part of the story if desired policy outcomes are to have a chance to succeed. A common thread in good policy processes (often not given due attention in the theory of policymaking) is careful consideration of the organisational structures and processes within which policy work occurs.

A successful policy adviser will give attention to both strategy and tactics, not just addressing the important or high level ends as well as means, but also tactics to deal with more immediate matters and to manage daily processes (see Behm 2015, pp. 197–8). In fact, the single most important lesson I learnt from my time as a public servant, as keen and impatient as I was to get desired outcomes, was the critical role of processes and structures if desired outcomes were to have any chance of success.

Ministers can tactically bypass interdepartmental committees and use other less conventional or more innovative mechanisms such as carefully selected task forces that might include not only public servants, but also ministerial advisers and or external experts, or taskforces of relevant ministers (see e.g. Edwards 2001, p. 185).

Some of the key questions I found that a policy adviser might need to assess include:

- What *structures* best fit the task? Are structures needed for a whole-of-government approach or something less cross-cutting? Is there to be an interdepartmental committee or a taskforce or some other arrangement?
- What *policy stages* are to be followed and in what order? Is there to be formal consultation or informal consultations? Are these to be ongoing or episodic? If a formal process, are meetings to be made public or just bilateral? Is the evaluation to be internal or external?
- If the *policy issue* has a longer-term objective, can it be achieved in one budget measure or should the policy objective be phased in over time?
- Should the policy issue from a line agency be shared first with central agencies and/or go before a minister or ministers for guidance?
- *Who* should be involved: Which agencies, public servants, ministerial advisers and non-government players? When in the process should they be involved? What accountabilities should they have?

These are examples of how a policy official can exercise agency as described by Mackie (this volume, Chapter 9). A key consideration is how policy advisers interact with ministerial staff, as described below.

Dealing with ministers and their staff

A minister (or group of ministers) is pivotal in the policy process; therefore, 'managing up' effectively to a minister can take considerable skill, including, critically, learning on-the-job about their relevant characteristics. Are they extravert or introvert? Do they think in pictures and need oral briefing or do they prefer reading words on a page? Are they highly intuitive or more analytical? Former minister Nicola Roxon provided some advice to public servants, including to be 'strategically smart and adapt advice' by framing it based on who you are talking to, and 'ascertain at the beginning if your minister is a talker or a reader when it comes to processing advice' (as cited in Donaldson 2018).

The relationship of ministers and their staff with the public service has evolved over the decades (see Edwards 2002; Holland 2006; Maley 2000; Nethercote 2002). In the 1980s, the attitude of some senior public servants with whom I worked was that 'ministers come and go, but we remain'. At that time, ministers answered for the actions of officials (as well as their advisers). By the early 1990s, as a consequence of a series of deliberate changes to public service tenure, departmental structures and reward systems, the balance of power had switched to the political executive. This put public servants in the frontline, defending ministers and their staff (Nethercote 2002). Today there are more ministerial advisers than ever before (although not necessarily with the same level of policy expertise as in the past).

A learning experience for me arose from a media article in 1996 that claimed that senior officials in the Department of the Prime Minister and Cabinet (PM&C) regarded the advisers in the Prime Minister's Office (PMO) as 'amateurish'. Of course, this claim sparked fury from the PMO and also from the prime minister himself. The article came some months after an intensive effort by senior PM&C officials to build up good relationships with the newly elected Prime Minister Howard and his staff (Edwards 2002). Such a setback can quickly destroy trust that might have taken months to build up. This illustrates how important it is to take care in building up and maintaining a respectful relationship with a minister's office, however time-consuming that may be. This is a precondition for being able to offer 'frank and fearless' advice.

Placing value on networks and relationships

The role of relationships and policy networks of players, at whatever stage of the policy process, should never be underrated in assisting policy development and affecting its outcomes (see Althaus, Bridgman & Davis 2018, p. 229–30; Behm 2015, pp. 215–16; Edwards 2004, p. 6). Aside from a minister or ministers, key players could include elected officials, public servants, interest groups, non-government organisations from the community, business and elsewhere, researchers, consultants and think tanks, and also the media. People who you know or have known in various capacities, both inside and outside government, can often turn out to be valuable later on in assisting a policy agenda move on.

Informal networks of key players were especially important in putting long-term unemployment on the agenda in the early 1990s, in which key ministerial advisers, bureaucrats and academics were in constant contact through informal processes (see examples in Edwards 2001, pp. 145–6, 188; Edwards & Stewart 2017, p. 341). They were also beneficial in the case of child support, in which informal contacts with the legal profession, social welfare and women's groups assisted in minimising adverse comments on the proposed reform.

Collaborating or 'managing across' with people from other agencies inside government to the outside and vice versa is needed if any complex policy issue is to move towards a resolution. Importantly, it needs to be a strategic process about why collaboration is needed, when it should occur, with whom and how. It may mean up-front informal bilateral discussions followed by broader collaborations depending on the sensitivity and complexity of the issue.

Today policy advisers' networks have widened as the sources of policy advice to ministers have broadened. Although policy advising remains a major function of public servants, increasingly they compete with private and other non-government advisers.

Managing the researcher–policy practitioner interface

Not all research is, or should be, attempting to inform policy. There currently exists a real conflict here for academics who, while wanting to have policy influence, face incentive structures in universities that emphasise publications in what are rated as quality journals.

However, there is considerable evidence that, if research is to better inform policy, it is not the written word as much as dialogue, interaction (e.g. in round tables) and ongoing related mechanisms (and relationships) between policy practitioners and researchers that work best (see Australia and New Zealand School of Government [ANZSOG] 2007; Head & Crowley 2015; Nutley, Walter & Davies 2007). Moreover, that dialogue is helped if the issues discussed are of concern to the government of the day. Busy policy people will use trusted experts, but otherwise are not in the habit of reading what are often dense research papers.

None of the major social policy exercises in which I was involved would likely have seen the light of day without the involvement of academic researchers at key stages in policy development. However, the success stories were of researchers going beyond their written words to interact and engage with policymakers and to convince them of the worth of their ideas. Hence the importance of dialogue and of building relationships and trust across the sectors.

In 2007, an ANZSOG project interviewed senior public servants and academics on both sides of the Tasman to find out what research they would most value. In the process the fragility of the academic–public servant relationship came to the fore, best illustrated by one humorous (if it were not so pointed) rhetorical question from a senior official: 'What is the difference between an academic and a terrorist? You can negotiate with a terrorist.' More positively, they identified the need for round tables with experts on issues of concern to them and also the use of knowledge brokers to assist in bridging the researcher–policy practitioner gap (ANZSOG 2007).

If policy influence is the goal, then, as unpalatable as it may seem to some, research cannot be a standalone activity; rather, it should be viewed, as policymaking is—more as part of a process. To be clear, for research to impact on policy, it needs to be part of the policy process and vice versa.

My case studies on developing policy indicate that policy ideas from academics can assist in moving a policy forward. For example, the idea of using the tax system to assess and collect child support came from an American researcher. But that is not to deny that the greatest value of academic policy research usually comes in assisting in identifying the problem and in analysis, if not also evaluation (Edwards 2010b, pp. 59–61).

Being pragmatic and managing ambiguity

A policy idea can at times assist ministers get out of a bind with a particular problem that has so far not been resolved, but it rarely translates into practice without significant modification. Second best or even third best solutions may need to be accepted. Hence, anyone involved in the policy process needs to be pragmatic about what can be achieved, including dealing with trade-offs and ambiguity—from policy objectives to policy decisions. French (2012, p. 538), a former minister in the Canadian Government, refers to 'fast and frugal forms of rationality that sacrifice any pretence to optimisation'.

Trade-offs are the name of the game for policy and political players. They come in many forms, for example, between exercising strong leadership and dealing collaboratively within networks; facing political demands, including short time-spans while also facing a shortage of resources; being responsive to a minister's agenda while the public support for it might be lacking; and managing risk or fearing failure while also being innovative.

Relationships get tested when there is more than one person to whom you 'manage up'. As a ministerial consultant working out of a department, I was answerable to the secretary of the department as well as the minister. I faced the same uncertainty when working from PM&C on youth allowance policy but reporting to a line minister who was assisting the prime minister on youth affairs.

A highly valued skill of a person who provides policy advice is good judgement. This is hard to define and is partly based on experience, but also in some ways it is innate. Good judgement relates to having clarity about the longer-term desired outcomes and being able to use both a strategic and tactical approach to get there, accepting trade-offs and being adaptable so as to take political sensitivities into account. An example would be involving those who are to be responsible for implementing a policy in the early stages of policy development: knowing when to take notice and when to challenge them on possible implementation hurdles (see e.g. Edwards 2001, pp. 84, 95).

There is a related need to be able to deal with ambiguity. A senior policy adviser will often leave a meeting with a minister or ministers without clarity around what was meant by what was said. How a policy adviser responds to that circumstance is obviously going to be critical. Good judgement is required on how to gain the needed clarification, including assessing whether the minister actually understood what was said at the briefing session or, rather, judged it best politically not to have that clarification.

Concluding observations

Coming towards the end of my working life, most of which has been spent either assisting in the development of policy or commenting on policy-related processes and issues, I remain of the view that a policy development framework can be invaluable in contributing to good policy processes being followed. However, even as a normative framework, it can be rather sterile, if not simplistic to follow, if used on its own. As indicated above, the organisational structures and processes within which policy analysis occurs is important. Also important is the combination of players for any policy exercise—ministers, their advisers, public servants, academics and other non-government players. Both academics wanting to be boundary players with the public sector and public servants wanting to be more outward focused need to engage in dialogue and interaction. Above all of this, of course, is the paramount importance of that least in control factor for policy advisers—the politics: it determines whether policy progresses from stage to stage and, if it does, at what pace.

Let me end on a most salutary reflection: regardless of hard you might try, any good policy outcome you may have had some input into can be eroded, if not reversed, sometime in the future. However, as this contribution has attempted to show, the more effort put into the process of developing policy, the more durable it is likely to be.

References

Althaus, C, Bridgman, P & Davis, G 2018, *The Australian policy handbook: A practical guide to the policy-making process*, 6th edn, Allen & Unwin, Crows Nest, NSW.

Australia and New Zealand School of Government (ANZSOG) 2007, 'Enhancing ANZSOG's contribution to better government: Future research directions', Research Reference Group, October.

Banks, G 2010, 'Successful reform: Past lessons, future challenges', Keynote address to the Annual Forecasting Conference of the Australian Business Economists, Sydney, 8 December.

Banks, G 2013, 'Good processes underpin strong innovative policy', *Australian Financial Review*, 22 March, p. 2.

Banks, G 2014a, *The governance of public policy: Lectures in honour of eminent Australians*, ANZSOG, Carlton, Vic.

Banks, G 2014b, 'Return of the rent-seeking society [Stan Kelly Lecture, The Economic Society of Australia, Melbourne, August 2013]', in G Banks, *The governance of public policy: Lectures in honour of eminent Australians*, ANZSOG, Carlton, Vic.

Banks, G 2018, 'Whatever happened to "evidence based policy making"?' Alf Rattigan Lecture 2018, ANZSOG, Carlton, Vic.

Beauchamp, G 2016, 'The role of government in innovation', in *Twelve speeches 2016: A year of speeches from public service leaders,* Institute of Public Administration Australia, Barton, ACT.

Behm, A 2015, *No, minister: So you want to be a chief of staff?*, Melbourne University Press, Carlton, Vic.

Botterill, L & Fenna, A 2019, *Interrogating public policy theory: A political values perspective*, Edward Elgar, Cheltenham, UK, doi.org/10.4337/9781784710088.

Bridgman, P & Davis, G 2003, 'What use is a policy cycle? Plenty, if the aim is clear', *Australian Journal of Public Administration*, vol. 63, no. 2, pp. 98–102, doi.org/10.1046/j.1467-8500.2003.00342.x.

Bromwell, D 2017, *The art and craft of policy advising: A practical guide*, Springer International Publishing, Cham, Switzerland, doi.org/10.1007/978-3-319-52494-8.

Burgess, V 2017, 'It has home-grown hindsight, but can the public change?' *Mandarin*, 4 October.

Cairney, P & Kwiatkowski, R 2017, 'The politics of evidence-based policymaking: How can we maximize the use of evidence in policymaking?', *Palgrave Communications Special Issue,* Palgrave, New York, NY.

Colebatch, H 2006, *Beyond the policy cycle: The policy process in Australia*, Allen & Unwin, Sydney, NSW.

Dennett, H 2017, 'Get ready for more disruption: Parkinson floats national citizen survey', *Mandarin*, 12 December.

Donaldson, D 2018, '"Urgent": Former secretaries assess public service capability', *Mandarin*, 12 February.

Edwards, M 2001, *Social policy, public policy: From problem to practice*, Allen & Unwin, Sydney, NSW.

Edwards, M 2002, 'Ministerial advisers and the search for accountability', *Canberra Bulletin of Public Administration,* no. 105, September.

Edwards, M 2004, *Social science research and public policy: Narrowing the divide,* Occasional paper, Policy paper no. 2, Academy of the Social Sciences, Canberra, ACT.

Edwards, M 2010a, 'The policy-making process', in D Woodward, A Parkin & J Summers (eds), *Government, politics, power and policy in Australia,* 9th edn, Pearson Australia, Frenchs Forest, NSW.

Edwards, M 2010b, 'Making research more relevant to policy: Evidence and suggestions', in G Bammer, A Michaux, A Sanson (eds), *Bridging the 'know–do' gap: Knowledge brokering to improve child well-being,* ANU E Press, Canberra, ACT, doi.org/10.22459/BKDG.08.2010.04.

Edwards, M, Halligan, J, Horrigan, B & Nicoll, G 2012, *Public sector governance in Australia,* ANU E Press, Canberra ACT, doi.org/10.22459/PSGA.07.2012.

Edwards, M, Head, B, Tiernan, A & Walter, J 2017, 'Policy capacity decline: Trends, causes and remedies', paper presented to the Australian Political Studies Association Conference, Monash University, 25–27 September.

Edwards, M & Stewart, M 2017, 'Pathways and processes: Toward a gender equality policy', in M Stewart (ed.) *Tax, social policy and gender*, ANU Press, Canberra ACT, doi.org/10.22459/TSPG.11.2017.11.

Everett, S 2003, 'The policy cycle: Democratic process or rational paradigm revisited?', *Australian Journal of Public Administration,* vol. 62, no. 2, pp. 65–70, doi.org/10.1111/1467-8497.00325.

French, R 2012, 'The professors on public life', *The Political Quarterly,* vol. 83, no. 3, pp. 532–40, doi.org/10.1111/j.1467-923X.2012.02320.x.

Head, B 2015, 'Toward more "evidence-informed" policy making?', *Public Administration Review,* vol. 76, no. 3, pp. 472–84, doi.org/10.1111/puar.12475.

Head, B & Crowley, K (eds) 2015, *Policy analysis in Australia,* Policy Press, Bristol, UK, doi.org/10.1332/policypress/9781447310273.001.0001.

Holland, I 2006, 'Parliamentary committees as an arena for policy work', in H Colebatch (ed.), *Beyond the policy cycle: The policy process in Australia,* Allen & Unwin, Sydney, NSW.

Keating, M 1996, 'Defining the policy advising function', in J Uhr & K McKay (eds), *Evaluating policy advice,* Federalism Research Centre, ANU and Commonwealth Department of Finance, Canberra, ACT.

Keating, M 2017, 'The Productivity Commission on more effective government. Part 2 of 2', *John Menadue – Pearls and Irritations*, 14 December, viewed 5 March 2020, johnmenadue.com/michael-keating-the-productivity-commission-on-more-effective-government-part-2-of-2/.

Kingdon, J 1995, *Agendas, alternatives and public policies,* Harper and Collins, New York, NY.

Maley, M 2000, 'Conceptualising advisers' policy work: The distinctive policy roles of ministerial advisers in the Keating government, 1991–96', *Australian Journal of Political Science*, vol. 35, no. 3, pp. 449–70, doi.org/10.1080/713649346.

Nethercote, JR 2002, 'What servants are for', *Sydney Morning Herald Web Diary,* 27 June.

Nutley, S, Walter, I & Davies, H 2007, *Using evidence: How research can inform public services,* Policy Press, Bristol, UK, doi.org/10.2307/j.ctt9qgwt1.

Productivity Commission 2017, *Shifting the dial: 5 year productivity review,* Productivity Commission, Canberra, ACT.

Shergold, P 2015, *Learning from failure: Why large government policy initiatives have gone so badly wrong in the past and how the chances of success in the future can be improved,* APSC, Canberra, ACT.

Strangio, P, 't Hart, P & Walter, J 2017, *The pivot of power,* Miegunyah Press, Carlton, Vic.

Wilenski, P 1986, *Public power and public administration,* Hale and Iremonger, Sydney, NSW.

8

Using the policy cycle: Practice into theory and back again

Russell Ayres[1]

USE LARGE MAPS. (Cary 1944, p. 374)[2]

Introduction: Context and focus

My professional practice as a senior public servant between 2004 and 2016 was very much informed by my knowledge of policymaking theory and research. In that period, I led several policy, evaluation and program design teams in the Australian Public Service (APS). The observations and conclusions outlined here are based on my 'lived experience' as a senior policy officer in Australian Government social policy departments. My approach was effectively a form of 'action research', which is a valuable

---

1   I am indebted to Professor Meredith Edwards and Dr Trish Mercer for invaluable comments on earlier drafts of this chapter.
2   In Cary's 1944 novel, *The horse's mouth*, the artist Gully Jimson gives this advice to his young protégé in the closing scenes. He tells Nosey that the world is unfair, messy and difficult to negotiate; the best you can hope for is to have a sense of humour, a willingness to press on regardless and a 'map'— which is, of course, an abstract simplification, a theory or mental model—to help guide you. And, according to Jimson, it is advisable to use 'large maps' (i.e. abstract depictions that nonetheless reflect the terrain you are seeking to traverse). Policymakers could do worse than heed Jimson's advice when trying to understand the complex, messy and difficult world of public policy analysis, advice and implementation.

approach when seeking to generate discussion and debate within and across the domains of practice and theory (Creswell & Poth 2018; Ely et al. 1991).

In the mid-1990s—following a 12-year career in the APS—I undertook doctoral research at the University of Canberra. Completing my PhD—'Policy markets in Australia'—involved gaining a deep and broad understanding of the theory and literature around how public policy is (or ought) to be created. Towards the end of my candidature, I began working as an independent public policy consultant and trainer, a role I maintained for five years. In 2004, I returned to the APS and completed another 10 years in the service, mostly at the senior executive service level.

Summary of the approach

Box 8.1 provides a summary of how I sought to bring policy theory into the APS. It was a somewhat 'covert' approach, whereby I used my various roles as a manager and leader in policy branches to introduce my colleagues to some of the ideas around policymaking. I focused on the policy cycle framework, but also discussed some other perspectives, especially from the literature around policy systems.

Box 8.1. Summary of the approach.

Premise: there is no such thing as a theory-free public service, but there can be 'theory blindness' among practitioners.

Observation: there is a culture of pragmatic scepticism in the APS that occasionally takes the form of a casual, cynical dismissal of 'academic' approaches, and is sometimes mirrored in academia by a dismissal of 'practitioners'.

Approach: I took an understated, low-key approach to theory mainly with more junior colleagues (i.e. less imbued with dominant culture).

Model: I used a version of the Australian policy cycle (Althaus, Bridgman & Davis 2018) mixed with a little disjointed incrementalism, a taste of 'garbage can' and, every now and then, a dash of complex systems.

In line with John Maynard Keynes's observation that 'practical men who believe themselves to be quite exempt from any intellectual influence, are usually the slaves of some defunct economist', I believe there is no such thing as 'theory-free' action in government. Indeed, it is oxymoronic to conceive of policymaking as unshaped by theory. That said, there can be a form of 'theory blindness', in which practitioners fail to reflect on the underlying rationale for their policymaking and what constitutes 'good' (i.e. effective, efficient) policymaking process and what does not. One of the reasons I sought to promote the theoretical underpinnings of policymaking was to help reduce the risk of theory blindness undermining a reflective, learning-based approach to policy development among the teams I led.

Linked to the risk of theory blindness is what I perceived as a tendency to 'pragmatic scepticism' as part of the APS mindset (Mercer this volume, Chapter 3). A pragmatic policymaking approach has much to recommend it, especially as an antidote to reflexive ideology in political decision-making, and it is very much a part of the Australian (and New Zealand) tradition in public administration (Davis et al. 1993; Fabian & Breunig 2018; Halligan 1995; Head & Crowley 2015).

The APS partakes of the general Australian scepticism about academia and the world of experts. In principle, scepticism is healthy and productive, but sometimes it tips into wilful blindness—an unwillingness to see that experts and academics might have useful things to say to those who are looking to improve their professional practice.[3] Given this culture, I generally took a low-key approach to policymaking theory as a factor shaping practice. However, from time to time, I ran information sessions on the theory of policymaking for my own staff, the content of which is the basis of this chapter.

The APS can be particularly sceptical about 'experts' or 'academics' who do not demonstrate a sufficiently grounded understanding of, or experience in, the realities of government. This is understandable, if somewhat frustrating to academics. A fast-moving, uncertain and ambiguous environment demands an approach that is flexible ('agile' in current parlance) and not overly constrained by the straightjacket of a rigid theory or prescription about how the work ought, in an ideal world, to proceed. Not dwelling too much on theory can also promote a 'bias to action' (or 'cut through'), allowing the APS to more rapidly and effectively

---

3   A sceptical mindset can also be a form of psychological defence. If you are given the task of taking a government's agenda and policy direction and finding ways to implement it, an analytical framework that encourages starting with deep questions around problem identification and questioning priorities can be distracting (or even disheartening) when dealing with the cut and thrust of government and public administration.

take the government's policy positions to implementation, achieving the 'deliverables' and 'outcomes' beloved of the new public management approach (Ayres 2001a; Hood 1995; Lane 2000).

Sometimes, official scepticism about the value of theory in the art and craft of policymaking can seem rather self-serving. Jocular references to laws being like sausages (in that it is best not to see how they are made— erroneously attributed to Otto von Bismarck) are occasionally used to deflect inquiry into how and why decisions of government are made. This tends to create a 'black box' effect around the decision-making process, shrouding it in mystery. This approach is sometimes coupled with references to the particular way of thinking that is required to 'do' policy in government. Officers are sometimes identified as possessing (or not possessing) a 'policy brain', without any real articulation of precisely what this is, or why it seems to be something inherent in the individual and not able to be learned. It can seem as though there is a 'priesthood' of elite policy officers, with their own secrets and specialist knowledge, acquired through being admitted to the inner sanctum of government and not to be divulged in any detail to external scrutiny or critique.

Implicit in this approach is a level of exclusivity: if you are inside the 'black box', the box does not have to be explained to you. You experience it every day of your professional life, and your knowledge of it is implicit and rarely examined or critiqued. This is 'learning by doing', with a quasi-apprenticeship model applied to the recruitment and on-the-job training of young public servants who are considered to have a 'policy brain' and concomitant skills of analysis and written and oral communication, and the capacity to take general propositions and create practical policy propositions, implementation plans and so on.

I do not want to overstate the case here; this tendency is neither uniform nor universal within the APS. Attitudes towards theorising about policymaking vary from individual to individual, between organisations and from issue to issue. Many public servants working in policy roles are curious about policymaking theory. They seek and consume academic literature on the topic and attend seminars, conferences and workshops to hear what academics, researchers and theoreticians have to say about policymaking. They take a critical interest in political, economic and business-based models of decision-making and implementation, adopting and adapting ideas from diverse disciplinary fields. But the underlying character of the institution remains sceptical, pragmatic and with a 'bias for action' that does not engage deeply or in a sustained way with theory, ideas or concepts.

As a senior public servant, I was on the continuum between 'theory-oriented' and 'practice-oriented', and found myself moving up and down it, depending on the circumstances. As a general preference, I gravitated to the rational-comprehensive approach embodied in the policy cycle. I did not do this because I thought the policy cycle is always the best explanation or description of how policy gets made and implemented. Rather, I thought the policy cycle approach was the best known and most easily communicated framework available to assist understanding and communicating how policy development and implementation might, in an ideal sense, be done.[4]

As a leader of several policy teams, I also thought that, for many public servants to properly grasp what the policy cycle is about, it was best to start with their own day-to-day experience. I sought to guide my colleagues towards a way of seeing theory as relevant, even useful, to their professional goals. The next section explains how I sought to do that.

Building a policy cycle from the bottom up

This section outlines the presentation I prepared for several teams I led in the APS, especially in the various incarnations of the current Department of Education, Skills and Employment. These included teams working on specific policy and implementation issues in early childhood education and care, and in research and development. I also used this presentation for teams working on program evaluation. These teams were generally working under tight timeframes with considerable pressure to deliver particular outputs, such as Cabinet submissions, Commonwealth–state agreements, program implementation plans and guidelines, or evaluation strategies and plans. The culture was generally action-oriented and task-

---

4   There is an extensive literature on different types of policy frameworks. I acknowledge considerable debt to authors such as Lindblom and Woodhouse (1993), Lasswell (1951), May (1998), Edwards (2001), Bridgman and Davis (2003), Considine (2005), Colebatch (2009), deLeon (1998), Di Francesco and Uhr (1996), Halligan (1995), Head and Crowley (2015), Parsons (2002), Peters (1998), Schon and Rein (1994) and Stewart (1999). I also draw on previous publications with Jenny Stewart (Stewart & Ayres 2001a, 2001b).

focused. I therefore decided to use inductive reasoning ('bottom up') rather than the usual deductive ('top down') approach that is common in presenting or explaining the policy cycle.

My aim was to take my colleagues' own experiences in their work as policy officers and resolve these down to their most fundamental components, before building them back up to a reasonably consistent heuristic they could use to understand at least some of the theory behind what they did on a day-to-day basis. I also encouraged them to exercise some of their natural scepticism to critique the theory when it did not seem to fit or help in their practice. The model towards which I built was a variant on the excellent Australian policy cycle devised by Althaus, Bridgman and Davis (2018). My aim was to draw out the implicit concepts and mental models that public servants use and blend them with the explicit policy cycle model.

Step 1: The two things public servants do

This is the starting point. Every public servant would acknowledge there are two fundamental things they collectively do in their day-to-day work (see Figure 8.1). Public servants:

- advise government so it has information on which to base its decisions
- implement government's decisions, including coordinating the work of third parties.

It is important to note that, even in this highly simplified model, there is a feedback loop between the two elements. This shows that the advice mode influences the implementation mode and vice versa. I included this feedback loop to allow for the later development of a form of complex systems thinking (as a more advanced version of my approach) if that seemed warranted. This feedback loop also reflected the importance of early and close involvement of those responsible for implementation—including public servants, service providers and other governments—to help ground policy advice in a sound understanding of the constraints and possibilities of implementation.

- Sometimes public servants advise
- Sometimes they implement
- Creates a feedback loop

Advise ———(influence/direct)———▶ Implement
(feedback/inform)

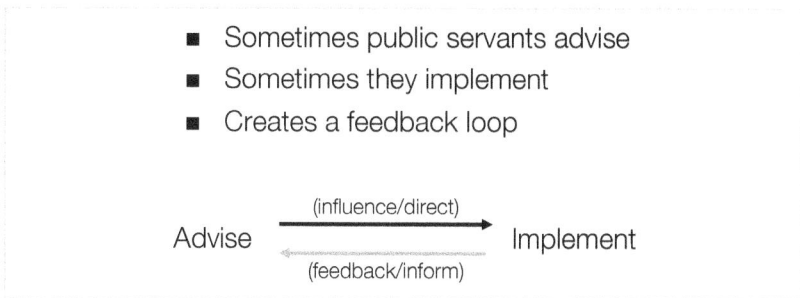

Figure 8.1. Step 1: The two things public servants do.

My 'real world' experience tended to greatly complicate this obviously oversimplified picture. For example, in 2013 I led a small policy team in the Department of Education tasked with advising the Abbott government on the terms of reference for a major Productivity Commission (PC) inquiry into childcare and early education. The team continued once the inquiry was established, managing the department's interactions with the inquiry team and providing advice and analysis to both the PC and the assistant minister for education, Sussan Ley. The PC's final report was released in October 2014.

In one sense, the team was in advising mode, as we were not implementing a program or initiative on behalf of the government. However, many of the policy parameters had already been determined. The Coalition had fought the 2013 election campaign in part on the basis of a commitment to hold a PC inquiry to advise on how the national system of childcare and early childhood education could be made more 'flexible, affordable and accessible' (Liberal Party of Australia 2013) for parents and more effective in supporting carers' (mainly mothers') workforce participation. The new government was also very keen to ensure childcare funding was fiscally sustainable, having previously issued draft terms of reference for the proposed inquiry (Liberal Party of Australia 2012).

From that standpoint, the team I led might be characterised as implementing an agenda already determined by the government. Many issues, however, were not well known or understood, and there was a need for significant analysis of the options around childcare funding and regulation. Therefore, I focused the team on analysis and modelling options rather than assuming that the policy position was fixed and clear.

Step 2: Add in 'decide'

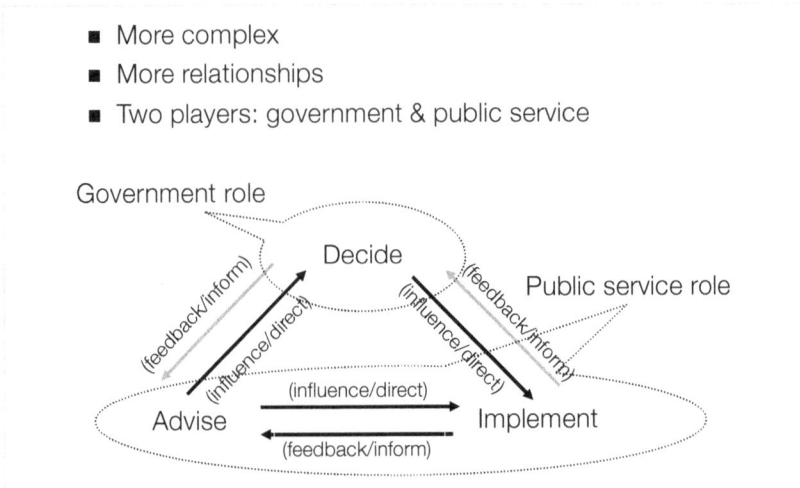

- More complex
- More relationships
- Two players: government & public service

Government role

Decide

Public service role

(feedback/inform)

(influence/direct)

(influence/direct)

(feedback/inform)

(influence/direct)

(feedback/inform)

Advise

Implement

Figure 8.2. Step 2: Add 'decide'.

Building on the simplified model derived from public servants' 'felt' experience in Step 1, I introduced the element of 'decision' and the role of government (see Figure 8.2). I would emphasise to my colleagues that this is still a highly idealised model—neither descriptive (empirical) nor normative (prescriptive). Rather, it is a heuristic: a rule of thumb guide. It borrows a little from the 'is' of empirical description (because it is grounded in how public servants tend to work) and a little from the 'ought' of normative prescription (because it refines the process to a set of steps or phases), but is not really either. Like all conceptual models, it cannot match the complexity and contingency of the real world. In conveying this point to colleagues, I would note that:

- governments obtain advice from many sources and they often use non-public service institutions and individuals to implement their agendas[5]
- public servants are empowered to make decisions, either through formal, legislative delegation or through convention

---

5   In 1997, Prime Minister John Howard articulated the principle of contestable policy advice in a speech on the Australian Government's expectations of the public service (Howard 1998).

- the functions of advice and implementation are not always distinct, especially in organisational structures within government, and sometimes within the briefs given to external agents, such as policy consultants and service providers.[6]

Nevertheless, the model as I presented it was getting closer to a framework that could be used as a rough guide in the real world of public policy and administration.

Step 3: Complete the basic problem-solving model

As shown at Figure 8.3, I add the evaluation function at this point. I do this partly because I have a background in program evaluation and I often lead teams with a role in evaluation, especially in education, early childhood and Indigenous programs. I also add evaluation because I have a background in total quality management, and I sometimes highlight W Edwards Deming's (1986) quality improvement model, which also has four elements:

- plan
- do
- check
- act.

While the Deming model does not directly map to the policy cycle, there are some interesting similarities at the level of project management and operations between the world of policy and its implementation on the one hand, and the world of systems management and engineering on the other.

I called this the 'problem-solving' stage of the model, because it is similar to the many problem-solving cycles used by management consultants, perhaps most famously developed and promoted by McKinsey & Company (see Chia 2018). The language and frameworks of management consulting are familiar to many public servants, as they are often exposed to the work of consultants and the implicit and explicit models they use.

---

6   See, for example, the role played by ACIL management consultants in driving industrial relations on the Australian waterfront in the 1990s (Ayres 2001b). Service providers are often engaged both as delivery agents of government and as participants in the policy development process, especially the larger not-for-profit organisations such as the Brotherhood of St Laurence.

- Add evaluation
- Basic problem-solving cycle

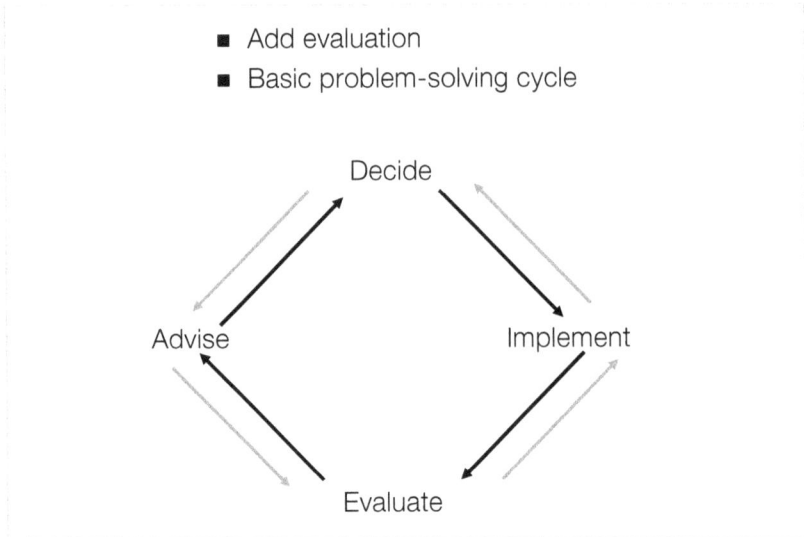

Figure 8.3. Step 3: Complete the basic problem-solving model.

Building evaluation into the model was always an important step for the research and evaluation teams I led, whether working at a whole-of-department level or within a specific policy stream. I found that evaluators responded well to the idea that their role is integral to the policy and implementation process. I also found that having this approach facilitated working across policy and program areas, with evaluation acting as the linchpin between the two.

Step 4: Refining the model

I completed the inductive development of a policy cycle by breaking down the 'advise' section. This is because the policy 'engine room' of the APS is quite complicated and involves the pursuit of several types of activity, often simultaneously. As shown in Figure 8.4, the five new elements I introduced were:

- identify the issue or issues
- analyse the issues and the instruments available to address them
- consult stakeholders
- coordinate across government
- recommend a course of action to government.

- Break down 'advise' into:
  - Identify issue
  - Analyse issue and instruments
  - Consult
  - Coordinate
  - Recommend
- Result: a generic policy cycle (based on the Australian Policy Cycle)

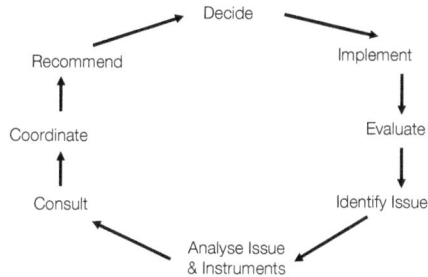

Decide

Recommend

Implement

Coordinate

Evaluate

Consult

Identify Issue

Analyse Issue & Instruments

Based on: Althaus, Bridgman & Davis (2018).

Figure 8.4. Refining the cycle.

This generates a variant on Althaus, Bridgman and Davis's Australian policy cycle (see Figure 8.5), but with some notable differences. I would combine 'analysis of the issues' with 'analysis of the instruments', as in my experience the two processes are often combined in the APS. In part, this is due to the way governments often constrain the choice of policy instruments, for example by determining a preference for competitive markets for service delivery over direct provision by government agencies.[7]

I would also add the step of making a recommendation to government. In my experience, the work that goes into crafting and negotiating a Cabinet or ministerial submission's recommendations can be quite exhaustive and complex. Leaving such a major task out when talking to public servants—especially public servants who work closely with ministers—risks leaving a large and obvious gap in the model.

These 'tweaks' of the Australian policy cycle may well be debated, but they do not materially change the foundations of the useful and well-known model presented by Althaus, Bridgman and Davis.

---

7   However, Meredith Edwards (this volume, Chapter 7) rightly observes that there is an important distinction to be drawn between the 'issue' and the 'problem'. The issue may be a large, systemic concern (e.g. homelessness), while the problem may be a specific factor underlying the issue (e.g. housing affordability).

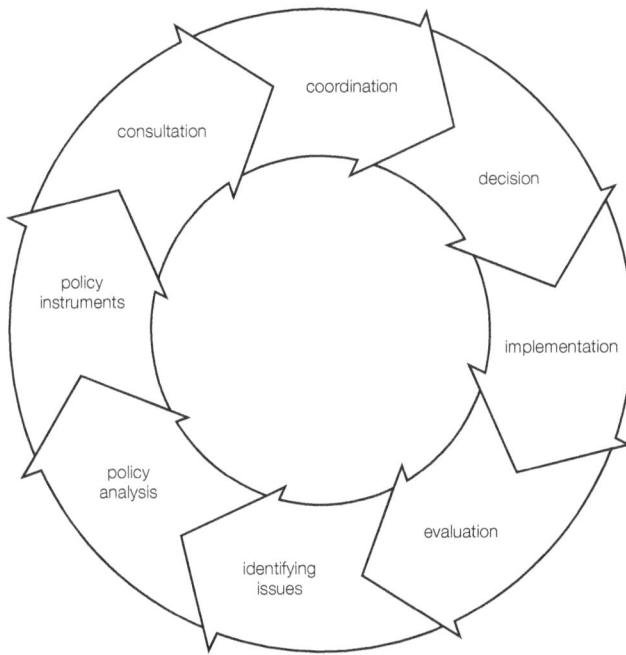

Figure 8.5. Australian policy cycle.
Source: Althaus, Bridgman and Davis (2018).

Step 5: 'Complexifying'[8] the model

As a final—somewhat tongue-in-cheek—stage in the process, I would take the model one step further (Figure 8.6). At the risk of echoing Barry Jones's notorious 'Noodle Nation' diagram (Australianpolitics.com 2001), I believe it is important to reflect the felt experience of many public servants who perceive their work lives as contingent and incremental rather than cyclical or linear—like Lindblom's (1959, 1979) 'muddling through'. Some of my colleagues were inclined to see the policy process as a jumble of post-hoc rationalisations and solutions looking for a problem, along the lines of the 'garbage can' model, as described by Cohen, March and Olsen (1972). For different reasons, many academics also criticise the

---

8   This term was coined by the secretary of the Department of Administrative Services in the 1990s, Noel Tanzer, who observed that public servants are very good at 'complexifying' issues that don't need to be that complex. I think this is certainly a tendency among public servants (I was not immune to it myself). Yet, the fact remains that many public policy issues are inherently complex, and there is considerable wisdom in HL Menken's observation that 'for every complex human problem there is an answer that is clear, simple, and wrong'.

rational-comprehensive approach as not being apparent in the empirical evidence, as discussed by McCool (1995). The problem seems to be a clash between description and prescription. A more accurate depiction of how policy development actually happens does not necessarily afford participants with a useful guide for how they *should* proceed in any given circumstance. The policy cycle at least helps to shape action, even if it may be seen as deficient as a description of what an external observer sees.[9]

In my presentation to colleagues I tried to reconcile this tension, at least to some degree. Many—perhaps all—'real world' policy processes progress in a nonlinear fashion, with shifts across and between elements of the cycle, and with various elements being conducted in tandem. It is this tendency that I try to depict at Figure 8.6.

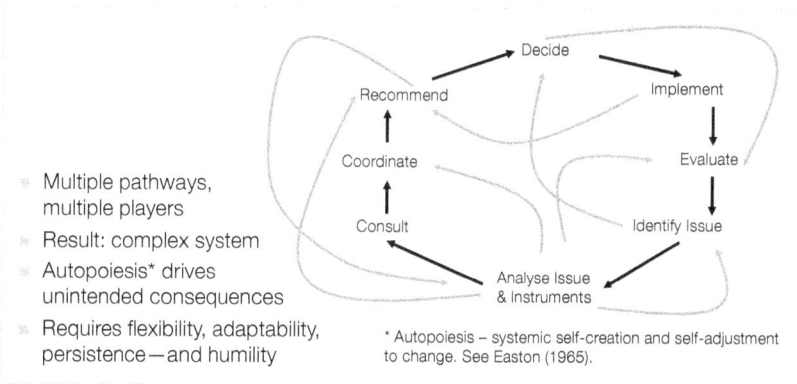

Figure 8.6. 'Complexifying' the model.

It was often important at this point to distinguish between chaotic randomness and systemic complexity. Recognising that the real world is not as neat as the policy cycle implies—and, indeed, asserting that it can never be thus—does not mean that policymaking is necessarily chaotic or random. As Kingdon (1995) shows, policy decisions can be seen as the product of several 'streams' (policy, politics and implementation) that coalesce at a 'window of opportunity' to generate momentum for change and a new policy direction or position. This description carries

---

9   I have some sympathy for Smith and May's (1993) proposition that the argument between rational and incremental models of policymaking is, in the end, somewhat artificial. Both approaches are valid, they simply seek to achieve different ends in the attempt to understand, explain and guide policymaking.

considerable empirical 'weight'—it 'feels' about right as a way of describing policymaking. It is, however, perhaps less successful in guiding action as participants operate within and across Kingdon's streams.

Normatively, it is desirable to impose a disciplined, structured way of thinking about policy analysis. When I presented my suggested way of seeing and applying the policy cycle to colleagues in the APS, it often generated interesting and productive discussions about specific cases and alternative pathways for difficult or challenging policy work. This blended model can help open the minds of practitioners working in public policy and implementation to more possibilities and more creative approaches to their work.

In my presentation to colleagues, I would also sometimes also introduce some concepts from complex systems approaches to the objects of policy, such as social systems, the economy or international relations. As outlined by a range of authors (Cairney & Geyer 2015; Easton 1965; Stewart & Ayres 2001b), there are some important concepts arising from complex systems theory that relate to large social systems, including:

- feedback (in which information cycles back and forth between elements or nodes in the system to reorient their trajectory or behaviour)
- autopoiesis (in which the system tends to be 'self-generative', adjusting and changing in response to developments within and around the system over time).

The notion of autopoiesis is especially important, even though the term is unfamiliar and can distract some audiences. As a concept, it helps to place government as an element *within* the system, rather than as a god-like manipulator outside the system. The tendency for the system to reorganise around new information and to find a new stasis is itself a signalling factor for the system as a whole and not simply a unidirectional causal process. This can help explain phenomena such as the unintended consequences of government action (or inaction).

I would generally conclude my discussions with colleagues by considering the qualities required from public servants working on policy development, analysis and advice, including flexibility, adaptability, persistence and humility.

Any impact? Possibly …

In preparing this chapter, I asked a former colleague who worked in several branches I led if he remembered me talking about the policy cycle. I was struck by his response:

> I do recall you talking about using policy cycle frameworks and interspersing the theory with practice.
>
> What I remember more clearly however, is the practice—and then reflection on the extent to which it departed from theory, and how individual effort and vision can, from time to time, 'bend the shape of things that haven't happened yet'.[10] (R Ciesniewski, personal communication, 2 July 2018)

This encapsulates the main point I want to make. The interplay between theory and practice is real and substantive, even if some practitioners may not always be conscious of that interplay, or the role of theory in the complex, highly contingent world of government. Theory can help practice, but in the APS practice is a deeply pragmatic activity. It deploys tacit knowledge, mixes analysis with trial and error, values persistence and judgement, and follows shifting pathways and purposes. Getting the job done starts with some level or form of normative theory—however sketchy or incomplete—but acting (and reacting) in the real world of government and administration is an exercise of will and negotiation that can never be adequately encompassed by theories, models or frameworks.

Conclusion: Implications for the profession

Reflecting on this aspect of my public service career, there may well have been more opportunities to introduce ideas from the growing body of theory around policymaking into the world of practice than I realised at the time. Certainly, in the past decade or more, several universities have increased the opportunity to study public policy, especially at the postgraduate level (Di Francesco 2015). Some departments and agencies have also undertaken organisational development work to deepen the connection between theory and practice, while others have encouraged their staff to undertake short courses in policy development.

---

10   The quotation is from a Neil Finn song, 'Faster than light'.

Given these advances, there are likely to be increasing numbers of public servants who are familiar with, or open to, some of the theories, models and frameworks that seek to explain or improve policymaking. There would seem, therefore, to be an opportunity to further explore these issues to determine to what extent public servants are aware of theories of policymaking, the ways in which they use those theories, and how effective they find the theories in the conduct of their day-to-day work in policy analysis and advice. Such analysis is likely to be valuable to theorists and practitioners alike, and it could help deepen and extend their mutual discourse.

References

Althaus, C, Bridgman, P & Davis, G 2018, *The Australian policy handbook: A practical guide to the policy making process*, 6th edn, Allen & Unwin, Crows Nest, NSW.

Australianpolitics.com 2001, *Liberals attack Beazley over knowledge nation*, viewed 4 September 2018, australianpolitics.com/2001/10/23/liberals-attack-beazley-over-knowledge-nation.html.

Ayres, R 2001a, 'Outcomes & outputs and policy advice in the Commonwealth', paper presented at the Annual Conference of the Public Policy Network, University of New South Wales, Sydney.

Ayres, R 2001b, 'Policy markets in Australia', PhD thesis, University of Canberra.

Bridgman, P & Davis, G 2003, 'What use is a policy cycle? Plenty, if the aim is clear', *Australian Journal of Public Administration*, vol. 62, no. 3, pp. 98–102, doi.org/10.1046/j.1467-8500.2003.00342.x.

Cairney, P & Geyer, R (eds) 2015, *Handbook on complexity and public policy*, Edward Elgar Publishing, Cheltenham, UK.

Cary, J 1944, *The horse's mouth*, Michael Joseph, London, UK.

Chia, A 2018, 'Distilling the essence of the Mckinsey way: The problem-solving cycle', *Management Teaching Review*, vol. 4, no. 4, pp. 355–70, doi.org/10.1177/2379298118779325.

Cohen, M, March, J & Olsen, J 1972, 'A garbage can model of organisational choice', *Administrative Science Quarterly*, vol. 17, no. 1, pp. 1–25, doi.org/10.2307/2392088.

Colebatch, HK 2009, *Policy*, Open University Press, Maidenhead, UK.

Considine, M 2005, *Making public policy: Institutions, actors, strategies*, Polity Press, Cambridge, UK.

Creswell, JW & Poth, CN 2018, *Qualitative inquiry and research design: Choosing among five approaches*, Sage Publications, Thousand Oaks, CA.

Davis, G, Wanna, J, Warhurst, J & Weller, P 1993, *Public policy in Australia*, Allen & Unwin, St Leonards, NSW.

deLeon, P 1998, 'The evidentiary base for policy analysis: Empiricist versus postpositivist positions', *Policy Studies Journal*, vol. 26, no. 1, pp. 109–13, doi.org/10.1111/j.1541-0072.1998.tb01927.x.

Deming, WE 1986, *Out of the crisis*, Cambridge University Press, Cambridge, MA.

Di Francesco, M 2015, 'Policy analysis instruction in Australia', in B Head & K Crowley (eds), *Policy analysis in Australia*, Policy Press, Bristol, UK, doi.org/10.1332/policypress/9781447310273.003.0017.

Di Francesco, M & Uhr, J 1996, 'Improving practices in policy evaluation', in J Uhr & K Mackay (eds), E*valuating policy advice: Learning from Commonwealth experience*, Federalism Research Centre (ANU) and Commonwealth Department of Finance, Canberra, ACT.

Easton, D 1965, *A systems analysis of political life*, John Wiley & Sons, New York, NY.

Edwards, M 2001, *Social policy, public policy*, Allen & Unwin, Sydney, NSW.

Ely, M, Anzul, M, Friedman, T, Garner, D & McCormack Steinmetz, A 1991, *Doing qualitative research: Circles within circles*, Falmer Press, London, UK.

Fabian, M & Breunig, R (eds) 2018, *Hybrid public policy innovations: Contemporary policy beyond ideology*, Routledge, New York, NY, doi.org/10.4324/9781351245944.

Halligan, J 1995, 'Policy advice and the public service', in BG Peters & DJ Savoie (eds), *Governance in a changing environment*, McGill-Queen's University Press, Montreal, Canada.

Head, B & Crowley, K (eds) 2015, *Policy analysis in Australia*, Policy Press, Bristol, UK, doi.org/10.1332/policypress/9781447310273.001.0001.

Hood, C 1995, 'Contemporary public management: A new global paradigm?', *Public Policy & Administration*, vol. 10, no. 2, pp. 104–17, doi.org/10.1177/095207679501000208.

Howard, J 1998, 'The 1997 Sir Robert Garran oration', *Australian Journal of Public Administration*, vol. 57, no. 1, pp. 3–11, doi.org/10.1111/j.1467-8500.1998. tb01359.x.

Kingdon, JW 1995, *Agendas, alternatives and public policies*, HarperCollins, New York, NY.

Lane, JE 2000, *New public management*, Routledge, London, UK.

Lasswell, H 1951, 'The policy orientation', in D Lerner & H Lasswell (eds), *The policy sciences*, Stanford University Press, Stanford, CA.

Liberal Party of Australia 2012, *Tony Abbott joint press release—terms of reference for proposed Productivity Commission review into child care,* Press release, 19 November, viewed 30 January 2020, pandora.nla.gov.au/pan/22107/ 20130812-1653/www.liberal.org.au/latest-news/2012/11/19/tony-abbott-joint-press-release-terms-reference-proposed-productivity.html.

Liberal Party of Australia 2013, *The coalition's policy for better child care and early learning*, viewed 4 June 2019, pandora.nla.gov.au/pan/22107/20130906-0245/ lpaweb-static.s3.amazonaws.com/The+Coalition%E2%80%99s+Policy+for+ Better+Child+Care+-+final.pdf.

Lindblom, C & Woodhouse, E 1993, *The policy-making process*, Prentice-Hall, Englewood Cliffs, NJ.

Lindblom, CE 1959, 'The science of "muddling through"', *Public Administration Review*, vol. 19, no. 2, pp. 79–88, doi.org/10.2307/973677.

Lindblom, CE 1979, 'Still muddling, not yet through', *Public Administration Review*, vol. 39, no. 6, pp. 517–26, doi.org/10.2307/976178.

May, PJ 1998, 'Policy analysis: Past, present, and future', *International Journal of Public Administration*, vol. 21, no. 6/8, pp. 1089–114, doi.org/10.1080/ 01900699808525336.

McCool, D 1995, 'The process of public policy making: Introduction', in D McCool (ed.), *Public policy theories, models, and concepts: An anthology*, Prentice-Hall, Englewood Cliffs, NJ.

Parsons, W 2002, 'From muddling through to muddling up: Evidence based policy-making and the modernisation of the British Government', *Public Policy & Administration*, vol. 17, no. 3, pp. 43–60, doi. org/10.1177/095207670201700304.

Peters, G 1998, 'Policy networks: Myth, metaphor and reality', in D. Marsh (ed.), *Comparing policy networks*, Open University Press, Philadelphia, PA.

Productivity Commission 2014, *Childcare and early childhood learning: Productivity Commission inquiry report*, Productivity Commission, Canberra, ACT.

Schön, DA & Rein, M 1994, *Frame reflection: Toward the resolution of intractable policy controversies*, BasicBooks, New York, NY.

Smith, G & May, D 1993, 'The artificial debate between rationalist and incrementalist models of decision making', in M Hill (ed.), *The policy process: A reader*, Harvester Wheatsheaf, New York, NY.

Stewart, J & Ayres, R 2001a, 'The public policy process', in C Aulich, J Halligan & S Nutley (eds), *Australian handbook of public sector management*, Allen & Unwin, Crows Nest, NSW.

Stewart, J & Ayres, R 2001b, 'Systems thinking and policy practice: An exploration', *Policy Sciences*, vol. 34, pp. 79–94, doi.org/10.1023/A:1010334804878.

Stewart, RG 1999, *Public policy: Strategy and accountability*, Macmillan, South Yarra, Vic.

9

Succeeding and failing in crafting environment policy: Can public policy theories help?

Kathleen Mackie

Introduction

> Mainstream Western accounts of the policymaking process often bear little resemblance to the realities of those who 'accomplish' the actual policy work on a daily basis. (Williams 2010, p. 195)

> It is worth talking to academics and others to understand policy, because people like me can't explain why we did what we did. We just did it. A lot of it is understanding the craft. You think everyone gets it. But it is amazing how many people don't. (Interview with a policy practitioner with 30 years experience in federal environment policy, as cited in Mackie 2014, p. 19).

Will training public servants in policy theory help to improve their capabilities and thereby contribute to achieving better policy outcomes? This question is increasingly important for environment policy, given that climatic and environmental threats to human survivability and biodiversity continue to escalate. If policy theorists can strengthen the capacity of policy officials to deliver innovative and effective policy advice and solutions, the benefits would be valuable. Indicators that we no longer have the luxury of lengthy ruminations over policy theory and policy practice can be found in two examples. First, the 2018 Intergovernmental Panel on Climate Change (IPCC) report highlights the truncated time frame available to avoid the most damaging impacts of climate change, and concludes that:

> If the global temperature rises by 1.5°C, humans will face unprecedented climate-related risks and weather events. We are on track for a 3–4°C temperature rise. To meet a goal of 1.5°C warming, this demands immediately cutting the planet's emissions to 45% below 2010 levels by 2030. (IPCC 2018)

Such action would require unprecedented global agreement to policy actions.

Second, in the Australian context, the graphic failure of the Murray–Darling Basin governance arrangements to avoid serious damage to that essential river system over many decades underscores the need to improve environment and natural resource management policy (Government of South Australia 2019). Phillip Glyde (2019, p. 19), chief executive of the Murray–Darling Basin Authority, recently argued that the basin plan is science-based. However, it has clearly failed in its implementation and in ensuring all the stakeholders play a constructive role. Successful 'policy' requires more than transparency and an evidence base.

Practitioners and policy theorists share a common desire to provide effective support for those new to the work of policy, and those who need to craft good policy in the context of significant and changing political and economic constraints. This chapter offers a practice-based perspective on how policy theories and frameworks can assist policy analysts to deliver good policy advice to ministers for their consideration and decision.

Academics in the public policy field are acutely aware of the disconnect between policy theory and policy practice. They know that many policy officials learn their craft on-the-job (Allen & Wanna 2016; Mercer this volume, Chapter 3). For my own part, I was trained in economics and geography and then found myself at the policy coalface with no background in policy theory, politics or political science. I kept quiet and watched, while continuing to make errors. In my early years, the machinations and manoeuvrings of senior policy officers higher up the Australian Public Service (APS) ladder were not transparent or explained. It was a matter of learning on-the-job as best as one could in a world in which policy development strategies were not made explicit, failures were not examined and policy successes were not mined for shared lessons.

The ways in which policy officials undertake and orchestrate their roles in the policy process are generally not revealed in the policy literature in a clear or systematic way that would encourage emulation (notable exceptions include studies on street-level bureaucrats and policy entrepreneurs). There is still a dearth of studies informed by a practitioner or 'insider' perspective. For example, Jarvie (personal communication, November 2013), in her work on policy learning, found that there has been surprisingly little systematic work in Australia on how public servants behave in complex policy environments. Samnakay (2017, p. 106) observed that 'the process of how national strategic policies are developed and implemented in Australia is unclear, and largely unattended in the literature'. Moreover, few studies have sought to identify the cues that policy officials pay attention to in assessing whether or not an environment policy is likely to succeed.

This chapter argues that policy theorists would do well to investigate exactly how policy officials go about their work.[1] Such research is difficult because, under the APS Code of Conduct and security requirements, public servants are significantly constrained in their right to divulge the inner workings of policymaking. Theorists such as Colebatch, Hoppe and Noordegraff (2010) and Williams (2010) have acknowledged that their understanding of policymaking has been held back by difficulties in documenting the actual experiences of policy officials (Mackie 2014, p. 9). As Williams (2010) noted, academics are acutely aware of their limited access to the core artefacts that move policy forward— the internal documents, people and processes of government. In her view, the academic is on the outside looking in. Yet, accessing insider perspectives, however difficult, is necessary if policy theory is to offer practitioners the tools, frameworks and understandings that underpin the craft of policymaking.

---

1   The findings in this chapter are drawn from doctoral research I conducted in 2011–14 into why some federal environment policies in Australia fail and others succeed (Mackie 2014, 2016). The research documented how federal environment policy officials avoided failure and pursued success over the period 1993 to 2013. Of relevance here, the research demonstrated that policy officials drew on their experience, instincts and intuition rather than the array of policy theories and frameworks in the public policy literature.

Changing policy dynamics

Questions relating to how policy theory can inform and support the work of policy officials are pertinent across all policy areas and jurisdictions. My doctoral research focused on the area of federal environment policy. Federal engagement in environmental policy is fairly recent. From a relatively small agency in 1971, a fledgling Department of the Environment grew during the 1980s. The 1996 Howard government gave its Minister for the Environment, Senator Robert Hill, a place in Cabinet for the first time. Hill proved to be a highly effective minister. He brokered the landmark *Environment Protection and Biodiversity Conservation Act 1999*; established the Natural Heritage Trust; improved Australia's fuel quality, thereby generating air quality and emission reduction benefits; and set in train Australia's national oceans policy agenda.

As it evolved over the next three decades, the department nurtured a distinctive generation of environment policy officials who were in the main passionate about protecting the environment but savvy enough to stay within Westminster boundaries. By contrast, over the last decade, the scope for creative environment policymaking appears much diminished, with a greatly reduced budget, increasing politicisation of the federal bureaucracy and climate change policy, and a series of less effective environment ministers than previously.

Trigger for the research

My research interests were triggered by the political and policy chaos arising from the then Department of the Environment's Home Insulation Program. Under the Rudd government, the program had aimed to insulate 2.7 million homes from its commencement in February 2009; however, the program was abruptly terminated in February 2010 after four young installers employed by private contractors under the program died. The Home Insulation Program was one of 12 environmental policies I researched. In October 2009, I was asked to assist to rebuild trust between Minister Peter Garrett and the Home Insulation Branch. After my first day, I came to the strong view that the program ought to be terminated. On my second day, 14 October 2009, the first death occurred, that of Matthew Fuller. One of the environment policy officials who crafted the initial policy proposal to fund home insulation as an energy efficiency measure told me that when she heard that $2.7 billion had been approved as a part of Rudd's stimulus package, she knew the program would fail and she quietly moved jobs. That clear prediction of failure triggered my interest in the policymaking process.

How to access the insider view

Accessing insider knowledge and experiences of how policy gets made requires a trusting relationship between the researcher and interviewee. I was able to interview the officials who had a core role in making policy over 20 years from 1993 to 2013. The interviews included all five secretaries of the department and the majority (nine) of the deputy secretaries from 1993 to September 2013. This coverage ensured the inclusion of policy officials who had access to ministers and their offices and were accountable for the implementation of Cabinet policy decisions.

All the policy officials who were invited to participate in the study agreed to be interviewed. This high acceptance rate may be explained by official support for the study, anonymity, a high level of interest in the topic and the fact that the researcher, as a former public servant, was known to the participants. All interviewees were aware of the support of the departmental secretary and board of management. Secretary of the Commonwealth Department of the Environment Dr Paul Grimes noted that my study had the support of the departmental management board, that respondents would not be asked to disclose any confidential information and that their anonymity was assured. That the study had ethics approval from the University of New South Wales, and that responses were treated confidentially and reported anonymously, provided further comfort to participants. Finally, all the interviewees had worked with me in a budget, corporate, program or policy capacity, or while in a central agency as a manager, subordinate or colleague. Taken together, these factors engendered a high level of trust and, thus, a willingness to talk openly about experiences of policymaking.

Interviewees were selected who had close exposure to, and could therefore comment on, the success or failure of six biodiversity and six energy/solar policies and programs (see Table 9.1). The interview canvassed which environmental policies (including but not restricted to the 12) had been successful, whether it was possible to predict success and what drove success or failure. By the 51st interview, there was a sense of convergence in the responses, albeit with a spread of views about particular policies. The sample comprised 31 senior executive service policy officers, and

20 executive level 1 or 2 officers. Over half the interviewees had more than 15 years experience in environmental policy. Nearly three-quarters had experience in Cabinet, budget or ministerial processes.

The interviewees considered the art of policymaking to be intuitive, perfected through a mix of policy nous, judgement and experience. They were highly qualified in areas such as law, economics and natural resource management, but few held formal qualifications in public policy. How they went about policy was, for the most part, learnt on-the-job, by observing or by osmosis. Notably, most interviewees struggled to define policy; this suggests an instinctual and experience-based approach rather than a theoretical approach. The one interviewee who was able to provide a ready definition had completed a masters of public policy. Most took time to think through how they would define policy (Mackie 2014, pp. 111–15).

Insights from the policy theory literature

As preparation for the interviews, I spent a year reading literature on public policy. I was keen to know whether any of the theories of public policy offered compelling explanations as to why policy failures occurred and how to avoid them. To my frustration, I found that little resonated with me. There were some great turns of phrase such as 'muddling through' (Lindblom 1959) and Cohen et al.'s 'garbage can' model (as cited in Dryzek 1983), but there was no coherent framework of policymaking that I could draw on to explore questions of what drives environment policy success and failure.

Kingdon's seminal 1984 work on agenda-setting struck a chord with me. Kingdon (2003, pp. 231–2) was able to uncover much about the intent, motivations and strategies of government officials and thus generate groundbreaking theory on agenda-setting through his in-depth interviews with United States government officials (Mackie 2014, p. 60). I liked the way Kingdon's three streams—problem (the policy issue), policies (the instruments and ideas) and politics (public opinion, stage of electoral cycle, degree of opposition)—could run in parallel, and that the policy entrepreneur, which could be a government official or lobbyist or other player outside the bureaucracy, could encounter considerable doses of 'messiness, accident, fortuitous connections and dumb luck' (Kingdon, 2011, p. 206; Mercer this volume, Chapter 3).

My interviewees shared some wonderful stories about the shadowy practice of how policy is made—sometimes serendipitously. For example, in 1999, as part of GST negotiations, Prime Minister John Howard misheard a statement to the leader of the Australian Democrats by his treasurer, Peter Costello. Costello stated: 'I'll give Meg Lees $400,000 for an environment package.' However, Howard heard $400 million (Mackie 2014, pp. 175–6). As a result, the Department of the Environment had an enormous windfall in the budget that year and the $400 million funded many environmental measures. Costello confirmed the veracity of this story of 'dumb luck'. This story raises the question: how does the policy theorist accommodate such seemingly random occurrences? Kingdon listened deeply to policy officials and, in doing so, was able to uncover much about their intent, motivations and strategies. He also revealed the value of interviews in a trusting relationship as a method of understanding policymaking. Yet, overall, I found no theory or set of theories that unpacked my experiences of policymaking in a way that meant success could be replicated and failure avoided.

A framework to assess policy success and failure

Marsh and McConnell (2010) provide a useful framework for analysing whether policy episodes can be categorised as success or failure. They measure success across three dimensions:

1. Process: how did the policy arise and what was its level of support?
2. Programmatic: was it implemented as per its stated objectives?
3. Political: was it popular with the electorate and therefore with politicians?

Marsh and McConnell's framework provided a coherent rubric to assess the 12 policies along a success–failure continuum to crosscheck what the interviewees were saying. Interviewee ratings of which policies were successful, had mixed outcomes or failed were compared to ratings I derived by applying Marsh and McConnell's framework (Mackie 2014). Table 9.1 sets out the interviewee assessments of the 12 policies grouped by Marsh and McConnell's framework (Mackie 2014, p. 108, 2018, p. 59).

Table 9.1. Targeted federal environmental policies and programs 1993–2013. Success–failure per Marsh and McConnell framework vs success–failure per interviewees.

Environmental policy or program	Interviewees' success/ failure nominations	
	Success	Failure
Rated towards success under Marsh and McConnell[a]		
Working on Country	23[b]	0
Fuel Quality Standards Act 2000	9	0
Rated mixed outcomes under Marsh and McConnell[a]		
Natural Heritage Trust	9	5
Regional Forest Agreements	16	5
Environment Protection and Biodiversity Conservation Act 1999	11	9
Marine Protected Areas	11	3
Caring for Our Country	5	6
Rated towards failure under Marsh and McConnell[a]		
Home Insulation Program	5	18
Green Loans Program	0	8
Solar Homes and Communities Plan	0	3
Solar Hot Water Rebate Program	0	3
National Solar Schools Program	0	3

[a] Rated 'towards success' means broadly successful on all three of Marsh and McConnell's dimensions (i.e. process, programmatic and political); 'mixed outcomes' means neither outstandingly successful nor unsuccessful on any one dimension but no major failings; 'towards failure' means broadly failed across all three dimensions.

[b] The interviewee nominations in each row add up to less than 51, as interviewees restricted such nominations to programs they had direct experience or some knowledge of.

Marsh and McConnell's framework provided a way of reality checking the interviewees' subjective assessments of policy success along structured process, program and political dimensions. The interviewees rated the Indigenous ranger Working on Country program (which provided award wages to Indigenous people to care for cultural and natural values on Indigenous tenure on behalf of all Australians) and National Fuel Quality Standards (which led to improved air quality, greenhouse emission and health outcomes) as notable successes. The Home Insulation Program and associated smaller Green Loans Program (which aimed to provide interest free loans to assist homeowners to invest in energy efficiency measures) were rated as absolute failures. While a few dissenters considered Home Insulation successful, a slew of public inquiries begged to differ

(Australian National Audit Office 2010; Australian Royal Commission into the Home Insulation Program 2014; Commonwealth of Australia 2010; Hawke 2010).

Interviewees had a strong sense of whether or not a policy was going to succeed based on a range of indicators. Among predictive factors in the policy literature, they validated the importance of engaging with stakeholders, having clear objectives and knowing the evidence base. In the context of environment policy, they played down factors such as adequate resources, nature of the policy origins and clear policy design.

Respondents emphasised the importance of the policy mandate, especially in the hands of a capable minister. Additionally, policy 'agency'—legitimate but incisive interventions by officials to get a result for the good of the environment—was cited as a key to success. Examples of this positive agency were adding a land-clearing moratorium into Commonwealth–state agreements; invoking clauses of the Environment Protection Act to unlock marine protection policy; and paying Indigenous people fair wages to maintain natural and cultural values on Indigenous lands (Mackie 2014, pp. 191–204). Conversely, poor outcomes in Home Insulation and Green Loans were attributed to a distinct lack of agency. In the Home Insulation Program, for example, sterile briefings to the minister on critical safety and fraud issues were represented as a kind of 'agency by omission'. One specific example of this was highlighted by the 2014 Royal Commission into the Home Insulation Program, in which a senior executive failed to attach the risk register to a critical April 2009 brief to Minister Garrett (Hawke 2010, p. 32; Mackie 2014, p. 208).

Agency of officials as a key driver of successful policy

Westminster conventions decree that officials advise and ministers decide. Ministers and governments rely on the discretion of policy officers. Politicians, their advisers and departmental senior executives need to be able to fully trust the officials providing advice and policy solutions. The hidden but vital role of officials, as they try to steer policy towards success, is difficult to see in practice or express in theory. The in-depth interviews with environment policy officials revealed that their deliberate manoeuvrings to get policies onto the minister's agenda, and to pursue policies though to success, were a key factor in whether environment policies failed or succeeded.

The interviewees revealed that they rarely drew on policy theory, models or frameworks to inform their policy work. Surprisingly, experienced and adept policy officers struggled to define 'policy'; they considered policy work instinctual—it was in their DNA. Sure, they were aware of the policy cycle and relied on it to keep an eye on the process steps needed to deliver a policy result. Some had even been trained in the concept (Mackie 2014, pp. 115–17). But, in the main, they learnt on-the-job. That learning ranged from a patient watchfulness for the opening of a 'policy window' to the masterminding of clever shortcuts and alternate routes to overcome the political, economic and resource barriers to delivering good policy.

A former departmental secretary interviewed for this study concluded that, although officials generally understood what constituted good public policy, responsibility for policy failure could be sheeted back to officials expending too much time and effort on formulating the policy framework, and not enough on crafting a policy narrative that dovetailed the government's political priorities with the interests of the primary stakeholders, enabling the politician to understand and sell the policy to the electorate. Climate change policy was his prime example of this fundamental failure to bring the political realm along by developing a policy narrative elegant and simple enough for the electorate to understand and accept. The interviewee stated:

> I think we spent at that time far too much time in formulating the policy framework for climate change and not on the communications and political leadership framework. On the whole, I would have to say that climate change was perhaps the most disappointing failure of mine. I worked on it for eight or nine years. (as cited in Mackie 2014, p. 229)

Through listening to the insider experience of policy success (and failure), this study generated clues on how to think about the instrumental role of officials in policy. That is not to say the interviewees were overplaying their role. They were mindful of the role and power of the federal environment minister and Cabinet, and circumspect about their reach as bureaucrats. A mid-level official, highly regarded by ministers and the departmental executive, and possessing extensive Cabinet and Department of Prime Minister and Cabinet experience, volunteered that:

> I can think of only one example of a policy process where I was able to have a role that made a difference. It was in the water process. It was the only single direct difference I made on environment policy the whole time I was working for the government. It was

when I was asked by the Prime Minister's Office to brief the PM on a demand by irrigators to change the water policy that was before Cabinet. I quickly orally briefed the Prime Minister's advisor. I briefed him to tell the PM not to agree to a water allocation for rice irrigators in a particular year when there was insufficient water, as to give them an allocation would have set a precedent. I knew a lot about the issue and I had all the facts and figures at hand and I was emphatic. My case was irrefutable. It was a simple story and a well-defined problem. I wrote a note for file. The irrigators were expecting the PM to agree to their demands. But he didn't. He took my advice. (as cited in Mackie 2014, p. 214)

As this quotation demonstrates, opportunities to pursue agency are scarce yet vitally important. Indeed, my analysis of the experiences of 51 interviewees suggests that the notion of official as 'policy agent' is underplayed in the theoretical literature. This is largely because of the mantra that 'politicians decide and officials implement'.

Implications for policy theory

As already stated, my research revealed that a high level of agency by officials is a key to understanding policy success and failure. This suggests that academics would be well served in their theory development if they made concerted efforts to access the insider world of policy officials. For policy theory to gain greater relevance, more focus on the tactical manner in which officials pursue policy agendas is needed. The findings remind policy practitioners that their skills and interventions (or failure to intervene) are vital in the policy process, notwithstanding contemporary pressures towards politicisation and marginalisation of the public service.

Legitimacy of officials' agency in policymaking processes

In regard to the legitimacy of their behaviour, interviewees were able to distinguish between 'understanding the politics' and 'acting politically', and between being apolitical and being politically savvy. One interviewee, for example, described the need to have a sense of how the politics of a policy issue might play out, while at the same time taking care to avoid being a part of the political landscape or being aligned with stakeholder positions.

The department secretaries interviewed for this project were comfortable with their actions in terms of taking a strong agency role in pursuing policy outcomes. They saw it as a necessary part of providing full advice to their minister. This behaviour of prudent autonomous policy is not necessarily inconsistent with the Westminster system of government. However, such behaviour is not identified to any significant degree in the policy literature. Colebatch (2006, p. 3), one of Australia's leading policy theorists, has argued that the well-recognised account of the Westminster system may not be consistent with the experience of policy workers.

This dissonance between the rhetoric of the Westminster tradition and the actual experience of policymaking is beginning to be acknowledged in analyses of, and official documents on, policy administration in Australia. Stephen Sedgwick, former head of the Australian Public Service Commission, observed a softening in approach to the convention that 'government decides' and 'officials implement' (Towell 2013). Sedgwick suggested that past approaches to policy development have been weak on the concept of 'strategic foresight capability'. This concept parallels the notion of agency. Sedgwick argued that some ministers and some governments are interested in a forward-looking public service that is more actively engaged in setting the strategic policy agenda and, therefore, can provide more than simple responsiveness to the agenda of the government of the day (Towell 2013).

Banks (2013, p. 4), when head of the Australia and New Zealand School of Government, reinforced the importance of policy officials finding the right balance in respecting the policy decisions of government and doing a 'solid job in advising and informing government policy decisions'. He saw that balance as important in addressing the mounting number of policy failures in Australian federal policy, such as the carbon and mining taxes, the National Broadband Network and key strands of immigration policy. Banks (2013, p. 9) argued that policy ideas need to be 'tested and contested before implementation—within the bureaucracy, the community, the Cabinet room and, ultimately, within the Parliament'.

Contrary to the perception of Canberra public servants (bureaucrats) as self-serving, the interviewees in this study revealed a high level of commitment to civic service. Most expressed a commitment to delivering meaningful and measurable environment policy outcomes for the public good through a high level of inventiveness and persistence. Collectively, the interviewees were public spirited and knowledgeable. The following statement by an interviewee is representative of the sentiments of all interviewees on their role as players in the policy process:

> Everyone pursues particular policy agendas to an extent. Everyone is a policy actor in a sense and each of us thinks that we are doing it in the public interest. And we just have to keep each other honest in that regard and remind each other of that. I don't see 'actor' as a pejorative term. Each of us has views. We are not value neutral. We all have views. Part of my motivation for working for the Commonwealth is I want to produce good public policy outcomes and they don't always align with what the Government wants. But ultimately I am accountable to my seniors here and to the Government and to the Minister actually, and through him to the Parliament. (as cited in Mackie 2014, p. 223)

In summary, although the policy officials interviewed for this study revealed a surprisingly high degree of agency, their intent in doing so was to deliver good public policy. Many of the interviewees had elected to work in the Department of the Environment because the portfolio function of protecting the environment aligned with their personal values. Instances of leaking confidential documents (e.g. as occurred in the Regional Forest Agreements process) or of improper behaviour (e.g. as exhibited by the rogue executive level 2 in the Green Loans Program) underscore how agency behaviour can be highly inappropriate, to the extent of contravening the *APS Code of Conduct* and the *Public Service Act 1999* (Mackie 2014, p. 223). High-profile examples are evident in other policy areas, such as the Australian Wheat Board scandal and the Children Overboard incident. With agency comes responsibility. As one interviewee argued, where policy failure does occur (provided that responsibility for failure can be attributed), public servants should be held to account.

Conclusion

This chapter has investigated a practitioner–academic study of federal environment policy episodes using Marsh and McConnell's framework for understanding policy success. My analysis demonstrates the absence of public policy theory in the tool kit of the 51 policymakers interviewed. Additional studies are needed to test the universality or uniqueness of this finding, and the implications of the disconnect between policy theory and practice.

This research, based on rare access to the inner workings of federal environment policymaking, unearthed multilayered descriptions of how officials go about their tasks in environment policy. The insights revealed by the officials have implications for the deepening of public policy theory. In particular, policy thinking would do well to be more inclusive of the intentions and strategies—the 'agency'—of officials, including their vital roles in attempting to steer policy away from failure towards success, drawing on their practical insights and collaborative practices to secure small and large policy wins.

My study found that policy officials were able to deliver policy successes even in the absence of a coherent policy theory or framework. Nevertheless, training in the art and craft of policy is essential. It is more efficient to train new policy graduates in what is known (lessons and good practices), rather than relying on the time-honoured APS practice of throwing graduates into the deep end of policy work. This chapter suggests the need for a focus on how a deeper study of practice can inform theory, which in turn can be used to assist in the training of practitioners, rather than focus on how current policy theory can enhance the work of policy practitioners.

These findings suggest that, for public policy theory to gain greater relevance, we could do well to focus on the tactical manner in which officials pursue policy agendas. These findings remind policy practitioners that their skills and interventions (or absence of action) are vital in the policy process, notwithstanding contemporary pressures towards politicisation and marginalisation of the public service. Further analysis in other policy areas (e.g. employment, education, health, tax reform and aged care) would test the wider relevance of these findings. The increasing turbulence and politicisation of the policy process make it all the more imperative for policy theories to assist in training officials in the art of evidence-based, compelling policy advice that can 'stick', and for officials to focus on providing sound policy advice that puts the long-term interests of all Australians above narrow and short-term vested interests.

Major policy problems facing the nation, from the treatment of Indigenous and displaced peoples to the impacts of climate change, require that policy practitioners need access to rapid support services to help them provide compelling and defensible options to decision-makers. It is important to build 'communities of practice' in which the policy client, the people who design and deliver policy, and those who seek to understand policy, can all work together.

In summary, policymakers learn on-the-job, not from theory; the agency of policymakers warrants more attention in theory; and practical experience (or 'dirty hands') make for better policy. In informing participants in the big debates on stability and change, policy officials have a critical role in presenting options and likely consequences to ministers. Public policy theorists and educators have an important role in arming the policy practitioners with the best knowledge kit possible. Persistence, courage and knowing where to draw the line between advocacy and advice are increasingly necessary tools in that kit.

References

Allen, P & Wanna, J 2016, 'Developing leadership and building executive capacity in the Australian public services for better governance', in A Podger & J Wanna (eds), *Sharpening the sword of state: Building executive capacities in the public services of the Asia-Pacific*, ANU Press, Canberra, ACT, doi.org/ 10.22459/SSS.11.2016.02.

Australian National Audit Office 2010, *Home insulation program,* audit report no. 12, ANAO, Canberra, ACT.

Australian Royal Commission into the Home Insulation Program 2014, *Report of the Royal Commission into the home insulation program*, Government of Australia, Canberra, ACT.

Banks, G 2013, 'Restoring trust in public policy: What role for the public service?' *Garran Oration for the IPAA,* 21 November.

Colebatch, HK 2006, 'Thinking about policy: Finding the best way', presentation to Govnet International Conference, 29 November, ANU, Canberra.

Colebatch, H, Hoppe, R & Noordegraff, M (eds) 2010, *Working for policy*, Amsterdam University Press, Amsterdam, The Netherlands, doi.org/10.5117/ 9789089642530.

Commonwealth of Australia, Senate, Environment, Communications and the Arts References Committee 2010, *Inquiry into the energy efficiency homes package ('ceiling insulation')*, Australian Government, Canberra, ACT.

Dryzek, J 1983, 'Don't toss coins in garbage cans: A prologue to policy design', *Journal of Public Policy*, vol. 3, no. 4, pp. 345–67, doi.org/10.1017/S0143814 X00007510.

Glyde, P 2019, 'Letter to the editor', *Sydney Morning Herald*, 24 July.

Government of South Australia 2019, *Report of the Royal Commission on the Murray–Darling basin,* Government of South Australia, Adelaide, SA.

Hawke, A 2010, *Review of the administration of the home insulation program,* Australian Government, Canberra, ACT.

Intergovernmental Panel on Climate Change 2018, *Global warming of 1.5°C,* special report, viewed 31 January 2020, www.ipcc.ch/sr15/.

Kingdon, J 1984, *Agendas, alternatives and public policies,* Little Brown, Boston, MA.

Kingdon, J 2003, *Agendas, alternatives and public policies,* 2nd edn, Longman, New York, NY.

Kingdon, J 2011, *Agendas, alternatives and public policies,* updated 2nd edn, Longman, Boston, MA.

Lindblom, C 1959, 'The science of muddling through', *Public Administration Review,* vol. 19, no. 3, pp. 79–88, doi.org/10.2307/973677.

Mackie, K 2014, 'Federal environment policymaking in Australia: Avoiding failure; pursuing success', PhD thesis, UNSW.

Mackie, K 2016, 'Success and failure in environment policy: The role of policy officials', *Australian Journal of Public Administration,* vol. 75, no. 3, pp. 291–304, doi.org/10.1111/1467-8500.12170.

Mackie, K 2018, *Succeeding and failing in Australian environmental policy,* Brou Lake Publishing, Canberra, ACT.

Marsh, D & McConnell, A 2010, 'Towards a framework for establishing policy success', *Public Administration,* vol. 88, no. 2, pp. 564–83, doi.org/10.1111/j.1467-9299.2009.01803.x.

Samnakay, N 2017, 'Thinking strategically in federal policy: Defining the attributes of high-level policies', *Australian Journal of Public Administration,* vol. 76, no. 1, pp. 106–21, doi.org/10.1111/1467-8500.12199.

Towell, N 2013, 'Challenges in a changing world', *Canberra Times,* 27 July.

Williams, A 2010, 'Is evidence-based policymaking really possible? Reflections for policymakers and academics on making use of research in the work of policy', in H Colebatch, R Hoppe & M Noordegraaf (eds), *Working for policy,* Amsterdam University Press, Amsterdam, The Netherlands, doi.org/10.1515/9789048513086-016.

10

Understanding the policymaking enterprise: Foucault among the bureaucrats

Craig Ritchie

Introduction

> Policy analysis can no longer afford to limit itself to the simplified
> academic models of explanation. Such methods fail to address
> the nonlinear nature of today's messy policy problems. They fail
> to capture the typically heterogeneous, interconnected, often
> contradictory, and increasingly globalized character of these issues.
> Many of these problems are, as such, appropriately described as
> 'wicked problems'. In these situations, not only is the problem
> wanting for a solution, the very nature and conceptualization of
> the problem is not well understood. Effective solutions to such
> problems require ongoing, informed deliberation involving
> competing perspectives on the part of both government official
> and public citizens. (Fischer & Gottweis, 2012, p. 6)

In 2009, as an Aboriginal senior public servant, I was looking for a way
to better understand the policymaking process in light of the seemingly
incorrigible policy failure in what I have termed the Aboriginal and Torres
Strait Islander policy enterprise. It seemed that we were then, and I contend
still are, hampered by limiting and ineffective models for understanding
the nature of the policy problems that confront us and what it is that

we actually do in the policymaking enterprise. As a consequence, at least in terms of the Aboriginal and Torres Strait Islander policy enterprise, we had hitched our wagon to a dying star and seemed destined to fall headlong into the void it creates, regardless of how much rebadging we undertook and how many 'this is a fresh start' photo opportunities we manufactured—and we have been very good at those!

Our chief practical and methodological deficits are twofold. The first is a tenacious adherence to a policymaking orthodoxy derived from the managerialist obsession prevailing in Canberra, which seemed to me to have little resonance either with the communities I came from or worked with. The second is an inability to see the role that culture plays in defining how we work, shaping everything from problem definition to policy formulation, implementation and evaluation, according to the dominant cultural perspective of the non-Indigenous other—white Australia in particular. This has blinded us to the opportunities that a better understanding of Aboriginal culture might offer as a solution to what one Commonwealth report described as a policy space characterised by 'good intentions, *flawed policies*, unrealistic assumptions, poor implementation, unintended consequences and dashed hopes' (Commonwealth of Australia 2009, p. 39, emphasis added).

Since 2008, the 'new' policy approach for Indigenous Australia has been to make Aboriginal and Torres Strait Islander people more like white people. We did not call this policy 'assimilation', as Hasluck (1953) did in the mid-twentieth century, or 'mainstreaming', as Howard did in the 1990s; instead, we called it 'Closing the Gap'. Whatever the label, as Maddison (2009, p. 2) has so appositely observed, the fundamental logic at play in Indigenous policymaking is that 'if Aboriginal people could just be more like white people [our] problems would be resolved'. The effect has been to continue the colonial logic that positions white Australia (i.e. the non-Indigenous other) as the point of reference, and as the designated locus for Aboriginal and Torres Strait Islander peoples' aspirations. Now, more than a decade after this reformulation, we are about to embark on a new policy journey framed around collaboration and the romance of 'co-design', but this egregiously flawed logic still underpins the way we work. In concert with our rusted-on managerialism, it threatens to undermine our efforts and undoubted goodwill, and result in us becoming a living example of the Einsteinian definition of insanity. Something has to give. As policymakers, we need a better way to understand our own business. Foucault's concept of the *dispositif* gives us just such a way. Having let Friedman and Hayek have their way with us for these many years, it is high time we let Foucault loose among the bureaucrats.

A history of failure

In his masterful analysis of the failure of large-scale state initiatives to foster social and economic development, James C Scott (1998) identifies a profound and radical cultural dissonance that ultimately undermines the effectiveness of these interventions. Central to his analysis is an active and interventionist state. The chief means by which the state achieves its objectives is public policy (Althaus, Bridgman & Davis 2018). The Aboriginal and Torres Strait Islander policy enterprise is an example of such an intervention. The cultural dissonance at the heart of this enterprise renders the usual ways of proceeding in the formation and implementation of public policy not merely ineffective, it can often make matters far worse. In Australia, the relationship between the settler-colonial state and Indigenous peoples is a substantially transactional one in which service delivery, hence policy, is the central feature. Indeed, it might be argued that this transaction constitutes the *exclusive* ground of this relationship and that, apart from our construction and representation within the policymaking complex, Aboriginal and Torres Strait Islanders figure scantily in the modern Australian imaginary. Aboriginal people are positioned existentially as policy objects with problems to solve rather than as a unique and constitutive part of a modern Australia whose core identity is doggedly, often belligerently, non-Indigenous and white in its form, history and function, including the operations of the state.

Given this situation, it should be no surprise that issues affecting Aboriginal and Torres Strait Islanders are notoriously resistant to change. Superficial reasons for policy failure in this area are relatively well documented. That these explanations have conspicuously failed to improve things speaks to the limits of contemporary instrumentalist policymaking. By claiming to be rationalist and systematic, policymaking denies, or at best sets to one side, the cultural and historical context in which it operates and that shapes the entire business of policymaking. The problem is the foundation of the policy enterprise in Western Enlightenment rationality and modes of action, which conflict in important and fundamental ways with the foundations and modes of action in Aboriginal and Torres Strait Islander communities.

Following on from this, I want to suggest four things. First, in the face of results that are decidedly elusive, we are not well served by allegiance to prevailing positivist, technocratic and managerialist paradigms in public policy. Second, public policymaking is, at its core, a profoundly paradigmatic, value laden and cultural endeavour, with origins in a normative view of the world that must be rendered subject to the analytical gaze. Third, policy failure, particularly in the Aboriginal and Torres Strait Islander policy enterprise, is primarily a failure to take account of this paradigmatic and cultural nature of the policy enterprise. Fourth, failing to take account of Aboriginal culture (norms, values and behaviours) in the policy process will continue to undermine policy efforts.

In this chapter I suggest that we need a new way to think about the practice of policymaking that liberates us from the limitations of the modernist instrumental rationality that characterises our profession. We need new ways to think about how we respond to the complex policy issues that confront us—ways that do not rest on the faulty assumptions that our understanding of these problems is settled and that any solutions can be taken for granted.

Policy well made: Policy*making* rather than policy

This chapter is based on the proposition that well-made policy is fundamentally transformative. At its heart is the idea that policy and policymaking matters and can make a difference. However, the chronic policy failure that characterises the Aboriginal and Torres Strait Islander policy enterprise would seem to indicate that we have a serious problem and that our policy is neither good nor well made. This is a diagnosis that we have conspicuously avoided. In our headlong rush to improve delivery and policy implementation, it has been too easy to rush past the idea of 'flawed policies' completely. In fact, the question of improved policy development was dismissed in the 'Strategic review of Indigenous expenditure' (Commonwealth of Australia 2009). Heaven forbid that we should delve into whether we were trying to improve delivery of a fundamentally flawed set of policy widgets! However, the question of flawed policies is critically important and should not be so easily glossed over. Identifying flawed policies and how they are produced is the *condicio sine qua non* for both Aboriginal people and policymakers to get to the more complex issue of root cause(s) of policy failure, including the fundamental issue of cultural dissonance, resulting in a more effective Aboriginal and Torres Strait Islander policy enterprise.

The questions of flawed policy on the one hand, and the transformative impact of policy well made on the other, brings the practice of policymaking squarely into the frame. According to Althaus, Bridgman and Davis (2018), there is a clear link between a better appreciation of the policy process and achieving better outcomes from policy. The crucial issue we confront in the Aboriginal and Torres Strait Islander policy enterprise concerns the issue of policymaking and the apparatus through which it takes place, rather than individual policy artefacts. Flawed products are the result of flawed processes, policy products included. Consequently, a better understanding of the deeper nature of policymaking—not just its methods or techniques—stands as a singularly pressing and largely unexamined area of analysis (Colebatch 2006).

I use the word 'understanding' advisedly. From the point of view of both practice and theory, mere knowledge is no longer enough, at least knowledge as it is understood in modernism—that is, universalised, abstracted, detached and synoptic. What is required is knowledge in the form of practical insights and cunning intelligence, which Scott (1998) identified as the Greek concept of *metis*. In Scott's (1998, p. 6) analysis, *metis* refers to the 'fund of valuable knowledge embedded in local practices'. He contrasts *metis* with 'thin, formulaic simplifications imposed through the agency of the state', which fail to deliver effective policy outcomes (Scott 1998, p. 309; Rhodes 2017).This form of knowledge has an 'indispensable role' in the actual functioning of social systems that state actors, working from within an 'imperial and hegemonic planning mentality', either cannot see or set aside to their cost.

Decentring the analysis of policy and bringing the process of policymaking to the fore, this chapter seeks to map the terrain of the policymaking system using Foucault's concept of *dispositif* as a guide. In doing so, it provides a desperately needed analytical model that facilitates four things: first, an understanding of policymaking as an integrated and dynamic system or enterprise; second, interrogation of policymaking at an enterprise level; third, identification of key points of interaction within the policymaking system and critical intervention points for system recalibration; and, fourth, and perhaps most importantly, it advances an overarching role for culture in policymaking.

The contemporary context

The contemporary policymaking landscape in Australia is an interesting mix of terrain. We remain dominated by the managerialism we inherited from the new public management reforms of the last quarter of the twentieth century. Predicated on predictability, authority and control, this mode of policymaking seems likely to maintain its hegemonic position, especially in light of the most recent prime ministerial address to the Australian Public Service (APS) (Morrison 2019), with its retreat to Blairite imperatives around delivery (Barber 2008, 2015). Anxiety about improved delivery is matched with an enduring anxiety about the policy capacity of the APS, although it is fair to say that this anxiety is shadowed by the delivery-at-all-costs mentality at work in Australian administrative and political classes. In terms of political imperatives, contemporary Australian political life is beset by a furious and unrelenting competition among major political players for 'the centre'. This competition has some interesting consequences. In policy terms, it has led to virtually indistinguishable policy prescriptions from both sides of politics, as politicians and parties abandon doctrinaire ideological positions in pursuit of pragmatic outcomes. This blurring of political ideologies further reinforces the need for a deeper understanding of the philosophical, conceptual and theoretical substrata of the policymaking enterprise.

Foucault's *dispositif* as a framework for understanding

The concept of *dispositif* first appeared in Foucault's *The archaeology of knowledge*, in which he was concerned to set out the 'density of the accumulation' or the contextual dynamics in which statements as embodiments of knowledge are enmeshed, shaped and transformed (Foucault 1972, p. 141). For Foucault, the *dispositif* was the central mechanism in the construction and deployment of knowledge. He defined the concept of *dispositif* in the following way:

A thoroughly heterogeneous ensemble consisting of discourses, institutions, architectural forms, regulatory decisions, laws, administrative measures, scientific statements, philosophical, moral and philanthropic propositions—in short, the said as much as the unsaid. Such are the elements of the apparatus. The apparatus itself is the system of relations that can be established between these elements. (Foucault & Gordon 1980, p. 196)[1]

Drawing on this definition, the constituent elements of Foucault's *dispositif* are illustrated in Figure 10.1.

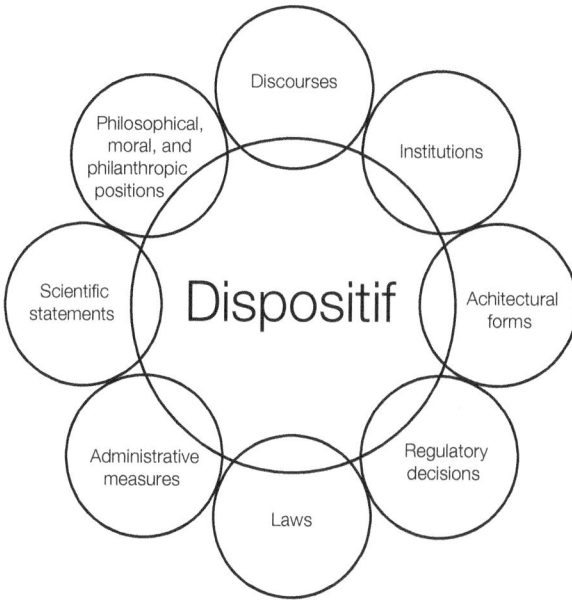

Figure 10.1. Foucault's *dispositif*.

Jäger's (2001) simplified description of the *dispositif* as consisting of three categories of constituents—discursive, non-discursive and materialisations—is illustrated in Figure 10.2. In either version, the relevance of the *dispositif* to understanding the foundational dynamics of policymaking is clear: we need to ask questions about what is said and why; what is done and why; the structures within which these practices are carried out; and, importantly, how these three domains interact.

---

1   Note that Foucault uses the word *apparatus* instead of the French *dispositif*; however, the terms are synonymous in his work.

Dispositives

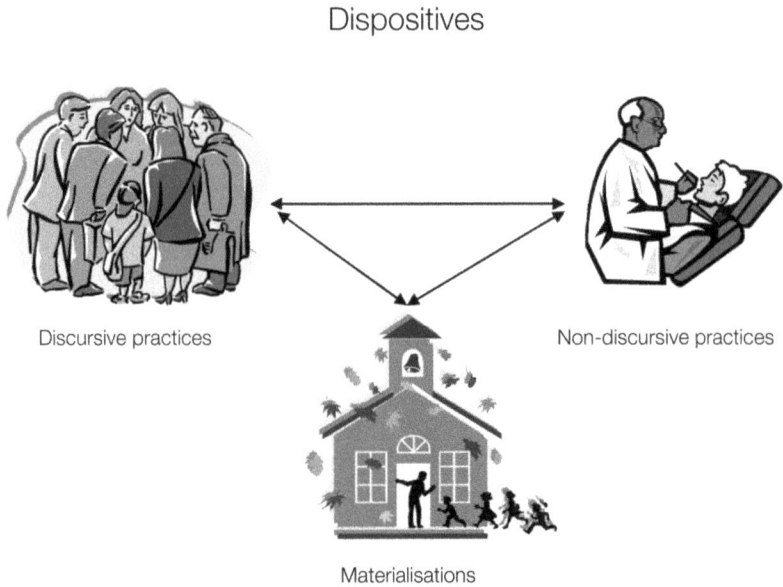

Discursive practices   Non-discursive practices

Materialisations

Figure 10.2. Jäger's *dispositif*.

I want to draw particular attention to Jäger's use of the word 'ensemble'. This is critical as it points to the mode of operation of the *dispositif*. It is not simply a cluster of independently functioning elements in proximity to each other, but an ensemble of independent and heterogonous elements functioning as a single entity (Stevenson 2007). The idea of ensemble also directs attention not just to the collectivity of the *dispositif* but also to the overall effect or impact of same. The point is that the disparate elements of the *dispositif* act in concert—though in differing ways to produce an effect.

Deploying the *dispositif*

Complex policy issues are deeply sociological in nature and are not easily susceptible to simplistic solutions that derive from the econo-legal mindset that dominates contemporary policymaking. We need the capacity to ask different questions, both about complex policy issues and the practice of policymaking itself, to avoid the uncritical pursuit of an ill-equipped analytical and professional practice that is failing us. We need to recognise 'we belong to social apparatuses [*dispositifs*] and act within them' (as cited in Armstrong 1992, p. 164).

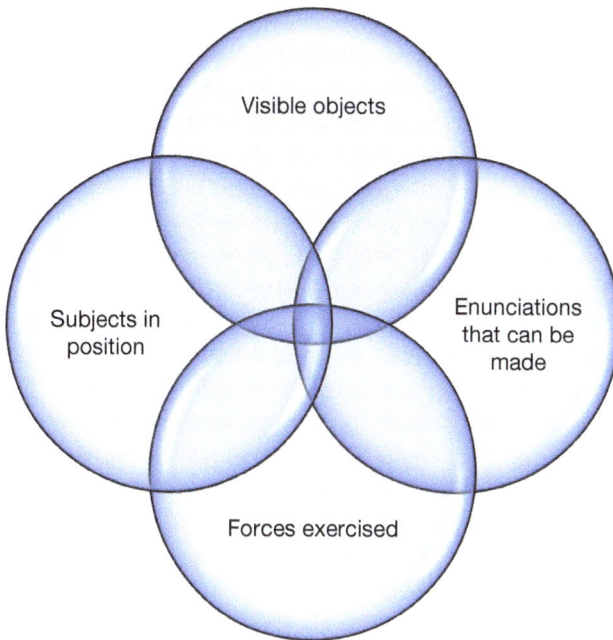

Figure 10.3. Foucault's concern (from Deleuze 1992).

If we belong to and operate within these social apparatuses, then understanding the way they work is critical. Deleuze draws our attention to the key interests Foucault was pursuing in his development and articulation of the *dispositif* as a concept: 'visible objects, affirmations which can be formulated, forces exercised and subjects in position' (as cited in Armstrong 1992, p. 159). As depicted in Figure 10.3, these modes of operation structure the *dispositif* and provide a suite of analytical lenses that help to sharpen our analytical and practical focus in respect of the policymaking enterprise. They represent four arenas of activity that describe the ways in which the *dispositif* works in policymaking. As such, they provide a useful guide to the kinds of questions that dispositive analysis generates.

Visibility and enunciation: What can and cannot be seen; what can and cannot be said

Policymakers respond to a particular version of reality in which some things can be seen and responded to, while others are obviated or not seen at all. In this sense, policymaking relies on a constructed reality in which objects are real insofar as they are meaningful to actors in particular contexts.

There are critical questions that must be asked, starting with the process that Schneider and Ingram (1993) described as the 'social construction of target populations'. As actors within the policymaking apparatus, we must ask questions about how policy problems and people are fashioned and constructed in and through what we do. Our professional conceit is that we are engaged in a profoundly rational, value free and evidence-based enterprise; however, in practice things are much less clear-cut.

The point is that a policy reality is a socially constructed artefact, a composite manufactured through a process of bricolage that draws on a variety of raw materials within an overarching framing narrative. In other words, reality is represented to be a certain way and understanding this is central to policy analysis (Bacchi 2009). *Dispositif* analysis demands that we interrogate what we are seeing and why. It recognises that the things we see, be they policy problems, people or solutions, reflect the way that light is structured and distributed within the apparatus that we are part of, and dares to ask: why is this so and might it be different? In this respect, narrative and discourse reign supreme.

This brings us to enunciation: what is said, how it is said and why. Australian academic Carol Bacchi (2009) challenges us to think more deeply about the normative foundations of policymaking by asking the simple question, 'what's the problem represented to be?', instead of asking what the problem is. In doing so, she raises the second mode of operation within the *dispositif*: 'lines of enunciation'. Enunciation refers to affirmations or statements that are made within the *dispositif*. There are two central dimensions to this aspect of dispositive function: the first concerns the content of what is said, the second concerns how it is said.

Discourse is how objects are framed, created and brought into view. We think through language and objects are formed discursively. We understand what is seen by what is said about areas or objects of policy concern. Language matters in the policy enterprise and social construction works through words more than through structure (Schneider & Ingram 1993). We see this in Australia through the words that are chosen to refer to particular policy issues or to particular policy objects. For example, ideas of a 'budget emergency' or a 'climate emergency' are embodied, not through data or information, but in and through what is said about data and deployment of the terms themselves. Consider how the active substitution of 'illegal arrival' for 'asylum seeker' in popular and policy discourses has served to construct policy problems and responses. In terms of the Aboriginal and Torres Strait Islander policy enterprise, consider, for example, how the notion of disadvantage has become discursively attached to the idea of Indigeneity. Such is the conflation of disadvantage and Indigeneity, even among some Aboriginal and Torres Strait Islander people, that the rising Indigenous middle class is rendered invisible or even illegitimate because these Indigenous Australians resist the dominant imagery (visibility) of the Aboriginal policy *dispositif* (Langton 2013).

The second dimension of enunciation concerns the manner in which things are said. By 'manner', I am not referring to media or mechanisms of delivery, even though these are not without significance. I have in mind instead the manner of speaking, the more nuanced and, I argue, more powerful aspects of narrative that go to questions of tonality, demeanour, gesture and expression. The way that something is said is as critical as what is said. Meaning, hence reality, is constructed from words and how they are used, including subjective elements such as tone and inflection, as well as word choice and how these are combined. Consequently, good analysis must have regard to the *how* of discourse as well as to its what! Hence, discourse is the location at which knowledge and power intersect (O'Farrell 2005).

Power and force: Actions taken or not taken

Power should be understood not only in terms of hierarchy and structure, position or office, but also as a deeply social phenomenon that emerges through interaction between actors within the *dispositif*. This perspective is often overlooked in the modern public sector. Deleuze's use of the word 'force' speaks to this missing perspective. In using this word, he points us not to the exercise of brute strength, or power as the possession of a particular individual, but to the physicist's understanding of force as the outflow of interaction between objects and the effect of that interaction on objects. Force is the push and pull that results from the interaction between objects. It is not inherent in a position but emerges as influence exerted. Force refers to the outworking of power not as the possession of an individual or the residual effects of an office but as that which emerges in and from processes of interaction within the *dispositif*.

Subjectification: Questions of identity and how we are understood

Subjectification is the process by which particular meanings are incorporated into the self or identity. Through this process, individual actors are positioned within the social space that the *dispositif* represents. This dimension concerns questions of identity both as to how individuals understand themselves ontologically and as a particular position or location within a set of social relationships. It concerns the roles that demarcate individual actors and groups of actors and the place they occupy in the policymaking regime; for example, policymaker versus policy object or decision-maker versus adviser. There is a powerful clue here about the potential for transformation of policymaking. Changing subjectifications can have a significant impact on the forms of knowledge and power that operate in and through the *dispositif*. New players entering the field, discursive shifts and variable engagement by actors reflect the ebbs and flows in how people see themselves and how they are seen within a particular social apparatus.

Analytical positions of dispositive analysis

While each of these represent a crucial analytical domain in the making and implementation of public policy, there is nevertheless a risk of conversion of the dynamism and responsiveness of the *dispositif* into a bloodless managerial technique; that is, the transformation of what is fundamentally a way of seeing and a mode action into a controlled process. One characteristic of modernist ideology is its ability to appropriate new ideas, apparently give credence to them but then organise the life out of them, subjugating them to its imperial epistemological and technical frameworks. Understanding the particular analytical dispositions that the *dispositif* produces reduces this risk. These dispositions are a repudiation of universals, a focus on becoming and the place of culture.

Repudiation of universals

Central to Foucault's thinking is the repudiation of the universal—or, more accurately, the 'universal universal'.[2] Social apparatuses no longer make an appeal to universal and transcendent foundations that sit

---

2   While Foucault rejected the idea of a universal standing outside of history and, therefore, being transcendent, he acknowledged that propositions arising from an historical epoch can take on the function of universals, which remain contingent and contextual.

outside of history. In the place of these universals the *dispositif* consists of multiplicities and draws from, and focuses attention on, knowledge that arises from context and place; is accessible only though relationships and belonging; and is characterised by subjectivity and contingency, rather than transcendence. This position is directly at odds with the modernist epistemic regime centred on formal, abstracted and propositional knowledge, and that purports to embody 'reason par excellence' (Armstrong 1992, p. 162). In such an epistemic regime, there are a number of things that are important and that bear on the professional practice of policymaking. The first of these is *place*, which needs to be understood as much more than simply geographical or spatial location. The second is context. Rhodes (2017, p. 116) makes the following observation: 'Human action is also historically contingent. It is: "Characterised by ineluctable contingencies, temporal fluidity and contextual specificity"'. Context needs to be understood more broadly than location. It must take account of the ideational and discursive context in relation to which policymaking is done. This should include historical context.

Lines of becoming

For Foucault, the *dispositif* is not predicated on eternal verities and their reproduction, but on the fundamental dynamic of becoming. The *dispositif* is about who and what we are becoming. In other words, there is a fundamental dynamism at work in the *dispositif* that adds to its analytical power. Foucault was deeply committed to the place that history (as opposed to the past) plays in discursive formation and the idea that every discourse has a history, or genealogy, that must be understood.[3] Without this perspective, the risk of reification is high, and likely to produce static and limited analysis and an unresponsive professional practice. At a minimum, this 'line of becoming' drives us to consider questions of change and transformation in the policymaking *dispositif* and to interrogate the social vision that drives our policymaking endeavours. In such a frame, knowledge that purports to be either settled or standing outside of history is deeply problematic. Identities that are posited as static and are either assigned or asserted, rather than negotiated over time, are similarly suspect.

---

3   This understanding was achieved via a process of archaeology.

There is a deeply embedded retrospectivity in much policy analysis. We look at data that describe phenomena as they have occurred and formulate policy responses on that basis. Little if any analysis takes account of the present situation and the operant knowledge systems that underpin the lived experience of intended policy beneficiaries, positioned exclusively as beneficiaries rather than participants or co-producers. In the case of Aboriginal and Torres Strait Islander people, this positioning is indisputable. In addition, little analysis, at least in my experience, takes account of where things may be going—other than the heroic assumption that what has been in the past will be in the future. This is the chief folly of rationalist thinking: having hit upon a universal, disinterested knowledge, one ought to be able to rely on it holding true at all times and in all places and apply it accordingly. What we discover in practice is that this is not the case and that knowledge, even of the settled kind, is really an artefact of time understood broadly as both an epoch and a continuum, and place beyond mere geography, to consider social and political location.

The third dimension that the idea of 'lines of becoming' invites us to consider is the question of social vision and the future state that is in the process of coming into view. Ideas about what might be, and certainly what ought to be, derive from deeply held social vision that, while filtered through political ideology, is fundamentally cultural in origin. We will return to this question later, but for now it is sufficient to bring the culture question into view.

The Policy Enterprise Model

Foucault's *dispositif* can be used in the Australian policymaking context, and it can help us map the functional terrain of contemporary policymaking, identifying the core components of this enterprise, and highlighting the points at which these components intersect and interact. I have developed the Policy Enterprise Model (Figure 10.4) to provide practitioners and analysts with a heuristic device designed to enable them to comprehend the nature of the policy enterprise. The model represents the arrangement of related elements that constitute contemporary policymaking. It locates policymaking in an interactive arena defined by five domains: policy actors, structures and systems, networks and alliances, policy paradigms and cultural context.

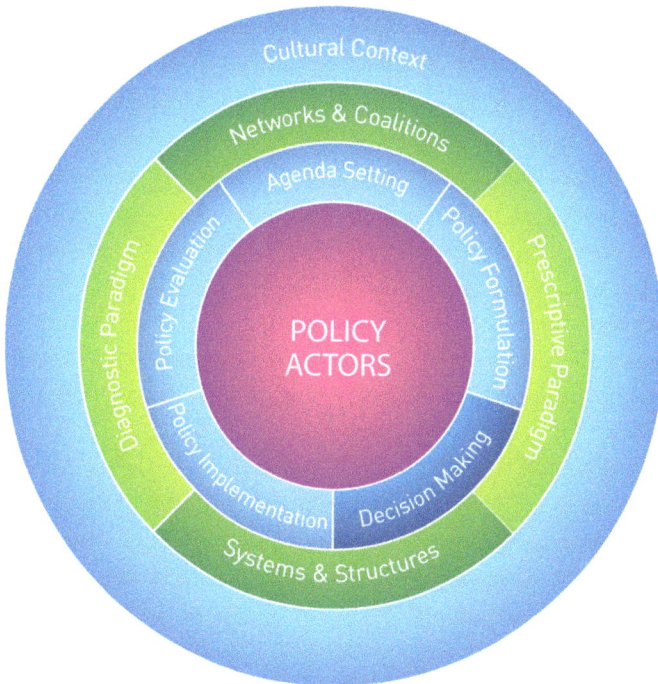

Figure 10.4. The Policy Enterprise Model.

The components

It is important to stress that this is an actor-centred model. It began as a way for thinking through the work of the public servant in policymaking terms. What is it that the public servant, as an intrinsic part of the policymaking process, actually does? The model posits the policy actor engaging in a number of discrete, though interrelated, bodies of work. In the model, these work domains are not presented as a cycle or a series of sequential phases, but as domains or kinds of work. None of this work takes place in a context-free environment, so it is important to recognise the key features of the context in which this work is done.

The immediate context consists of four elements.[4] The first, 'systems and structures', refers to the institutional and organisational context that characterises particular polities. The second, 'network and alliances', refers

---

4   There is an extensive literature covering questions of 'policy actors' (see, e.g. Althaus, Bridgman & Davis 2018; Howlett, Ramesh & Perl 2009; Sabatier 2007; Sabatier & Jenkins-Smith 1993).

to particular alignments of actors within a particular policy domain. The third and fourth, the 'paradigmatic core', refers to two primary policy paradigms, one diagnostic and the other prescriptive. More will be said of these below.

Finally, the outer ring of this model refers to the cultural context in which policymaking is done. The model posits culture as occupying a crucial, all-encompassing position relative to the other elements. Culture sits over, around, between and underneath the other elements of the *dispositif* shaping and influencing their complexion and function. Any serious effort to understand the nature of the policymaking process, including thinking through the potential to transform this process, must pay attention to culture.

Paradigmatic core: Diagnostic and prescriptive paradigms

At its core, policymaking is a profoundly paradigmatic enterprise (Béland & Cox 2013), involving shared ways of understanding the world that embody a priori intellectual commitments and behavioural imperatives (O'Leary 2007). In such an enterprise, what and how policymakers 'think' influences what they do in policy terms (Campbell 2002; Finlayson 2006). This thinking takes the form of 'taken for granted descriptions and theoretical analyses that specify cause and effect relationships that reside in the background of policy debates and that limit the range of alternatives policy-makers are likely to perceive as useful' (Campbell 2002, p. 22). The model posits a diagnostic paradigm through which policy problems and target populations can be comprehended, and a prescriptive paradigm through which policy responses can be developed and authorised.[5]

Paradigm has been defined as a set of 'received beliefs' held collectively (Kuhn & Hacking 2012). Kuhn posits that knowledge develops through disruption and displacement of paradigms rather than through accretion (as cited in Lakatos & Musgrave 1970). Hence, paradigms are governmental, underpinning conceptual and methodological continuity or 'normal science' operating within the authorising boundaries of the paradigm to regulate methodology, knowledge and inclusion in the scientific community (Kuhn & Hacking 2012; Cairney 2012). To understand the operation of paradigms we need to examine how paradigms are structured.

---

5   This proposition is similar to Snow and Benford's (1988). They identified three frames at work in policymaking: diagnostic framing, prognostic framing and motivational framing.

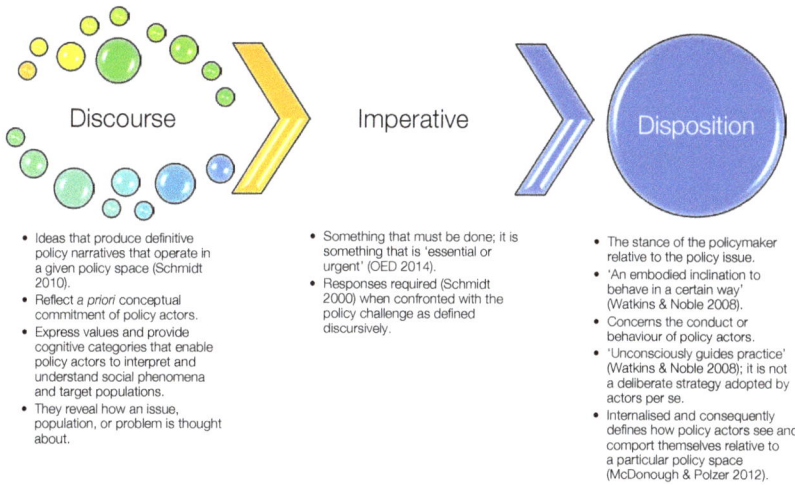

Discourse

- Ideas that produce definitive policy narratives that operate in a given policy space (Schmidt 2010).
- Reflect *a priori* conceptual commitment of policy actors.
- Express values and provide cognitive categories that enable policy actors to interpret and understand social phenomena and target populations.
- They reveal how an issue, population, or problem is thought about.

Imperative

- Something that must be done; it is something that is 'essential or urgent' (OED 2014).
- Responses required (Schmidt 2000) when confronted with the policy challenge as defined discursively.

Disposition

- The stance of the policymaker relative to the policy issue.
- 'An embodied inclination to behave in a certain way' (Watkins & Noble 2008).
- Concerns the conduct or behaviour of policy actors.
- 'Unconsciously guides practice' (Watkins & Noble 2008); it is not a deliberate strategy adopted by actors per se.
- Internalised and consequently defines how policy actors see and comport themselves relative to a particular policy space (McDonough & Polzer 2012).

Figure 10.5. The anatomy of the paradigm.

Policy paradigms consist of three interacting elements: discourses, imperatives and dispositions, as set out in Figure 10.5. These are stable conceptual structures that identify particular kinds of ideas and questions, necessary actions and specified roles for actors in the policy enterprise (Campbell 1998; Colebatch 2006; Howlett, Ramesh & Perl 2009; Sabatier 2007; Sabatier & Jenkins-Smith 1993).

The point is that the 'reality' encountered by actors is socially and discursively constructed. In the same way, while discourses shape meaning for actors, they also generate ideas about what must be done when confronted with the reality they define. These imperatives in turn inform policy objectives within a particular policy enterprise. These policy imperatives also define the role of, and enable, the policymaker. Policymaking is, therefore, the policy actor embodying a particular role derived from the discursive framework within which the actor operates.

Cultured beings

Policy actors are members of social networks and, consequently, are cultured beings—which is to say that we are socially and culturally positioned and that we function within, and from, a cultural context. None of us operates in a sociocultural vacuum and the idea that, in the practice of policymaking, we escape the influence of this is nonsensical and, in terms of the Aboriginal and Torres Strait Islander policy enterprise, dangerous.

According to Bennett (2008), 'culture is there, and it is there first'. If policymakers operate (inevitably and inescapably) in contexts in which culture exerts a pervasive influence,[6] it follows that policymaking is inevitably a cultural enterprise (Hood 1998; Wildavsky 1987; Wildavsky, Ellis & Thompson 1997), and that the products of this activity (i.e. policies) are themselves cultural artefacts with meanings and effects that are fundamentally cultural in nature. To understand our enterprise in this way provides us with a different and valuable analytical purchase on the question of improved policymaking and, via this, better outcomes for Aboriginal and Torres Strait Islander people. To pretend that what we are engaged in is a value free exercise in scientific objectivity risks exactly the kind of epistemological and practical imperialism described by Scott (1998) as sitting at the heart of the failure of the large-scale reform he examined in his magisterial work *Seeing like a state*.

Critical though it may be, the culture question stands as one of the most egregiously underdone areas of inquiry in the policy sciences. Seeking to understand why particular issues are framed and understood in particular ways, and to interrogate the underpinning social vision that animates policy work, demands serious engagement with the question of policy, as all of these questions have their origins in the cultural context in which actors operate. In this respect, culture is as inevitable as it is inescapable. Each of us is a cultured being and comprehending our own cultural positioning, as well as that of the intended beneficiaries of our efforts, is singularly important. I argue that this is indispensable because culture is an all-encompassing dynamic and there is no area of life that culture does not go (Fornas 2017, p. 2). Culture shapes behaviour (Kroeber 1963), cognition (Geertz 1983), how we govern (Geertz 1966), our public administration (Hood 1998) and the ways our social systems operate (Matsumoto 2001). To leave this question to one side because it is difficult seems fundamentally self-defeating.

---

6   This influence covers all behaviour including both what they think and how they act (see Finlayson 2006). This is not to say, however, that social actors are passive. Social structures, such as culture, are themselves the products of human interaction and also condition this action. This means that we shape our contexts as much as those contexts shape us.

Conclusion

Whether policy and policymaking ever lives up to its transformative potential is, of course, an open question. It requires the capacity to understand the nature of policy enterprise so as to transform it, and thereby produce policy that effectively addresses the challenges that confront Aboriginal and Torres Strait Islander people.

Driven as we are by fairly unsophisticated imperatives around delivering 'whatever works', a sharpening of our professional vision is in order. We need to cease the credulous application of approaches drawn from the increasingly indefensible, though imperial, high modernism of the kind Scott (1998) critiques, with its entrenched scientism, obsession with metrics, narrow intellectual parameters and ignorance of the role that culture plays in the policymaking enterprise. Instead, as outlined in this chapter, we need to consider other, often overlooked, analytical lenses that take a holistic view/systems perspective, position policymaking as an interactive arena and provide a role for culture.

References

Althaus, C, Bridgman, P & Davis, G 2018, *The Australian policy handbook: A practical guide to the policy-making process*, 6th edn, Allen & Unwin, Crows Nest, NSW.

Armstrong, TJ 1992, *Michel Foucault, philosopher: Essays translated from the French and German*, Harvester Wheatsheaf, New York, NY.

Bacchi, CL 2009, *Analysing policy: What's the problem represented to be?*, Pearson, Frenchs Forest, NSW.

Barber, M 2008, *Instruction to deliver: Fighting to transform Britain's public services*, Methuen, London, UK.

Barber, M 2015, *How to run a government: So that citizens benefit and taxpayers don't go crazy*, Allen Lane, London, UK.

Béland, D & Cox, RH 2013, 'The politics of policy paradigms', *Governance: An International Journal of Policy, Administration, and Institutions*, vol. 26, no. 2, pp. 193–5, doi.org/10.1111/gove.12034.

Bennett, T 2008, *Culture and governmentality: Critical trajectories,* Blackwell, Oxford, UK.

Cairney, P 2012, *Understanding public policy: Theories and issues*, Palgrave Macmillan, Houndmills, UK, doi.org/10.1007/978-0-230-35699-3.

Campbell, JL 1998, 'Institutional analysis and the role of ideas in political economy', *Theory and Society*, vol. 27, pp. 377–409, doi.org/10.1023/A:100 6871114987.

Campbell, JL 2002, 'Ideas, politics, and public policy', *Annual Review of Sociology*, vol. 28, pp. 21–38, doi.org/10.1146/annurev.soc.28.110601.141111.

Colebatch, HK 2006, *Beyond the policy cycle: The policy process in Australia*, Allen & Unwin, Crows Nest, NSW.

Commonwealth of Australia 2009, 'Strategic review of Indigenous expenditure: A report to the Australian Government', in Department of Finance and Administration (ed.), *Administration*, Commonwealth of Australia, Canberra, ACT.

Deleuze, G 1992, 'What is a dispositif?', in TJ Armstrong (ed.), *Michel Foucault philosopher*, Harvester Wheatsheaf, New York, NY.

Finlayson, A 2006, '"What's the problem?": Political theory, rhetoric and problem-setting', *Critical Review of International Social and Political Philosophy*, vol. 9, pp. 541–57, doi.org/10.1080/13698230600942034.

Fischer, F & Gottweis, H 2012, *The argumentative turn revisited: Public policy as communicative practice*, Duke University Press, Durham, doi.org/10.1215/9780822395362.

Fornas, J 2017, *Defending culture: Conceptual foundations and contemporary debate*, Palgrave Macmillan, Cham, Switzerland, doi.org/10.1007/978-3-319-57810-1.

Foucault, M 1972, *The archaeology of knowledge*, Tavistock, London, UK.

Foucault, M & Gordon, C 1980, *Power/knowledge: Selected interviews and other writings, 1972–1977*, Harvester, New York, NY.

Geertz, C 1966, 'The impact of the concept of culture on the concept of man', *Bulletin of the Atomic Scientists*, vol. 22, no. 4, pp. 2–8, doi.org/10.1080/00963402.1966.11454918.

Geertz, C 1983, *Local knowledge: Further essays in interpretive anthropology*, Basic Books, New York, NY.

Hasluck, PS 1953, *Native welfare in Australia: Speeches and addresses*, Paterson Brakensha, Perth, WA.

Hood, C 1998, *The art of the state: Culture, rhetoric, and public management*, Clarendon Press, Oxford, UK.

Howlett, M, Ramesh, M & Perl, A 2009, *Studying public policy: Policy cycles & policy subsystems*, Oxford University Press, New York, NY.

Jäger, S 2001, Discourse and knowledge: Theoretical and methodological aspects of a critical discourse and dispositive analysis', in R Wodak & M Meyer (eds), *Methods of critical discourse analysis*, SAGE, Thousand Oaks, CA.

Kroeber, AL 1963, *Anthropology: Culture patterns & processes,* Harcourt, New York, NY.

Kuhn, TS & Hacking, I 2012, *The structure of scientific revolutions*, University of Chicago Press, Chicago, IL, doi.org/10.7208/chicago/9780226458144. 001.0001.

Lakatos, I & Musgrave, A (eds) 1970, *Criticism and the growth of knowledge*, Cambridge University Press, Cambridge, UK, doi.org/10.1017/CBO 9781139171434.

Langton, M 2013, *The quiet revolution: Indigenous people and the resources boom*, ABC Books, Sydney, NSW.

Maddison, S 2009, *Black politics: Inside the complexity of Aboriginal political culture*, Allen & Unwin, Crows Nest, NSW.

Matsumoto, DR 2001, *The handbook of culture & psychology*, Oxford University Press, New York, NY.

McDonough, P & Polzer, J 2012, 'Habitus, hysteries, and organizational change in the public sector', *Canadian Journal of Sociology*, vol. 37, pp. 357–79.

Morrison, S 2019, 'Prime Minister's address to the Australian Public Service', 19 August, Institute of Public Administration Australia ACT Division, viewed 16 April 2020, www.act.ipaa.org.au/2019-pastevent-primeminister.

O'Farrell, C 2005, *Michel Foucault*, SAGE, Thousand Oaks, CA.

O'Leary, Z 2007, *The social science jargon buster*, SAGE, London, UK, doi. org/10.4135/9780857020147.

Oxford English Dictionary 2014, *Oxford English Dictionary*, viewed 8 June 2014, www.oed.com/.

Rhodes, RAW 2017, *Interpretive political science: Selected essays*, Oxford University Press, Oxford, UK, doi.org/10.1093/oso/9780198786115.001.0001.

Sabatier, PA 2007, *Theories of the policy process*, Westview Press, Boulder, CO.

Sabatier, PA & Jenkins-Smith, HC 1993, *Policy change and learning: An advocacy coalition approach*, Westview Press, Boulder, CO.

Schmidt, VA 2000, 'Values and discourse in the politics of adjustment', in FW Scharpf & VA Schmidt (eds), *Welfare and work in the open economy: Volume 1: From vulnerability to competitiveness*, Oxford University Press, Oxford, UK.

Schmidt, VA 2010, 'Taking ideas and discourse seriously: Explaining change through discursive institutionalism as the fourth 'new institutionalism'', *European Political Science Review*, vol. 2, pp. 1–25.

Schneider, AL & Ingram, HM 1993, 'Social construction of target populations: Implications for politics and policy', *The American Political Science Review*, vol. 87, no. 2, pp. 334–47, doi.org/10.2307/2939044.

Scott, JC 1998, *Seeing like a state: How certain schemes to improve the human condition have failed*, Yale University Press, New Haven, CT.

Snow, DA & Benford, RD 1988, 'Ideology, frame resonance and participant mobilization', in B Klandermans, H Kriesi & S Tarrow (eds), *From structure to action: Social movement participation across cultures*, JAI Press, Greenwich, CT.

Stevenson, A (ed.) 2007, *Shorter Oxford English dictionary: On historical principles*, Oxford University Press, Oxford, UK.

Watkins, M & Noble, G 2008, *Cultural practices and learning: Diversity, discipline and dispositions in schooling*, University of Western Sydney, Sydney.

Wildavsky, A 1987, Choosing preferences by constructing institutions: A cultural theory of preference formation', *The American Political Science Review*, vol. 18, no. 1, pp. 3–22, doi.org/10.2307/1960776.

Wildavsky, AB, Ellis, R & Thompson, M 1997, *Culture matters: Essays in honor of Aaron Wildavsky*, Westview Press, Boulder, CO.

11

The practical realities of policy on the run: A practitioner's response to academic policy frameworks

Louise Gilding

Policy on the run is an oxymoron. It is a given that policy based on robust qualitative and quantitative evidence is more likely to succeed. It is also a given that gathering and analysing evidence requires time and resources. However, the reality is that policy developers no longer have the luxury of time and resources. Decision-makers want answers to complex problems: fast. How can robust policy be delivered with limited time and resources?

The following is a practical reflection of my 20-plus years of experience in developing and leading strategy and policy across a wide array of governmental portfolios. It discusses how I made *sense* of many policy models, and how I iteratively developed my own blended approach based on *four questions and a triangle*.

My approach is by no means a perfect model, but is a reflection on how I have reconciled the constraints of time and resources with a desire to deliver policies that make a difference for my community. I will outline my approach by covering the following topics:

- my working definition of policy
- communicating policy to effect change

- a blended approach: four questions and a triangle
- what is the problem?
- what does the evidence tell us?
- listening for evidence
- multidisciplinary teams
- what should we do?
- what does success look like?

I then offer an example of applying the four questions and a triangle approach, in the form of a case study drawn from the experience of being involved as the executive group manager Housing ACT in developing the *ACT housing strategy: Growing and renewing public housing 2019–2024* (Housing ACT 2019).

My working definition of policy

'Policy is rather like the elephant—you recognise it when you *see* it but cannot easily define it' (Cunningham 1963). Working in the ACT Government is my vocation. My purpose is to serve my community. My mission is to solve problems by developing policies and systems that help solve people's issues and make this city a better place. What I have *seen* is that the essence of strategy and policy development is solving problems.

Good policy makes a difference for people. People intuitively recognise solutions to their problems, and when they hear a government policy that sounds right, it resonates. A further characteristic of good policy is that it requires minimal regulation because its design encourages buy-in and incentivises behavioural change. Often, when it is the right thing to do, policy is self-enforcing and does not actually need to be highly regulated. There are many different policy interventions such as 'tools, instruments, methods, measures, and interventions to change the behaviour of individuals and groups' (Freiberg 2010, p. 82). As a policymaker, it is my task to understand how these interventions can be used to achieve more or less of a certain (desired or un-desired) behaviour. To express this in economic terms, policy interventions should decrease negative externalities or increase positive externalities. In summary, my definition of policy is solving people's problems by incentivising different individual and community behaviours so that this city is a better place to live and work.

Communicating policy to effect change

One of the things I regularly say to my policy team—and this is perhaps a provocative statement—is that policy that cannot be implemented is not actually policy because it cannot effect change. Often policies sit in the bottom drawer, not being implemented because they are so complicated that even the experts cannot explain them. As Albert Einstein stated: 'If you can't explain it simply, you don't understand it well enough' (Goalcast 2017).

When I finished my Australia and New Zealand School of Government (ANZSOG) masters, my head was laden with policy models, frameworks and triangles. Asked to present my work on public sector transformation to key decision-makers, I wrote a short, high-level 'pitch'. At the end of the discussion, the following comment was made: 'This is great. Just don't let the policy wonks get hold of it'. Sage advice for any senior public servant—don't let the policy wonks get hold of it. Interestingly, that is precisely what I am: a policy wonk!

A blended approach

My response is 'yes, of course'. But the words have had great impact. As complicated as a problem or an issue may be, my job is to understand the complexity *and* to communicate it with simplicity so that decision-makers can actually effect change. Scott and Baehler (2010, p. 35) put it this way: 'High performing public officials succeed in balancing these competing imperatives on a daily basis in their professional practice … developing various integrated and blended models". There are many ways to develop policy and numerous policy models: intervention logic, policy cycle, eight-fold path of policy analysis, the rational and participatory approaches, the panic loop, cost–benefit analysis, multi-criteria analysis, systems mapping economic modelling and forecasting, scenario analysis and others. Present these models and the majority of decision-makers' eyes glaze over. Ignore them and risk throwing the 'baby out with the bathwater'. Equally, over-privileging a particular or favoured model reduces or limits options. By bringing together my academic study and the practical reality of working with time-poor decision-makers, I developed my own 'blended approach'. It is an amalgamated, flexible method. Importantly, when under pressure, I can remember it. When confused by multiple presenting problems, drowning in data, swamped with unrealistic recommendations and flailing for direction, it provides me with a way to stay on track and deliver results. In short it is four questions and a triangle.

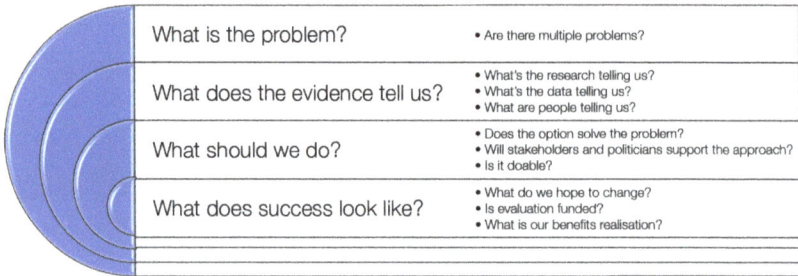

What is the problem?	• Are there multiple problems?
What does the evidence tell us?	• What's the research telling us? • What's the data telling us? • What are people telling us?
What should we do?	• Does the option solve the problem? • Will stakeholders and politicians support the approach? • Is it doable?
What does success look like?	• What do we hope to change? • Is evaluation funded? • What is our benefits realisation?

Figure 11.1. The four questions.

Question 1: What is the problem?

There might be multiple problems or sub-problems. Problem definition is an iterative process. As literature reviews, environmental scans and desktop analysis are commenced, the problem or problems to be solved are illuminated. There are many problem definition frameworks that can be employed at this point such as intervention logic and triple bottom line analysis. In my experience, it is worthwhile spending as much time as possible to understand, and revisit throughout policy development, this fundamental question. In his book *The regulatory craft*, Malcolm Sparrow (2000, pp. 137–54) implores readers to 'pick important problems and fix them'. It is tempting to move ahead to solutions without a thorough problem definition. However, one of the greatest and obvious policy pitfalls is to be working on a solution to the wrong problem.

Question 2: What does the evidence tell us?

Sources of evidence can generally be arranged into three main groups:

- research and literature
- qualitative data
- quantitative data.

There are many frameworks that can be employed to collect and analyse evidence, but 'fitness for purpose acts as the main criterion for determining what counts as good evidence' (Nutley 2009, p. 5); in other words, what suits the available time, resources and scope of the problem. Time spent answering Question 1 (what is the problem?) helps to clarify the evidence collection and analysis task required.

For many years I have used the *Triple bottom line assessment for the ACT Government* (ACT Government 2012a) as a framework to quality assure problem definition and identify evidence requirements by answering a series of questions about potential environmental, economic and social impacts. Within the framework, there is a multidimensional scan against which a proposal can be assessed. While often used at the back end of policy development, using the scan up-front provides a mechanism to identify what evidence is needed. When operating in time critical situations, the scan can provide a solid ready reckoner, particularly in relation to what evidence is known and unknown.

In January 2019, the ACT Government announced that it would establish a wellbeing index to monitor economic progress and guide its budget allocations (Burgess 2019). A first for an Australian jurisdiction, the index, which follows on from New Zealand's wellbeing budget, will monitor a range of indicators including homelessness rates and housing affordability, health outcomes, gender parity, environmental sustainability, social capital and participation in community activities. These indicators will no doubt drive evidence requirements for policy teams. A spokesperson for the ACT Government explained that: 'Drawing them together as a set of indicators that are regularly monitored and reported against will see them play a greater role in driving how we design and deliver both policy and service delivery' (Burgess 2019).

Good policy needs good evidence—qualitative and quantitative. What are the numbers telling us? What are people telling us? Do the numbers and people tell a consistent story? Stakeholder engagement is fundamental to good policy, and I am passionate about listening intently to what people are telling us. What are people's stories? Who are we actually listening to? Who do we actually need to ask? Engagement with people is key. There are so many different ways we can engage, and with the advent of social media and technology, these techniques are evolving and providing new opportunities for evidence collection.

Listening for evidence

There is much insight to be gained from actually (and deeply) listening to people and hearing the threads of the different things they say and the wisdom and insight that each individual brings. I find that it is from these conversations that recommendations start to form. These conversations can also triangulate the other evidence: literature, research and data.

By listening with clean (i.e. without bias) intent, I often hear people reflect in their own words what the theories, data and research says. For example, when engaging with stakeholders to develop *Growth, diversification and jobs: A business development strategy for the ACT* (ACT Government 2012b), I would often hear: 'there's not enough money to commercialise my idea', reflecting classic market failure. Academics express it like this:

> This more active government role is justified by the identification of market failures that hamper innovation. The existence of market failure is one of the principal rationales for government regulation. Suboptimal innovation occurs when market mechanisms are unable to yield socially optimal levels of investment in innovation either because the market is not getting or seeing the right signals or there are bans to diffusion and adoption. By its very nature innovation is steeped in risk. Only a small number of entrepreneurs succeed. Nevertheless, the successes more than compensate for the failures along the way. Indeed, in the innovation process the failures are just as important. Without investor willingness to experiment and risk their capital and the capital of others, there would be no innovation process. The role of government is to actively support this process by countering the market failures that describe innovation investment. (De Rassenfosse 2011)

In short, lack of investment makes it difficult to bring an idea to market. That is all a time-poor decision-maker has to hear. But that short statement needs a foundation of literature, research and data. One of the roles of a policy team is to be 'clean' (without bias) translators of evidence.

When consulting outside government, I find it is best to drop the rhetoric. Stakeholders need the genuine you—not the political spin and not the rhetoric of academics. Methodology matters less than building genuine rapport with stakeholders. It is important to hear the quiet voices. The squeaky stakeholders get attention but, for me, it is the unobtrusive voices, without hidden agendas, that can often articulate the underlying problems and potential solutions better than anyone else.

Strong stakeholder relationships are imperative, particularly when operating on the run. Stakeholder relationships formed in times of relative calm are lifelines in times of policy crisis. On many occasions, I have called a trusted community representative to test and triangulate what I am hearing and what the operational data is showing. I want to know what people are actually experiencing, and why. Keeping in touch and having a finger on the pulse is a given for any policy officer wanting to provide up-to-date intelligence and evidence to decision-makers.

Finally, a word about frontline workers (both internal to government and external): they are critical yet often overlooked stakeholders. Without frontline input and know-how, policy implementation will most likely fail. Listening and engaging with frontline workers and ensuring their perspective is part of the evidence base and used to inform program design is akin to 'insuring' for success.

Multidisciplinary teams

'Innovation happens at the cross-section of disciplines' (Gilding 2018). If we are to find solutions to complex problems such as homelessness, we need input from a broad range of disciplines and experts. Typically, policy teams within the public sector and in academic and research institutions only attract people from within their portfolio area. Justice departments have lawyers, planning department have planners and human services departments have social workers. For many years, I have intentionally built multidisciplinary teams bringing together lawyers, economists, planners, social workers, psychologists and behavioural economists. I deliberately bring different expertise, training and thinking into one division with the aim of sparking innovative thinking.

A word of warning: multidisciplinary teams are harder to manage. A cross-section of disciplines brings a cross-section of personalities, thinking styles, communications styles and cultural belief systems that can be difficult to coordinate. Nonetheless, the rewards of building such teams are great, as they deliver creative responses to policy problems. Moreover, and in my experience, multidisciplinary teams tend to have higher rates of successful implementation.

Question 3: What should we do?

A natural human tendency is to jump straight from the problem to the solution. However, successful solutions are found in understanding the problem and analysing the evidence. From these first two questions, the potential answers to the third become evident. Once possible options are established, I often use Moore's (1995) 'strategic triangle' as a criteria to judge options and establish a preferred recommendation. It sets out three broad tests (Alford & O'Flynn 2009) for any public sector strategy:

1. Does the option create *public value* (i.e. does it solve the problem)?
2. Is the option aligned with the *authorising environment* (i.e. will politicians and stakeholders support the approach)?
3. Are the *operational capabilities* available (i.e. is it doable)?

Options that meet these tests are preferred.

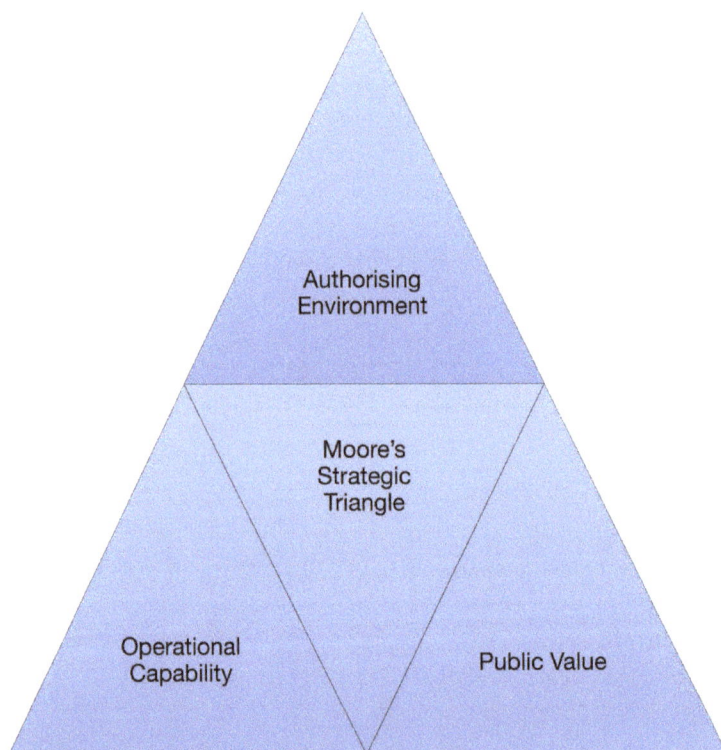

Figure 11.2. Moore's strategic triangle.
Source: Author's diagram based on Moore (1995).

The strategic triangle concept has caused disagreement between public managers and academics: 'Moore has noted that one aim of the Kennedy project[1] was to make sense of what is was that managers *actually* did; not what academics *thought* they did' (Alford & O'Flynn 2009, p. 175). Regardless of Moore's motivation, reflecting on my policy successes and failures, there is a correlation with whether the triangle is aligned or misaligned.

The following two examples illustrate my point:

- At the ACT level of government, an attempt by one minister to legislate for note acceptors on poker machines without a cash input limit was reversed by her own government, as it failed to provide for harm minimisation (Westcott 2015). This shows a clear misalignment between public value and the authorising environment.
- At the federal level of government, the Commonwealth's Home Insulation Program was misaligned in terms of operational capability: industry did not have the capacity to deliver the required volume and regulatory requirements were insufficient to ensure safe installation.

It is an illuminating exercise to review policy failures in relation to what part of the triangle was misaligned.

Question 4: What does success look like?

Rather than as an afterthought, the determinants of success need to be identified as part of policy development. Funding for evaluation is now commonly accepted and, more frequently, demanded. Understanding what the policy is designed to change and establishing benchmarks and data collection to measure success is essential and accepted as good practice.

---

1   The Kennedy project brings together 15 years of Moore's research, observations and teaching about what public sector executives should do to improve the performance of public enterprises.

Case study: *ACT housing strategy: Growing and renewing public housing 2019–2024*[2]

A recent Productivity Commission (2017) inquiry into human services declared that 'the social housing system is broken'. There is no doubt that public housing in Australia faces many challenges. In 2017, the ACT Government committed to developing a housing strategy to address housing affordability across all tenures and income ranges. My Housing ACT policy team was responsible for work in relation to homelessness and public housing. The policy and strategy development took over two and a half years. We used my four questions and triangle approach as a broad guide that integrated other tools and approaches to deliver the *Growing and renewing public housing 2019–2024* plan (Housing ACT 2019). The elements under each stage are described below.

Question 1: What's the problem?

After many months of discussion and data analysis, the multiple problems facing the public housing enterprise were synthesised into several key issues, including that:

- a growing population and increasing demand for affordable housing without corresponding property supply means growing waiting times
- an ageing property portfolio means that houses are increasingly expensive to maintain and expensive for tenants to heat and cool
- there is a mismatch between current stock and what tenants actually need (this is seen in high underutilisation rates [people are in houses that are too big for them] and overcrowding [people are in houses that are too small] and many tenants want a transfer)
- public housing provides sub-market rent, which means the portfolio, while asset rich, does not have the cash flow to address the three issues above unless it uses capital for ongoing costs.

---

2   I would like to acknowledge the various policy officers and experts who contributed tirelessly to developing the *Growing and renewing public housing plan*, a genius team who delivered an outcome that will make a significant difference for vulnerable people in Canberra.

1	2
A growing population and increasing demand	An ageing portfolio with inefficient dwellings with high maintenance costs

3	4
A mismatch between current stock and tenant need	Decreasing revenue base and increasing costs

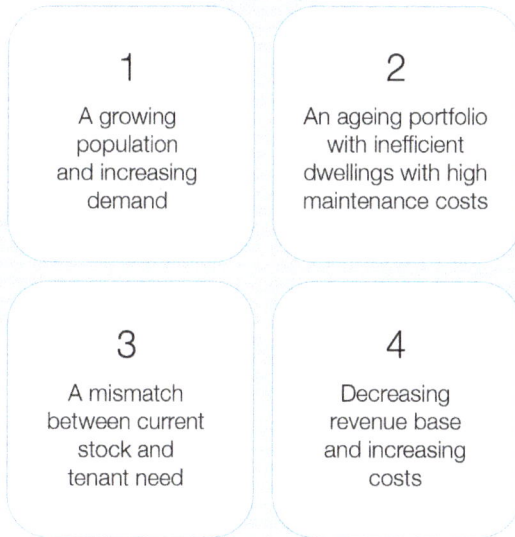

Figure 11.3. What is the problem?

Question 2: What does the evidence say?

An extensive evidence base was compiled as part of developing the housing strategy that included careful consideration of the key influences on the ACT housing market. This key land and economic data is outlined in the *ACT housing strategy* (ACT Environment, Planning and Sustainable Development Directorate [EPSDD] 2018), and showed that households in income quintiles 3–5 have a crowding-out impact on incomes 1–2, placing the latter in housing stress—that is, the lowest 40 per cent of income earners are spending more than 30 per cent of their incomes on housing. Translated from 'policy wonk', this means that, 'on average, the ACT is Australia's most affordable jurisdiction to buy and second most affordable for renting … but there's no doubt that there are people on low incomes and facing disadvantage who remain left behind in the current housing market' (EPSDD 2018, p. 1).

A substantial evidence base was developed that included reviewing the extensive national and international housing research and literature; and spatial, feasibility, portfolio, financial and demographic modelling. Accompanying the extensive literature and quantitative analysis was a lengthy qualitative engagement that included the establishment of a Ministerial Affordable Housing Consultative Group with representatives across the housing continuum, a housing and homelessness summit, small focus groups and workshops, and surveys and submissions (EPSDD 2018, pp. 11–12). These extensive qualitative data were analysed by the Housing ACT team to produce an engagement report that, in many instances, aligned with the quantitative data, crystalised the problems and then pointed to possible interventions and strategies.

Question 3: What should we do?

Using this evidence base, we developed three options papers addressing each of the challenges: context and challenges, our viability and funding, and growth and renewal. The papers outlined a broad range of options. These were judged using criteria similar to Moore's strategic triangle and, importantly, the quantitative and qualitative evidence fed into this process. These papers enabled busy decision-makers to quickly assess and consider possible solutions.

A critical part of the work was presenting the extensive evidence so that it was accurate and could be quickly understood. If you can say it in 30 pages, do not say it in 78 pages. If you can say it in one sentence, do not say it in three sentences. If you can say it in a picture, do. We included Figure 11.4 in our work. Even though the public housing business model is described every year in a plethora of annual report pages, it is largely and greatly misunderstood. This picture, which tells the story at a glance, has resulted in a new understanding of how public housing works and the incredible benefit that is provided to the most vulnerable people in our community.

The picture clearly shows the viability problem faced by all public entities in Australia (albeit using ACT data). What it also shows is the extent of public value that is delivered—that is, the investment in social inclusion and equity provided by the ACT Government on an annual basis (Scott & Baehler 2010). Financial statements do not do this. The story of public housing had not previously been presented to decision-makers in this way. It is the responsibility of 'policy wonks' to wrestle with the problem, evidence and options and present them in such a way that decision-makers have what they need. Pictures and diagrams that are designed with clean intent and based on evidence are a powerful tool to that end.

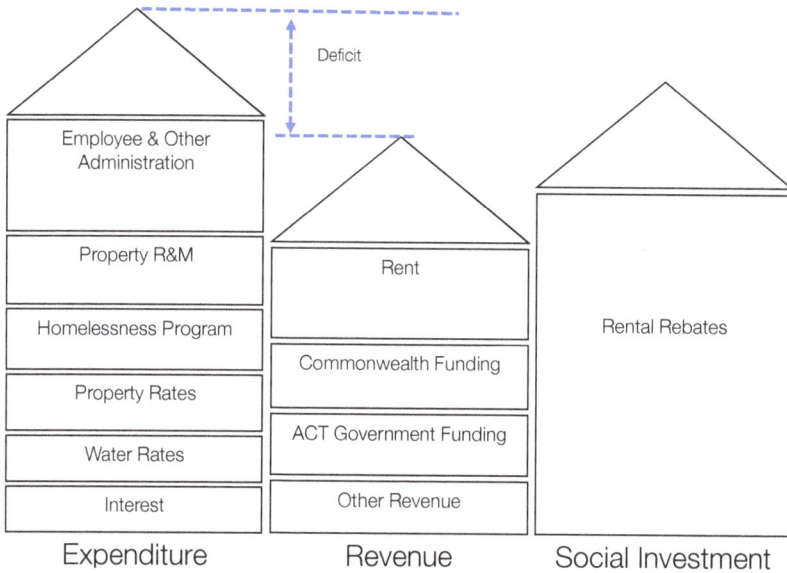

Figure 11.4. Visualisation of balance sheet data and social investment.[3]

The result is that the ACT Government is now investing $100 million to grow public housing in the ACT. I would posit that public housing is not broken when approached and funded as social infrastructure.

Question 4: What does success look like?

There are many benefits that will be realised from the implementation of the *Growing and renewing public housing 2019–2024* plan (Housing ACT 2019). These will be articulated against the wellbeing indicators and examined in a benefits realisation plan. In short, this plan will deliver 1,000 renewed properties and grow the portfolio by 200 properties to be dispersed throughout Canberra's suburbs and town centres. Our objective is to deliver homes that better match tenants' needs and provide a range of housing options. 'Having the right mix of social infrastructure means we are better equipped to provide vulnerable members of our community with the housing stability we need' (Housing ACT 2019).

---

3 I would like to acknowledge my South Australian housing colleague, Phil Fagan-Schmidt, who shared a similar diagram and sparked my thinking to adapt it and add the third 'house'.

Conclusion

I keep those four questions and triangle at the top of my mind. I find it a useful framework to draw on when I have 90 seconds to brief a minister or when I have three years to deliver a strategy. It is scalable across problems, timeframes and resources. It allows for integration with other models, frameworks and approaches while providing a true north to fall back on when immersed in complexity.

References

ACT Environment, Planning and Sustainable Development Directorate (EPSDD) 2018, *ACT housing strategy,* ACT Government, Canberra.

ACT Government 2012a, *Triple bottom line assessment for the ACT Government,* viewed 19 January 2020, www.cmtedd.act.gov.au/__data/assets/pdf_file/0020/331373/TBL_Assessment_Framework.pdf.

ACT Government 2012b, *Growth, diversification and jobs: A business development strategy for the ACT,* viewed 19 January 2020, www.business.act.gov.au/__data/assets/pdf_file/0017/430424/Business_Development_Strategy.pdf.

Alford, J & O'Flynn, J 2009, 'Making sense of public value: Concepts, critiques and emergent meanings', *International Journal of Public Administration,* vol. 32, nos 3–4, pp. 171–91, doi.org/10.1080/01900690902732731.

Burgess, K 2019, 'ACT government to introduce wellbeing index', *Canberra Times,* 16 January, viewed 20 January 2020, www.canberratimes.com.au/story/5997331/act-government-to-introduce-wellbeing-index/.

Cunningham, G 1963, 'Policy and Practice', *Public Administration,* vol. 41, no. 3, pp. 229–38, doi.org/10.1111/j.1467-9299.1963.tb01786.x.

De Rassenfosse, GJ 2011, *Understanding innovation: The role of policy intervention, a report for the Victorian Department of Treasury and Finance,* Melbourne Institute of Applied Economic and Social Research: Intellectual Property Research Institute of Australia, Melbourne, Vic.

Freiberg, A 2010, *The tools of regulation,* The Federation Press, Sydney, NSW.

Gilding, L 2018, 'Practical realities of policy on the run', *ANZSOG: Building communities of practice: Exploring how practitioners access and respond to academic policy frameworks,* ANZSOG, Canberra, ACT.

Goalcast 2017, 'Top 30 most inspiring Albert Einstein quotes of all times', viewed 19 January 2020, www.goalcast.com/2017/03/29/top-30-most-inspiring-albert-einstein-quotes/.

Housing ACT 2019, *ACT housing strategy: Growing and renewing public housing 2019–2024,* ACT Government, Canberra.

Moore, M 1995, *Creating public value: Strategic management in government,* Harvard University Press, Cambridge, MA.

Nutley, SW 2009, 'Past, present and possible futures for evidence-based policy', in G Argyrous, *Evidence for policy and decision-making: A practical guide,* UNSW Press, Sydney, NSW.

Productivity Commission 2017, *Introducing competition and informed user choice into human services: Reforms to human services,* Report no. 85, Commonwealth of Australia, Canberra, ACT.

Scott, C & Baehler, K 2010, *Adding value to policy analysis and advice,* UNSW Press, Sydney, NSW.

Sparrow, M 2000, *The regulatory craft: Controlling risks, solving problems & managing compliance,* Brookings Press, Washington, DC.

Westcott, B 2015, 'Minister bypassed officials advice', *Canberra Times*, 2 April, pp. 1, 5.

12

Documenting the link between policy theory and practice in a government department: A map of sea without any land

Andrew Maurer[1]

Introduction

In 2015, I was asked to develop a document that described the approach of the Commonwealth Department of Communications and the Arts to policy development. It would be used as an input in a new training course for departmental officers delivered through the Crawford School of Public Policy. I was chosen partly because I was regarded as having great policy expertise within the department, and partly because I had worked with the human resources area previously in delivering internal policy training. Mostly though, I had recently been moved to a sort of 'odd jobs' position in which I was expected to do whatever was needed to make the department work more smoothly. This was one of those odd jobs. The three parts of this chapter describe:

- the department's changing structure and policy training needs
- considerations that influenced the drafting of a 'policy handbook'

1   Thanks to Dr Trish Mercer, Dr Russell Ayres and Professor Brian Head for their encouragement and guidance. Thanks also to the Department of Communications and the Arts for agreeing to this chapter being written.

- the process through which the handbook was adopted as an accurate portrayal of departmental policy practice.

My background

My public service career up to this point had been moderately eclectic. Unlike many of my colleagues, after university I started in the Australian Public Service (APS) as a base grade clerk in a photocopy room, rather than entering through a graduate program. In the next 10 years I moved through a number of public service positions that might be seen as 'administrative' rather than 'policy' roles: trademark examiner, computer system tester, business analyst, technical writer, trainer, information technology team leader, internal auditor, project manager and general troubleshooter. I led a six-month mission in India for a United Nations agency, and then joined the Communications portfolio. Once there, I moved into a purely policy stream, mostly working in areas where the intersection of technology, law and economics called for new public policy approaches. After an interlude as the department's liaison officer in the minister's office, I returned to the department and led policy and program branches as well as areas responsible for international relations. When the department went through an extensive restructure, I spent a few months setting up a new policy branch, and then moved to a support role for the department's senior leadership—assisting with strategic planning, designing and implementing a new business planning process, and improving internal communication.

Mercer's (this volume, Chapter 3) description of a public service in which policy expertise is gained either through a mentored apprenticeship or serendipitous 'learning by doing' matches my experience. In my career, I had not received training in policy or policy theory. For the most part, when working as a policy officer, I was told to achieve a particular outcome and left to figure it out. Through practical work, I developed my own understanding of how to 'do policy' and got moved to increasingly difficult work at the conclusion of each task. There was an almost spartan 'with your shield or on it' attitude that is perhaps part of what contributes to the pragmatic mindset developed by policy practitioners in the public service. The work was a pleasure and a privilege, but at the same time I saw others develop very different concepts of a policy officer's role, and sometimes fail to develop a mental map of how to 'do policy' altogether. Over time, I sought out different descriptions of policy theory to better enunciate the underlying conceptual structure of my work. I read Productivity Commission reports on policy issues for insights on information gathering and analysis, and Australian National Audit Office administrative reviews to improve implementation techniques.

There came a point when I was transferred to lead a branch where the majority of staff were very good, but did not seem to understand *why* they were doing certain tasks—they did not have the mental context linking those tasks to an overarching policy process. I wanted to take the branch from a position where four or five team leaders and senior policy officers had policy expertise to a point where everyone in the branch was empowered to make an intellectual contribution to policy work. It was at that point that I really delved into policy theory, looking to build shared concepts of the policy process, and designing practical ways in which those concepts could improve the delivery of the branch's work. It provided something of a template for my later work on the departmental policy guide.

The path taken

For reasons noted below, I thought a useful approach for developing a departmental policy guide was to take one theoretical account of the policy process—Althaus, Bridgman and Davis's (2018) Australian policy cycle in their *Australian policy handbook*—and describe how different areas within my department contributed to each step of the cycle. It quickly became clear that, although I was developing a resource for the Crawford School course, the document could be a useful point of reference within the department itself to aid daily work during a time of extensive change.[2]

Triggers and influences

The brief I was given was simple: write a document describing the concepts and practices used by the Department of Communications when developing and implementing policy. There were a couple of immediate challenges:

---

2   In 2015, when the work being discussed here took place, the 2018 edition of *The Australian policy handbook* was not in existence; an earlier edition of the text was used. The most recent edition is referenced here for ease of access for readers who wish to follow up the reference.

- The department included various localised areas of expert policy practice, but did not have a department-wide approach—policy skills were mostly developed through a mixture of 'apprenticeships' and learning through doing.
- The department had undergone an extensive restructure that had shaken up all previous practices and corporate knowledge.

There were, however, some countervailing circumstances that could assist the exercise:

- The Australian Public Service Commission (APSC) had recently conducted a capability review of the department, which documented some clear strengths and made straightforward proposals to further improve the department's policy capabilities and practices.
- The departmental restructure had involved the creation of new areas—a chief economist-led research bureau, and separate market analysis teams—to improve the department's evidence-based policy capacity.
- After months of uncertainty, there was a strong appetite among the department's staff for any information or guidance that would establish 'a new normal' for how teams would interact with each other and how the department as a whole would successfully undertake its work.

There appeared to be an opportunity to deliver a 'policy handbook' that would not only be useful for the Crawford School's 'Policy Essentials' course, but would also address issues raised by the restructure, the APSC Capability Review and the ongoing operational needs of the department.

Restructure

The department went through extensive change in 2014 and 2015. Staff numbers across the board were reduced by 30 per cent, and all remaining policy positions were reshuffled so that most policy staff were working on different subject matter and in a newly formed team. Policy teams were further reduced in size to contribute staff to a new 'Bureau of Communications Research' led by a chief economist, and to create separate 'market analysis' teams with commercial knowledge and technology expertise.

The intent of the restructure was to move from having policy areas that specialised in communications industry sectors (i.e. telecommunications and broadcasting) to a model that holistically addressed cross-cutting policy issues (i.e. infrastructure, competition, consumer protection and content). There was to be greater consideration of the communications sector's contribution to the wider economy—reflected in the creation of the economic and commercial teams, as well as a new 'digital productivity' division. A great emphasis was placed on the department moving from a program and policy function to being a pure policy department.

All of this would require a new way of working—a division of labour would be applied to policy development. Reduced-size policy teams would no longer have to possess an all-round skillset; however, through communication and collaboration with other areas (particularly the research bureau and market analysis teams), they were expected to deliver superior results.

Review

The APSC, an agency tasked with ensuring that the public service is sustainable and effective in carrying out the work of government, had been undertaking a series of 'capability reviews' of government agencies since 2011. It developed a standardised framework to describe capability (see Figure 12.1), and agencies were individually evaluated in terms of leadership, strategy and delivery. The APSC undertook a capability review of the department while it was being restructured.

Given its timing, the APSC based its capability assessment on the department's future plans and how well it was tracking towards the outcomes of the restructure (APSC 2015, p. iv). The February 2015 report was positive about the department's ability to deliver government agendas, and optimistic about how the restructure would improve on that capability.

The review identified several areas for improvement, and advised that staff needed a better explanation of how the new structure and new ways of working would operate on a day-to-day basis. There needed to be improved mechanisms to plan and collaborate on work shared across different areas, and to track the achievement of objectives. The review also noted that the department's reliance on local 'policy apprenticeships' had a certain utility, but was not sufficient for its future ambitions. Managers needed additional support in mentoring their teams' policy skills, and there needed to be a more systematic approach that built a consistent set of skills across the department.

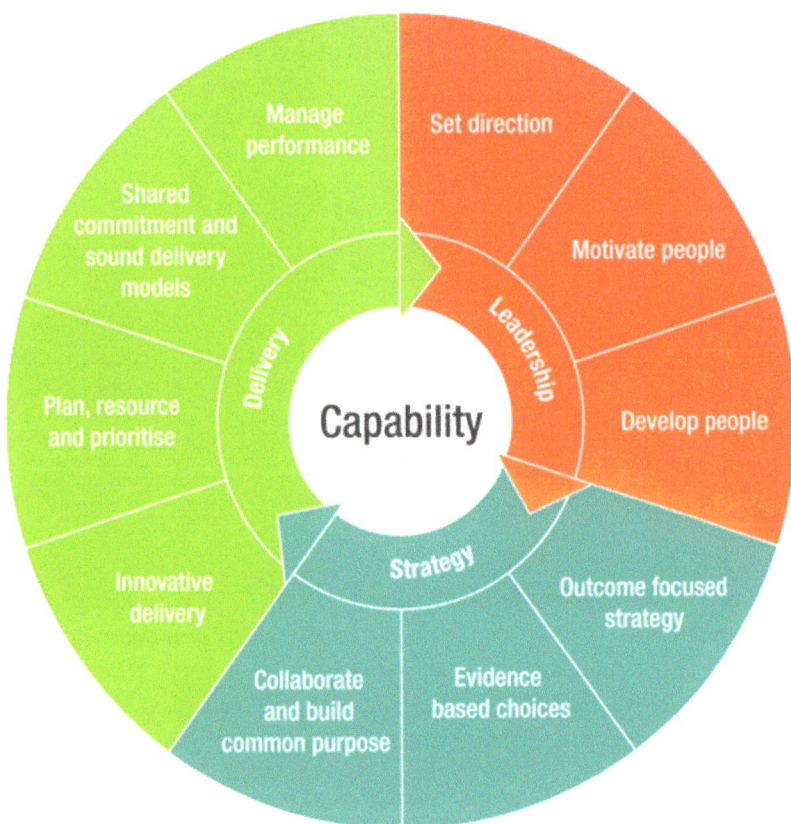

Figure 12.1. APSC model of capability.
Source: APSC (2015).

Further change

In September 2015, the department changed minister and secretary. The Digital Productivity Division was moved to a different government portfolio. The Ministry for the Arts was brought into the department as a policy and program division. Incoming staff were keen to get an idea of how the department, now called the Department of Communications and the Arts, conducted its work, and how to navigate its structure. Having gone through two years of restructure and uncertainty, remaining staff had the sense that, once again, they were in a very different department. They too wanted a guide to what the 'new normal' would be.

Developing a policy handbook

> Policy is enunciated in rhetoric; it is realized in action.
> (Kaufman 2006, p. 3)

During the restructure, the secretary of the department, Drew Clarke, established an executive committee consisting of himself, his two deputy secretaries and their direct reports, the department's first assistant secretaries. The executive committee addressed departmental resourcing and strategic management, and, at a high level, the development and implementation of policy. In May 2015, Clarke and the executive committee asked me to develop a document that would be used by the Crawford School's 'Policy Essentials' course. I provided progress reports to the executive committee as the work proceeded.

Initially, the request envisaged the target audience for the document to just be the new policy officers attending the course and the lecturers delivering it. However, the people attending the course would be working with other policy officers in teams led by experienced managers and practitioners. Those teams, in turn, were grouped by subject matter into branches led by assistant secretaries, who reported to the department's first assistant secretaries. These branch heads and team leaders were the ones making detailed plans and managing the day-to-day work of policy officers. No-one wanted there to be a disconnect between what people were taught in the Crawford policy course and their lived experience in the department, so the target audience was broadened to include all policy officers, team leaders and branch heads, as well as those areas that were not directly involved but provided support to the department's policy work.

Scope

I had been asked to document the department's approach to policy development. The reality was that an explicit departmental approach did not exist. For the most part, good policy work was done through individuals acquiring a thoroughgoing knowledge of the subject matter at hand, and an informal culture of collaboration and ad hoc information exchange. Individuals had their personal mental constructs that they used as a framework for organising their policy work, and long-established teams tended to share and follow common practices. The department's restructure meant that a lot of assumed and implicit knowledge fell away, as did the informal channels of communication and cooperation.

Obviously, branch heads, team leaders and their teams would work to re-establish these networks in the course of their daily work, but it would be a slow, organic process, made more tentative by the fact that everyone was learning new subject matter. The policy handbook was an opportunity to provide some points of common reference and signposts for the people creating new norms for departmental work and policy capability.

Process

The policy handbook went through a few iterations. In late May 2015, I circulated the first draft to the people leading departmental branches, the research bureau and the market analysis teams, and then held meetings to brief them on the content and purpose of the handbook. I suggested that they discuss the draft with their branches and teams and encouraged them to make changes—particularly in the chapters that described different areas' roles and how they would work together in delivering policy outcomes. There were a lot of proposed changes, mainly because people started treating the descriptions of areas' responsibilities and modes of interaction as a roadmap for their everyday interactions.

Over several weeks, I redrafted the various suggestions into a coherent version, and released it as an editable 'track-changes' draft to the entire department. I also provided progress reports to the department's executive committee, and to the department's audit committee. There was a brief period of renewed drafting, consultation and briefing during machinery-of-government changes in September and October 2015; this is when the Ministry of Arts was incorporated into the renamed Department of Communications and the Arts. The final product was provided to the Crawford School of Public Policy to use in the training course it was delivering to departmental staff, and republished on the department's intranet in November 2015.

Drafting

The policy handbook mapped the department's different work areas and described their operation using the Australian policy cycle as the organising principle. The handbook contained four chapters:

1. an introduction that outlined the purpose of the document
2. a description of the department's structure, and the thinking behind the division of labour between policy teams, market analysis teams and the research bureau

3. a thumbnail sketch of Althaus, Bridgman and Davis's (2018) policy cycle, illustrated by a description of the roles, actions and interactions of different areas of the department at each stage of the cycle

4. a final chapter describing 'additional practices within the department' that, strictly speaking, were not existing practices, but were additional reflections on policy techniques and theory that arose when drafting the handbook.

Why choose the Australian policy cycle?

There were several reasons that I used the Australian policy cycle as the foundation for the department's handbook. As a theoretical construct, it attempted to cover the entirety of the policy process, rather than 'deep-diving' into a single aspect. As a policy practitioner, I could not see a step in the cycle that I could readily omit, or additional material that needed to be added—it had a good internal logic and practitioners could see its relevance to most of the daily activities involved in policy development. I particularly liked the fact that it did not merely describe and analyse past policy work, but could be used as a tool to design new policy processes and to develop supporting project plans and work structures. To my mind, the Australian policy cycle was very well suited to planning and coordinating the work of multiple people or several teams: there was not an implicit assumption that a single entity would make decisions or undertake work all the way through.

Finally, I wanted the policy handbook to be used by the entire department, not just those attending the Crawford policy course, so it needed to overcome any innate scepticism about policy theory, and be taken on board by stressed people learning new subject matter in a new job. The basics of the Australian policy cycle could be readily picked up, and I felt that people with a reasonable amount of policy experience could feel confident in training others in it, or explaining their current work in its terms. Although not extensively cited in day-to-day work, I could point to examples of the policy cycle being referenced or utilised in work across the APS, and the extent of its adoption made people more confident in its legitimacy and utility.

The role of policy theory in the APS—a riddle wrapped in a mystery inside an enigma

The Australian policy cycle has clear strengths; however, in academic literature, it has also drawn criticism (summarised nicely in Mercer this volume, Chapter 3) for providing far too simple, idealistic and linear a picture of policymaking. The reality of policymaking involves a far greater complexity of action and policy actors. Cairney somewhat provocatively suggests that '*policymakers engage in a policy process over which they have limited knowledge and even less control* ... we need to give up on models that project simplicity and central control (such as the policy cycle)' (Cairney this volume, Chapter 13). In the case of the department's policy handbook, why not use a model that emphasises complexity and the absence of central control?

Cairney (this volume) notes a divergence between policy theories that 'help *explain* policymaking rather than seek to promote what *should* ... happen'. I think the distinction between the more advanced theories that help *explain* policy, and those that help *do* policy is a useful one.

In seventeenth-century Russia, there was a concern in some quarters that masses were taking too much time—some liturgies were up to eight hours long. It was considered wrong to skip any elements, so the cunning solution was to split the liturgy into smaller parts and have them all sung at the same time by different teams of priests. Masses were admirably fast, all elements of the liturgy were present. Unfortunately, from the congregation's point of view, this practice of *mnogoglasie* made masses a mad, incomprehensible cacophony with up to six teams of priests trying to make themselves heard and the beginning, middle and end of the mass happening at the same time. The priests generally knew what they were doing and why, but it was impossible for congregations to either understand what was going on or to meaningfully participate.

Policy work in government can be equally confusing. Language can be arcane, many activities are conducted in parallel and it is not always clear to participants how different activities relate to the overarching public policy process. The Russian Church eventually put aside *mnogoglasie*. In the public service, and possibly in all policymaking, it is here to stay. From my perspective, the Australian policy cycle's selling point is that, for policy novices, it brings clarity out of pure howling chaos. The recognition and comprehension of key concepts enables meaningful participation; this in turn leads to a more sophisticated understanding of policy and the policy environment. For the more experienced practitioner, it provides mental maps and concepts that can be used as an organising principle when planning and undertaking policy work. The fact that those maps and concepts are held in common with other practitioners enables collaboration across the organisation.

It was my view that a policy theory that emphasised complexity and lack of agency might be more accurate but would not enable proactive and confident policy work to be pursued consistently across the department. Essentially, the Australian policy cycle as described by Althaus, Bridgman and Davis (2018, para 21) is 'a heuristic … designed to help answer the daunting question "What do I do now?"'. At the time of its restructure, that was exactly what the Department of Communications and the Arts needed. The policy handbook was intended to be the starting point, not the culmination, of building policy capability in the organisation. This meant that its primary value would not be in its content, but in how it was read and used by its audience. Focusing on its audience, the handbook needed to:

- introduce novices to essential policy concepts
- give more experienced practitioners a shared language for describing policy work
- establish common expectations of how policy areas would work with each other
- provide the Crawford Policy School a point of departure to explore a more complex world of policy.

However, it was highly dependent on the concepts described in the handbook being incorporated into the department's everyday work.

Deployment

To be successful as a departmental resource, the handbook needed to be supported by the people who coordinated the work of policy officers—the branch heads. Both Cairney (2015) and Ayres (this volume, Chapter 8) have described a certain innate scepticism about policy theory among policy practitioners in the public service. At the beginning, there were similar sentiments from the branch heads, not from any sort of anti-intellectualism, but reflecting different concerns, namely, that the policy theory in the handbook would not do enough or that it would do too much. On the 'not doing enough' front, there was the worry that the use of policy theory would not improve the quality or ease of doing policy work, but would require additional time and effort so that people could demonstrate compliance with a newly minted but untried departmental approach to policy. On the 'doing too much' side, there was a worry that people in the department might be so concerned with following steps laid out in the handbook that they would not exercise judgement or develop their own expertise in the course of policy work.

Selling points

The branch heads' most pressing concerns were largely allayed when they read the handbook—their fears of a complex document requiring the doctrinaire application of irrelevant checklists had not eventuated. However, they were still lukewarm on the document. Many remained dubious about how the policy theory component of the handbook would be applied in their daily work. My initial thought was that unless there were some very clear 'selling points' that showed the policy cycle's utility for their future work, the branch heads might be inclined to ignore that part of the document.

I prepared (and tried) various arguments and explanations, but it became clear that regardless of how eloquent or well-reasoned my talking points were, they were not doing the job; it was less a question of whether the policy handbook was acceptable to the branch heads, and more a question of whether they were intellectually and emotionally ready to accept it. Advocacy from the author of the handbook was going to be taken with a grain of salt or discounted altogether. I decided instead to focus on giving the branch heads and the rest of the department a mechanism to build their familiarity and ownership of the handbook. The parts of the handbook covering the role and interactions of different areas of the department were regarded as having practical use and interest. I encouraged the branch heads to discuss with each other whether these parts of the handbook were accurate, and to return with edited text.

The handbook becomes a source of truth

The branch heads were quite positive about meeting to discuss the roles and interactions of different areas of the department. The new areas—the research bureau and the market analysis teams—were particularly keen to have their function documented and understood in the department. However, immediately following the restructure, they did not have work on hand to discuss and negotiate with the different areas of the department. Many parts of the department had the same issue. During the restructure, most areas had focused on tying up loose ends so that their successors would have an easier transition. It changed the nature of discussions.

In the absence of an immediate task that needed doing, most areas in the department found that the Australian policy cycle provided a good proxy to outline how future work would be handled.

In my initial draft, I had attempted to make the descriptions of different areas' contribution to the policy process as clear as possible, but had made it plain that I would be very happy to accept any change that improved accuracy and clarity. There was an initial flurry of edits as people suggested additional detail to describe their areas' responsibilities. This was followed by a slightly smaller flurry of reversions back to the original text. I had not expected it, but as soon as the handbook was released to branch heads for comment and update, it was latched onto as an authoritative guide to who within the department should be doing what work. The handbook was simple, it was practical and there was no other written description of how the department should work. People believed its narrative and started making choices based on it. The 'division of labour' approach to policy work was new and had some teething issues to work out. The handbook was used as a commonly agreed starting point when arbitrating disagreements between areas about how to take work forward. This meant that people were cautious about claiming too much (or too little) of a role in the policy process, and quickly became aware that any sweeping changes they put forward would be the subject of forensic scrutiny and discussion with the other areas they would be working with. The majority of edits ended up clarifying points of demarcation and making sure the descriptions of work would not be misconstrued by team members or by the department's senior leadership.

The process of wrangling out respective roles, responsibilities and expectations meant that people did not focus too much on critical analysis of the handbook's theory component—the policy cycle. They used the handbook as a whole as a starting point for their discussions and grew comfortable with treating the policy theory component as 'a given'. I think it established a usefully pragmatic attitude: the policy cycle was increasingly regarded as a useful heuristic rather than an omniscient oracle. It was not a set of instructions to be followed by each different policy team in every circumstance, but instead provided a consistent overall structure and set of concepts that could be used when planning future work.

Further feedback—the 'selling points' show up at last

From my perspective, a major change in the branch heads' collective view of the handbook came around the time of the first flurry of edits. I had approached a couple of people who I regarded as policy mavens: expert, fascinated by all aspects of the policy process and highly respected in the department. I asked that they reflect on what the department needed from the document and provide an unvarnished critique of the handbook to their fellow branch heads. One of them sent a late night email with some points that strongly influenced the subsequent edits suggested by branch heads. The points were:

- The handbook was written in a lively style. Descriptions were brief, clear and to the point. This should be maintained. Individual areas could put more detail in their business plans or internal documents if they wanted, but it was not desirable for the handbook.

- The Australian policy cycle was a well-structured, pragmatic construct that could readily be used to train staff in policy work.

- Linking the policy cycle to the department's structure and operation was a good idea, as it helped the theoretical component feel 'real'.

- The fact that the Australian policy cycle was relatively well known meant that it would be useful in discussing work with a variety of stakeholders.

- The description of the role and interaction of different areas of the department would be useful in orienting staff to the restructured department.

- People should be wary of 'drafting by committee'—inconsistencies and double-ups had crept in when different areas had edited the text.

- Although the handbook and the policy cycle both made it clear that policy development did not consist of a fixed sequence of actions, it would be good if that message were emphasised. Novice policy practitioners tended to apply the things they learnt in a mechanical fashion. Adaptability and judgement were key. Checklists and anything that implied a rigid sequence should be avoided.

I think that, unconsciously, the branch heads had started to accept the handbook. The late night email perceptibly repositioned the branch heads' conscious thinking about the document. They no longer approached the handbook as a passive audience; they started thinking about it as a tool to be used—whether to negotiate roles across the department, develop their staff or communicate the nature of their work with internal and external stakeholders.

Organic circulation and an anticlimactic launch

As part of their collaboration and consultation across different areas, teams and branches started describing their future work to each other in terms of the policy cycle—it was increasingly being used as a common language across the department's policy work. When I redesigned the department's business planning process (another odd job that I had been assigned) or briefed the audit committee on the department's response to the APSC Capability Review, I included cross-references to material covered in the handbook. It meant that, when departmental staff undertook business planning or reporting to the audit committee, they could do so using the handbook's structure and concepts as a commonly understood frame of reference. The policy cycle was subtly becoming pervasive and, at the same time, less exciting and less foreign. People were using it to plan future activities in a matter of fact way—they were not thinking about it as a theoretical model, but as a way of organising policy work that was congruent with the way the department did things.

At the beginning of the consultation process, I had encouraged branch heads to give early copies of the handbook to their staff: some did, some did not. During the course of discussions between different areas of the department, everyone was talking about future work in terms of the handbook's contents, and branch heads and section heads often continued to use the same language and concepts for their areas' internal planning. Staff involved in these planning sessions had a very strong sense that, if they read the mysterious handbook that was being alluded to, they would have an inside track on understanding what was going on. The more enterprising staff that had not yet received a copy started seeking it out, either from me or from fellow staff in areas where it had been more generally shared. They also tended to make a point of passing it on to their friends and colleagues.

As it became apparent that slightly different versions were starting to circulate, I released a final draft to the entire department for a last round of review and comments. By this stage, the Ministry of Arts had joined the portfolio. Their response was that the handbook was useful for orienting staff to how the department worked, and that the way they worked matched (more or less) the policy cycle, although they had not referenced it as explicitly as the rest of the department seemed to. The rest of the department seemed a bit puzzled by the final round of consultation. The handbook accurately described the policy process and division of policy work between areas; it matched what everyone knew—what more was needed?

The final release of the document in November 2015 was pleasantly low-key. A copy was added to the department's intranet, and a copy provided to the Crawford School of Public Policy so that they could include it in the new policy course they would deliver to selected departmental staff.

I had early feedback from course participants: the handbook helped them to better understand the department and matched how their fellow team members and their managers were tending to talk about policy development. However, they would have liked to see some checklists or flowcharts to use when they returned to work.

I had been using the department's electronic file management system to keep track of accesses and edits to the handbook during the consultation phase. There had been a lot of different people reading it in the month immediately before and after its finalisation. After that, the number of people accessing the document dropped off, with some upticks each time a new Crawford Policy School course started (interestingly, it was not just course attendees who were opening the document), each time we had an influx of new staff or graduates join the department, and at certain stages in the annual business planning process. Mostly though, the contents of the handbook seemed to have become the 'new normal' for the department, and the document itself did not need to be referred to.

Conclusion: Reflections on policy theory and the policy handbook

I was asked to document the department's approach to policy, and found that, while there was a diversity of policy practitioners, some highly expert, there was no universally held theory or practice. Instead, there was a certain mystique attached to policy work and what Ayres describes as 'being inside the "black box"'—a combination of everyday experience and implicit knowledge that meant some and not others were regarded as possessing a 'policy brain' (Ayres this volume, Chapter 8).

The APSC Capability Review had identified that the department's traditional approach of policy apprenticeships and 'learning by doing' worked to a certain extent, but that to strengthen the organisation's capability, a more systematic approach was needed. I have not mentioned it previously, but there were a series of publications questioning whether the APS more generally had been suffering a decline in public policy capability, institutional memory and, on an individual level, the analytical and communication skills needed to fulfil its role in the Australian polity (Behm 2015; Button 2012; Shergold 2015; Tingle 2015). There was a degree of self-examination within the department on whether these concerns were true, and what might be done. At the same time, all previous practices and corporate knowledge had been shaken up by a radical restructure and downsizing, which had taken close to a year to put in place. People wanted to know how the restructured department would operate, so they could get on with their work. A clear map of how things would work on a day-to-day basis did not exist. The handbook needed to address a present organisational need.

Was the handbook a success?

From my perspective, the most substantive work associated with the handbook was undertaken by the branch heads and team leaders when they adopted its concepts into everyday practice. The text of the handbook did not change radically between its first draft and final release, but in that time I saw it move from being a dubious and theoretical document, to a charter for how things ought to be, to a basis for negotiating work and, finally, ending as a factual report of how policy work was handled in the department.

I would say that the handbook was most successful when it was still being edited and haggled over. The inclusion of the policy cycle gave the handbook a clear structure and intellectual rigour. The matching description of roles and responsibilities within the department made the theoretical component relevant to the handbook's audience. The fact that everyone knew the handbook's contents, and everyone was using it, was the thing that made it real. The policy cycle became a common language across the department, people knew their own role and the role of other areas, and there were clear structures for communication and collaboration to take work forward.

Jorge Luis Borges (1985) wrote a short story, 'On exactitude in science', about an empire that sought to create more and more accurate maps of its territory: 'the Map of a Single province covered the space of an entire City, and the Map of the Empire itself a single Province'. These were regarded as deficient and so the cartographers created a map that was precisely the same scale as the empire. It proved too cumbersome to use or maintain over time, and so the story reports that it was abandoned.

There are a lot of thoughts that can be taken from the story, such as: when you have the reality of lived experience, you do not need a 1:1 map. The readership of the handbook declined over time, partly because the reality it described was so apparent and well understood. Perhaps a more positive way of looking at it is put forward by Althaus, Bridgman and Davis (2018, para 19) in the introduction to their text:

> The policy cycle is just a starting point for understanding. Its role is to teach policy to those for whom it is not a familiar companion from a lifetime of practice and study … a simple model helps order reality and provide a sense of direction … With time, it may seem too simple—but by then the model has done its work.

The departmental handbook was something that individual policy practitioners could learn from, internalise and grow beyond.

From an organisational perspective, the success was having the department adopt commonly understood policy concepts and heuristics, and build a larger pool of people with a shared understanding of the fundamentals of the agency's policy work. The challenge in future will be entropy: humans forget and organisations change. New staff join, other staff move on, organisational structures and everyday practices adapt to meet new needs. Maintaining the currency of written documentation can be nearly as onerous as Borges's map. Periodic mechanisms like the APSC Capability Review may operate as a suitable trigger for agencies to identify when their policy capability needs to be refreshed.

References

Althaus, C, Bridgman, P & Davis, G 2018, *The Australian policy handbook: A practical guide to the policy making process*, 6th edn, Allen & Unwin, Sydney, NSW.

Australian Public Service Commission 2015, *Capability review: Department of communications*, viewed 10 January 2020, www.apsc.gov.au/capability-review-department-communications.

Behm, A 2015, *No, minister: So you want to be a chief of staff?* Melbourne University Press, Melbourne, Vic.

Borges, JL 1985, 'On exactitude in science', in NT di Giovanni (trans.), *A universal history of infamy*, Penguin Books, Harmondsworth, UK.

Button, J 2012, *Speechless: A year in my father's business*, Melbourne University Press, Melbourne, Vic.

Cairney, P 2015, 'How can policy theory have an impact on policymaking? The role of theory-led academic-practitioner discussions', *Teaching Public Administration*, vol. 33, no. 1, pp. 22–39, doi.org/10.1177/0144739414532284.

Kaufman, H 2006, *The forest ranger: A study in administrative behavior*, Resources for the Future, Washington, DC.

Shergold, P 2015, *Learning from failure: Why large government policy initiatives have gone badly wrong in the past and how the chances of success in the future can be improved*, APSC, Canberra, ACT.

Tingle, L 2015, 'Political amnesia: How we forgot how to govern', *Quarterly Essay*, 60, Black Inc., Collingwood, Vic.

PART 3

How can theory better inform practice and vice versa?

13

Taking lessons from policy theory into practice

Paul Cairney

Introduction

Policy theorists and policy practitioners could learn from each other continuously if they could communicate more frequently and effectively. They could build on some promising developments, which suggest that there is scope for mutual learning between policy theorists and practitioners (see Threlfall & Althaus this volume, Chapter 2). Academics draw general and relatively abstract conclusions from multiple cases, and their work has *some* impact on practitioner experience (such as via early career development training). Practitioners draw conclusions from rich descriptions of direct experience in specific cases, and these experiences can often inform policy studies (such as via elite interviews). How can we bring together their insights and use a language that we all understand and appreciate?

This chapter focuses on the role of policy theory in that conversation. Many policy theories could be valuable to policy practitioners if communicated more effectively (or, as Ayres [this volume, Chapter 8] describes, if they use them directly to describe their own task). In other words, the implications have to be relevant and feasible to practitioners, the language needs to be clear to a wider audience and the presentation needs to compete well with other models (such as the classic policy cycle). To maximise their impact, we need to turn two potential obstacles into advantages.

First, policy theories provide relatively abstract insights, producing general conclusions that are not immediately obvious to practitioners if they seek more concrete advice. However, we can use their broad insights to identify the extent to which individual practitioner experiences are specific to their own context or part of a 'universal' experience. In particular, some general stories of policymaking have profound implications about the limits to policymaker attention and the lack of government control over policy processes.

Second, policy theories focus primarily on explaining policymaking, and few studies offer practical guidance. As such, they are often ignored in favour of less accurate but more user-friendly models. Further, guidance from policy theory tends to appeal to policymakers' sense of pragmatism (about adapting to the limits to their powers) without accounting for key pressures, such as the electoral environment in which all policy practitioners operate, and in which elected policymakers in government have to project power. However, we can at least use theories to identify key ethical and practical issues, partly to assess the value of simpler and allegedly more practical models.

No single account of policy theories can cover their depth and variety. Rather, I outline one story, based on key elements of many policy theories. Its main message is that policymakers can only pay attention to a small proportion of their responsibilities, and they engage in a policy process over which they have limited knowledge and even less control. I use this story to identify key implications for two main reference points in academic–practitioner discussions:

1. to question the descriptive and practical value of the 'policy cycle' image of policymaking via a series of stages
2. to reject the slogan 'evidence-based policymaking' as a useful or realistic way to describe governance.

I conclude by describing some examples—from personal experience—of how academics and practitioners can engage with each other to consider the role of evidence and governance in a political process.

Policy theory: A story of policymaker psychology and policymaking complexity

Some models are popular because they provide a low-jargon message about how policymaking could, and perhaps should, be made (Cairney 2015). More sophisticated policy theories may be more accurate, and potentially more useful, but 'they are also less accessible to researchers seeking conceptual clarity and to practitioners looking for useful knowledge of policymaking' (Cairney, Heikkila & Wood 2019, p. 1). Therefore, my first task is to project the sense that we can synthesise key policy theory insights to produce a low-jargon story of policymaking with practical value.

Put most simply, *this story is that policymakers engage in a policy process over which they have limited knowledge and even less control.* If so, we need to give up on models that project simplicity and central control (such as the policy cycle) and be clear on what the meanings of popular aims—such as 'evidence-based policymaking'—are, or could be, in practice.

This story is based on two factors (see Cairney 2020, ch. 13). The first relates to 'bounded rationality' (Simon 1976) and policymaker psychology. The world contains an almost infinite amount of information, but humans have finite cognitive abilities. By necessity, they must combine cognition and emotion to limit information searches and make choices (Cairney & Kwiatkowski 2017; Gigerenzer 2001, pp. 37–8; Kahneman 2012, p. 20). We can spin this process negatively, with reference to the 'cognitive biases' that prompt humans to make suboptimal decisions (such as by engaging only with information they already understand or being vulnerable to 'groupthink'), or positively to describe 'fast and frugal heuristics' and the human ability to make efficient choices based on emotion, values and simple strategies such as trial and error (Gigerenzer 2001, pp. 37–8).

In policy studies, bounded rationality translates into a variety of assumptions or expectations, but a key story is that policymakers can only pay attention to a tiny proportion of their responsibilities, and policymaking organisations struggle to process all policy-relevant information. They must prioritise some issues and information and ignore the rest (Baumgartner, Jones & Mortensen 2018). They do so in a variety of ways: drawing on fundamental beliefs such as ideologies, paradigms, hegemons and core beliefs; relying on organisational rules;

listening only to their allies; engaging in trial and error strategies; making quick emotional judgements in relation to social stereotypes; and telling or following simple stories that limit attention to a small number of a) preferred ways to frame policy problems and b) politically feasible ways to solve them (Cairney 2020; Jenkins-Smith et al. 2018; Ostrom 2007; Schneider et al. 2014; Shanahan et al. 2018).

The second factor relates to complex policymaking environments (see also Geyer & Cairney 2015, on 'complex systems'). We can describe this environment with reference to five constituent parts, summarised in Table 13.1, and accompanied by a possible moral for each factor. Combined, the story is that policymakers struggle to understand (far less control) an environment in which there are many actors spread across many venues, each with their own rules, ideas, networks, and responses to socioeconomic conditions and events.

Table 13.1. Bounded rationality in a complex policymaking environment.

Concept	Academic summary of each concept	One moral of the story
Bounded rationality	Policymakers combine cognition and emotion to limit information searches and make choices.	Policymakers cannot process all policy-relevant information.
Actors	There are many actors—including policymakers and influencers—spread across many types of policymaking venues (venues are sources of authoritative choice).	Power is not concentrated in a single centre of government.
Institutions	Each venue contains its own 'standard operating procedures' or 'rules of the game'. Some are formal, written and understood easily. Others are informal, unwritten and often taken for granted or communicated through socialisation.	There is no single rule book.
Networks	Each venue can produce its own networks of policymakers and influencers, and the lines between formal responsibility and informal influence are blurry.	There is no singular process of consultation or simple way to coordinate action.
Ideas	Actors in each venue draw on a different set of core ideas or beliefs about the nature of policy problems and the acceptable range of solutions.	A language in good currency in one venue may have no value in another.
Context and events	Natural, social and economic factors limit policymakers' abilities to address and solve policy problems. Routine and non-routine events help to set the policy agenda and influence the resources available to actors.	Policymakers do not control key events and socioeconomic conditions.

Source: Adapted from Cairney (2020), John (2003, p. 495), Heikkila and Cairney (2018), and Ostrom (2007).

Lindblom's (1959, 1979) incrementalism is a classic way to describe how policymakers address bounded rationality in such policymaking environments: they adopt pragmatic ways to a) gather and use information, b) engage in strategic analysis and c) negotiate political settlements that do not depart radically from the status quo. In other words, policy change is incremental because people see the benefits of only studying in-depth the changes that would be *technically feasible*, in relation to available resources, and *politically feasible*, in relation to current policy and the balance of power. Further, Lindblom's phrase 'muddling through' is popular among many practitioners, perhaps because it sums up the idea that their options are limited but they are still making key choices about how to deal with their environment. 'Muddling through' highlights pragmatism and realism without giving up on the idea of some degree of central direction. Similarly, 'disjointed incrementalism' describes many pragmatic strategies that will be familiar to practitioners, including the intensive analysis of a small number of options (rather than a heroic sweep of all possible choices) and trial and error learning.

Yet, this interpretation of Lindblom's account is potentially misleading in two main ways. First, 'punctuated equilibrium theory' (PET) shows that policymaking systems actually produce 'hyperincremental' *and* non-incremental policy change, or the combination of long periods of policymaking stability and bursts of instability (Baumgartner, Jones & Mortensen 2018). Second, PET is one of many approaches that highlight the lack of policymaker awareness of the processes over which they ostensibly have control. PET studies highlight the role of 'disproportionate information processing', in which policymakers and organisations devote minimal attention to most issues (and maximal attention to some), or their attention lurches from one issue to another without a proportionate shift in information on the size of a problem. Policymakers set goals but 'they are not generally effective in judging the connections between [their] goals and the complex reality they face' (Jones & Thomas 2017, p. 49). All policy actors communicate their particular expertise within a much larger system of which they have almost no knowledge (Sloman & Fernbach 2017). In any situation, 'most members of the system are not paying attention to most issues most of the time' (Baumgartner 2017, p. 72).

This scarcity of attention and environmental awareness helps explain why the 'centre' will always be subject to limits to their coordinative capacity (see Cairney 2020):

- *Limited choice.* Policymakers inherit organisations, rules and choices. Most 'new' choice is a revision of the old (Hogwood & Peters 1983; Rose 1990).

- *Limited attention.* Policymakers must ignore almost all of the policy problems for which they are formally responsible. They pay attention to some, and delegate most responsibility to civil servants. Bureaucrats rely on other actors for information and advice, and they build relationships on trust and information exchange.

- *Limited central control.* Policy may appear to be made at the 'top' or in the 'centre', but in practice policymaking responsibility is spread across many levels and types of government (many 'centres'). Policy outcomes appear to 'emerge' locally despite central government attempts to control their fate. This diffusion of power is partly through choice (such as in federal systems), but also borne of necessity (Cairney, Heikkila & Wood 2019).

- *Limited policy change.* Most policy change is minor, made and influenced by actors who interpret new evidence through the lens of their beliefs. Well-established beliefs limit the opportunities of new solutions. New solutions succeed only during brief and infrequent windows of opportunity.

This *description* of policymaking must inform *prescription*: seeking policymaking solutions based on the idea of an all-knowing and all-powerful centre is like trying to fly unaided rather than designing and using a plane (Lindblom 1964). One frequent source of advice is via complexity theory, in which scholars generally encourage policymakers to accept and describe their limits: accept routine error, reduce short-term performance management, engage more in trial and error, and 'let go' to allow local actors the flexibility to adapt and respond to their context (Cairney 2012). In other words, to give up on the idea of being 'able to manipulate systems in a god-like way', in favour of coordinating the action of many autonomous actors within a policymaking system (Stewart & Ayres 2001, pp. 80, 87).

Implications for the policy cycle

This story of limited awareness and control is straightforward to *tell* but not to *sell*. Communication is only one part of the problem. The other is that it does not help policymakers tell a story about what governments are elected to do. It is a particular problem for governments operating in the Westminster tradition, who need to balance two inevitable but competing tensions: to engage in pragmatic policymaking and maintain an image of governing competence built on central control (Cairney 2015). Central government policymakers may accept the descriptive accuracy of policy theories emphasising limited central control, but not the recommendation that they should let go, share power and acknowledge their limits to the public.

In that context, the cycle metaphor appears to endure because it provides a way to project a particular form of policymaking to the public: you know how we make policy, and that we are in charge, so you know who to hold to account (see also Mercer [this volume, Chapter 3] and Wanna [this volume, Chapter 4] on the cycle as an aid to new public servants who learn on-the-job and in 'in-service' training; and Maurer [this volume, Chapter 12] on its role, within government, in boosting confidence, providing a common language, and setting cross-departmental expectations). It also provides a simple model of policymaking with stages that map onto important policymaking functions: identify and define problems that require government attention; identify the costs and benefits of solutions; legitimise your choice of solution; ensure sufficient resources for implementation; establish if the policy was successful; and decide if the policy should be continued, modified or discontinued.

Yet, if we take seriously the policy theory story, it is difficult to conclude that the cycle metaphor can actually endure in a meaningful or practical sense. At some point, it becomes too difficult to project the sense that policy is made from the centre, via a series of orderly stages, when this projection is so clearly inaccurate. For example, one of the formerly strongest proponents of this image—the European Commission— now describes a far messier reality (Topp et al. 2018). If so, the idea of centralised policymaking gives way to a focus on 'multi-level governance', 'polycentric governance' or 'multi-centric policymaking' to describe the need to accept the limited coordinative capacity at the 'centre' and explore ways to establish governing legitimacy when many policy practitioners have a clear role (Cairney, Heikkila & Wood 2019). Central government policymakers often *decide* to share power, and often seem to *like the idea* of delegating responsibility to other actors while finding pragmatic ways to legitimise actions by unelected bodies (John 1998, p. 29; Jordan & Richardson 1987, p. 233). However, modern policy theories suggest that key forms of power sharing are *necessary* and *inevitable*, rather than in their gift (Cairney, Heikkila & Wood 2019).

If we accept this story, the only enduring advantage to the policy cycle image relates to the *functions* associated with its stages, since they provide a way for civil servants to manage their work and turn elected government aims into reality (Althaus, Bridgman & Davis 2013; cf. Ritchie [this volume, Chapter 10] whose Policy Enterprise Model situates the cycle within a wider policymaking and cultural context). Yet, the policy theory story helps us reject the idea that we can use such an artificial model to plan civil service work. The usual image of a policy cycle is of a *single* cycle, to represent either a) a single process overseen by a small group of policymakers and analysts, who are in possession of the facts and control of the policy process, carrying out their aims through a series of stages; *or, more realistically*, b) a huge set of policy cycles that connect with each other in messy and unpredictable ways. Picture a kaleidoscope or Spirograph rather than a single circle. If so, what could be the point of 101 policymakers each being at the centre of their own policy cycles if they do not engage with the policy processes of their colleagues? What happens in cross-cutting issues when the cycles of one unit are out of sync with another?

In that context, perhaps the most we can expect of the policy cycle's stages is to treat them as a *checklist* of functions to carry out at some point (i.e. define problems, identify solutions, legitimise your work and evaluate policy processes) without expecting to be able to apply them rigidly or in order, and while remaining cognisant of the bigger picture in which any such planning would take place (cf. Edwards's [this volume, Chapter 7] discussion of 'covering all stages in the policy process, although not necessarily in any order'). If so, the policy theory story has much to offer the checklist, including:

- find out where the action is (establish the policymakers and influencers with whom to engage)
- form networks and seek allies (establish whose support you need, and how to get it)

- learn the language of debate and rules of the game in multiple venues (establish how best to engage with multiple policy actors in and out of government).

This kind of 'intelligent policymaking' (Sanderson 2009), built on awareness of your position in a complex system over which you have no control, seems like a more useful focus of training than a simple set of functions built on a too simple understanding of policy processes (see also Koski & Workman 2018 on ways for governments to process information more effectively).

Implications for 'evidence-based policymaking'

This shift of focus should also have a major effect on the discussions people have about 'evidence-based policymaking' (EBPM). One part of the problem with the idea of EBPM is that many of its advocates describe it from the perspective of actors who are primarily outside of government, looking in. As such, they compare their unrealistic expectations for policymaking (based on simple models like the policy cycle) with the far less rewarding processes that they actually experience. Oliver, Lorenc and Innvær's (2014) systematic review finds that a) few scholars outside of policy studies rely on policy concepts and b) almost all of those scholars engage primarily with the policy cycle. If they seek to engage with policymakers, who also project this sense of centralised and orderly policymaking, they will expect to find several opportunities to present evidence to help to define the nature and urgency of a policy problem, weigh up the costs and benefits of solutions, and evaluate the chosen solution before a debate on whether or not to continue.

This fiction of order and control provides a false sense of security to evidence advocates, who will soon be disappointed with their engagement. If so, they may refer primarily to the alleged problems with politicians (who do not listen to or understand evidence, or do not have the political will to do something with it), rather than their own lack of knowledge of complex policymaking environments, to explain their limited impact. It may warp their views on why policy practitioners seek and use a wide variety of sources of information rather than simply trying to base policy on narrowly defined scientific evidence (see e.g. Gilding's [this volume, Chapter 11] description of *triple bottom line assessment*).

In contrast, a policy theory story allows us to think about three main processes to which all policy advocates must respond:

1. Policy practitioners necessarily have a broader view on what counts as good evidence, since they need to identify the policy relevance of information, and engage in some process of deliberation to manage societal beliefs or preferences. In other words, they are not simply technocrats looking for technically feasible solutions.

2. They have to ignore almost all information, almost all of the time, and seek efficient ways to manage and use evidence.

3. They do not fully understand or control the process in which they seek to use evidence. Rather, they are part of a large and complex policymaking environment in which many policy actors have influence. If things appear to go wrong, we should not assume it is their fault.

This story allows policy actors to engage with a policy process that exists, rather than an orderly and predictable process that they would like to see. Instead of seeking to supply evidence at formally defined stages, they would instead develop a series of strategies to deal with uncertainty:

- There are many policy practitioners and influencers spread across government, so find out where the action is, or the key venues in which people are making authoritative decisions.

- Each venue has its own 'institutions'—the formal and written, or informal and unwritten rules of policymaking—so learn the rules of each venue in which you engage.

- Each venue is guided by a fundamental set of ideas—paradigms, core beliefs, monopolies of understanding—so learn that language and its implications.

- Each venue has its own networks—the relationships between policy practitioners and influencers—so build trust and form alliances within networks (or venue shop, to find a more sympathetic audience).

- Policymaking attention is often driven by changes in socioeconomic factors or routine/non-routine events, so be prepared to exploit the 'windows of opportunity' to present your solution during heightened attention to a policy problem.

It prompts actors to consider how far they are willing to go to pursue EBPM, when they know that the evidence will not speak for itself. For example, are they willing to emulate interest groups to frame issues, tell stories, close off debate, and/or exploit social stereotypes to gain the attention and support of policymakers (see Cairney 2018a)? It also allows actors to manage their expectations, since:

> Policy studies recommend investing your time over the long term—to build up alliances, trust in the messenger, knowledge of the system, and to seek 'windows of opportunity' for policy change—but offer no assurances that any of this investment will ever pay off. (Cairney & Oliver 2019, p. 8)

Further, even if successful, evidence advocates may find it difficult to pinpoint and measure their own impact.

Implications for practitioner–academic exchange

If academics and practitioners accept this policy theory story, how can they engage with each other to consider the role of evidence and governance in a political process over which no one has full control and many actors need to find ways to cooperate effectively? In this section, I describe some examples of possible responses, based on work I have done with practitioners such as civil servants.

First, policy theories can be used to lead small group discussions during executive training. For example, I have found that civil servants in the UK and Scottish (central) governments tend to agree that 1) the policy cycle is a useful starting point to describe what does not happen, and 2) we need some way to describe a far messier and complex policymaking process. In other words, the cycle is more of an ideal type to compare with reality than an ideal state to which to aspire. If so, it prompts a period of reflection, in which civil servants discuss how to operate within a more complex process, to balance being pragmatic about their limited role with the need to help ministers project a sense of central control (Cairney 2015, pp. 33–5). These discussions tend to promote critical thinking, or 'intelligent policymaking' (Sanderson 2009), and civil service networking, rather than blueprints or specific models of behaviour based on policy theories.

Second, policy theories inform wider strategies for policymaking organisations. For example, with the European Commission's Joint Research Centre, I co-authored a discussion of eight key skills or functions for an organisation seeking to bring together the supply and demand of policy-relevant knowledge (Topp et al. 2018, p. 1):

> (1) *research synthesis*, to generate 'state of the art' knowledge on a policy problem; (2) *management of expert communities*, to maximise collaboration; (3) *understanding policymaking*, to know when and how to present evidence; (4) *interpersonal skills*, to focus on relationships and interaction; (5) *engagement*, to include citizens and stakeholders; (6) *effective communication* of knowledge; (7) *monitoring and evaluation*, to identify the impact of evidence on policy; and (8) *policy advice*, to know how to present knowledge effectively and ethically.

This agenda is particularly relevant to academics, since its main messages are about how to produce policy-relevant knowledge, increase its perceived legitimacy (as part of wider scientific or stakeholder engagement), operate effectively in a policy process and provide policy advice in political settings. Further, if policy practitioners accept a messy and uncontrollable policy process (rather than an orderly cycle) as a starting point, it prompts them to think in new ways about how to gather policy-relevant knowledge, engage more widely with stakeholders *and* reflect on the limits to their policy impact.

Third, policy theories can help us think through the ways in which we discuss EBPM in relation to governance (as described in the Policy Project's (2018) write-up of our workshop with civil servants from the New Zealand government). Some of this discussion is so straightforward that a reference to policy theory jargon would get in the way. For example, there are common descriptions of the gap between academic and policymaker cultures based on factors such as technical languages, timescales, professional incentives, relative comfort with uncertainty, and assessments of scientific evidence in relation to other forms of policy-relevant information and values or beliefs. In that context, I suggest to civil servants that many academics might be interested in more engagement, but might be put off by the overwhelming scale of their task, and—even if they remained undeterred—would face some practical obstacles:

1. *They may not know where to start*: who should they contact to start making connections with policymakers?

2. *The incentives and rewards for engagement may not be clear.* The UK's 'impact' agenda has changed things, but not to the extent that any engagement is good engagement. Researchers need to tell a convincing story that they made an impact on policy/policymakers with their published research, so there is a notional tipping point of engagement in which it reaches a scale that makes it worth doing.

3. *The costs are significant.* For example, any time spent doing engagement is time away from writing grant proposals and journal articles (in other words, the outputs that still make careers).

4. *The rewards and costs are not spread evenly.* Put most simply, white male professors may have the most opportunities and face the fewest penalties for engagement in policymaking and social media (Cairney & Oliver 2019; Oliver & Cairney 2019; Savigny 2019). Or, the opportunities and rewards may vary markedly by discipline. In some, engagement is routine. In others, it is time away from core work.

Therefore, civil servants should provide clarity on what they expect from academics, when they need information and what they can offer in return. They should also show some flexibility with deadlines. Better still, they should engage continuously with academics to help form networks and identify the right people needed at the right time.

However, there is also a clear role for policy theories in thinking through the relationship between evidence use and governance. Table 13.2 provides one case study to identify consistent models of evidence use when we combine political choices about what counts as good evidence *and* what counts as 'good policymaking' when we assume complexity rather than control (Cairney 2016, 2017, 2018b). For example, one aim is to use evidence of success in one area and 'scale up' the program to a wider area. There are three approaches in good currency: use evidence from randomised control trials to diffuse the same model; use storytelling to describe experiences, assuming that each new intervention takes place under new conditions, and explicitly rejecting uniformity; or train practitioners to experiment with policy solutions based on promising but incomplete evidence.

In this case, the policy theory story may help make one approach more competitive and defendable than we would otherwise expect. If we were to make the problematic assumption that some policymakers could exert their power to roll out the same model uniformly, and that the model has a uniform effect, then approach 1—driven primarily by randomised control trials (RCTs)—would be relatively attractive. In contrast, if we assume the absence of central control, and that the same policy introduced in two places can have very different effects, then approach 2—driven by experiential knowledge, storytelling and governance principles (such as localism and respect for service-user design)—becomes more competitive. So too does approach 3, in which the idea is that central governments give practitioners 'on the ground' the freedom to experiment and learn what works in their experience.

Table 13.2. How should you combine evidence and governance to 'scale up' policy?

	1. Implementation science	2. Storytelling	3. Improvement method
How should you gather evidence?	Hierarchy and RCTs	Practitioner knowledge Service-user feedback	Evidence and 'experimentation'
How should you 'scale up' from best practice?	Uniform model Fidelity to the model	Tell stories, invite people to learn	If it is working, keep doing it
What aim should you prioritise?	Evidence of active ingredient of a dosage	Governance principles	Training and feedback

Conclusion

Most policy theories help *explain* policymaking rather than seek to promote what *should*, or predict what *will*, happen. As such, on their own, they do not provide direct advice on how to act, or try to set the direction of travel, within policy processes. Yet, they provide some useful pointers for actors seeking influence—frame issues to make them policy relevant, find out where the action is, learn the rules and language, find allies—and explain why these actions matter. Different theories also help explain to civil servants the patterns they may see while in government. For example, elected policymakers can ignore an issue or evidence for long periods, then suddenly pay high attention and demand a solution almost as soon as they describe a problem. Or, the same evidence-informed story may generate full support from one coalition but energetic opposition from another. In some cases, we know who will support or oppose a story; in others, they reflect an identity, or set of beliefs, that is difficult to anticipate.

Further, we can use policy theories to generate stories of policy processes with profound relevance to practitioners. Put most simply, they encourage us to dispense with the imagery of order and government control associated with models such as the policy cycle. Instead, policymakers can only pay attention to a small proportion of their responsibilities, and they engage in a policy process over which they have limited knowledge and even less control. If we accept this story, we accept that practitioners need new ways to think about old ways of doing things. The policy cycle's functions may remain relevant, but as part of a kaleidoscope of activity in which problem definition and solution generation is part of a far larger and more collaborative process, rather than a self-contained cycle. It often makes little sense to evaluate policy as if implementation could be achieved from the top down. 'The evidence' matters, but the complex nature of the policy process has a major influence on what evidence counts.

In that sense, stories from policy theory primarily provide a lens through which to understand all forms of practical advice, often as a *way of thinking* more than a blueprint for action. However, they also help set a new agenda to consider how policy should be made. There comes a point when models such as the policy cycle become so unrealistic as to provide little normative guidance. If practitioners begin with this mindset, they can consider more realistic ways in which to juggle the need to be pragmatic *and* foster accountability in political systems.

References

Althaus, C, Bridgman, P & Davis, G 2013, *The Australian policy handbook: A practical guide to the policy-making process*, 5th edn, Allen & Unwin, Sydney, NSW.

Baumgartner, F 2017, 'Endogenous disjoint change', *Cognitive Systems Research*, vol. 44, pp. 69–73. doi.org/10.1016/j.cogsys.2017.04.001.

Baumgartner, F, Jones, B & Mortensen, P 2018, 'Punctuated equilibrium theory', in C Weible & P Sabatier (eds), *Theories of the policy process*, 4th edn, Westview, Chicago, IL, doi.org/10.1016/j.cogsys.2017.04.001.

Cairney, P 2012, 'Complexity theory in political science and public policy', *Political Studies Review*, vol. 10, no. 3, pp. 346–58, doi.org/10.1111/j.1478-9302.2012.00270.x.

Cairney, P 2015, 'How can policy theory have an impact on policy making?', *Teaching Public Administration*, vol. 33, no. 1, pp. 22–39, doi.org/10.1177/0144739414532284.

Cairney, P 2016, *The politics of evidence-based policymaking*, Palgrave Pivot, London, UK.

Cairney, P 2017, 'Evidence-based best practice is more political than it looks: A case study of the "Scottish approach"', *Evidence and Policy*, vol. 13, no. 3, pp. 499–515, doi.org/10.1332/174426416X14609261565901.

Cairney, P 2018a, 'How far should you go to privilege evidence?', *Paul Cairney: Politics and Public Policy*, viewed 11 January 2020, paulcairney.wordpress.com/2018/07/20/how-far-should-you-go-to-privilege-evidence-2-policy-theories-scenarios-and-ethical-dilemmas/.

Cairney, P 2018b, 'Teaching evidence based policy to fly: How to deal with the politics of policy learning and transfer', *Paul Cairney: Politics and Public Policy*, viewed 11 January 2020, paulcairney.wordpress.com/2018/10/11/teaching-evidence-based-policy-to-fly-how-to-deal-with-the-politics-of-policy-learning-and-transfer/.

Cairney, P 2020, *Understanding public policy*, 2nd edn, Palgrave, London, UK.

Cairney, P, Heikkila, T & Wood, M 2019, *Making policy in a complex world*, Cambridge University Press, Cambridge, UK, doi.org/10.1017/9781108679053.

Cairney, P & Kwiatkowski, R 2017, 'How to communicate effectively with policymakers: Combine insights from psychology and policy studies', *Palgrave Communications*, vol. 3, no. 37, viewed 11 January 2020, www.nature.com/articles/s41599-017-0046-8, doi.org/10.1057/s41599-017-0046-8.

Cairney, P & Oliver, K 2019, 'How should academics engage in policymaking to achieve impact?' *Political Studies Review*, special issue, vol. 18, no. 2, pp. 1–17, doi.org/10.1177/1478929918807714.

Geyer, R & Cairney, P (eds) 2015, *Handbook on complexity and public policy*, Edward Elgar, Cheltenham, UK, doi.org/10.4337/9781782549529.

Gigerenzer, G 2001, 'The adaptive toolbox', in G Gigerenzer & R Selton (eds), *Bounded rationality: The adaptive toolbox*, MIT Press, Cambridge, MA, doi.org/10.7551/mitpress/1654.001.0001.

Heikkila, T & Cairney, P 2018, 'Comparison of theories of the policy process', in C Weible & P Sabatier (eds), *Theories of the policy process*, 4th edn, Westview, Chicago, IL.

Hogwood, B & Peters, BG 1983, *Policy dynamics*, St Martin's Press, New York, NY.

Jenkins-Smith, H, Nohrstedt, D, Weible, C & Ingold, K 2018, 'The advocacy coalition framework: An overview of the research program', in C Weible & P Sabatier (eds), *Theories of the policy process*, 4th edn, Westview, Chicago, IL.

John, P 1998, *Analysing public policy*, Continuum, London, UK.

John, P 2003, 'Is there life after policy streams, advocacy coalitions, and punctuations: Using evolutionary theory to explain policy change?' *Policy Studies Journal*, vol. 31, no. 4, pp. 481–98, doi.org/10.1111/1541-0072.00039.

Jones, B & Thomas, H 2017, 'The cognitive underpinnings of policy process studies', *Cognitive Systems Research*, vol. 45, pp. 48–51, doi.org/10.1016/j.cogsys.2017.04.003.

Jordan, AG & Richardson, JJ 1987, *British politics and the policy process*, Allen & Unwin, London, UK.

Kahneman, D 2012, *Thinking fast and slow*, Penguin, London, UK.

Koski, C & Workman, S 2018, 'Drawing practical lessons from punctuated equilibrium theory', *Policy and Politics*, vol. 46, no. 2, pp. 293–308, doi.org/10.1332/030557318X15230061413778.

Lindblom, C 1959, 'The science of muddling through', *Public Administration Review*, vol. 19, no. 2, pp. 79–88, doi.org/10.2307/973677.

Lindblom, C 1964, 'Contexts for change and strategy: A reply', *Public Administration Review*, vol. 24, no. 3, pp. 157–8, doi.org/10.2307/973641.

Lindblom, C 1979, 'Still muddling, not yet through', *Public Administration Review*, vol. 39, no. 6, pp. 517–26, doi.org/10.2307/976178.

Oliver, K & Cairney, P 2019, 'The dos and don'ts of influencing policy: A systematic review of advice to academics', *Palgrave Communications*, vol. 5, no. 21, viewed 11 January 2020, www.nature.com/articles/s41599-019-0232-y, doi.org/10.1057/s41599-019-0232-y.

Oliver, K, Lorenc, T & Innvær, S 2014, 'New directions in evidence-based policy research: A critical analysis of the literature', *Health Research Policy and Systems*, vol. 12, no. 34, doi.org/10.1186/1478-4505-12-34.

Ostrom, E 2007, 'Institutional rational choice', in P Sabatier (ed.), *Theories of the policy process*, 2nd edn, Westview Press, Cambridge, MA.

Policy Project 2018, 'Maximising collaboration between public servants and academics in evidence-based policy making', viewed 11 January 2020, paul cairney.files.wordpress.com/2018/10/paul-cairney-roundtable-conversation-tracker.pdf.

Rose, R 1990, 'Inheritance before choice in public policy', *Journal of Theoretical Politics*, vol. 2, no. 3, pp. 263–91, doi.org/10.1177/0951692890002003002.

Sanderson, I 2009, 'Intelligent policy making for a complex world: Pragmatism, evidence and learning', *Political Studies*, vol. 57, no. 4, pp. 699–719, doi.org/10.1111/j.1467-9248.2009.00791.x.

Savigny, H 2019, 'The violence of impact: Unpacking relations between gender, media and politics', *Political Studies Review*, vol. 18, no. 2, doi.org/10.1177/1478929918819212.

Schneider, A, Ingram, H & DeLeon, P 2014, 'Democratic policy design: Social construction of target populations' in P Sabatier & C Weible (eds), *Theories of the policy process*, 3rd edn, Westview Press, Boulder, CO.

Shanahan, E, Jones, M, McBeth, M & Radaelli, C 2018, 'The narrative policy framework', in C Weible & P Sabatier (eds), *Theories of the policy process*, 4th edn, Westview, Chicago, IL, doi.org/10.4324/9780429494284-6.

Simon, H 1976, *Administrative behavior*, 3rd edn, Macmillan, London, UK.

Sloman, S & Fernbach, P 2017, *The knowledge illusion: Why we never think alone*, Penguin, London, UK.

Stewart, J & Ayres, R 2001, 'Systems theory and policy practice: An exploration', *Policy Sciences*, vol. 34, no. 1, pp. 79–94, doi.org/10.1023/A:1010334804878.

Topp, L, Mair, D, Smillie, L & Cairney, P 2018, 'Knowledge management for policy impact: The case of the European Commission's Joint Research Centre', *Palgrave Communications*, vol. 4, no. 87, doi.org/10.1057/s41599-018-0166-9.

14

Synthesising models, theories and frameworks for public policy: Implications for the future

Allan McConnell

Introduction

The worlds of academic theory and policy practice are often portrayed as two remote endeavours, each barely acknowledging the other and more comfortable with scepticism than mutual respect. In this volume's first chapter, the editors identify the key goal of the book: to shed light on this 'two worlds' relationship and examine actual and potential opportunities that would help policy theory speak to practitioners and vice versa. It is clear from all the contributions in this volume that, while stereotypes do indeed have some basis in reality, there is also goodwill on both sides and, indeed, there are not inconsiderable elements of enthusiasm. The present chapter is a step along the road towards the goals of the book. It reflects on the chapters in aggregate, drawing out five general themes and examines reasons to be cautious and realistic, but also reasons to be pragmatically optimistic.

Theories and practitioners have their limits: We need realistic expectations

Much of public life and public policy is full of promises—occasionally 'cast iron' ones, such as UK Prime Minister Boris Johnson's guarantee that Brexit would be delivered by 31 October 2019. Politicians and policymakers can produce, and get caught up in, the heady rhetoric of partisanship and cultures of 'we can deliver'. Academia also talks of 'ground breaking' and 'truly innovative' research. Yet, despite many undoubted achievements on all sides, it is worth making a key but often-ignored point. No one has perfect solutions for all scenarios and, therefore, it is important to have realistic expectations of what is possible. One might call this a pragmatic optimism, rather than a blinded optimism that can never be fulfilled. The issues are huge, but let us consider a few brief points that typify.

Our first port of call is to consider the limits of academic theories of public policy and policy processes. In policy studies, there is no 'theory of everything' that would be able to capture the circumstances and variables of every scenario, accompanied by a definitive statement on causal factors and a prediction of what might happen in any particular situation. As Cairney and Geyer (2015) argue, policy systems and their environments are characterised by multiple, complex interdependencies and individual behaviours that can—even with small variations—lead to innumerable outcomes. For example, I cannot think of any academic theory that could be used to say 'if we do X it can be guaranteed that a new road tunnel will be built in exactly three years time' or 'we can set welfare benefits levels at Y and it can be guaranteed that Z number of children will no longer live in poverty'. Implementation is a relatively neglected aspect of policy processes, yet huge vulnerabilities can incubate because there are a multitude of small issues with potentially large and damaging consequences (such as ambiguous wording in policy goals or training shortfalls around issues of service delivery). Successful implementation of any program cannot be guaranteed (Hill & Hupe 2009). Indeed, one of the lessons of Wildavsky (1984), in recognising the 'muddiness' of competing evidence bases, issue complexity and differences in underlying assumptions and values, is the absence of a 'secret' to policy analysis that will apply at all times in all contexts. Understanding policy involves craft and informed judgement.

In a similar vein, many of the chapters in this book point to academia being limited in its relevance to the world of practitioners. In research undertaken for Chapter 9, Mackie (this volume) conducted interviews with policymakers in a study of environmental policies over the period 1993–2013. She found that they rarely drew on policy frameworks or concepts to help inform their work. A survey of policy practitioners in New Zealand, conducted by Löfgren and Bickerton (this volume, Chapter 5) found that the biggest barrier to using academic outputs was being unable to convert academic frameworks into policy outputs. They also found that some of the main constraints faced by practitioners in using academic theories included academic work being too technical, abstract, difficult to apply and difficult to interpret.

Despite such misgivings, we should not 'throw the baby out with the bathwater'. Although some academics may be very protective of their theoretical models and assumptions, it is better, I would argue, if we think of these theories as suggesting tendencies rather than iron laws. For example, in a recent book on policy success, Luetjens, Mintrom and 't Hart (2019) argue that there are six emerging patterns in successful projects (including problems being well-defined and allowing issues to 'ripen' before acting), but they acknowledge that the presence of such characteristics increases the likelihood of success rather than guaranteeing it. This example typifies the contribution that public policy scholars and theories can make. Overall, therefore, we should have realistic expectations about what academic theory can bring rather than thinking it has a ready-made solution for every policy problem or every scenario that a decision-maker faces.

A parallel line of reasoning can also be applied to policy practitioners who do not have guaranteed interventions for every policy issue or decision-making predicament. In Chapter 1, Mercer, Ayres, Head and Wanna (this volume) note a broader dissatisfaction among politicians and commentators in relation to lack of policy capacity on the part of public servants. There is undoubtedly some validity in this view, and it makes sense to have a public service that is fit for the purpose of addressing the trials and tribulations of modern policymaking, which often encompass high complexity and political uncertainty in a world in which many policy challenges are multi-jurisdictional and global. But it also brings an undercurrent of unfortunate personalisation, as though 'weak' policy capacity can be attributed to the inherently weak attributes or the behavioural inclinations of public servants. As cited in Chapter 7 by Edwards (this volume), the head of the Department of Prime Minister and Cabinet asked public servants to: 'Think big. Aim high. Experiment. Be Ruthless'. Yet, as Halligan (2019) argues, the reality is that the public service is typically risk-averse because it operates in highly politicised environments with major consequences for failure.

To take this point further, rhetoric with inferences that public servants are part of the problem because they do not fully grasp complex situations and cannot navigate them with relative ease, belies the reality that carving out policy 'solutions' and finding a way through a maze of ambiguous and contested issues can be tough—even for the most experienced public servants. One reason is that many policy problems, such as Indigenous disadvantage, drug abuse and gender inequality, are 'wicked', because there are high levels of contestation on the root causes of the problem, the interventions needed to address them, as well as high levels of uncertainty about whether any 'solution' will actually work (Head 2008; Head & Alford 2015; McConnell 2018). Practitioners may also have 'boundedly rational' limits (such as lack of time and resources) in being able to comprehensively examine every issue from every angle and work out the most appropriate means of intervention. Indeed, as Edwards (this volume) argues in Chapter 7: 'too often policy development stalls because policy advisers put policy options to ministers without taking account of the values that will govern their decisions'. Politics is part of the landscape of policy processes, and it seeps by a process of osmosis into every area of the public sector. Politics is not just 'party politics' or 'what the minister wants'. Politics is also the business of governing, in which governments and public authorities need to manage crowded policy agendas and issues that exceed their capacity to prioritise and deal forcefully with each one. Hence, much of the business of governing is about redefining issues, making them manageable and even pushing them to the margins (or beyond) of policy agendas in the hope that they will stay there—at least for a while (McConnell & 't Hart 2019; Stringer & Richardson 1979).

Importantly, we should not dismiss the value of practitioner insights just because they do not have guaranteed solutions for every situation. Many have years of experience across multiple portfolios and epitomise what Rhodes (2016, p. 638) describes as the craft skills of 'counseling, stewardship, prudence, probity, judgement, diplomacy, and political nous'. Further examination of such issues is provided below, but—mirroring the academic experience—the point is that practitioners are well placed to exercise good judgement on what will tend to work and what will not. We should not expect them to have 'all the answers', in the same way that we should not expect academic theories to conceptualise and provide guaranteed practical advice for every scenario. In some instances, the combined value can be greater than their individual contributions, but the best way of gaining insights and advancing the relationship is through realistic and achievable (rather than utopian) assumptions about what is possible.

The two worlds are not completely separate: Beware of stereotypes

As Mercer, Ayres, Head and Wanna indicate in Chapter 1, there is a widely held belief in the contrast between the 'ivory tower world' of academia and the 'real world' of policy practitioners. The former is often considered to be focused on explaining broader trends and patterns, too frequently in abstract and difficult-to-understand terms that are divorced from the realities of policy practice. Meanwhile, practitioners are focused on 'doing' and addressing day-to-day challenges (from the strategic to the operational), with little time to read and interpret theoretical frameworks that have potentially limited value. Indeed, such a distinction can be inferred from work on why practitioners do not use academic research (albeit not the only reason). As Löfgren and Bickerton outline in Chapter 5, based on their empirical studies in New Zealand on the extent to which policy practitioners draw on academic research, some of the constraints include academic work being too technical, too abstract, difficult to apply and difficult to interpret.

There is undoubtedly some distance between these two worlds, cultivated not least by the respective roles and jobs performed by academics and policy practitioners. As Threlfall and Althaus suggest in Chapter 2, the disconnect is fuelled by institutional factors such as (some) academics not valuing practical effects, and practitioners being unable to access articles that are hidden behind paywalls. Nevertheless, a persistent theme throughout this volume is the existence of spaces of intersection, akin to overlapping circles in a Venn diagram. As indicated in Chapter 1 by Mercer, Ayres, Head and Wanna, and Chapter 4 by Wanna, there is a rich seam of policy programs across many Australian universities with a particularly important one being the Australia and New Zealand School of Government (ANZSOG)—a leader in providing boutique training and study for senior public servants. In Chapter 2, Threlfall and Althaus point to the artificiality of a theory–practice divide because the two realms are part of a shared enterprise with each involved in critical thinking and reflection to build understanding and seek policy improvement. Newman, Cherney and Head (2015), in a major survey of over 2,000 public officials (supported by 16 in-depth interviews), found considerable overlap and diversity. Dissemination practices varied within academia, and uptake of academic research varied within the practitioner world.

An important point, but one which is barely mentioned in this volume, is that 'on-the-job' learning comes with the inference that public servants are 'blank slates' when they arrive in the public sector. Clearly this is not the case and, indeed, apart from their lived experiences and reflections, almost two-thirds of the Australian Public Service have an undergraduate degree or higher, and many of these will be in the social sciences broadly defined (Australian Public Service Commission 2016).[1] A key value of such degrees is being able to navigate uncertainty, ambiguity, competing evidence bases, opposing arguments and accept that there are typically no magical understandings. Such issues of complexity and differences of opinion are at the very heart of public policy. Therefore, even without exposure to policy theories per se, many public servants already have—via their prior education—some of the transferable skills needed to navigate complex and fast-moving public sector issues.

Overall, therefore, while there are credible reasons to distinguish between the world of academic theory development and the world of policy practitioners, we should beware of over-amplifying the differences and stereotyping the separation.

High-profile theories are the tip, not the iceberg: Opportunities are greater than we think

One of the clear signals throughout this volume is the existence of a handful of theories that are pervasive in many public sectors (see particularly Chapter 3 by Mercer). Arguably, at the top of the list is the policy cycle

---

1   This figure is calculated from the data in Table 21 and excluded public servants for which no educational background was available.

or stages approach, which has its origins in Lasswell (1956, 1971) and the development of policy sciences in the decades after World War II in which breaking down the policy decision process into a sequence of quasi-rational tasks (such as intelligence, promotion and prescription) was a means of harnessing policy expertise for societal betterment. Chapter 12 by Maurer provides a clear example of the value of the policy cycle as the starting point for the development of a policy handbook for the Department of Communications.

High on the radar of policy practitioners also is Mark Moore (1995, 2013) and his public value framework. Moore provides a guide to public sector strategy, based on managers aligning the goals of delivering substantive public value, enabling legitimacy/political sustainability, and ensuring operational/administrative feasibility. At the heart of the public value framework is the vision of a positive role for the public sector, as an antidote to the burgeoning rejection of 'big government' that had begun under the Reagan presidency in the US (as exemplified in Osborne & Gaebler [1992]). As indicated by Mercer, Ayres, Head and Wanna in Chapter 1, the public value framework has, despite some criticism and ambiguities, resonated for many public servants by helping legitimate, guide and enable policy development. Indeed, the very ambiguity of the term 'public value' may be, drawing on Stone (2012) from her work on policy symbols and meaning, the 'glue' that allows different views and interpretations to cohere.

Incrementalism, a concept originating with Lindblom (1959, 1965) and taken further by Braybrooke and Lindblom (1970), is another pervasive theory, with its emphasis on the value of incremental change driven by the administrative practicalities and democratic principles of bargaining, negotiation and trade-offs. As argued by Mercer in Chapter 3, it probably remains one of the best descriptors of how policy is made, despite being challenged by the new public management model, with its emphasis on competition, efficiency and cost-containment.

The multiple streams framework originating with John Kingdon (1984, 2011) is perhaps not so prevalent, but it certainly resonates with many. Kingdon shows how timing is crucial. On occasions such as new public moods, changes of government or crises, problems, potential solutions and politics can coalesce to produce 'windows of opportunity' that can act as vehicles for change or, equally, can be closed when the circumstances are not aligned. In Chapter 9, Mackie indicates how the framework was highly useful in helping uncover the intent and motivations of public officials. Kingdon's multiple streams framework is simple and accessible in making us think about an 'idea whose time has come' (Kingdon 2011, p. 1).

There are certainly other theories and concepts to be found in the public sector. Some are scattered throughout this book, including wicked problems (Ritchie this volume, Chapter 10), evidence-based policymaking (Threlfall & Althaus this volume, Chapter 2), policy success and failure (Mackie this volume, Chapter 9) and the eight-fold path of policy analysis (Gilding this volume, Chapter 11) Yet, there are others not mentioned (such as nudge theory and risk management) as well as numerous theoretical frameworks with insights around issues such as accountability, transparency, resolving intractable controversies, policy design, policy inaction and learning, as well as frameworks addressing sectoral specific issues, such as disability, farming, security, transport and housing.

There is no suggestion here that practitioners *should* draw on insights from such theoretical frameworks. As we know, public servants have difficulty in accessing them or considering them, for whatever reason, to be of practical value. Rather, the point to be made is that academic insights are more than just a handful of well-travelled concepts that circulate routinely within the public sector and appear regularly in workshops. They do not equate with academia, in the same way that a few top Hollywood actors do not equate with the acting profession as a whole. Hence, the potential for academic theories to add value to the work of the public sector is much greater than we might think.

Using theory is not all or nothing: Minimalism and flexibility can be of high value

Academic theories may be seen by some as grand, rigid and written for academic purposes rather than practitioner relevance. Notwithstanding the veracity of this point for many academic works, some can offer insights that help inform others who may use these in deep or light ways, as they see fit. Therefore, academic theories do not need to be implanted in the public sector as though they are intellectual experiments. Many chapters in this book reveal theories and concepts that are used in partial, minimalist ways, while adapting to the particular context in which they are considered to be of value. Chapter 3 by Mercer points to the value of 'rules of thumb'. Chapter 8 by Ayres, a senior public servant with well over a decade of experience, sets out in detail how his work and leadership across various social policy departments, was shaped by modifying the core elements and principles of the policy cycle. Gilding, a policy practitioner with over 20 years experience across a range of portfolios, outlines in Chapter 11 how she was able to adapt an array of policy models into a 'blended' approach, including the policy cycle and Moore's public value approach.

One of the lessons of the current volume, therefore, is that academic theories and concepts can be useful and flexible simply by helping to provide insights into the opportunities/risks of different approaches to tackling policy challenges. Cairney (2013) addresses this issue in a major work on what we should do with multiple policy theories, each tackling issues from different directions and underpinned by different assumptions about how we understand the world. Hence, rather than searching for a grand unifying 'theory of everything', or engaging in endless comparisons between 'apples and oranges', we should be comfortable with theory offering 'insights'. Indeed, using 'just enough' theory, and being flexible in doing so to fit practitioner purposes, can be worth the investment. In fact, Cairney's chapter in this volume (Chapter 13) points to the value of theory as a novel lens to help think about practical problems, rather than being a blueprint for action. It is clear that academic analyses can help inform the 'real world' of thinking about, and addressing, complex social challenges. In Chapter 7, Edwards recounts her time as a policy adviser in the Hawke–Keating years and suggests that many major social policy initiatives may not have seen the light of day if not for the involvement of academic researchers at multiple stages of the policy process.

The two worlds do not collide as much as we think: Sharing the same space can often be successful

Following on from the above, it is clear that there are useful synergies between the two worlds and that the outcomes can be successful. For example, the policy cycle remains the most pervasive and useful concept in the Australian public sector, exemplified in the success of the *Australian policy handbook* by Althaus, Bridgman and Davis (2018), which is now in its sixth edition with sales in excess of 30,000 (see particularly Mercer, Ayres, Head & Wanna this volume, Chapter 1). Its strength, despite much critique, is that it is a starting point for grasping some of the core ingredients of the policy processes (from initial problem definition through to implementation and evaluation). It also provides a normative starting point in seeking to recommend a sense of order to how policymakers can address undesirable social conditions/policy problems.

The concept of public value has become a mainstay in ANZSOG's Executive Master of Public Administration and Executive Fellows Program. As Barrett indicates in Chapter 6, the public value approach has been a useful means of enabling parliamentary actors to think of themselves as public managers, rather than simply as custodians of parliament. In Chapter 12, Maurer outlines how he was tasked with producing a handbook for the Department of Communications that could be used for policy development. In doing so, he relied heavily on the policy cycle, with much success to the point that it became incorporated into everyday practice. Incrementalism has also been a useful tool in avoiding policy paralysis and proceeding pragmatically in policy development (Mercer this volume, Chapter 3). Certainly, there have been instances when the relationship did not work out, but shared spaces can bring about mutual benefit.

Conclusion

This volume has been exceptionally useful in airing and examining issues around the interface between academic theory and practitioners, as well as the capacity for, and constraints on, further synergies. It is clear to me that, while there is some understandable and legitimate truth in the distinction between the worlds of academic theory and policy practice, there is a danger in exaggerating the separation and diminishing areas of commonality. Both have an interest in trying to figure out what government does (and does not do) and both would like to see policy outcomes that are beneficial to society as a whole, regardless of whether they may disagree on the best means of doing so. Academics do not need to be practitioners and practitioners do not need to be academics. We should be realistic rather than utopian in our expectations. There is value in their differences, but there is also value and mutual benefit in exploring further opportunities for interaction and shared spaces.

References

Althaus, C, Bridgman, P & Davis, G 2018, *The Australian policy handbook: A practical guide to the policy-making process*, 6th edn, Allen & Unwin, Crows Nest, NSW.

Australian Public Service Commission 2016, *Shape of the APS,* viewed 2 February 2020, www.apsc.gov.au/shape-aps.

Braybrooke, D & Lindblom, CE 1970, *A strategy of decision: Policy evaluation as social process,* The Free Press, New York, NY.

Cairney, P 2013, 'Standing on the shoulders of giants: How do we combine the insights of multiple theories in public policy studies', *Policy Studies Journal,* vol. 41, no. 1, pp. 1–21, doi.org/10.1111/psj.12000.

Cairney, P & Geyer, R 2015, 'Introduction', in P Cairney & R Geyer (eds), *Handbook on policy complexity,* Edward Elgar, London, UK.

Halligan, J 2019, 'Nadir or renaissance for the Australian Public Service?', in M Evans, M Grattan & B McCaffrie (eds), *From Turnbull to Morrison: The trust divide*, Melbourne University Press, Melbourne, Vic.

Head, BW 2008, 'Wicked problems in public policy', *Public Policy*, vol. 3, no. 2, pp. 101–18.

Head, BW & Alford J 2015, 'Wicked problems: Implications for public policy and management', *Administration & Society,* vol. 47, no. 6, pp. 711–39, doi.org/10.1177/0095399713481601.

Hill, M & Hupe, P 2009, *Implementing public policy: An introduction to the study of operational governance,* 2nd edn, SAGE, London, UK.

Kingdon, JW 1984, *Agendas, alternatives and public policies,* Little, Brown and Company, Boston, MA.

Kingdon, JW 2011, *Agendas, alternatives and public policies,* 2nd edn, Longman, Boston, MA.

Lasswell, HD 1956, *The decision process: Seven categories of functional analysis,* University of Maryland, College Park, MA.

Lasswell, HD 1971, *A pre-view of policy sciences,* Elsevier, New York, NY.

Lindblom, CE 1959, 'The science of "muddling through"', *Public Administration Review,* vol. 19, no. 2, pp. 79–88, doi.org/10.2307/973677.

Lindblom, CE 1965, *The intelligence of democracy,* The Free Press, New York, NY.

Luetjens, J, Mintrom, M & 't Hart, P (eds) 2019, *Successful public policy: Lessons from Australia and New Zealand,* ANU Press, Canberra, ACT, doi.org/ 10.22459/SPP.2019.

Moore, MH 1995, *Creating public value: Strategic management in government,* Harvard University Press, Cambridge, MA.

Moore, M 2013, *Recognizing public value,* Harvard University Press, Cambridge, MA, doi.org/10.4159/harvard.9780674067820.

McConnell, A 2018, 'Rethinking wicked problems as political problems and policy problems', *Policy & Politics,* vol. 46, no. 1, pp. 165–80, doi.org/10.1332/ 030557317X15072085902640.

McConnell, A & 't Hart, P 2019, 'Inaction and public policy: Understanding why policymakers "do nothing"', *Policy Sciences,* vol. 52, no. 4, pp. 645–61, doi.org/10.1007/s11077-019-09362-2.

Newman, J, Cherney, A & Head, B 2015, 'Do policy makers use academic research? Reexamining the "two communities" theory of research utilization', *Public Administration Review,* vol. 76, no. 1, pp. 24–32, doi.org/10.1111/ puar.12464.

Osborne, D & Gaebler, T 1992, *Reinventing government: How the entrepreneurial spirit is transforming the public sector,* Addison-Wesley, Reading, MA.

Rhodes, RAW 2016, 'Recovering the craft of public administration', *Public Administration Review,* vol. 76, no. 4, pp. 638–47, doi.org/10.1111/puar.12504.

Stone, D 2012, *Policy Paradox,* 3rd edn, WW Norton, New York, NY.

Stringer, JK & Richardson, JJ 1979, 'Managing the political agenda: Problem definition and policy making in Britain', *Parliamentary Affairs,* vol. 33, no. 2, pp. 23–39, doi.org/10.1093/oxfordjournals.pa.a051831.

Wildavsky, A 1984, *Speaking truth to power: The art and craft of policy analysis,* Transaction, New Brunswick, NJ.

15

Public policy theory, practice and skills: Advancing the debate

John Wanna, Russell Ayres, Brian Head
and Trish Mercer

Learning without thought is labour lost; thought without learning is perilous. (Confucius)

A theory must be tempered with reality. (Jawaharlal Nehru)

Circumstances give in reality to every political principle its distinguished colour and discriminating effect. (Edmund Burke)

Debates around developing policy skills in government

Debates about the need for developing better policy capacities and skills in government gained momentum in the 1950s and 1960s. At this time, there was a proliferation of interest in 'policy sciences' thinking and systemic approaches, popularised primarily by US scholars and 'pracademics'. Much of the policy theory–making emanating from the US was a legacy of the New Deal planning agendas of the mid-1930s and later strategic planning approaches developed by public and private organisations that helped to plan and strategise the war effort in the 1940s and the subsequent Cold War. Cognisant of calls for administrative reform in the public and private sectors (especially the Hoover Commission of 1949), large private corporations—such as the RAND Corporation, General Motors and other defence-related organisations that later inspired Robert McNamara's innovations under President Johnson (see Schick 1966, pp. 243–54)—promulgated a rationalist and systemic planning approach to policy sciences drawing on multidisciplinary expertise, including management and organisational planning, administrative science, economics, accounting, cost-benefit analysis, cybernetics and informational technologies.

From the 1960s onwards, the term 'policy' became identified as a professionalised set of analytical activities, which attracted several alternative theories and approaches. The previous overly rationalistic approaches extolling centralised planning were critiqued and amended but not entirely substituted (Dror 1968; Dye 1978). Other less rationalistic and more institutional approaches such as incrementalism were added, which acknowledged organisational behaviour, bounded rationalities, contingencies and opportunism. Policy was seen as an intentional set of activities that could be carefully designed and planned, studied intensively and professionally crafted through astuteness and prudence. Importantly, the principles and lessons could be taught or transmitted to practitioners working in real-life situations. Policy was seen as a mixture of actions, plans, promises, principles, motivations and desired intents, but, above all, it was guided by the practicalities of what was considered possible. Policy development, then, became a core function of government, and modern governments were urged to invest resources to enhance their policy capacities.

These intellectual developments around improving policy decision-making contributed an important 'supply-side factor' or 'push factor' to the growing international interest in the topic. Prior to that, of course, public servants had still contributed to 'policymaking', but generally described their work through a variety of other lenses, such as providing public financial resources, providing essential services, reviewing and drafting legislation, adopting technical improvements, setting community standards and enforcing regulatory arrangements. Significantly, in those days, the range of government responsibilities was relatively narrow (at least in the US) and closely linked to the provision of public good and market failure initiatives.

The other influence to generate interest in policy skilling was the 'demand factor' emanating from governments themselves (and, to a certain extent, from pressure groups and the wider electorate interested in various policy ideas or frameworks). Demand for better policymaking and policy skills became a significant 'pull factor'. Postwar governments became increasingly committed to social change, the development of more extensive welfare states and improved living standards across the community (through amelioration policies and 'quality of life' concerns) (Castles 1998; Hogwood & Gunn 1984; McEachern 1990). Policy goals and strategies signalled how governments wished to change living conditions and human behaviour—with policy programs the main means of effecting desired social change. Policy was often seen as a purposeful endeavour, with a focus on clarifying proposed or desired changes and planning their delivery more systematically. Policy was an organising concept that could span widely or narrowly depending on priorities and policy choices, but was also dependent on circumstances (as the third epigram above from Edmund Burke reminds us).

Given this historical background, what are the current and emerging debates around developing policy skills in government agencies? Three main topic areas may be distinguished. First, there has been concern over the *levels of policy capacity* a government might display or wish to achieve. For instance, capacities may be strong or weak, declining or improving, reactive or anticipatory, or there may be capacities for policy analysis or implementation.[1] Second, there has been much written on the *types of desired policy skills* that may be needed, especially prospectively. This can include the range and mix of professional disciplinary expertise that may be required, as well as analytical and operational skills such as systems thinking, project management and 'life cycle' management for asset stewardship (see, for example, Adams et al. 2015). Third, there is considerable interest in how *policy skills are transmitted and learnt*, and what is the best way to address shortcomings and to prepare for new demands and emerging situations. Debates also focus on the degree to

---

1   In recent times, many governments have attempted to assess their relative capacities through formal assessment reviews with initiatives such as 'capability reviews'. These formal reviews began in the mid-2000s in the UK across departments and in the US, Canada and the Netherlands in relation to defence readiness. These ideas spread around 2010 to other nations such as Australia, New Zealand and Singapore. Some research/think tank institutes helped promote the idea and develop alternative methodologies, for instance the Institute for Government in the UK (see Panchamia & Thomas n.d.). However, in some jurisdictions the commitment to sustaining capability reviews waned after the initial enthusiasm.

which academic theories percolate into the thinking and practices of public servants or whether practical experience feeds into broader intellectual thinking on the topic. A commitment to policy skills development represents an investment in future capacities and capabilities including an anticipatory preparedness for new eventualities and aspirations. These topics are crucial aspects of any custodial 'stewardship' practised by government agencies and policy advisers.

A stewardship approach implies that decision-makers and participants in public policy take responsibility not only for developing the current skills, capabilities and productivity of their organisations and staff, but also for future capabilities (Makhlouf 2017; Moon et al. 2017). For instance, key considerations might include how to broaden the skills mix of an organisation; how to identify and invest in new skills and capabilities; how to develop analytical and critical thinking skills that have longer-term benefits; and how to enhance evaluative capabilities, which can potentially have a positive influence on the quality of decision-making, policy adaptation and operational performance.

At various times, the investment in new ways of thinking about policy may appear less important: a second-order priority or peripheral concern, outweighed by the exigencies of immediate demands confronting an organisation. Dealing with present-day expediencies will generally outweigh investments in future capabilities, which might be unknown or subject to much volatility or revision. Academic treatises may sit on shelves, perhaps only read by a handful of scholarly colleagues, critics or protégés. Nevertheless, as John Maynard Keynes (1936, p. 383) once observed, 'practical men who believe themselves quite exempt from any intellectual influence, are usually the slaves to some defunct economist … [or] some academic scribbler of a few years back'. Keynes added that it took time for new ideas and theories to percolate 'so that the ideas which civil servants and politicians and even agitators apply to current events are not likely to be the newest' (p. 383).

One of the effects of the rise of professions is the tendency for every profession to have its own concomitant body of discrete theory about itself. The professions involved in public policy or public administration are no different. It is difficult to imagine that any profession would not develop a 'shadow' body of theory among its members most likely spreading into the world of intellectuals and professional academics. As discussed in Chapter 1, in Australia the adoption and development of a competency-based 'professions model' (along the lines of the UK government for its civil service) was recommended by the *Independent review of the APS* in 2019 (Department of the Prime Minister and Cabinet 2019) and accepted by the Morrison government, and is a further indication of investment in this important direction.

Many practitioners may work in relatively close alignment with policy theory models without fully appreciating the scholarly antecedents of their approach, and perhaps recognising the limitations of these models. For instance, many happily work with strategic planning norms, or follow incrementalist paths of development, or use project and risk management techniques, all of which are founded upon a body of theory. However, what is lost or neglected in uncritically applying a single model is the possibility of having a range of options available for government, various public authorities charged with policy responsibilities and parliament itself as the ultimate arbiter. Policy capabilities and approaches informed by policy theories constitute a professional toolkit of available means to achieve desired ends (see Mercer this volume, Chapter 3). Many public service training/professional development programs are at least partly based on one theoretical framework or another. A command of such knowledge helps to lift the sights of practitioners beyond the here and now.[2]

To whom are these debates important?

Understandably, policy practitioners (inside and outside government) are the main targets and intended recipients of policy theory. For existing or intending public servants, the development of policy skills is a vital component of their professional practice and of developing a 'community of practice' to deepen professional competencies and professional pride in the services performed (Hughes 1998). While practitioners are generally the intended market of 'academic scribblers', they can often be quite hard to reach or enthuse.

---

2   One characteristic that may have distinguished the more successful early responses to the COVID-19 pandemic (at least in the West) is the presence of an administrative class that has a reasonably deep understanding of the capabilities and roles of government, and the capacity to deploy those capabilities in an emergency.

Departmental executives and line managers have long complained about the lack of policy capabilities of staff, and the lack of analytical skills or the ability to think outside the box (see Chapter 1 this volume; see also Peters 1996; Tiernan 2011). While their concerns are subjective impressions, their perspectives are generally accumulated from decades of experience and are often widely shared by colleagues. Many executives adopting a stewardship perspective have long argued for the need for formalised training programs to teach policymaking and improve the analytical capacities of the next generations of public service leaders (Moran 2017; Podger 2019).

Further down the public service hierarchies or at line manager levels, officials often initiate their own training, mostly through attending university courses and various forms of professional training and accreditation. Often such attendance in educational institutions is work-related studying, but not necessarily in fields developing knowledge of policy theory or policy application per se. More tailored introductions to policy approaches are often delivered by public service commissions, specialist training institutes or via consultants in executive development courses (see Di Francesco 2015; Stewart 1999; Vromen & Hurley 2015).

Nevertheless, the debates about the quality and development of policy skills in government are not restricted solely to policymakers in public sector employment. Academics and other public commentators have frequently joined this debate, often criticising perceived shortcomings in governmental decision-making and highlighting suboptimal examples of poor policy development. There is a rich literature on policy fiascos and policy failure written with the benefit of hindsight, but far less on successful policy outcomes (but see Luetjens, Mintrom & 't Hart 2019). Many critics blame management fads in government for the supposed deterioration of policy capacity, displaced by the preoccupation with instrumentality and process-driven concerns (Ferguson 2019). The principal culprits are often cited as the preoccupation with new public management and the resort to outsourcing and contracting out (Boston 1995; Considine & Painter 1997).

So, who else ought to find these debates to be of some importance? There are many audiences who could benefit from a better understanding of policy processes, how government decisions that affect them are made, and the potentialities and limitations of traditional government decision-making. As the processes of government policymaking become more porous and collaborative we might want to broaden the circle of stakeholders to whom policy theory is relevant. These interested stakeholders will include researchers, major interest groups and peak industry bodies, non-public sector operatives especially in the not-for-profit and charities sectors, as well as consultants, lobbyists, ministerial staffers, media commentators, political party operatives and interested members of the public anxious to improve their understanding of policy.

What are the important contours of the debates?

As many contributors to this volume attest, much of the debate about the relevance of policy theory and policy approaches generally concerns the existence of 'two world orders of discrete practice': academics and practitioners who operate seemingly as ships passing in the night. As a number of contributors also point out (see e.g. Threlfall & Althaus this volume, Chapter 2; McConnell this volume, Chapter 14), this is a largely sterile and limiting controversy because the 'two worlds' may be differentially interconnecting—indeed, contributing to a volume such as this implies a recognition of the connection. There is ample evidence that policymakers in different fields of work form frames of reference informed by methods, tried and tested processes, analytical skills, design thinking, systems thinking and, to some extent, policymaking frameworks even if inchoate (Gill & Colebatch 2006). Having said that, there is also considerable scope to assess the practical relevance and utility of specific policy theories or rival approaches.

The normative crux of the debates tends to be how applicable academic policy theories are to practitioners in the field in offering theory-informed advice for practice. There is a school of thought that academic theories *are* relevant to practitioners, even if practitioners have not directly experienced them, due to the percolation of ideas over time. Institutions in particular may hold to more rationalist policy concepts such as the classic policy cycle, as Mercer and Maurer discuss in this volume (see Chapters 3 and 12, respectively). Others question whether 'one theory' or 'one policy model' is applicable or sufficient in itself or whether some range of theories might be useful in different contexts (see Cairney this volume, Chapter 13).

Hence, an important contour in the debates concerns whether a single theory is most relevant to inform practice or whether practitioners can selectively draw on a mix of concepts ('mix-and-match' or 'horses for courses') depending on circumstances. Some areas of policy are complex and rapidly changing while others are fairly stable and predictable; different theories may be appropriately applied to different contexts. Certainly, Cairney suggests that there is no perfect solution to any problem, and that we should 'synthesise the insights' from different approaches, taking care not to accept at face value claims that a simplified model is adequate to understanding or guiding action in the real world. Equally, care should be exercised in combining multiple theoretical insights, given, for instance, that the same terms can mean different things in different theoretical contexts, and the lack of agreement as to *how* they can/should be combined. One approach might be to employ multiple theories to provide complementary perspectives on the same event (Cairney 2019, pp. 236–8). Within this volume, contributors have explored or employed theoretical approaches ranging across the spectrum from a rationalist focus on centralised decision-making to multiple actors operating within a complex process, and, in some instances (see Chapters 8 and 11, by Ayres and Gilding, respectively), have combined more than one theoretical approach to aid their policy analysis.

What range of policy skills are we talking about?

Much academic discussion in this domain necessarily takes place at a high level of abstraction, involving stylised models, policy cycles and frameworks, comprehensive planning methods and project management techniques. In practice, many policy professionals are engaged in deeply pragmatic ways in very specific areas of policymaking or seeking to solve discrete policy problems. Overly generic models or theories may be of limited relevance to such practitioners and circumstances, and could impede action where it is needed to respond to an urgent need or there is a political imperative to act. There are also well-recognised cognitive limitations inherent in theory-making. As McConnell (this volume, Chapter 14) writes:

> In policy studies, there is no 'theory of everything' that would be able to capture the circumstances and variables of every scenario, accompanied by a definitive statement on causal factors and a prediction of what might happen in any particular situation.

He advises that well-informed practitioners can take the insights from academic theories in 'deep or light ways—as they see fit'. As for academics, they may be well advised to get closer to the 'coalface' of government decision-making and action, not only to gain insights for their own research, but also to find ways to bring their insights to bear in helping practitioners seeking to improve their decision-making, to better use methods and techniques, and to understand the risks and downsides of suboptimal outcomes.

This discussion also raises the issue of whether there are distinct policy skills that are sui generis to different policy fields, and whether using abstract, generic theory to inform practice may require much greater differentiation of the work of policy itself. Governments have a wide and ever-changing set of responsibilities, mandates and policy purviews; their officials and organisations are managing many different functions, activities, processes and business practices, using different policy levers or policy tools, and with different levels of resources and imperatives (Peters 1996). Government is not singular or uniform, nor are the possibilities of policymaking evenly spread across its various functions and organisations, with specialist areas tending to focus on the subject matter of their policy focus, such as the economy, the environment, global security or industry sectors.[3]

---

3   A few examples will serve to illustrate this point:
   • an official in Finance or Treasury working on public finances or macroeconomic focused on a highly specialised policy space, with its own parameters and specific concerns generic policy theories may be of little use in their day-to-day calculations (on the other hand, these officials may be 'captured' by prevailing orthodoxies and fail to countenance the bigger policy picture or political realities).
   • ministers insisting on a particular course of action (e.g. stimulus spending, fiscal consolidation and a return to budgetary surpluses, or a pay-down of debt levels) will also constrain policy options, overriding any policy model or theory that might otherwise seem relevant.
   • public servants concerned with matters dominated by scientific or technological challenges tend to focus on scientific calculations and advice, and may be relatively naive about the realpolitik of policy.
   • policymakers in regulatory functions or in areas of compliance or taxation may not see policy models about how policy is made as relevant to the complex issues for which they are responsible and legally accountable; rather, their focus may be on regulatory augmentation, parameter adjustments, compliance strategies and operating under changing legal interpretations and determinations.

Notwithstanding the role of specialist capacities and approaches, most practitioners will have some involvement in policy adjustment or development, and some policy theories will provide them with a better handle on making these decisions and taking actions. At a fundamental level, all forms of understanding, all analytical and communication skills, are crucial aspects of a practitioner's conceptualisation of the policy process. They may not express such interpretations in terms of theories, models or approaches but they inform their practice and the sense-making abilities of government policy, even while their articulated concerns may be more about methods of decision-making, authorisations to proceed, risk assessments, things that might go wrong or the unintended consequences of whatever action might be deemed appropriate.

The contributions of this volume

The successful workshop in 2018, on which this volume is based, began with the premise that the relationships between policy theory and actual practice were far from straightforward and linear. It was recognised from the outset that the relationships were complicated and sometimes combative in many areas of public policymaking. It was often recounted that theoreticians felt frustrated that their insights seemed not to be valued or widely applied by practitioners (and, if they were applied, that their theoretical insights were not generally acknowledged). Further, it was alleged that many practitioners, if they were aware of policy theory, found the products of the academy impracticable, whatever their intellectual and analytical merits. We were aware that these views were an article of faith for many observers and had become the stereotypical view of the relationship between these 'two worlds'. However, we were also motivated to search for the spaces of intersection between theory and practice, and for better ways of bridging the 'two worlds'.

This volume goes well beyond the defence of a particular model or theory, or the 'war stories' that practitioners routinely recount to defend a view that no model captures the chaos and complexity of practice. The contributions to this volume show that the reality of what practitioners rely on to make decisions is much more complex than the stereotype would have us believe. Often when we delve into frontline policy work, experience may sometimes be worse than the stereotype suggests, but also, in places, perhaps better than we might expect. Certainly the picture that emerges here is that the range of experiences and the perceptions across the divide between theory and practice are many and varied, and resist simple classification or summary. This complexity is reinforced in this volume in chapters by David Threlfall and Catherine Althaus (Chapter 2) and also Karl Löfgren and Sarah Hendrica Bickerton (Chapter 5). Allan McConnell reminds us that we should 'beware of over-amplifying the differences and stereotyping the separation' between these two worlds (Chapter 14). What emerges is the realisation that the trend to seek better knowledge of policy and information about alternative possibilities seems to be broadly headed in the right direction. There are now many theoreticians who either have personal experience of the practicalities of policymaking or are very open to understanding the perspectives of those who have had such experience. Meanwhile, there are also many practitioners who have immersed themselves in the literature and emerged considerably wiser, if not struck by a single and overwhelming bolt of enlightenment. In assessing the current state of affairs in the Australian context, they are well represented in this monograph. To many practitioners, the glass may seem only half full, yet there is every prospect that it may become fuller.

It is true that a number of the contributions to this book stress that the tasks of applying policy theory to practice are fraught and difficult to achieve for a variety of reasons, and that it can be hard to trace the influences when they do occur (see also Colebatch 2010; Parsons 2004; Wanna 2015). Examples include Kathleen Mackie's exploration of succeeding and failing in crafting environmental policy, and, at a deeper philosophical and cultural level, Craig Ritchie's critique of the Western Enlightenment assumptions underpinning the contemporary policy enterprise (Chapters 9 and 10, respectively). In her fieldwork into policymaking in the Commonwealth's Environment department, Mackie found her interviewees rarely drew on policy theory to inform their policy work; even experienced and adept policy officers 'struggled to define "policy"; they considered policy work instinctual—it was in their DNA' (Chapter 9).

Val Barrett, in her review of the attitudes to public management in complex and hard to 'steer' institutions like the Australian and British parliaments (Chapter 6), concludes that the differences between parliament and other public institutions are not as great as parliamentary practitioners might imagine, and that the contemporary public management theories they tend to shun could be very relevant for strategic reform initiatives.

In particular, she argues that the public value approach and associated paradigms 'lend themselves as well to parliamentary administration as to public administration'.

Contrasting with and leavening this picture, are chapters by Russell Ayres (Chapter 8), Meredith Edwards (Chapter 7), Louise Gilding (Chapter 11), Andrew Maurer (Chapter 12) and Trish Mercer (Chapter 3). All demonstrate that theoretical work can resonate for individual public servants who find a framework (or frameworks) to draw on—one that 'strikes a chord'—to support them to understand real policy world issues and dilemmas. On the continuum between academics and practitioners, these contributions are generally of the blended, 'pracademic' sort. This practitioner-cum-academic is perhaps a type that would bear more study, just as the notion of the 'policy entrepreneur' has been a focus of discussion in recent decades, especially in North America where much more interaction and career exchanges between town and gown occurs.

Many contributors ask whether a more explicit understanding of the full range of policy frameworks would help policy workers to do their jobs better. Kathleen Mackie and Trish Mercer both pose such questions in their chapters. This is surely worth further exploration, given the ongoing angst expressed at the political and commentating level (discussed earlier) as to the policy capacity of the public services in Australia and other Westminster jurisdictions. This also reinforces the significance of understanding the breadth of the target group for such policy theory. This is not simply about breaking down the elitist hegemony of the so-called 'Canberra bubble' as many of our political leaders are fond of suggesting. Policy work is done at many levels across the public services, involving various stages of policy exposure, and various actors and stakeholders. Crucially, it involves many non-public sector policy advisers and influential operatives across the community and globally.

Overall, the contributions to this volume tend to suggest that policy theory needs to describe and engage with 'policy in action', an emphasis on the practical doing of policy work that resonates throughout the *APS capability roadmap* prepared for the APS Secretaries Board in March 2019 (Australian Government 2019) and discussed in Chapter 1. There are also chapters here that should give practitioners and those tasked with training and developing future practitioners serious pause for thought. John Wanna, for example, in Chapter 4, provides a constructive critique of the pedagogical challenges in offering senior executive education including in presenting relevant theories in such a teaching and learning setting. As discussed earlier, Paul Cairney in Chapter 13 and elsewhere (2019) makes some strong and clear-eyed observations about how some practitioners risk uncritical or inappropriate application of superficially attractive models if they do not explore, understand and adapt to the underlying assumptions and preferences of those models.

Future directions

We know comparatively little about what participants are offered in formal public policy teaching, other than perhaps the core offerings in the Australia and New Zealand School of Government (ANZSOG) programs, and even less about how those students with policy experience respond to this. Following Di Francesco's comprehensive survey of tertiary institutions teaching policy studies (2015), we could extend his analysis to discover what is actually taught under the banner of public policy theory. Di Francesco discusses at a general level the types of courses and subject matter taught across tertiary institutions (i.e. key components of policy analysis instruction), but, perhaps of necessity, does not delve into the coverage of theories or particular approaches, although he does produce typologies based on course titles offered.

But, as well as enhancing our understanding of specific policy theories within formal tertiary training, there is, as Cairney suggests, value in undertaking interactive discussions with current public servants to communicate the complexity of policy and distil the insights from the diverse range of policy theory (Cairney 2015, p. 33). Academics are often not clear as to how practitioners can deploy theory. Beyond the suggestions made earlier in this conclusion, one means of offering practical lessons to time-poor practitioners could be in the form of 'policy theory–bites'—short training sessions aimed at conveying useful policy concepts (sometimes embedded within a policy framework), such as:

- how better to undertake policy 'on the run', which tends to be produced during 'issue attention cycles' associated with relentless media attention
- the importance of always being ready for a 'policy window' to open
- the insights into 'fast policy thinking', which can be gleaned from behavioural economics and psychology studies

- how to develop reflexive capacities and encourage curiosity and inquiry
- appreciating the value of policy evaluation and making desired outcomes and impacts transparent and measurable
- exploring what makes a problem seem 'wicked' and what range of interrelated initiatives are appropriate for such multidimensional problems
- how to work comfortably in the 'purple zone', which can create tensions between public servants and ministers (see Alford et al. 2017; Alford & Head 2017; Althaus, Bridgman & Davis 2018; Cairney & Weible 2017; Kingdon 2011).

There have been frequent calls, as Threlfall and Althaus remind us in Chapter 2, to shed more light on the broader area of how theory can be tested against practice. Both Gilding and Maurer (this volume, Chapters 11 and 12, respectively) provide rare insights into this area. Mackie (see Chapter 9) has highlighted the significance of the agency exercised by policy officials within environmental policymaking as a key driver in the success or failure of specific policies and programs; this is an area that warrants more attention in theory, notwithstanding the difficulties in accessing the insider world of public servants to understand their capacity to act as 'policy agents' within a Westminster system. A further challenge for us is: can we move beyond the individual case studies that only explore this link in specific contexts? Paul 't Hart and colleagues, using an adapted policy success assessment framework by McConnell, have recently compiled a series of international studies on learning from policy success, including a volume on Australia and New Zealand (see Luetjens, Mintrom & 't Hart 2019). While most of their illustrative cases are long-term policy trajectories, there are many valuable lessons in such comparative assessments.

We might wish to encourage the practice of preparing 'learning briefs'—written heuristically to disseminate specific learnings and good practices across agencies.[4] Some Commonwealth departments require middle and senior staff engaged in successful policy work to prepare and disseminate learning briefs that capture practical learnings for colleagues to consider. It could be instructive, perhaps through a practitioner–academic partnership,

---

4   In some government departments these written 'learning briefs' already exist but are internal documents and not made public or widely disseminated across government. Many of these would make valuable case studies to wider audiences even if some critical reflections may be divulged.

to examine whether embedding a theoretical framework into such briefs might enhance the insights to be garnered: for instance, running the ruler of McConnell's assessment framework over the particular policy outcomes, or employing the multiple streams approach to investigate the role of ideas and entrepreneurial policy actors in agenda-setting. This would complement, and potentially reach a wider audience, than the 'action-learning' teaching cases such as those employing public value as a prism for diagnosis produced by ANZSOG and other training institutes. We can augment these efforts with pracademic podcasts, policy 'bites', policy 'windows' and more use of visualisation approaches to summarise complex concepts and processes (e.g. flow charts and concept maps).

Whatever the specifics, there is a considerable body of applied research that could profitably be done to advance our understanding of the value of policy theory to develop policy skills. In particular, partnerships could be formed between academics and practitioners to explore how various policy theories are actually used, both in the workplace and as a language for communicating shared concepts and approaches. For instance, while scholars have raised the issue of public value encouraging bureaucrats to exercise spontaneous agency, we still have little direct evidence to discover the extent to which this may help to explain the strong appeal this approach holds for senior public servants in Westminster systems, particularly in Australia and New Zealand. As the exponents of public value theory have themselves been quick to recognise, this empirical research agenda as yet lacks grounding in rigorous studies. A much needed research agenda:

> Could test empirically whether the tools of public value truly have an impact on the thoughts and actions of public managers, or is this simply a conceit of public management teachers. (Hartley et al. 2017, pp. 671, 680–1)

Within this applied research agenda, we might wish to conduct significant studies to examine whether, how and to what effect policy frameworks, models or theories offered through graduate and postgraduate study or training courses are influencing and being applied by policy practitioners working in the intergovernmental space, encompassing both Commonwealth and state public servants in Australia and across central and line agencies, policy developers and implementers, both metropolitan and regional. A partnership between ANZSOG and a university with a dedicated public policy school would be an ideal platform to develop this research proposal in consultation with key public service agencies.

Attempting all of these areas of applied research may be ambitious, perhaps overly so—yet, to shed light on the interaction or not between theory and practice, it is essential. Without such work being undertaken and published we will remain largely in the dark about how the 'two worlds' connect and influence each other, and how each might work with the other to improve the crucial work of government and policymaking.

A concluding comment

As a field of scholarly research and theoretical interest, public policy is avowedly multidisciplinary and interdisciplinary. As this book amply demonstrates, it is also concerned with reaching across the divide that inevitably lies between theory and practice. These are among the strengths of the applied field of study, although they do undoubtedly raise challenges, too. Where, perhaps, there remains the most work to be done—if the contributions in this book are a guide—is in deepening our understanding of what *actually* happens when policy is developed and deployed, and especially *why* it happens the way it does. What do practitioners think they are doing and why they are doing it? Is there a collective set of norms and expectations among public servants and the myriad others involved in generating policy advice, or is this an irredeemably heterogeneous group who engage in policy with differential values and behavioural practices? What changes if we shift our focus from specific, individual cases or actions and try to understand what is happening at a broader and more systemic level? If these difficult-to-answer empirical and analytical questions can in some measure be answered, then what do the answers mean, normatively? Is there a need to build a more coherent profession of policymakers, analysts and advisers and encourage the development of communities of practice? If so, what would be the core characteristics of such a profession? What would it 'profess' and what would its value be to our polity and to the wider community? These are, of course, questions that this publication certainly does not fully answer, but it does, we hope, make clear the need to seek some answers along these lines, even as the Australian policy enterprise continues to grapple with major policy challenges (demonstrated most recently by the COVID-19 pandemic).

References

Adams, D, Colebatch, HK & Walker, CK 2015, 'Learning about learning: Discovering the work of policy', *Australian Journal of Public Administration*, vol. 74, no. 2, pp. 101–11, doi.org/10.1111/1467-8500.12119.

Alford, J, Douglas, S, Geuijen, K & 't Hart, P 2017, 'Ventures in public value management: Introduction to the symposium', *Public Management Review*, vol. 19, no. 5, pp. 589–604, doi.org/10.1080/14719037.2016.1192160.

Alford, J & Head, BW 2017, 'Wicked and less wicked problems: A typology and a contingency framework', *Policy and Society*, vol. 36, no. 3, pp. 397–413, doi.org/10.1080/14494035.2017.1361634.

Althaus, C, Bridgman, P & Davis, G 2018, *The Australian policy handbook: A practical guide to the policy-making process*, 6th edn, Allen & Unwin, Sydney, NSW.

Boston, J 1995, 'Inherently governmental functions and the limits to contracting out', in J Boston (ed.), *The state under contract*, Bridget Williams Books, Wellington, NZ.

Cairney, P 2015, 'How can policy theory have an impact on policymaking? The role of theory-led academic-practitioner discussions', *Teaching Public Administration*, vol. 33, no. 1, pp. 22–39, doi.org/10.1177/0144739414532284.

Cairney, P 2019, *Understanding public policy theories and issues*, 2nd edn, Red Globe Press, London.

Cairney, P & Weible, C 2017, 'The new policy sciences', *Policy Sciences*, vol. 50, no. 4, pp. 619–27, doi.org/10.1007/s11077-017-9304-2.

Castles, F 1998, *Comparative public policy: Patterns of post-war transformation*, Edward Elgar, Cheltenham, UK.

Colebatch, H 2010, *Policy*, Open University Press, Maidenhead, UK.

Considine, M & Painter, M (eds) 1997, *Managerialism: The great debate*. Melbourne University Press, Carlton, Vic.

Department of the Prime Minister and Cabinet (PM&C) 2019, *Our public service, our future. Independent review of the Australian Public Service*, viewed 4 June 2018, www.apsreview.gov.au/about.

Di Francesco M 2015, 'Policy analysis instruction in Australia', in B Head & K Crowley (eds), *Policy analysis in Australia*, Policy Press, Bristol, UK, doi.org/10.1332/policypress/9781447310273.003.0017.

Dror, Y 1968, *Public policy making re-examined*, Chandler, San Francisco, LA.

Dye, TR 1978, *Understanding public policy*, Prentice-Hall, Englewood Cliffs, NJ.

Ferguson, B 2019, *Competing for influence: The role of the public service in better government in Australia*, ANU Press, Canberra, ACT, doi.org/10.22459/CI.2019.

Gill, Z & Colebatch H 2006, '"Busy little workers": Policy workers' own accounts', in H Colebatch (ed.), *Beyond the policy cycle*, Allen & Unwin, Sydney, NSW.

Hartley, J, Alford, J, Knies, E & Douglas, S 2017, 'Towards an empirical research agenda for public value theory', *Public Management Review*, vol. 19, no. 5, pp. 670–85, doi.org/10.1080/14719037.2016.1192166.

Hogwood, B & Gunn, L 1984, *Policy analysis for the real world*, Oxford University Press, Oxford, UK.

Hughes, P 1998, 'A spirit of service', Paterson Oration, ANZSOG, Melbourne.

Keynes, JM 1936, *The general theory of employment, interest and money*, Macmillan, London, UK.

Kingdon, J 2011, *Agendas, alternatives and public policies*, 2nd edn, Little Brown, Boston, MA.

Luetjens, J, Mintrom M & 't Hart P 2019, *Successful public policy: Lessons from Australia and New Zealand*, ANU Press, Canberra, ACT, doi.org/10.22459/SPP.2019.

Makhlouf, G 2017, 'The importance of stewardship for public sector productivity', Paper presented to the New Zealand Public Sector Finance Leadership Conference, Wellington.

McEachern, D 1990, *The expanding state: Class and economy in Europe since 1945*, Harvester Wheatsheaf, London, UK.

Moon, K, Marsh, D, Dickinson, H & Carey, G 2017, *Is all stewardship equal? Developing a typology of stewardship approaches,* Public Service Research Group Issues Paper, no. 2, viewed 1 June 2020, www.unsw.adfa.edu.au/public-service-research-group/sites/cpsr/files/uploads/Issues%202%20Stewardship.pdf.

Moran, T 2017, 'Back in the Game', IPAA Fellows' Oration, IPAA, Melbourne, 21 November.

Panchamia, N & Thomas, P n.d., *Capability reviews*, Institute for Governance, viewed 2 June 2020, www.instituteforgovernment.org.uk/sites/default/files/case%20study%20capabilities.pdf.

Parsons, W 2004, *Public policy*, Edward Elgar, Aldershot, UK.

Peters, G 1996, *The policy capacity of government*, CCMD, Ottawa, Canada.

Podger, A 2019, 'Protecting and nurturing the role and capability of the Australian Public Service', Parliamentary Library Lecture, Canberra, 10 September.

Schick, A 1966, 'The road to PPB: The stages of budget reform', *Public Administration Review*, vol. 26, no. 4, pp. 243–58, doi.org/10.2307/973296.

Stewart, R 1999, *Public policy: Strategy and accountability*, Macmillan, Melbourne, Vic.

Tiernan, A 2011, 'Advising Australian federal governments: Assessing the evolving capacity and role of the public service', *Australian Journal of Public Administration*, vol. 70, no. 4, pp. 335–46, doi.org/10.1111/j.1467-8500.2011.00742.x.

Vromen, A & Hurley, P 2015, 'Consultants, think tanks and public policy', in B Head & K Crowley (eds), *Policy analysis in Australia*, Policy Press, Bristol, UK.

Wanna, J 2015, 'Policy analysis at the federal government level', in B Head & K Crowley (eds), *Policy analysis in Australia*, Policy Press, Bristol, UK, doi.org/10.1332/policypress/9781447310273.003.0005.